Psychology
Basics

Psychology Basics

Volume 2

Intelligence Tests—
The Visual System

Index

edited by

FRANK N. MAGILL

SALEM PRESS, INC.
Pasadena, California
Englewood Cliffs, New Jersey

Essays originally appeared in *Survey of Social Science: Psychology*, 1993; new material has been added.

∞ The paper used in these volumes conforms to the American National Standard for Permanence of Paper for Printed Library Materials, Z39.48-1984.

Library of Congress Cataloging-in-Publication Data
Psychology basics / edited by Frank N. Magill.
    p.   cm. — (Magill's choice)
Includes bibliographical references and index.
ISBN 0-89356-963-1 (set : alk. paper). — ISBN 0-89356-964-X (v. 1 : alk. paper). — ISBN 0-89356-965-8 (v. 2 : alk. paper)
    1. Psychology—Encyclopedias. I. Magill, Frank Northen, 1907-1997. II. Series.
BF31.P765   1998
150'.3—dc21   97-39249
                                     CIP

Third Printing

PRINTED IN THE UNITED STATES OF AMERICA

TABLE OF CONTENTS
Volume 2

Psychology Basics

INTELLIGENCE TESTS

Type of psychology: Intelligence and intelligence testing
Fields of study: Ability tests; intelligence assessment

Individual intelligence tests are used by psychologists to evaluate a person's current cognitive ability and prior knowledge. The intelligence testing movement has a long history, including the development of numerous group and individual tests to measure one aspect of a person's overall intelligence, which frequently changes over time.

Principal terms

AGE NORM: on an aptitude test, the median score made by children of a specific chronological age

COGNITION: ways of knowing and intellectual processes; thinking, problem solving, remembering, and understanding

INTELLIGENCE: among many definitions, David Wechsler's "the aggregate or global capacity of the individual to act purposefully, to think rationally and to deal effectively with the environment" is widely accepted

INTELLIGENCE QUOTIENT (IQ): a unit showing the relative standing of an individual's ability as measured by intelligence tests

MENTALLY GIFTED: a person significantly above average in intellectual functioning, with an IQ of 130 or higher

MENTALLY HANDICAPPED: a person significantly below average in intellectual functioning, with an IQ of 69 or below

PERCENTILE: a score or point in a distribution at or below which a given percentage of individuals will fall; for example, if a student has a test score at the 99th percentile, his or her score is equal to or higher than scores of 99 percent of cases

PERFORMANCE TESTS: tests on which the examinee is required to manipulate various objects

SENSORIMOTOR TESTS: tests designed to measure sensory, perceptual, and psychomotor skills separately or in juxtaposition

VERBAL TESTS: tests requiring written, oral, or numerical answers

Overview

Although means for measuring mental ability date as far back as 2000 B.C., when the ancient Chinese administered oral tests to determine a candidate's fitness for carrying out the tasks of civil administration, the modern intelligence test has its origins in the nineteenth century, when Jean-Étienne-Dominique Esquirol drew a clear distinction between mentally deranged people ("lunatics") and mentally retarded people ("idiots"). Esquirol believed that it was necessary to devise a means of gauging "normal" intelligence so that deviations from an agreed-upon norm could be ascertained, and he pointed out that intellectual ability exists on a continuum extending from idiocy to genius. His work coincided with studies in Europe and the United States that were designed to develop a concept of "intelligence" and to fashion a means of testing this capacity. Work done by Sir Francis Galton in the United Kingdom on hereditary genius, by James McKeen Cattell in the United States on individual differences in behavior, and by Hermann Ebbinghaus in Germany on tests of memory, computation, and sentence completion culminated in the 1905 Binet-Simon scale, created by Alfred Binet and Théodore Simon. It was the first practical index of intelligence measurement as a function of individual differences. This test was based on the idea that simple sensory functions, which had formed the core of earlier tests, are not true indicators of intelligence and that higher mental processes had to be included.

French psychologist and educator Binet founded the first French psychological laboratory. He was a pioneer in the study of individual differences in abilities and introduced intelligence tests that were quickly accepted and widely used in Europe and the United States. His work stemmed from a commission from the minister of education in Paris, who gave him the task of devising a way to distinguish between idiocy and lunacy, as Esquirol had defined them, and normal intelligence, so that handicapped students could be given special instruction. He and Simon used many items that had been developed by earlier examiners; the key advances they made were to rank items in order of difficulty and to register results in terms of age-based cognitive development. Their scale reflected the idea that intelligence was a combination of faculties—judgment, practical sense, and initiative—and contained measures related to memory, reasoning ability, numerical facility, and object comparison.

Binet and Simon's work demonstrated the feasibility of mental measurement, assessing intelligence for the first time in general terms rather than measuring its component parts. Binet revised the test in 1908, and another revision was published in 1911, the year of his death. Advances in his basic design led to the development of tests that could be used for all children (not only those considered mentally limited) in assessing their "mental quotient," a ratio adapted by Lewis Terman of Stanford University. It was obtained by dividing mental age (as determined through scores on a test) by chronological age. Terman renamed the term the intelligence quotient (IQ), and his 1916 version of the Binet-Simon scale became known as the Stanford-Binet test, the most common intelligence test administered in the United States during the twentieth century. It was revised and updated in 1937, 1960, 1972, and 1986, when a point-scale format was introduced for the first time.

Binet's test depended on an age scale; that is, the questions which were answered correctly by a majority of ten-year-old children were assigned to the ten-year age level of intelligence. A more sophisticated version of the test was devised by Robert Yerkes, which depended on a point scale for scoring; this format was fully developed by David Wechsler. While the Binet-Terman method used different tests for different age groups, Wechsler worked toward a test to measure the same aspect of behavior at every age level. The goal of his test was to measure intelligence in a holistic (encompassing the larger whole of personality) fashion that did not depend on the verbal skills that the Stanford-Binet tests required. Wechsler thought of intelligence as a multifaceted complex of skills, the total of an effective intellectual process; he wanted his test to show the way intelligent people behaved as a consequence of an awareness of the results of their actions. He thought that those actions would be more rational, worthwhile (in terms of social values), and meaningful than those of less intelligent people.

Wechsler's first test (the Wechsler-Bellevue Intelligence Scale) was published in 1939, and it awarded points for each answer depending on the level of sophistication of the response. The test consisted of six verbal subjects (information, comprehension, arithmetic, similarities, vocabulary, and digit span) and five performance subtests (picture completion, picture arrangement, block design, object assemblies, and digit symbols). The division into verbal and performance skills permitted the calculation of three intelligent quotients: a verbal IQ based on the sum of the verbal tests, correlated with norms of age, a performance IQ based on the sum of performance tests, and a full-scale IQ derived from the sum of all the answers. The test was standardized on a sample of adults, and it could be used to test individuals who had linguistic or sensorimotor handicaps. The pattern of scores on the separate tests could also be used to diagnose learning disability or, in some situations, clinical disorder or dysfunction.

The original test was limited by the sample used for standardization, but the 1955 Wechsler Adult Intelligence Scale (WAIS) provided a basis for testing adults from sixteen to seventy-five. Further revision in the standard scale (including the WAIS-R, 1981) updated the test to coincide with changes in cultural experience. In addition, a Wechsler Intelligence Scale for Children (WISC) was designed to cover ages five to fifteen in 1949 and was revised (WISC-R) in 1974 to cover ages six to sixteen. In 1991, another revision was introduced. Subsequent modifications also led to a test suitable for preschool children, the Wechsler Preschool and Primary Scales of Intelligence (WPPSI) of 1967, which covered ages four to six-and-one-half and included mazes, animal figures, and copying geometric designs. This test was revised in 1981 (WPPSI-R) to extend its range over three years to seven years, three months. Further adjustments have also been made to account for a candidate's sociocultural background in a test called the System of Multi-Cultural Pluralistic Assessment (SOMPA, 1977).

Recent definitions of intelligence have resulted in further development of testing instruments. Raymond Cattell's proposal that intelligence could be divided into two types—fluid (or forming) and crystallized (fixed)—led to a test that used figure classification, figure analysis, and letter and number series to assess the essential nonverbal, relatively culture-free aspects of fluid intelligence; it used vocabulary definition, abstract word analogies, and general information to determine the skills that depend on exposure to cultural processes inherent in crystallized intelligence. Other theories, such as Jean Piaget's idea that intelligence is a form of individual adaptation and accommodation to an environment, led to the development of a test which measures mental organization at successive ages.

Applications

There has been a tendency at various times during the twentieth century to regard intelligence assessment as an answer to questions of placement and classification in almost every area of human experience. The most effective and scientifically valid uses of tests, however, have been in predicting performance in scholastic endeavor, in revealing disguised or latent ability to assist in career counseling, in determining the most appropriate developmental programs for handicapped or mentally handicapped individuals, in locating specific strengths and weaknesses in an individual, in measuring specific changes associated with special programs and forms of therapy, and in comparing a child's mental ability with other children observed in a similar situation to establish a profile of cognitive skills.

One of the most widespread and effective uses of intelligence tests is the determination of possible problems in a child's course of basic education. As reported by Lewis Aiken in his *Assessment of Intellectual Functioning* (1987), a typical case involved an eight-year-old boy with a suspected learning disability. He was given the WISC-R test in 1985, and his full-scale IQ was figured to be 116, placing him in the high average classification. This provided an assessment of general intelligence and scholastic aptitude. His verbal IQ was 127, placing him in the ninety-seventh percentile, indicative of exceptional verbal comprehension. This suggested that he could reason very well, learn verbal material quickly, and process verbal information effectively. His performance IQ of 98 placed him in the average category, but the magnitude of the difference between his verbal and performance IQs is very unusual in children of his age. It pointed to a need for additional interpretive analysis, as well as further study to reveal the reasons behind the discrepancy. Close scrutiny of the test results showed that low scores on the arithmetic, digit span, and coding subtests might indicate a short attention or memory span, poor concentration, or a lack of facility in handling numbers. While no absolute conclusions could be drawn at this point, the results of the test could be used in conjunction with other procedures, observation, and background information to determine an appropriate course of action.

Another common use of an intelligence test is to help an examinee determine specific areas of ability or aptitude which might be useful in selecting a career route. As reported in Aiken, a college senior was given the Otis-Lennon School Ability Test (O-LSAT, Advanced Form R) just before her twenty-second birthday. She planned to enroll in a program in a graduate business school and work toward a master of business arts degree. The O-LSAT is designed to gauge general mental ability, and it includes classification, analogy, and omnibus (a variety of items to measure different aspects of mental functioning) elements. The omnibus includes verbal comprehension, quantitative reasoning, and the ability to follow directions. The examinee was able to complete the test in thirty-five minutes and used the remaining allotted time to check her answers. Her raw score (number of items answered correctly) was 64 (out of 80), her school ability index was 116—which approximated her IQ—and her percentile rank among candidates in the 18-plus range was 84. These scores were in the average range for college seniors, indicating an overall intellectual ability that could be classified as "high average" in terms of the general population. Of the sixteen items answered incorrectly, a superficial analysis pointed toward some difficulty with nonverbal reasoning, but no conclusions could be reached without further examination in this area. There was no significant pattern of errors otherwise, and the random distribution offered no additional guide to areas of weakness. The initial conclusion that was drawn from the test was that a career in business was appropriate, and that with hard work and the full application of her intellectual abilities, she would be able to earn an M.B.A. at a reputable university.

A particularly important application of intelligence assessment is the identification and guidance of a child with advanced intellectual abilities. In a case reported in Jerome M. Sattler's *Assessment of Children* (1988), a three-year-old boy was tested repeatedly from that age until his sixth birthday. This procedure required the implementation of the Stanford-Binet Form L-M, the WPPSI, and the Peabody Individual Achievement Test (PIAT) for grade equivalents. The Stanford-Binet scores were 127 (at age three), 152, 152, and 159+ (with a linear extrapolation to 163). During his first test he was anxious and did not give long verbal responses, but the range of his scores indicated a very superior classification. He did not cooperate with the examiner on the WPPSI vocabulary and animal subtests (the examiner believed that he was not interested), but his performance at age four placed him in the superior range. On the PIAT, he was consistently above average, earning a grade equivalent above 4.0 at the age of six, with a grade equivalent of 7.4 (his highest score) in mathematics; the average grade equivalent for age six is 1.0.

As Sattler points out, the case illustrates "a number of important principles related to testing and assessment." In the largest sense, it illustrates the way different tests measuring general intelligence may yield different results (although all pointed toward superior mental development). The same test may also yield different scores at different age levels. The child's motivation (among other factors) may also play an important part in his results. More specifically, since the boy showed more interest in reading at age three and mathematics at age six, the test could not be considered a useful predictor of later interest, although an interest in solving perceptual-logical problems remained consistent throughout. Finally, since the parents had kept a detailed record of the boy's early development in a baby book, the rich history recorded there was corroborated by the test results which reaffirmed their initial suspicions that the boy was unusually gifted. During his first year in school, he tended to play alone and had frequent minor tantrums which affected his performance in school subjects. When he became accustomed to the social process of school life, however, he was able to demonstrate the ability that his parents had observed at home and which the initial tests validated.

Context

While intelligence tests of some sort appeared in human history as early as the Old Testament Book of Judges (7:3-7, 12:6), which indicates that early Jewish society used questions and observations in personnel selection, the intelligence test as it is known today can be traced to Renaissance Europe. In 1575, the Spanish physician Juan Huarte wrote *Examen de Ingenios*, a treatise concerning individual differences in mental ability with suggestions for appropriate tests. His work, and that of other investigators and theorists, was the result of the rise of a middle class with aspirations to productive employment. Previously, the aristocracy had controlled everything, and fitness for a position was determined by lineage. Once this monarchical rule began to break down, other means were necessary for determining who was fit for a particular occupation and what might be the most productive use of a person's abilities. When it became apparent that royal blood was no guarantee of competence, judgment, or mental acuity, the entire question of the origins of intelligence began to occupy members of the scientific community. For a time, the philosophy of empiricism led scientists toward the idea that the mind itself was formed by mental association among sense impressions, and sensorimotor tests were particularly prominent. As the results of these tests failed to correlate with demonstrations of mental ability (such as marks in school), however, other means were sought to measure and define intelligence. The interest in intelligence testing in the nineteenth century was an important aspect of the development of psychology as a separate scientific discipline, and the twin paths of psychometric (that is, the quantitative assessment of an individual's attributes or traits) and statistical analysis on one hand and philosophical conjecture concerning the shape and operation of the mind on the other were joined in experimentation concerning methods of assessing intelligence.

From their first applications in France as a diagnostic instrument, intelligence tests have been used to help psychologists, educators, and other professionals plan courses of action to aid individuals suffering from some mental limitation or obstacle. This role has been expanded to cover the full range of human intellectual ability and to isolate many individual aspects of intelligence in myriad forms. The profusion of tests has both complicated and deepened an understanding of how the mind functions, and the continuing proposition of theories of intelligence through the twentieth century has resulted in an increasingly sophisticated battery of tests designed to assess and register each new theory.

In addition, technological developments, particularly the growing use of computers, will permit a wider use of flexible testing in which the decision about what item or task to present next depends on the previous answer. Computers are also useful in "number crunching," so that such basic components of a test system as norms, derived scores, and reliability and validity coefficients (the basic statistical material behind the calculation of scores) can be assembled more quickly and efficiently. Computers will also make it possible to administer tests at multiple sites simultaneously when an individual examiner's presence is not necessary. Nevertheless, the human capacity for judgment and analysis in the interpretation of results will remain crucial to test procedures.

Intelligence testing is likely to continue as a primary means of predicting educational or vocational performance, but tests designed to measure the mind in terms of its ability to process information by shifting strategies in response to a changing environment are likely to become more prevalent. The proliferation of more detailed, separate sets of norms for different groups (age, sex, ethnic origin, and so on) is likely to continue. Also, the relationship between intelligence per se and behavioral attitudes that seem to resemble aptitude rather than personality measures is part of the heredity-environment controversy that will continue. Finally, advances in studies on the neurophysiological bases of intelligence will be reflected in tests responsive to a growing understanding of the biochemical aspects of cognition. As an operating principle, though, professionals in the field will have to be guided by a continuing awareness that intelligence testing is only one aspect of understanding a person's total behavior and that the limitations involved in the measuring process must be understood to avoid incorrect or inappropriate diagnoses that might prove harmful to an individual.

Bibliography

Aiken, Lewis R. *Assessment of Intellectual Functioning.* Boston: Allyn & Bacon, 1987. An extremely good source, clearly written and comprehensive; with a historical overview, descriptions of crucial tests, many examples, theoretical discussions of concepts of intelligence and useful statistical tables. Includes a glossary of terms, a list of standard tests, a detailed bibliography, and several indexes.

Cohen, Ronald Jay, et al. *Psychological Testing: An Introduction to Tests and Measurement.* Mountain View, Calif.: Mayfield, 1988. A basic book providing the reader with background information on assessment issues, including intelligence and personality assessment. Also provides the reader with an excellent chapter on the science of technological measurement.

Fraser, Steven, ed. *The Bell Curve Wars: Race, Intelligence, and the Future of America.* New York: Basic Books, 1995.

Modgil, Sohan, and Celia Modgil, eds. *Arthur Jensen: Consensus and Controversy.* New York: Falmer Press, 1987. A must for anyone interested in the effects of cultural differences on the science of measurement, with an emphasis on African-American experiences. The volume is a collection of essays by outstanding contributors in the field of contemporary intelligence assessment. The last chapter is a competent response to the previous essays by Jensen, an extremely controversial figure in the field.

Sattler, Jerome M. *Assessment of Children.* 3d ed. San Diego, Calif.: Author, 1988. An outstanding text, including a thorough history of intelligence tests, a survey of issues involved in measurement, specific discussions of many individual tests, considerable scientific and statistical material, many tables, photographs, extensive references, and separate name and subject indexes.

Seligman, Daniel. *A Question of Intelligence: The IQ Debate in America.* New York: Carol Publishing Group, 1994.

Wolman, Benjamin B., ed. *Handbook of Intelligence: Theories, Measurement, and Applications.* New York: John Wiley & Sons, 1985. A very good source, containing thirty-five contributions by experts covering the entire field of measurement and assessment. The book was written as a tribute to David Wechsler and honors his pioneering work. The first section covers theories and conceptual issues, and the second addresses measurement issues and specific tests (and their limitations). The conclusion deals with the application of various tests to specific settings.

Leon Lewis
James R. Deni

See also:

Creativity and Intelligence, 176; Intelligence: Definition and Theoretical Models, 321; Intelligence: Giftedness and Retardation, 327; Race and Intelligence, 495.

Intimacy in Adulthood

Type of psychology: Developmental psychology
Field of study: Adulthood

Erik Erikson theorized that, during early adulthood, the critical psychological growth that must occur is the development of the capacity for intimacy. If one is successful, one becomes a genuinely loving person; if not, one suffers isolation.

Principal terms

COMMITMENT: the forming and keeping of concrete affiliations and partnerships that require significant sacrifices and compromises

INTIMACY: the capacity for a mutually satisfying openness, interest, and acceptance of a loved other

ISOLATION: the experience of finding oneself unable to be intimately involved with another

LOVE: the specific psychological strength that develops as one resolves the crisis of intimacy

MUTUALITY: the experience of one's partner's satisfaction as being intrinsically satisfying to oneself as well

PSYCHOSOCIAL CRISIS: a time in which a basic theme of psychological development becomes ascendent and is resolved in the context of a particular psychosocial relationship

PSYCHOSOCIAL DEVELOPMENT: the favorable resolution of a particular psychosocial crisis at the stage when it is the ascendant issue

PSYCHOSOCIAL DIMENSION: a dimension of one's basic psychological relations with particular others that has a formative and lasting impact on one's development

Overview

Within his eight-stage model of human development, Erik Erikson articulated three stages of adult development. The first of these stages he named "early adulthood"—roughly the period of one's twenties and thirties. Each stage has its own crisis, during which a particular kind of psychological growth happens. In early adulthood, the critical growth is to become a person capable of intimacy. Facing the issue of intimacy in early adulthood is no mere coincidence. As with every stage, the timing of this crisis has two bases. First, it arises from the person's readiness for it, achieved by having resolved the crisis of the preceding stage. Second, the new crisis is propelled into ascendancy by changes in one's psychosocial situation as one begins a new stage of development.

In the preceding stage, adolescence, the critical issue was the search for personal identity. This "identity crisis" is resolved when the youth succeeds in integrating previous childhood identifications into an original synthesis, a sense of inner consistency and coherence, a sense of direction, and a feeling of place. This identity allows the youth to enter the next stage of early adulthood, wherein one's identity must be risked. As always, the precious gain of the preceding stage allows entry into the next stage, but it also must be risked to resolve the next crisis.

By attaining a sense of who he or she is, the new adult is ready to make commitments to others—the very task demanded by the new psychosocial situation. Entering adulthood means above all that the experimenting orientation of adolescence must give way to the increasingly serious requirements of marriage, family, and career. In contrast to adolescent dating relationships, becoming a spouse and parent with another is not a step to be taken casually. One cannot simply walk away from these commitments as one could from one's boyfriend or girlfriend in high school. Nor can a career, once embarked upon, be changed as easily as switching one's major after starting college. As Richard Knowles noted, one becomes aware "that the commitment is open-ended, that it involves a history, not just a moment." Whereas adolescent involvements are characterized by the fluidity and easy movement needed for exploring one's personal identity, the involvements into which one enters upon becoming an adult have a binding power that requires a new characteristic: an investment of oneself such that one risks being changed, in unforeseeable ways, by the involvement. In other words, commitment requires being willing to sacrifice the very identity gained previously, as one advances toward a more encompassing union with another beyond oneself.

It is possible to initiate adult tasks, such as marriage, family, and career, without yet having resolved the adolescent crisis of identity. It is fairly common for youths who have not yet resolved their own identity crises to get married and even have children. They may hope to grow and find themselves through their marriage and/or children. More typically, however, the reverse happens: Such persons become so overwhelmed with the new demands of being a spouse and parent that they can only foreclose, rather than truly resolve, their identity crises. The requirements to "act like" an adult interfere with the needed exploratory context, thereby preventing the completion of a real development of personal identity. As Erikson has said, "the condition of a true twoness is that one must first become oneself."

The new adult's readiness to make commitments and the increasing demand from the world to do so form the situation that propels into ascendancy the psychosocial crisis of this stage. Erikson has labeled it a crisis of "intimacy versus isolation" to communicate the task of the young adult: develop a capacity for intimacy or suffer isolation. By "intimacy," Erikson means something much broader than the usual connotation, of being sexually involved, though he points to good sexual relations as a prototypical example of intimacy. A good sexual experience is characterized by mutual satisfaction, with the other person's satisfaction being as pleasing and important as one's own. This sense of "mutuality" is the key to Erikson's understanding of intimacy. Intimacy is a "mature devotion" to another—not as a negation of oneself, but as the context within which one will grow, beyond the egocentric concerns of adolescent identity, into an authentic appreciation of being open to and truly available for an "other." This fundamental openness is what Richard Alapack meant by the term "infinite relationship": a relationship that is not bounded by any limits on knowing or being known by the other. Maggie Scarf has defined intimacy very plainly, as "a person's ability to talk about who he really is, and to say what he wants and needs, and to be heard by the intimate partner."

For many, this challenge is daunting. Such openness and commitment entails many risks, not only of committing oneself too narrowly and inappropriately but also of being misunderstood or rejected. Life does not wait, however; time never stands still. If adults do not develop intimacy they will, over time, feel an increasing sense of isolation. One will feel cut off from deep human connection, lonely, without anyone with whom to share one's deepest self. People will then retreat psychologically, to a "regressive reliving" of earlier conflicts and a using of other people in a self-centered way.

By identifying this as a "psychosocial crisis," Erikson emphasizes that it is resolved within a concrete relationship. For most, this relationship will be a marital one, though many other types of relationships can also be the context for resolving this crisis. For example, one may make deep commitments of oneself to the priesthood, to a cause, to one's life work, to an idea, or to a friendship. In whatever form, the individual must experience in that relationship a deep affiliation calling for significant compromises and sacrifices.

When this crisis of intimacy is successfully resolved, the result is the development of a new "psychological strength" (or "virtue," in the old sense of that term). The unique new strength of this stage is what Erikson calls "love." To be a truly loving person means, for Erikson, to have a "mutuality of mature devotion"—in other words, the capacity for being genuinely interested in and openly available to an other. Only by such an "experiential union" can the partners resolve the ordinary antagonisms inherent in everyday functioning together.

Applications

Erikson has called the lack of intimacy "the core pathology of early adulthood." In that sense, his depiction of intimacy and isolation is especially applicable in understanding many relationship problems in adulthood. To understand these applications, however, it is first important to grasp Erikson's key distinction between isolation and "distantiation." To Erikson, distantiation means the capacity to make or keep one's distance, and it fits on the side of intimacy in the resolution of this crisis. When one develops the capacity for intimacy, one also develops the sense that one can reject the pseudo-intimacy of a bad relationship. One is then not driven by the fear of loneliness to settle for "anyone" rather than "no one." Once one has developed the capacity for intimacy, being alone no longer necessarily means being lonely.

Isolation may develop in either of two ways, which may be demonstrated by examples. First, one may simply be psychologically unable to be involved with a partner. Robin spends her evenings in the utter loneliness of encounters with her television set rather than a genuine other. Though she craves contact, her life is mostly an avoidance of it. A second way to experience isolation is what Erikson calls "isolation a deux"—isolation as two. One may be factually involved with another person and yet still be isolated. That may occur in any of three variations. For example, Mark has four dates every week, but they never result in lasting relationships. Though his "little black book" is filled with names and telephone numbers, Mark remains profoundly isolated. A second variation is the case of Alice, who has a series of relationships, none of which ever grows very deep. A closer look reveals that the course of these relationships is very stereotyped: On each date, Alice knows exactly what she will do, what she will talk about, and how involved she will become. Everything is prescripted, and Alice plays out the role. The problems arise when the script runs out and Alice must suddenly be herself. It is at that point that the relationship becomes boring, problematic, or too serious and finally breaks up.

In a third variation, this isolation a deux may even pervade a long-term marriage. This variation is the most tragic: Two people are seeking to love and be loved, yet are going through life merely side by side without really letting the other in. The incidence of infidelity in such marriages is high, but, as Scarf has noted, there are two very different reasons for this. A partner may become involved in an affair either to avoid intimacy with the spouse or out of a hunger for intimacy.

Psychology's understanding of intimacy is most concretely applicable for people wanting to have more fulfilling intimate relationships. There is a vast sense of yearning in contemporary society for intimacy; as wider social supports, such as communities and extended families, collapse, adults must rely more and more on their marriage for such support. Yet, sadly, those same pressures have made it harder for spouses truly to be there for each other.

One result has been an increase in the number of marriage therapists, who consequently have emerged as experts with much to say about the nurturing of intimacy in marriage. Psychiatrists Thomas and Patrick Malone, for example, have pointed out that intimacy means being in one's own space while also being in a shared space. It is not a loss of oneself, but a sharing that transforms one's own self. Through the process of being known by the other, one comes to know oneself in the other's presence; this nourishes one's own self. The Malones note that such a relationship requires reciprocity in that both members must be actively involved in what is happening. They also list other characteristics that, "if increased, make intimacy more likely": free choice, morality, acceptance, self-responsibility, attentiveness, risk-taking, presence, naturalness, participation, personal surrender, engagement, systemic detachment, and creativity.

Context

Erikson received his training from Sigmund Freud's Psychoanalytic Institute in Vienna when it was at its peak, during the years around 1930. This psychoanalytic background provided the foundation from which he created an original view of psychological development, one that took key elements from psychoanalysis yet also varied in important ways from Freud's. Erikson's own theory stresses three central features that have had a major impact on psychology, namely that development is lifelong, psychosocial, and epigenetic.

Erikson pioneered the view of psychological development as a process that does not come to an end when one reaches adulthood, as major theorists (such as Freud and Jean Piaget) had previously supposed (and is even expressed in the term "grown-up" for an adult). Rather, Erikson saw development as a never-ending lifetime process, a series of stages extending across a person's entire life span. Prior to Erikson's influence, "developmental psychology" was synonymous with "child psychology." Now, the subfield of the psychology of adult development is perhaps the greatest growth area in psychological research. Though Erikson's actual writing on adulthood has been rather brief, what he said captured so well its essential crises that it has formed the basis for later psychologists' more extensive analyses, such as that of Daniel Levinson.

Erikson also deviated from Freud's emphasis on the psychosexual dimension of development, in which each stage was anchored by a bodily zone of psychosexual arousal. Erikson added a psychosocial dimension, by his discovery of the special relationship issues at the heart of each developmental stage. He did not do so as a refutation of Freud's psychosexual theory. Indeed, he explicitly says that the two are complementary and that nothing in Freud's theory precludes the addition of this psychosocial dimension.

Erikson also specified an "epigenetic principle" as governing psychological development. By that he meant that the issues of each stage are not merely sequentially connected. Rather, they are constituents of a more holistic or "organismic" development, evident in two senses. First, the issue of each stage emerges from and is built upon all those that preceded it, and is in that sense implicated in every other. Second, the resolution of each crisis involves the reintegration of all earlier ones, so that each crisis is genuinely a confrontation with every other crisis. Thus, to learn to love in early adulthood, one must again confront all the earlier crises from childhood and adolescence: those of trust, autonomy, initiative, industriousness, and identity.

Bibliography

Douglas, Jack D., and Freda Cruse Atwell. *Love, Intimacy, and Sex.* Newbury Park, Calif.: Sage, 1988. In the past several years, there has been a virtual flood of books for the general reader about how to improve intimate relationships. This one is a representative example but perhaps is a bit better than most. It offers many examples rather than superficial techniques, and it is more literate and insightful.

Erikson, Erik Homburger. *Childhood and Society.* Rev. ed. New York: W. W. Norton, 1964. This revision of a book that first appeared in 1950 is the most widely used basis for understanding Erikson's work. It includes a variety of separately written essays, covering such topics as life history, infantile sexuality, childhood in Native American cultures, play, cultural identity and its exemplification in the personal identities of two historical figures (Adolf Hitler and Maxim Gorky), and Erikson's first detailed presentation of his own psychosocial theory of life-span psychological development.

_____. *Identity and the Life Cycle.* New York: W. W. Norton, 1980. This collection of three previously written papers of Erikson is considered one of the best introductions of his work. The first part consists of clinical notes from field studies with Native Americans and a longitudinal study of children. The second part presents Erikson's stages of life-span psychosocial development in terms of its contributions to the development of a healthy personality. The third part addresses specifically the problem of the accomplishment of ego identity in adolescence.

_____. *The Life Cycle Completed: A Review.* New York: W. W. Norton, 1982. This work presents Erikson's updated outline of his theory of psychosocial development, written when he was already in his eighties. Interestingly, this time he depicts his life-span theory from the final stage—old age—and works backward from it, in order to show "how much sense a re-view of the completed life cycle can make of its whole course."

Evans, Richard I. *Dialogue with Erik Erikson.* Reprint. Northvale, N.J.: Jason Aronson, 1995.

Knowles, Richard T. *Human Development and Human Possibility: Erikson in the Light of Heidegger.* Lanham, Md.: University Press of America, 1986. The philosophical bases of this book will be too difficult in parts for a general reader, but it provides an insightful reinterpretation of Erikson's work. Knowles examines each of Erikson's psychosocial stages of development and adds an additional, existential level of understanding to each.

Levinson, Daniel J. *The Seasons of a Man's Life.* New York: Alfred A. Knopf, 1978. An excellent deepening of Erikson's sketch of adulthood. Levinson's understanding is based on in-depth interviews with adult males over a ten-year period. On that basis, he has been able to specify in great detail the essential phases of development in the twenties, thirties, and forties.

Malone, Thomas Patrick, and Patrick Thomas Malone. *The Art of Intimacy.* New York: Prentice-Hall, 1987. These two psychiatrists draw upon their work with adults having marital difficulties to present the meaning of intimacy and its connection with the growth of the self. The book also offers a careful analysis of ways of being in relationships, along with key distinctions between the "I, me, and self" modes of being with another.

Psychoanalysis and Contemporary Thought 19, no. 2 (1996). A special issue entitled "Ideas and Identities: The Life and Work of Erik Erikson," edited by Robert S. Wallerstein. A variety of insightful perspectives on Erikson; includes a selection of photographs.

Scarf, Maggie. *Intimate Partners: Patterns in Love and Marriage.* New York: Random House, 1987. A thoughtful analysis of problems in intimate relationships, especially of problems that have long-standing roots. Scarf depicts the essential types of interactions underlying typical problems and shows how they often perpetuate issues from one's parents' marriages.

Tribe, Carol. *Profile of Three Theories: Erikson, Maslow, Piaget.* Dubuque, Iowa: Kendall Hunt Publishing, 1995.

Christopher M. Aanstoos

See also:

Adolescence: Cognitive Skills, 13; Adolescence: Sexuality, 19; Cognitive Development Theory: Jean Piaget, 135; Ego Psychology: Erik Erikson, 223; Generativity in Adulthood, 260; Identity Crises, 284; Integrity, 315; Moral Development, 399; Psychoanalytic Psychology, 471; Trust, Autonomy, Initiative, and Industry, 633.

LANGUAGE
The Developmental Sequence

Type of psychology: Language
Field of study: Infancy and childhood

Like any ability, a child's skill with language does not appear all at once but emerges in stages of development. The child proceeds through babbling, single-word speech, and two-word sentences, and then learns to elaborate and combine these primitive sentences. The field of language acquisition has studied the development of this sequential process in children learning a number of different native languages.

Principal terms

ARTICULATION: the physical process of producing a speech sound

FUNCTION WORD: a word which has little meaning in itself yet signals relationships between other words in a sentence, such as an article ("the" or "a") or a preposition (for example, "in," "on," "of")

GRAMMATICAL MORPHEME: a minimal unit of meaning whose principal function is to signal relationships among elements in a sentence; function words and inflections are both grammatical morphemes

INFLECTION: an addition to the stem of a word which indicates subtle modulations in meaning, such as plurality (more than one) or tense (present time or past time); in English, inflections are all suffixes (that is, they are added to the end of the word stem)

OVEREXTENSION: the application of a word to more instances in the world than ordinary adult usage allows

PASSIVE VOICE: a sentence structure in which the agent of the action does not serve as the grammatical subject of the sentence; the sentence "The ball was thrown by the boy" is a passive-voice sentence (as opposed to its active counterpart, "The boy threw the ball")

PROPOSITION: an utterance having a subject and a predicate; often used as a synonym for "sentence," although a sentence may actually contain more than one proposition

REFERENT: an object in the real world to which a word refers

SALIENT: characterized by something which stands out from the background because it is perceptually prominent

Overview

Even before they are ready to walk, most babies are busily engaged in acquiring their native languages, and they do so with startling rapidity. The typical four-year-old child is already in command of most of the major structures that characterize the language of adults. The details of exactly how children are able to extract such complex rules from the language of the community into which they have been born are largely unknown; however, there is considerable information about the stages—the developmental sequence—of language development.

Young infants do not talk, but an observer witnessing a "conversation" between mother and baby might think they do, for a mother treats a tiny baby as a conversational partner, allowing the baby's burps, coughs, or cries to stand for a "turn" in the communication exchange and responding to these vegetative sounds with comments such as "Oh, you're hungry, aren't you?" or "Well, excuse you!" As the infant matures, the mother ceases to respond to involuntary noises and treats only higher-quality vocalizations such as babbling as a conversational turn. By the time a child reaches one year, a mother accepts only words or approximations to them as attempts at language. In the first year of life, then, the child is encouraged to talk through the speech exchange known as conversation.

Although infants burp, cough, and cry, such noises are not in fact language, nor are the earliest additions to this repertoire, such as cooing and babbling. Babies coo in the early weeks of extrauterine life, but they do not actually begin to utter intentional strings of what might be called speech sounds until around the middle of the first year, at about six or seven months of age. These intentional sequences of sounds are called babbling, and they usually consist of a repeated, or reduplicated, consonant-vowel string, such as "bababababa" or "dadadada." The purpose of such babbling seems to be vocal play or practice. Children will babble to themselves or take turns babbling with a playful adult, using various pitch patterns on the babble to indicate glee, anger, discomfort, and so on. Typically, babies babble only a limited number of possible speech sounds, favoring consonants formed at the front of the mouth, such as /b/, /m/, /p/, or /d/, and avoiding those produced at the back, such as /k/ or /g/. Their preferred vowel sounds are those represented by the letter *a* in the words "father" or "daddy" (different sounds, in spite of the use of the same letter).

Although some variation exists, children generally produce their first real words based on the adult language around one year of age. These early words usually contain the same speech sounds the child favored in babbling. If, for example, a child's preferred babble string was "dadadada," a list of the child's first words might include "duck," "daddy," "shoe," and "sock," not necessarily because the concepts housed in these words are inherently interesting to the child but because they begin with /d/ or with consonants produced at nearly the same place in the mouth.

Children typically pass through a phase during which they speak one word at a time. In some ways, these utterances are not true words at all since they tend to convey much more information than a single word would. For example, if a child says "Cookie!" he or she probably wants to be given one, so the word is not a mere label for an object. Moreover, many of these one-word utterances demonstrate an "overextension" of the meaning of the adult word. For example, the child may use "duck" to indicate a duck, a sea gull, a mug with a protruding handle, or Daddy holding a cookie between his teeth. That is, the child may identify the word not with the entire original referent but with one or more salient features associated with it.

The one-word period is rapidly supplanted by the two-word stage. During this stage, the child unites two words in a single utterance. "Cookie allgone" or "Airplane bye-bye" are utterances typical of English-speaking children in the second half of the second year of life, and similar two-word sequences have been found in the speech of many different children acquiring many different native languages. Some children seem to use a formulaic approach; that is, they use one or two words frequently and combine these with a large number of other words. Children who take this approach may be heard to say "Hi Daddy," "Hi doggie," "Hi kitty," "Hi car," or "See car," "See duck," and so on. Other children tend to use two-word utterances to express a number of relationships they have observed, such as actor-action ("Doggie run") or possessor-possessed ("Baby blanket").

Regardless of which strategy the child employs, he or she quickly moves beyond the two-word stage. English-speaking children typically add to the length of their sentences by combining two or more two-word utterances and by adding one or more of the grammatical morphemes of English to the words comprising their utterances. That is, whereas previously the child may have said "Daddy drive," and "Drive car," he or she can now combine these two utterances into one: "Daddy drive car." In addition, the child's speech ceases to be telegraphic; that is, it no longer resembles a telegram in its omission of function words such as "the" and "is," and inflections such as -*s*, -*ed*, and -*ing*. Thus, forms such as "eating," "cookies," and "baby's" begin to enter the child's utterances. A sentence such as "That baby eating cookies" is not in the least unusual for a child at this stage.

It is important to understand that the child acquiring language is not parroting adults but is formulating a set of rules which will allow him or her to produce an indefinite number of novel utterances. One indication that children's language is rule-governed behavior and not imitation is the overgeneralization they so frequently produce. Having learned that -*s* signals plural and that -*ed* marks past tense in English, for example, children typically add these morphemes to exceptional nouns and verbs that are differently inflected. Thus, a child is likely to say "maked" instead of "made," "drawed" instead of "drew," "foots" instead of "feet," and so on, even though he or she has never heard these forms in the speech of adults. Moreover, a child is likely to resist correction of these forms, being certain that his or her own extraction of the rules is correct and that the rules apply without exception. These errors are creative, and, while they are errors, they indicate that the child has accurately assessed the rules of the language. Similar overgeneralization has been observed in children acquiring many different native languages, and thus appears to be a universal tendency. Children are left with the developmental task of determining the exceptions to their rules.

By the time a child is three years old, he or she probably has a fair-sized vocabulary and has mastered many of the grammatical morphemes. Whereas previously the child combined words to form two-word sentences, and two-word sentences to form more complete simple sentences, the child now begins to combine sentences by the process of coordination (tying ideas together through the use of function words such as "and") and through subordination (having one proposition serve as a modification for another). The child begins to make utterances such as "I played tag and I singed a song," "I'll be right there after I eat my cookie," "That's a man that wears a hat," and "I'd better eat my nuts before the dinosaur eats them." The child uses language to explain, to lie, to pretend, and to tell a story. Passive forms also appear, usually in shortened and colloquial form: "I got put in time-out."

By the age of five, a child has many of the forms of adult speech under his or her command. The child must still learn to make sentences cohere to produce a good story, to specify appropriately the antecedents (the full nouns) for pronouns, and to apply language skills to reading and writing.

Applications

The study of language acquisition has applications in the fields of education, second-language teaching, and speech pathology. How successful a child may be in learning to read and write may depend on how closely the teaching-learning situation resembles the situation in which the primary linguistic skills of talking and comprehending were acquired in the home. Many educators contend that the schoolroom should provide as natural a context as possible for the acquisition of reading and writing, and so teachers create situations in which children have to write real letters to real people, not just learn the form of letter writing by copying sample letters. Teachers who take this approach help children learn to read and write by having them compose their own stories and produce their own books. In other words, the children learn in a context where their words will be read by others as well as themselves, and so the material they learn from has intrinsic value; it is written by the children for the purpose of communication, just as early language is spoken by children in order to communicate. Language, after all, is acquired not for its own sake but to express desires, needs, hopes, and, eventually, thoughts. That literacy skills should be similarly acquired is the guiding principle of the school of educational practice called "whole language." Children are given a chance to make their own progress, perhaps halting at first, just as their progress with talking was. They are encouraged to produce whatever level of literacy they can, just the way mothers encourage their babies' vocalizations, and they are encouraged to move up to higher levels of abilities. The idea is to make the learning natural and to respect the child's own degree of progress.

In addition, knowledge of language development has enhanced the teaching of second languages in the classroom. Since the acquisition of second languages has often been studied by comparing the sequence of second-language acquisition to that of first-language acqui- sition, the explanations of similarities and differences can then be used to improve instruc- tion in second-language teaching. In particular, the teaching of English as a second language in the United States to children from newly immigrated families has benefited from a knowledge of developmental sequence. How can educators make the learning situation in the second language as natural and effortless as was the acquisition of the native language? Will drills work? What about teaching the child to translate or memorize?

Such methods are only minimally successful, if at all. Children acquiring their native languages do not memorize vocabulary in context-free drills, nor do they practice meaning- less changes in the forms of sentences—exercises frequently employed in the second- language classroom. Children acquiring both first and second languages learn by attempting utterances and modifying them when not understood, by trying out new words to see if they really understand them, and by attempting to get things done with words—explaining, requesting, and expressing ideas. Because children acquire their first language in the process of trying to communicate, they can acquire a second language most successfully when they are similarly immersed in the language and learn to "swim" in it. Children learn their way around a second language in the same manner as they master the first. They have no other option if they want to communicate.

A third area of application is a clinical one. Speech pathologists use the insights gained from language acquisition studies to help children who are having difficulties in normal speech development. For example, research on normal language development shows that many children pass through a phase in which they substitute the consonants /t/ and /d/ in all places where the adult language has /k/ and /g/; eventually, they learn the correct tongue positions for the correct articulation of various consonants. The question is, When should such substitutions cease? When is intervention by a trained practitioner necessary? The answers lie in what language behavior is typical of a sample of children at a particular age.

Speech pathologists are trained to assess the developmental progress of children's language on the basis of what is normative so that they can recommend some specific steps for clinicians, parents, teachers, and other care givers to take. In this way, faulty articulations and problems with syntax which get in the way of the child's comprehensibility and social acceptance—and subsequent success in school—can be remedied.

Context

Parents with an eye for detail have recorded their children's progress with language at least since evolution theorist Charles Darwin took notes on his son's development and published his observations in 1877. In 1907, the German psychologists Clara and Wilhelm Stern published the first edition of their masterful analysis of their own children's acquisition of German in *Die Kindersprache* (child language). Other parents around the world similarly kept track of their children's development in their native languages, but a systematic scientific investigation of the acquisition process did not actually begin until 1962, when Harvard psychologist Roger Brown, equipped with tape recorders, gifted student assistants, and Noam Chomsky's theory of generative transformational grammar, set out to chart the course of development of three English-acquiring children, who were given the pseudonyms "Adam," "Eve," and "Sarah." Through careful systematic analysis, Brown charted the children's first stages of language development, and a developmental order for the acquisition of the grammatical morphemes of English was established. Brown published the findings of his research group, along with a discussion of the methodology they used, in a book called *A First Language: The Early Stages* (1973).

In the late 1970's and 1980's, as knowledge about the early form of children's utterances increased, research began to turn toward factors responsible for the shape and content of children's speech. Investigators studied the meanings of early words and sentences and how these meanings change with time. They studied the "pragmatics" of young children's speech, that is, the particular forms children use to accomplish specific goals. For example, researchers sought to determine the developmental sequence of request forms and other speech acts and to study the development of extended discourse such as conversation and narrative.

In addition, many students of child language began to examine the sequence of acquisition of semantic (meaning) notions cross-linguistically. That is, they studied children acquiring the native languages of many different cultures in order to separate acquisition factors caused by constraints in cognitive development from factors that result from the structure of particular languages. They sought to determine whether children acquiring a particular language expressed a specific type of idea late because its meaning was difficult for a child to grasp conceptually or because the language itself had a means of expressing the notion that was especially difficult for children to learn. By comparing how children acquiring a number of different types of languages developed, investigators attempted to separate the universal from the particular—the strategies all children everywhere tend to use as opposed to the strategies which the structure of a particular language may suggest.

A third area of interest to have emerged is that of individual differences. During the 1960's and 1970's, the theoretical foundation for the study of language laid by linguist Noam Chomsky led researchers to assume that all children proceeded in the same way. As work progressed, however, it soon became evident that children may take alternate routes to the same goal. For example, as has been discussed, when children begin combining words to form primitive sentences, they may take a formulaic approach ("Hi car") or a relational approach ("Mommy do"). Even before the two-word stage, however, children may differ from one another in their approach. Some children at the one-word stage are "referential": Their early vocabularies include primarily words for objects, and they acquire new words relatively rapidly. Other children are "expressive": They use fewer nouns, preferring pronouns, modifiers, and function words. It should be kept in mind that these categories are ends of a continuum; children are rarely all one or all the other, but are more or less referential or expressive.

Since its inception in the early 1960's, the field of language acquisition study has grown enormously, and so has knowledge of the strategies children around the world use in developing what is quite possibly their most important intellectual skill, fluency in their native language.

Bibliography

Brown, Roger William. *A First Language: The Early Stages*. Cambridge, Mass.: Harvard University Press, 1973. This account of early language development in English and in several other languages is a classic, and it is accessible to the careful reader interested in the early work which laid the foundation for modern language acquisition research.

Bruner, Jerome S. *Child's Talk: Learning to Use Language*. New York: W. W. Norton, 1983. Looks at the acquisition process from the point of view of pragmatics; investigates how a child comes to use language to accomplish various goals in the world and how, from limited beginnings, the child learns to expand his or her uses of language. A well-written and succinct contrast to the syntactic approach espoused by Roger Brown.

De Villiers, Peter A., and Jill G. de Villiers. *Early Language*. Cambridge, Mass.: Harvard University Press, 1979. Written specifically for the nonspecialist. Provides a clear and accessible account of children's first sounds, words, and sentences, as well as a discussion of the nature of speech addressed to children and its possible role in facilitating language development.

Kessel, Frank S., ed. *The Development of Language and Language Researchers: Essays in Honor of Roger Brown*. Hillsdale, N.J.: Lawrence Erlbaum, 1988. An anthology of essays written by former students and colleagues of Roger Brown. Includes overviews of several of the subfields of language acquisition, as well as autobiographical accounts of several researchers' own development in thinking about language development issues. Of particular interest to the beginner are the selections by Dan I. Slobin, Melissa Bowerman, and Jill de Villiers.

Werner, Heinz, and Bernard Kaplan. *Symbol Formation*. New York: John Wiley & Sons, 1963. Uses information provided by numerous diary studies of language and language acquisition to provide a psychological account of the development of language, connecting changes in expressive language with developmental change in general. The first two parts of this five-part account will be of particular interest to the novice trying to understand the cognitive basis of language acquisition.

Marilyn N. Silva

See also:

Cognitive Development Theory: Jean Piaget, 135; Language Acquisition Theories, 352; Motor Development, 410; Speech Disorders, 576.

LANGUAGE ACQUISITION THEORIES

Type of psychology: Language
Fields of study: Behavioral and cognitive models; infancy and childhood

Three theories of how children learn to talk have provided differing interpretations of the roles played in this acquisition by inborn predispositions and by particular features of the environment. The debate among these theories, known as the behaviorist (or empiricist) approach, the innatist (or rationalist) approach, and the interactionist approach, echoes the controversies in other fields of psychology concerning the nature of knowledge.

Principal terms

CONDITIONING: a process by which a behavior comes to be paired with an environmental event; if a behavior results in a positive outcome (reward), the organism will tend to repeat that behavior; if the behavior results in a negative outcome (punishment), the organism will tend to avoid it

EMPIRICISM: a philosophical position which maintains that knowledge is a sum of sense impressions; that is, knowledge is derived from experience

NATURE: a philosophical term for the particular genetic endowments—the inborn capacities—of an organism

NURTURE: the philosophical term for the effect of the environment on knowledge, personality, and so on

REINFORCEMENT: the reward provided in a conditioning situation; negative reinforcement is the punishment that may be provided in a conditioning situation

SCAFFOLDING: a term used to describe the structured interaction by which American babies, at least, are introduced to language

Overview

Children all around the world, regardless of ethnicity or national origin, acquire the language of the group into which they are born with seeming ease and in essentially similar ways. Explaining exactly how two- to three-year-old children, who are as yet incapable of abstract reasoning, formulate the complex and abstract principles which allow them to comprehend and produce language has been the goal of three broad explanations of linguistic development. These explanations include the behaviorist approach, in which nurture is given paramount importance, the innatist approach, in which nature is given prominence, and the interactionist approach, in which nature and nurture are given equal importance, with both considered necessary and neither sufficient.

In the behaviorist view of language acquisition, imitation and conditioning account for language development. That is, proponents of this school of thought claim that children try to imitate the language they hear around them and pair the words and sentences they hear with environmental events. They receive social rewards such as smiles and other forms of approval for being increasingly correct in both pronunciation and meaning, and their initially babyish attempts at language eventually become replaced with appropriate adult forms. As is consistent with the behaviorist approach, the mental events which may accompany such responses are not included in this account of language development, because mental events are not open to direct observation. The basics of this theory are the stimulus, which may be an environmental occurrence such as the appearance of a cat and the expression of the word "cat" by an adult, and the response, the child's attempt to imitate the word he or she hears.

The behaviorist account seems plausible, but certain observations about what children actually do in the process of acquiring a language present a number of problems for the contention that imitation plays a significant role in language learning. For example, children will produce—and retain, even in the face of correction by adults—such erroneous forms as "throwed" or "readed," which they never hear in the language of the adults around them and which cannot therefore be the result of imitation. Second, when children have been explicitly asked to imitate adult sentences, they frequently substitute forms more in line with their own systems of language for some of the appropriate adult forms. Finally, the most damaging evidence against the behaviorist position is that in ordinary everyday interaction children produce completely novel utterances, utterances which they have not previously heard in the speech of adults. The creative nature of children's errors, imitations, and spontaneous utterances argues quite cogently against the contention that imitation plays the primary role in language acquisition.

The problems for the behaviorist account do not end with imitation, for it has been widely observed that parents reward truthfulness rather than grammatical correctness in the speech of their children. That is, children usually learn to speak quite grammatically without any reinforcement for their syntactic errors. The reinforcement component of the behaviorist tradition thus seems to be largely inoperative in language acquisition.

A second account of language acquisition is the innatist position advocated by the linguist Noam Chomsky. Using as evidence the idea that every sentence uttered is novel rather than a routine memorized by rote and the fact that native speakers of a language have intuitions about whether sentences never heard before are grammatical, Chomsky held, unlike the behaviorists, that linguistic science must investigate the source of this creativity and intuition, namely the set of mental events that are called "grammar." Furthermore, pointing to the numerous false starts, hesitations, and errors that occur in the speech around them, Chomsky contended that only an innate language faculty would enable children who could not deal with abstraction in other contexts to extract from this impoverished data a grammar capable of generating a potentially infinite and completely well-formed array of sentences. Chomsky, therefore, posited that human beings are born with a faculty he called the "language acquisition device" (LAD), which, equipped with a set of possible forms that grammars of human languages can take, allows children, on the basis of very limited data, to choose those rules of sentence formation which best characterize the sentences of the language to which they are exposed.

Since Chomsky's goal was to account for the ability of the finite human organism to produce a potentially infinite set of sentences, his emphasis fell on the syntax of language—that is, those rules of language which determine appropriate word order for sentences and which govern how certain sentences are systematically related to other sentences. For Chomsky, syntax was the central concern of language science. Implicit in this account is the notion that the child's interaction with others is not crucial to the theory of language acquisition. This model assumes that all that is necessary is for the child to be exposed to a language, and LAD will take over. With interaction not an essential component, it is clear that the innatist approach focuses on the structure of language (which is unique in all the communication systems found in nature) rather than on the function of language, communication.

No child acquires language in a vacuum, however, and many researchers contend that interaction is the crucial ingredient in the acquisition recipe. The interactionists do not dispute that humans are innately predisposed to acquire language, but they do question the necessity of positing anything so definite as a language acquisition device. Instead, the interactionist solution takes one of two forms, the cognitivist school or the social interactionist school.

The cognitivist position follows the theory of the Swiss psychologist Jean Piaget in that it contends that the child constructs language just as he or she constructs knowledge in other cognitive areas—by interacting with the environment. Through such interaction, innate reflexes begin to be elaborated and transformed into higher-order cognitive structures. The particular course that cognitive development takes is uniquely and universally human. Language, however, does not have a privileged position in this development; as a cognitive achievement among other important cognitive achievements, it rests on the same foundation and therefore is not separate from cognitive development, but rather follows from it.

The social interactionist approach, on the other hand, gives language special status yet does not focus on what might be innate. Instead, the focus of the social interactionists is the social rather than the physical environment. Researchers who subscribe to this approach have found that from the earliest days in the life of her child, the mother treats her baby as a conversational partner, giving meaning to the baby's vocalizations before these utterances have any conventionalized form. That is, she initiates the baby into the communicative exchange and introduces the baby to the idea that he or she can use vocalizations to refer to aspects of the environment as well as to demand or to express emotion.

Applications

A distinction must be made between what adherents of a particular school of thought know about real-world events and what they consider to be theoretically relevant. That is, behaviorists know that mental events accompany language responses, but they do not consider these mental events relevant within the constraints of their model. Similarly, innatists recognize that the environment is involved in language acquisition, because if it were not, all people would speak the same language. Thus, for innatists, the environment simply provides the raw data for LAD to analyze and is not a crucial part of the model. Finally, interactionists recognize that the child probably receives approval, at least for correct vocabulary, and that the child must acquire the rules of syntax in order to produce well-formed utterances. They point to the interaction between child and caretaker, however, as creating the meaningful situation in which such acquisitions must occur. Thus, no school of thought about language acquisition denies that children acquire language in a particular environment, or that the syntax of human languages is unique among animal communication systems, or that children interact with their caretakers. Each does dispute the relative importance and theoretical significance of these factors.

In fact, each model has features that are useful in explaining certain facets of the acquisition process. The behaviorist approach may be better than the other two for explaining certain aspects of vocabulary development. For example, nearly all parents have heard their child parrot back some expression they have used (and possibly regret using) at the most inopportune moment—perhaps during Grandma's visit. Moreover, psychologists Anat Ninio and Jerome Bruner, advocates of the social interactionist approach, writing in the *Journal of Child Language* in 1978, point out that the mother of the mother/child pair they studied reinforced 81 percent of her child's correct attempts at labeling, and she did so by repeating a more accurate version of the label back to the child, by saying "yes," and by laughing.

Yet behaviorism cannot account for other aspects of acquisition, and Ninio and Bruner claim that providing a child with a word to imitate actually lessens the chances that the child will utter the word at all in an immediate response. Thus, although they can verify the significance of social reward in vocabulary development, they discount the significance of imitation. Their position is that social interaction provides the "scaffolding"—the framework which makes the acquisition possible in the first place. Since, in their view, development is nurtured by conversational exchange, the practical rules guiding such exchange also guide the development of vocabulary. Thus if one partner, in this case the mother, utters a name (a "label") for a picture in a book, there is no need for the other partner, the child, to do so; immediate imitation on the part of the child, therefore, tends not to occur. Moreover, the reinforcement provided by the mother also takes place within the confines of the conversation. Ninio and Bruner do not discount reinforcement, but they reinterpret it as part of interaction.

As important as interaction seems to be for language development, it does not really explain how it is that the child acquires syntax, the set of rules that account for sentence construction. That is, whereas it is likely that interaction plays a crucial part in the language acquisition process, interaction alone cannot account for the fact that children use correct word order in their utterances, come to understand alternate versions (paraphrases) of the same proposition, and have the potential to talk about a never-ending array of possibilities. Only a theory which could describe the mechanisms underlying this skill would be powerful enough to explain the structural component of the acquisition process.

None of these theories can account for all the details of language acquisition. Undoubtedly, a larger theory which can integrate the data reported by the three schools in a meaningful way will replace these fragmentary accounts. That is, the behaviorist, innatist, and interactionist accounts are not wrong, only incomplete.

Context

Thanks largely to the influence of John B. Watson in psychology and Leonard Bloomfield in linguistics, behaviorism dominated much of the thinking about language and language acquisition during the first half of the twentieth century. In the 1950's, however, a challenge was issued to behaviorist approaches by linguist Noam Chomsky, who, in a slender but revolutionary monograph entitled *Syntactic Structures* (1957), argued against the behaviorism advocated by Bloomfield and his followers.

Virtually simultaneous with the appearance of *Syntactic Structures* was the publication of *Verbal Behavior* by B. F. Skinner, then the most influential advocate of behaviorism.

Verbal Behavior was an ambitious attempt to account for the acquisition of language in a behaviorist framework. In a scathing review published in 1959, Chomsky pointed to the "creative" aspects of language—the novelty of utterances—and attacked the basic tenets of Skinner's approach to language and language acquisition.

The debate between Chomsky and the behaviorists is one of the oldest debates in the history of ideas, echoing the philosophical disagreement in the seventeenth and eighteenth centuries between the British empiricists John Locke, George Berkeley, and David Hume, who claimed that knowledge of the world is attributable to a passive registration of sense impressions, and rationalists such as the French philosopher René Descartes, who claimed that much of human knowledge is attributable to innate "ideas" not derived from experience. Indeed the roots of innatism (or rationalism, as it is called in philosophical circles) go back to ancient Greece—to Plato, who originated the notion of innate ideas.

The debate between Chomsky and the interactionists, however, is more recent. In the early twentieth century, before Chomsky achieved prominence in linguistics, Jean Piaget looked at the empiricist (behaviorist) and rationalist positions and found them unable to explain the development of human knowledge. Because Piaget wrote in French, he was not much read in the United States, and the behaviorist tradition in psychology remained primary. Chomsky's challenge to behaviorist assumptions and his contentions about the nature of language acquisition had the effect of recruiting to the study of children's language a number of gifted researchers who set out to collect and interpret child language data in the light of Chomsky's model.

Much of the early work in this new field—called "developmental psycholinguistics"—involved recording and transcribing samples of young children's speech. Because the notion of the language acquisition device lay at the foundation of the model proposed by Chomsky, researchers initially kept few contextual notes about what a child was doing when speaking, and they frequently omitted or ignored what the child's adult caretaker said and did. It soon became apparent, however, that the context of the child's utterances was critical to interpretation. In 1970, language acquisition researcher Lois Bloom published *Language Development: Form and Function in Emerging Grammars,* in which she argued for "rich interpretation." That is, she contended that researchers had to do more than merely keep track of sentence growth; in order to describe a child's grammatical abilities, they had to examine the situation in which sentences occurred. Her evidence was a pair of identical two-word utterances spoken on two different occasions by the same child: "Mommy sock." On one of these occasions, the child's mother was putting a sock on the child; on the other, the child was talking about a sock that belonged to Mommy. Thus the first utterance meant approximately "Mommy is putting on my sock," and the second meant something like "Here is Mommy's sock." The relationship between the two words of the child's own utterance is clearly different on the two occasions, and only "rich interpretation" would allow the researcher to know how to provide the appropriate structural description for each utterance.

Such findings led to increasing attention to the details of context and conversation. Researchers found that mothers actually spoke quite clearly and grammatically to their babies and young children, so Chomsky's claim about the poor quality of the speech children hear was shown to be overstated. As researchers looked at mothers' speech to children, they also began to find that interaction was clearly structured to provide children with "scaffolding" to help them acquire language.

The debate continues, but since the early days of Chomsky's critique, behaviorism has generally been regarded by language acquisition researchers as lacking explanatory power, even though certain facets of the behaviorist paradigm may have become reinterpreted within a competing framework. The core of the criticism is that even if imitation and reinforcement could be shown to be crucial factors in the acquisition process, the question of how the child manages to imitate behavior as complex as language remains, as does the problem of explaining exactly how reinforcement works as a motivating device: How does the child come to make the connections between behavior and environmental reward?

These sorts of problems are not unique to the behaviorist model, however; one can aim similar ammunition at the rationalist/syntactic approach. How, for example, do children come to segment the continuous stream of speech into individual words in order to determine word order, if not through the repetition and even isolation of words that mothers and fathers provide in interacting with them? Nor is the interactionist school immune to criticism, for interaction alone cannot account for the acquisition of the most complex part of human language, its syntax, which provides language with its infinite potential.

Bibliography

Bohannon, John Neil, III, and Amye Warren-Leubecker. "Theoretical Approaches to Language Acquisition." In *The Development of Language,* edited by Jean Berko Gleason. Columbus, Ohio: Charles E. Merrill, 1989. This chapter in a language acquisition textbook provides a comprehensive overview of the theoretical approaches, outlining their general assumptions and evaluating each in terms of supporting and contrary evidence. It critically discusses the most plausible formulation of the rationalist approach, learnability theory.

Cairns, Helen Smith. *The Acquisition of Language.* 2d ed. Austin, Tex.: Pro-Ed, 1996.

Campbell, Robin, and Roger Wales. "The Study of Language Acquisition." In *New Horizons in Linguistics,* edited by John Lyons. Harmondsworth, Middlesex, England: Penguin Books, 1970. This essay constitutes an early critique of Chomsky and the psychologists he influenced, faulting them for not attending to the communicative function of language.

Erneling, Christina E. *Understanding Language Acquisition: The Framework of Learning.* Albany: State University of New York Press, 1993.

Gleitman, Lila R. "Biological Dispositions to Learn Language." In *Language Learning and Concept Acquisition,* edited by William Demopolous and Ausonio Marras. Norwood, N.J.: Ablex, 1986. In a highly readable article, Gleitman describes a number of observations which support the notion of the innateness of language-specific faculties.

McNeill, David. "The Creation of Language." In *Language,* edited by R. C. Oldfield and J. C. Marshall. Harmondsworth, Middlesex, England: Penguin Books, 1968. NcNeill provides a succinct, nontechnical discussion of language acquisition from the Chomskyan perspective. Although some particulars of linguistic theory presented here are somewhat dated, the thought which guides the rationalist approach, including a discussion of the language acquisition device, is clearly presented, along with some data supporting the rationalist thesis.

Piattelli-Palmarini, Massimo, ed. *Language and Learning: The Debate Between Jean Piaget and Noam Chomsky.* Cambridge, Mass.: Harvard University Press, 1980. Represents the proceedings of a conference held in October, 1975, which constituted the only meeting between Piaget and Chomsky. Given that they are the founders of two radically different theories involving the nature of knowledge, this book is required reading for anyone interested in the debate. It is lengthy (more than four hundred pages long) and not easy, but the fact that practitioners of different disciplines and methodologies were meeting face-to-face means that the language employed in the book does not become overly technical. Of great value are the discussions at the ends of the presentations and an entire section devoted to commentary on the debate.

Marilyn N. Silva

See also:

Cognitive Development Theory: Jean Piaget, 135; Language: The Developmental Sequence, 346; Speech Disorders, 576.

LEARNED HELPLESSNESS

Type of psychology: Learning
Fields of study: Cognitive learning; critical issues in stress; problem solving

The concept of learned helplessness, first observed in laboratory animals, has been applied to humans in various situations; in particular, it has been applied to depression. The idea holds that feelings of helplessness are often learned from previous experience; therefore, it should also be possible to unlearn them.

Principal terms

ATTRIBUTION: assigning a quality or characteristic to a person or situation
HELPLESSNESS: a perception of not being able to help oneself or others
LEARNING: gaining knowledge or skill and being able to exhibit it to another person
PERSONALITY: the total physical, intellectual, and emotional structure of an individual; exhibited through consistent behavior patterns
SELF-CONCEPT: a person's view of himself or herself; it can differ from how others perceive the person

Overview

The concept of learned helplessness originated with experiments performed on laboratory dogs by psychologist Martin E. P. Seligman and his colleagues. Seligman noticed that a group of dogs in a learning experiment were not attempting to escape when they were subjected to an electric shock. Intrigued, he set up further experiments using two groups of dogs. One group was first given electric shocks from which they could not escape. Then, even when they were given shocks in a situation where they could avoid them, most of the dogs did not attempt to escape. By comparison, another group, which had not first been given inescapable shocks, had no trouble jumping to avoid the shocks. Seligman also observed that, even after the experiment, the dogs that had first received the unavoidable shocks seemed to be abnormally inactive and had reduced appetites.

After considerable research on the topic, Seligman and others correlated this "learned" helplessness and depression. It seemed to Seligman that when humans, or other animals, feel unable to extricate themselves from a highly stressful situation, they perceive the idea of relief to be hopeless, and they give up. The belief that they cannot affect the outcome of events no matter what force they exert on their environment seems to create an attitude of defeat. Actual failure eventually follows, thereby reinforcing that belief. It seemed that the reality of the situation is not the crucial factor: What matters is the perception that the situation is hopeless.

As research continued, however, Seligman discovered that exposure to uncontrollable negative situations did not always lead to helplessness and depression. Moreover, the results yielded no explanation of the loss of self-esteem frequently seen in depressed persons. To refine their ability to predict helpless attitudes and behavior, Seligman and his colleagues developed a measuring mechanism called the attributional style questionnaire. It involves twelve hypothetical events, six bad and six good.

Subjects involved in testing are told to imagine themselves in the situations and to determine what they believe would be the major cause of the situation if it were to happen to them. After subjects complete the test, their performance is rated according to stability versus instability, globality versus specificity, and externality versus internality. An example of stable, global, internal perceptions would be a feeling of stupidity for one's failure; an unstable, specific, and external perception might consider luck to be the cause of the same situation. The questionnaire has been used by some industries and corporations to identify people who may not be appropriate for certain positions requiring assertiveness and a well-developed ability to handle stress. The same questionnaire has also been used to identify individuals who may be at high risk for developing psychosomatic disorders so that early intervention can be implemented.

Perhaps the primary significance of learned helplessness is its model of how a person's perception of a life event can influence the person's behavior—and can therefore affect his or her life and possibly the lives of others. Seligman believes that the way people perceive and explain the things that happen to them may be more important than what actually happens. These perceptions can have serious implications for a person's mental and physical health.

Applications

The human mind is so complex, and the cognitive process so unknown, that perception is one of the most confusing frontiers facing social scientists. Why do people perceive situations as they do—often as events far different from the ones that actually transpired? If a person is convinced that an event occurred the way he or she remembers it, then it becomes that person's reality. It will be stored that way and may be retrieved that way in the future—perhaps blocking opportunities for positive growth and change because the memory is based on an inaccurate perception.

If children are taught that they are "stupid" because they cannot understand what is expected of them, for example, then they may eventually stop attempting to understand: They have learned that their response (trying to understand) and the situation's outcome are independent of each other. If such helpless feelings are reinforced, the individuals may develop an expectation that no matter what they do, it will be futile. They will then develop a new feeling—hopelessness—which can be generalized to a new situation and can interfere with the future. Various studies have indeed shown that many people have been "taught" that, no matter what their response, the outcome will be the same—failure—so there is no reason to bother to do anything.

One example of this can be demonstrated in the area of victimized women and children. Halfway houses and safe houses are established in an attempt both to protect and retrain battered women and children. Efforts are made to teach them how to change their perceptions and give them new feelings of potency and control. The goal is to teach them that they can have an effect on their environment and have the power to administer successful positive change. For many women, assertiveness training, martial arts classes, and seminars on how to make a strong positive statement with their self-presentation (such as their choice of clothes) become matters of survival.

Children, however, are in a much more vulnerable situation, as they must depend on adults in order to survive. For most children in the world, helplessness is a reality in many situations: They do not, in fact, have much control over what happens to them, regardless of the response they exhibit. Adults, whether they are parents, educators, church leaders, or older siblings, have the responsibility of being positive role models to help children shape their perceptions of the world. If children are allowed to express their feelings, and if their comments are listened to and considered, they can see that they do have some power over their environment and can break patterns of learned helplessness.

A therapist has described "Susan," a client who as a youngster had lived with the belief that if she argued or asserted her needs with her parents they would leave her. She became the "perfect" child, never arguing or seeming to be ungrateful; in the past, if she had, her parents would often get into a fight and one would temporarily leave. Susan's perception was that if she asserted her needs, she was abandoned; if she then begged the parent who remained to tell the absent parent that she was sorry and would never do it again, that parent would return. In reality, her parents did not communicate well and were using their child as an excuse to get angry and leave. The purpose was to punish the other adult, not hurt the child.

When Susan became an adult, she became involved with a man who mistreated her, both physically and emotionally, but always begged forgiveness after the fact. She always forgave him, believing that she had done something wrong to deserve his harsh treatment in the first place. At her first session with a therapist, she was reluctant, having been referred by a women's shelter. She missed her second session because she had returned to her lover, who had found her at the shelter. Eventually, after a cycle of returns to the shelter, the therapist, and her lover, Susan was able to break free and begin the healing process, one day at a time. She told the therapist repeatedly that she believed that no matter what she did the outcome would always be the same—she would rather be with the man who abused her, but paid attention to her, than be alone. After two difficult years of concentrating on a new perception of herself and her environment, she began to experience actual power in the form of positive effectiveness on her life. She became able to see old patterns before they took control and to replace them with new perceptions.

Another example of the power that perceptions of helplessness can have concerns a man ("John") who, as a young boy, was very attached to his father and used to throw tantrums when his father had to leave for work. John's mother would drag him to the kitchen and hold his head under the cold water faucet to stop his screaming; it worked. The child grew up with an impotent rage toward his mother, however, and disappointment in his father for not protecting him. He grew up believing that, no matter how he made his desires known, his feelings would be drowned, as they had been many years before. As a teenager, John grew increasingly violent, eventually getting into trouble; he did not realize that his family was dysfunctional and did not have the necessary skills to get better.

John was never able to believe in himself, even though—on raw rage and little confidence—he triumphed over his pain and terror to achieve an advanced education and black belt in the martial arts. He even developed a career teaching others how to gain power in their lives and how to help nurture the spirit of children. Yet after all this, he still does not have much confidence in his abilities. He is also still terrified of water, although he forces himself to swim.

Feelings of helplessness can also affect a person's health. Research is being conducted on ways of healing that involve perceptions of helplessness or power; in a sense, this involves healing by positive thinking, a very controversial area of science. There has been evidence that the mind and body are inseparable, that one influences the other even to the point of breakdown or healing. There have been many anecdotal reports of people who successfully combat cancer for years after it has been diagnosed as terminal. On the other hand, many people have learned to react in helpless ways to stress, becoming afflicted with migraine headaches, ulcers, and severe back problems, and possibly even causing certain types of terminal illnesses in themselves. Tremendous amounts of money are spent treating stress-related disorders, many of which could be avoided if people could learn that they can have a positive effect on their environment and themselves. There are many effective ways that people can assert power over their lives. Learned helplessness need not be terminal.

Context

The concepts of helplessness and hopelessness versus control over life situations are as old as humankind. The specific theory of learned helplessness, however, originated with the experiments conducted by the University of Pennsylvania in the mid-1960's by Martin E. P. Seligman, Steven F. Maier, and Bruce Overmier. The idea that helplessness could be learned has opened the door to many exciting new approaches to disorders formerly considered personality or biologically oriented, such as psychosomatic disorders, victimization by gender, depression (the "common cold" of mental disorders), and impaired job effectiveness.

The idea that they actually do have an effect on their environment is of tremendous importance to people suffering from depression, because most such people mention a general feeling of hopelessness, which makes the journey out of this state seem overwhelming; the feeling implies that one is powerless over one's reactions and behavior. Research-based evidence has shown that people do have the power to influence their perceptions of their environment and, therefore, change their reactions to it.

Research has provided validity to the suspected link between how a person perceives and influences his or her environment and the person's total health and effectiveness. Leslie Kamen, Judith Rodin, and Seligman have corroborated the idea that how a person explains life situations (a person's explanatory style) seems to be related to immune system functioning. Blood samples were taken from a group of older persons who had been interviewed about life changes, stress, and health changes. Those whose interviews revealed a pessimistic or depressive explanatory style had a larger percentage of suppressor cells. Considering the idea that suppressor cells are believed to undermine the body's ability to fight tumor growth, these discoveries suggest a link between learned helplessness (as revealed by attitude and explanatory style) and susceptibility to diseases.

Studies have also been conducted to determine whether learned helplessness and explanatory style can predict illness. Results, though inconclusive, suggest that a person's attitude and perception of life events do influence physical health some twenty to thirty years later and can therefore be a valuable predictor and a tool for prevention. Particularly if an illness is just beginning, a person's psychological state may be crucial to healing.

If the research on perception and learned helplessness is accurate, a logical next step is to find out how explanatory style originates and how it can be changed. Some suspected influences are how a child's first major trauma is handled, how teachers present information to be learned (as well as teachers' attitudes toward life events), and parental influence.

Perhaps the most promising aspect of the research on learned helplessness is the idea that what is learned can be unlearned; therefore, humans really do have choices as to their destiny and quality of life. Considerable importance falls upon those who have a direct influence on children, because it is they who will shape the attitudes of the future.

Bibliography

Abram, Harry S., ed. *Psychological Aspects of Stress*. Springfield, Ill.: Charles C Thomas, 1970. In this collaboration of chapters on six different stressful situations and how they affect the human being, the different contributors, all medical doctors, examine and discuss the human response to stressful events in life, both pathologically and physiologically. Covers topics from human precognitions to outer-space stressors and intimates that preconceived thought influences future perceptions. Excellent references at the end of each chapter.

Applebee, Arthur N. *The Child's Concept of Story, Ages Two to Seventeen*. Chicago: University of Chicago Press, 1978. An innovative approach and eight thought-provoking chapters give this book an edge on some of the classics in this field. The author examines the use of language and how perceptions can be influenced by it. Demonstrates an adult's and child's sense of story, as well as the responses of adolescents. The author shows how perceptions are easily manipulated by skillful use of phrasing. There are three appendices: a collection of analysis and data, elements of response, and a thorough supplementary table.

Bammer, Kurt, and Benjamin H. Newberry, eds. *Stress and Cancer*. Toronto: Hogrefe, 1981. This edited group of independently written chapters presents thirteen different perspectives from a variety of professionals working in the field of cancer and stress. Well-written; achieves its goal without imposing editorial constraints. Perception of events is emphasized as a major determinant of healing. Excellent resources.

Coopersmith, Stanley. *The Antecedents of Self Esteem*. San Francisco: W. H. Freeman, 1967. Emphasizes the importance of limits and boundaries of permissible behavior in the development of self-esteem. Discusses the mirror-image idea of humans emulating society as it develops through the parent/child relationship. There are four very helpful measuring devices in the appendix.

McKean, Keith Joseph. "Using Multiple Risk Factors to Assess the Behavioral, Cognitive, and Affective Effects of Learned Helplessness." *Journal of Psychology* 128, no. 2 (March, 1994): 177-184.

Seligman, Martin E. P. *Helplessness: On Depression, Development, and Death*. San Francisco: W. H. Freeman, 1975. This easily read and understood book was written by the master researcher in the field of learned helplessness. Covers such areas as anxiety and unpredictability, education's role in emotional development, experimental studies, and how perception influences everyday life. Excellent references. This book is a must for anyone interested in the topic.

Frederic Wynn

See also:

Avoidance Learning, 93; Depression: Theoretical Explanations, 200; Habituation and Sensitization, 266; Instrumental Conditioning: Acquisition and Extinction, 309; Learning, 364; Learning: Generalization and Discrimination, 370; Pavlovian Conditioning, 433.

LEARNING

Type of psychology: Learning
Fields of study: Cognitive learning; instrumental conditioning; Pavlovian conditioning

The psychology of learning examines change in behavior and its causes. The field is primarily limited to changes that result from an organism's experiences and not from biological causes, but the two can interact; learning is one of the most fundamental areas in all of psychology and is critical to such fields as education and psychotherapy.

Principal terms

BEHAVIOR MODIFICATION: the application of learning principles to solve or prevent problems by changing the stimuli that control maladaptive behavior in order to teach new behaviors

BEHAVIORISM: a theoretical approach which states that the environment is the primary cause of behavior and that only external, observable stimuli and responses are available to objective study

COGNITION: mental processes such as attention, thinking, problem solving, and perception; cognitive learning emphasizes these processes in the acquisition of new behaviors

CONDITIONING: the formation of new associations between stimuli and responses that result in behavior change

INSTRUMENTAL CONDITIONING: learning to respond voluntarily to stimuli because of the consequences of the behavior

PAVLOVIAN CONDITIONING: learning to emit reflexive responses to novel stimuli that were paired with naturally eliciting stimuli

PUNISHMENT: a consequence in instrumental conditioning that reduces the probability that a response will recur

REINFORCEMENT: a consequence in instrumental conditioning that increases the probability that a behavior will recur

RESPONSE: a unit of behavior; it may either be specific—for example, a physiological event—or be a functional act without reference to particular actions

STIMULUS: an environmental circumstance to which an organism may respond; it may be as specific as a physical event or as global as a social situation

Overview

Learning is traditionally defined as a relatively permanent change in behavior or behavior potential that occurs as a result of experience. This statement contains three different qualifications, each of which raises interesting and difficult questions.

Learning is relatively permanent. That is, the change in behavior must last for a sufficiently long time before it can be considered learning. Temporary changes do not qualify. For example, one occasionally acquires information that one forgets almost immediately. If one were to call directory assistance for a person's telephone number, one would be able to dial it quite easily. If the line were busy and one did not record the number, however, one probably would be unable to dial it correctly a few minutes later. One was able to dial the number only after calling directory assistance, so it was a change in behavior resulting from experience; yet it is not considered learning because it was not sufficiently permanent.

A question arises as to how long new information must be retained for it to be considered learned. It would be incorrect to say that only permanent changes qualify. One frequently forgets information that one once knew for long periods. If a friend moves and changes her telephone number, one will forget the old one in favor of the new. It would be illogical to say that one had not really learned the old one simply because it was not permanent. This problem is yet to be resolved in psychology. Cognitive psychologists continue to study how learned behavior is retained, under the category of memory research; among other issues, they study how memories are stored, retained, retrieved, and lost.

Learning is a change in behavior or behavior potential. The question here is one of performance and competence. Behavior changes may indicate that learning has occurred, but the actual performance may not be necessary. Some learning theorists, such as Gregory A. Kimble, believe that a change in behavior potential is sufficient. One may possess a capacity that, for whatever reason, is not demonstrated. A classic example of this situation was demonstrated in 1929 by Hugh Blodgett, a student of Edward C. Toleman, at the University of California, Berkeley. Blodgett compared the performances of rats as they learned mazes. The critical difference between the subjects was that some received reinforcements as they finished the mazes while others did not. As training continued, the animals that were reinforced showed the expected improvements; that is, they ran the mazes with fewer errors and in quicker times. Similarly, the unreinforced rats also performed as expected; they did not show these improvements.

After a number of days under these conditions, Blodgett introduced reinforcements to those who had not been receiving any. On the very next trial, these animals showed remarkable improvements. They performed almost as well as the rats that had been receiving reinforcements all along. In fact, they matched those other subjects after only one more day of reinforced training. Yet it had taken the other group almost one week to reach that level of accuracy.

It would be unreasonable to believe that the formerly unreinforced animals learned the maze on only those two trials. Blodgett concluded that they had been learning all along but were not demonstrating their abilities (this is now called latent learning). In short, their performance did not reveal their competence—hence the phrase "or behavior potential" in the definition of learning. This issue is a controversial one. Behaviorists (who prefer to study only what can be observed) tend to leave this phrase off the definition. Cognitive learning theorists, on the other hand, add it. They claim that learning occurs not when a behavior change is evidenced but when information is acquired. A potential for behavior change occurs during the experience which will be demonstrated only at the appropriate time. The problem is that the only way to measure potential is to measure performance.

Learning results from experience. Psychologists normally define experience as interactions with the environment, but not those that are biological in nature. For example, consider behavior changes that result from fatigue or illness. The running style of a marathon runner at the end of a race shows marked changes from the beginning of the race, clearly the result of the experience of having just run more than twenty-six miles. This new running style was not learned; it is caused by fatigue. Similarly, new behaviors such as hallucinations from a high fever are not learning, even though they result from an experience with some bacteria or virus.

These examples fail on two counts: They are not the proper kinds of experience, and they are temporary. Other examples include behavior changes that are caused by maturation. For example, infants begin babbling between four and six months of age. This is even true of children who are born deaf; it is obvious that such children never heard those sounds. Their new behavior of making languagelike sounds results from maturation, not learning.

Applications

Because the concept of learning is so broad and difficult to work with, psychologists usually refer to a specific kind of learning, such as conditioning or cognitive learning. These terms have the advantage of being more narrowly defined and therefore more easily understood. Psychologists identify numerous kinds of learning, but most agree that there are three basic types: Pavlovian conditioning, instrumental conditioning, and cognitive learning.

Conditioning is the formation of associations between stimuli and responses. In fact, many psychologists define learning according to these associations. Pavlovian conditioning is named for Ivan Pavlov, a Russian physiologist who discovered it in 1906. Pavlovian conditioning can be defined as the formation of associations between new stimuli and reflexive responses. Thus, as Pavlov demonstrated, dogs will salivate over food because of a natural, reflexive association between the food stimulus and the salivation response. With proper training, new associations can be formed, and the dogs will salivate at the sound of bells. This type of conditioning is generally understood to be limited to reflexive behavior but still clearly fits the definition of learning. It will last for some time, salivating at the sound of bells is certainly new, and it only occurs if the dogs experience a pairing between the bell and the food in the proper sequence.

Pavlovian conditioning is much more prevalent in everyday life than laboratory examples might suggest. It is likely that most human emotional responses are classically conditioned. In 1920, John B. Watson and Rosalie Rayner taught an eleven-month-old boy, Albert, to fear a rat through the use of Pavlovian conditioning. They paired the presentation of the rat with a loud, startling noise. Albert associated the fear-causing stimulus (the noise) with the new stimulus (the rat) and became frightened of the rat itself, even when there was no noise. Ethical considerations aside, this experiment certainly demonstrates the power of Pavlovian conditioning.

Some psychologists believe that phobias (irrational fears that cause great anxiety) and fetishes (abnormal sexual arousal from inanimate objects) are developed through this type of learning. Also, researchers have recently discovered that the body's immune response system and pain management can be conditioned. Thus, treatment for diseases, infections, and allergies can include Pavlovian conditioning.

Psychotherapy techniques that utilize conditioning principles are called behavior modification. Flooding and systematic desensitization are Pavlovian methods in which maladaptive associations are broken and replaced with other, healthy stimulus-response relations. For example, people who react with irrational fear to heights can be conditioned to replace the fear with relaxation by pairing the formerly fear-causing stimulus (height) with a relaxation stimulus (calm music, soothing thoughts, muscle relaxation, and so on). With careful and systematic training, clients will no longer experience such fear.

The field of instrumental conditioning was most influenced by B. F. Skinner. He found that voluntary behaviors, such as running in a maze, are learned by forming associations between the stimulus situation, the response, and the consequence that results. The consequence causes learning by changing the probability of the response. Reinforcement is a consequence that makes the response more probable; punishment makes it less likely. By varying the rules governing the consequence (the number of responses necessary, their timing, whether the consequence was pleasant or aversive, whether it was a delivery or a removal, and so on), Skinner found that behavior rates changed in specific ways.

Instrumental conditioning is used every time someone is rewarded for a desired behavior or punished for an undesired one. For example, the legal system is largely based on an attempt to dissuade citizens from breaking laws by threatening punishment. (Whether these efforts employ effective use of these principles is certainly an open question.) Similarly, parents and teachers use instrumental conditioning, whether knowingly or not, every time they attempt to instill proper behavior. Discipline techniques such as time-outs, restrictions, suspensions, rewards, and privileges all are attempts to use instrumental conditioning techniques.

One of the more interesting applications of instrumental conditioning is biofeedback training. Even though the behavior systems in biofeedback are not voluntary, the changes that occur are caused by the consequences delivered. Many people have benefited from such training. For example, if diagnostic equipment such as an electrocardiogram is made to produce a tone whenever a desired heart rate is achieved, the tone will act as a reinforcer. The patient will work to maintain the tone, thereby achieving a healthy heart rate. This type of therapy has proved especially useful for people with high blood pressure, migraine headaches, muscle tension, and nerve and muscle damage.

Cognitive learning is a much more ambiguous concept than conditioning. Learning theorists have identified such varieties as concept learning, insight learning, modeling, and observational learning, among others. All have in common the idea that the behavior change may not be observable because the important changes are internal to the organism. That is, learning is not the behavior change; it *causes* the behavior change. Cognitive psychologists identify learning as the acquisition of information.

Most human learning is probably cognitive in nature. Much of what people know they have learned by watching their parents, friends, and teachers. Social skills are learned largely by imitation. People know gender-appropriate behavior because they modeled their parents. They learned to talk because they were surrounded by people who talked. Whenever one learns by watching someone else perform a task, one must employ an understanding of the situation in order to gather the important information. Thus, one learns what to do, when to do it, and why it is important. Until such time as one chooses to demonstrate this new knowledge, there is no outward evidence of this learning. Nevertheless, most psychologists would agree that much has been learned.

Using language, reading, doing arithmetic, and behaving correctly in various social situations are all valuable and necessary skills in society. The use of these skills is very sophisticated and requires knowledge of concepts and symbols. Learning and using these concepts and symbols involve cognitive processes.

Context

Learning is one of the most fundamental areas in psychology. The theorists named already—Pavlov, Toleman, Watson, and Skinner—are some of the most influential in the entire discipline. The history of learning theory is, in many ways, the history of psychology.

Some of the earliest psychological research came from studies in animal learning conducted by Edward L. Thorndike in the 1890's, Edwin R. Guthrie in the early 1900's, and from Toleman, Pavlov, and others. One of the most important movements in psychology, behaviorism, was largely a learning-based approach. Watson founded this school of thought, described in his book *Behaviorism* (1925), in an effort to make psychology an objective and scientific field of research. He believed that all behavior could be explained by learning principles. Skinner extended and continued this field of thought beginning in the 1930's, and behaviorism dominated psychology for most of the next few decades.

Many of the early learning theorists attempted to generate grand, all-encompassing explanations of entire behavior systems. They believed, as was common in psychology at that time, that all behavior could be explained with a few well-formed principles. Modern learning theory is much more limited in scope. Most current theorists believe that human behavior is far too complex to be explained in any simple fashion and attempt to explain only specific aspects of the learning process.

Another relatively modern trend is to integrate neurological research into learning studies. Many modern researchers investigate brain anatomy and chemical changes that result from experience and study how these physiological adjustments are maintained and translated into behavior.

Perhaps the most obvious feature of modern learning theory is the inclusion of cognitive concepts into what was once mainly a behavioristic endeavor. Research into how information is gathered, stored, processed through our perceptual systems, and later retrieved forms a major part of the psychology of learning today.

Even though modern learning theory depends more on cognitive learning principles and higher-order mental functioning than on conditioning, these early ideas about simple learning by association have not been abandoned. Many of the empirical and theoretical formulations of the early researchers have become part of the accepted canon in psychology, and important basic research in Pavlovian and instrumental conditioning continues today.

Bibliography

Chance, Paul. *Learning and Behavior*. Belmont, Calif.: Wadsworth, 1988. This is an introductory text intended for the first course in learning. It is easy to understand and very accessible to the novice. Chance's purpose is to present the basic principles of learning theory, not to review current research. His bibliography reflects this and is not as complete as in many texts.

Donahoe, John W., and David C. Palmer. *Learning and Complex Behavior*. Edited by Vivian Packard Dorsel. Boston: Allyn & Bacon, 1994.

Estes, W. K. "Learning." In *Fifty Years of Psychology: Essays in Honor of Floyd Ruch*, edited by Ernest R. Hilgard. Glenview, Ill.: Scott, Foresman, 1988. Estes' chapter in this book is rather short (eighteen pages), and this is truly unfortunate. It is an excellent review of the field, written by one of the pioneers of learning theory. As a participant in the field, he offers an informative and insightful perspective. Though this essay will be understandable by anyone who has taken an introductory psychology course, sophisticated readers will find more to appreciate. Estes' bibliography includes the most important and influential works in learning.

Hebb, Donald Olding. *The Organization of Behavior*. New York: John Wiley & Sons, 1949. Hebb was one of the first to theorize about the relationship between brain mechanisms and learning. This book was one of the first (and is still one of the best) efforts to explain what happens in the brain between the stimulus and the response. Hebb intended the book for professionals in psychology, biology, and medicine; therefore, it is rather advanced.

Hergenhahn, B. R. *An Introduction to the Theories of Learning*. 3d ed. Englewood Cliffs, N.J.: Prentice-Hall, 1988. As a text for undergraduate psychology-of-learning classes, Hergenhahn's book is unusual. Instead of organizing the text into traditional chapters on conditioning, reinforcement, memory, and so on, he arranges by theory. Thus, there are chapters describing Thorndike's theory, Skinner's, Pavlov's, Toleman's, Jean Piaget's, Hebb's, and so on. Similar theories are placed in units with descriptions about their historical and theoretical relationships. The text assumes only an introductory course as background. Because of the theoretical nature of the book, the bibliography includes many of the most important early works in psychology.

Schwartz, Barry. *Psychology of Learning and Behavior*. New York: W. W. Norton, 1984. Schwartz presents a philosophical and empirical review of learning theory. Though the book is intended for students with only an introductory course background, it is probably more advanced. A very thorough book, it reviews considerable literature. The bibliography reflects this detail.

Skinner, B. F. *About Behaviorism*. New York: Alfred A. Knopf, 1974. Skinner intended this book for the layperson. It is extremely well written and is understandable even by those with no background in psychology. The book presents Skinner's ideas about the philosophy of behaviorism and argues that this approach is a productive and objective method for explaining and analyzing human behavior.

Watson, John B. *Behaviorism*. New York: W. W. Norton, 1925. This book introduced the school of behaviorism and, as such, is one of the most important and influential works in all of psychology. One can still learn much from it, though in the many years since its publication, considerable thought and research have eclipsed some of Watson's theses.

Salvador Macias III

See also:

Avoidance Learning, 93; Habituation and Sensitization, 266; Imprinting and Learning, 290; Instrumental Conditioning: Acquisition and Extinction, 309; Learned Helplessness, 359; Learning: Generalization and Discrimination, 370; Pavlovian Conditioning, 433.

LEARNING
Generalization and Discrimination

Type of psychology: Learning
Fields of study: Instrumental conditioning; Pavlovian conditioning

Generalization results in the transfer of learned behaviors to new situations, whereas discrimination results in the restriction of learned behaviors to specific situations. Both mechanisms are essential if learned behavior is to be maximally adapted to the circumstances in which it occurs.

Principal terms

DISCRIMINATION: the process by which behavior becomes specific to a stimulus or situation
GENERALIZATION: the process by which behavior learned in one situation is transferred to new situations
INSTRUMENTAL CONDITIONING: learning in which behavior becomes more or less frequent depending upon its consequences
PAVLOVIAN CONDITIONING: learning in which a conditioned stimulus comes to elicit a conditioned response through pairing with an unconditioned stimulus that automatically elicits an unconditioned response
REINFORCEMENT: the process by which a stimulus strengthens the behavior that it follows

Overview

Once a behavior has been learned in one situation, that behavior may occur in other, related situations. This tendency for behavior to spread to new situations is called generalization. The reciprocal process, in which behavior becomes more specific to a situation, is called discrimination.

Generalization occurs in Pavlovian conditioning when a conditioned response occurs to stimuli not present during training. Suppose a conditioned salivary response is established in a dog by pairing a 4,000-hertz tone with the presentation of food. A series of test trials is then given, during which tones ranging from 2,000 to 6,000 hertz are presented. Typically, the dog will salivate to a range of tones. If a graph is drawn plotting amount of salivation against tone frequency, a gradient of generalization is found, with the most salivation occurring to the original training stimulus, and less and less salivation occurring to tones that are more and more dissimilar.

In everyday life, generalization is ubiquitous. A child who is bitten by a collie may become afraid of all large dogs. A diner who becomes ill after eating crab may be nauseated by lobster and shrimp. An infant who is comforted by his mother's voice may be comforted by the sound of similar female voices. One's favorite song usually heard played on a piano also produces enjoyment when it is played on a violin or guitar.

Generalization is also found following instrumental conditioning. For example, a pigeon trained to peck a lighted disk of a particular color will also peck at a disk illuminated with a different color, though less vigorously. Again, generalization gradient will result, with the highest rate of pecking occurring to the original disk color and response rates declining as the color becomes more and more dissimilar to the original training stimulus.

Everyday examples abound. After learning to button her shirt, a child can also button her dress, sweater, and coat. A person who learns to read a book in school can also read a magazine, newspaper, or street sign. That same individual can read not only in school but also in a library, at home, or at work. Thus, her reading behavior has generalized across types of reading material as well as across locations. Similarly, a driver who has learned to drive a car on the streets of one city can also drive similar vehicles on the streets of other cities.

Although generalization is usually necessary for human adaptation, there are instances when generalization is not adaptive and people need to learn to behave differently in the presence of different stimuli and situations; that is, they need to discriminate.

In Pavlovian conditioning, discrimination training involves consistently pairing a specific conditioned stimulus with an unconditioned stimulus and consistently omitting the unconditioned stimulus following the presentation of all other stimuli. To train a dog to salivate exclusively in the presence of a 4,000-hertz tone, tones of 2,000, 2,500, 3,000, 3,500, 4,000, 4,500, 5,000, 5,500, and 6,000 hertz may be presented in random order, but only the 4,000-hertz tone would be followed by the unconditioned stimulus (food). In time, the animal would learn the discrimination and salivate only when it hears the 4,000-hertz tone.

Pavlovian discrimination learning occurs outside the laboratory as well. Consider the case in which a boy who misbehaves is always given a whipping by his father. Immediately afterward, the mother hugs and soothes the child. After several such experiences, the child learns a differential emotional response to his parents. His father becomes a signal for punishment and elicits a fear response; his mother becomes a signal for comfort and elicits pleasurable emotions. A diner who consistently becomes ill after eating in a certain restaurant but never after eating at other restaurants will begin to feel nauseated at the sight or thought of that one restaurant but may frequent others with impunity.

In instrumental conditioning, discrimination training involves learning that different environmental stimuli are associated with different conditions of reinforcement. To teach a pigeon a color discrimination, periods during which a disk is illuminated with a green light could be alternated with periods during which the disk is illuminated with a red light. Pecking the green disk would be reinforced by food delivery; pecking the red disk would never produce food. In time, the bird would learn to peck only when the disk is green.

The same procedure is responsible for instrumental discrimination learning in humans. The infant who calls her mother "mama" is reinforced with maternal affection, but she is ignored when the word is used to address her father, brother, or uncle. A child who swears in the presence of his peers may be rewarded with laughter and approval; swearing in the presence of his parents may be followed by punishment. As a consequence, swearing has a high probability of occurrence in the company of friends and low probability in the company of parents. Thus, through exposure to differential contingencies of reinforcement, people learn behavior that is appropriate to specific situations.

Applications

Generalization and discrimination are crucial to successful behavior in everyday life. Concept formation, for example, critically depends upon both these processes. In language development, when a child learns the meaning of a noun, she must learn that the noun is attached to a class of objects. When shown a dog and taught the word "dog," the child does not learn the word as a name for one specific dog but generalizes the term to other dogs as well. Initially, however, she may also overgeneralize, using the word to describe a variety of four-legged animals that are not dogs. As her use of the word is corrected by adults, she learns to discriminate between animals that are dogs and those that are not dogs. Her concept of "dog" becomes more and more refined.

Linguists have been aware of these phenomena in the learning of grammar as well. When learning English, children learn that the past tense is formed by adding -ed to the present tense form of a verb. Thus, a child may be taught the forms "smile/smiled" and "talk/talked," whereupon he will correctly use the forms "jump/jumped" and "walk/walked." This is successful generalization. Overgeneralization typically occurs, however, and the child will use forms such as "go/goed" and "run/runned." Discrimination learning now comes into play as the child learns the correct forms of these irregular verbs. In school, when the child begins studying a second language, he will face the same problem all over again.

Indeed, to be successful, all learning must involve elements of generalization and discrimination. Stimuli and situations are never identical from one occasion to the next. Without generalization, every stimulus or situation would be perceived as novel, and one would have to learn a response to fit each of these new occasions. Imagine the time and effort involved in having to relearn the meaning of a word every time it was used in a different sentence or how to operate a pair of scissors each time a different pair was used or a different material was to be cut. Generalization allows one to transfer learning across situations and facilitates efficient performance in a rapidly changing world.

Similarly, to learn an appropriate conditioned response, a person or animal must learn to discriminate the conditioned stimulus from among the welter of irrelevant background stimuli that are always present. One learns to salivate in anticipation of food when hearing bacon sizzling in the pan but not when hearing static on the radio or a fly buzzing overhead. In operant conditioning, one must learn the situational cue that means reinforcement is available, the so-called discriminative stimulus for reinforcement. Soda machines supply very distinctive discriminative stimuli, and people learn that when they see them they can insert coins into the slot and get a soft drink. They do not insert coins into the slots on radiators or cigarette machines to get something to drink. People also learn to pick up the telephone and speak into it only after it rings and to drive through an intersection only when the light is green.

Although generalization and discrimination usually occur automatically as the result of natural contingencies of reinforcement, they cannot always be counted on in applied settings and must sometimes be specifically programmed. An important issue in therapeutic settings is whether behavior changes will generalize to the client's natural environment. Many individuals who have made impressive gains in treatment revert to inappropriate behaviors after treatment terminates. For example, a client with a drug addiction may remain drug-free while in a rehabilitation program where drug abstinence behaviors are reinforced. If that client returns to an environment in which drug use is once again reinforced, resumption of drug use is likely. Similarly, a shy child may learn assertive behaviors in the presence of the therapist, but if assertiveness is ignored by the child's parents, teachers, and peers the behavior will extinguish.

To facilitate generalization of treatment gains, many therapists specifically program for it. One approach is to increase the similarity between the treatment environment and the natural environment. Significant individuals who will be interacting with the client outside the therapeutic setting may be specially trained to model and reinforce appropriate behaviors. The client may also receive discrimination training, thus learning to approach people and places that will support positive behavior changes and to avoid people and places that encourage inappropriate behaviors.

In industrial settings, discrimination learning is important in areas such as quality control. Often very fine discriminations must be made on sight between defective and nondefective products. This work can be very tedious, and fatigue is a major factor in decreased productivity. Animals have been trained to do such discriminations, however, and can work at them for hours on end. Thom Verhave has described several experiments in which pigeons were trained to discriminate between defective and nondefective pills based on their size, shape, color. The pigeons were very successful at removing defective pills from the assembly line, with an accuracy rate of 99 percent. B. F. Skinner has also described the use of pigeons to guide missiles to enemy ships. The pigeons had been taught to discriminate enemy ships from friendly ones and corrected the trajectory of the missile by pecking at an appropriate target.

Context

The processes of generalization and discrimination in Pavlovian conditioning were first described by Ivan Pavlov in his classic *Conditioned Reflexes* (1927). One intriguing area of research was work on experimental neurosis. Dogs were trained to salivate when the experimenter presented a circle as the conditioned stimulus and not to salivate when an ellipse was presented. After the discrimination was learned, the ellipse was gradually made more circular. Eventually, the discrimination broke down, and the dogs' behavior became disturbed. They whined and struggled against the conditioning harness. Subsequent conditioning was disrupted. This effect has been replicated in pigs, goats, and sheep. Even outside the conditioning environment, the sheep experienced heart arrhythmias, their social behavior was disturbed, and they often failed to flee from predators. Some researchers believe that this phenomenon is relevant to psychological pathologies in humans. It is known, for example, that humans placed in situations where they are unable to make important discriminations suffer anxiety, depression, or other negative emotional effects.

In 1920, John B. Watson and his student Rosalie Rayner described one of the first experiments demonstrating generalization following Pavlovian fear conditioning. An infant named Albert was conditioned to fear a white rat by pairing the rat with an unexpected loud noise. After only a few conditioning trials, Albert developed a fear reaction to the rat which generalized to other small, furry animals and objects, including a rabbit and a ball of cotton. In the absence of knowledge of the conditioning history, these fears would have been impossible to understand. This experiment demonstrated that pathological emotional responses do not always result from Freudian conflict or other mechanisms arising from the depths of the psyche but can result from simple conditioning.

In operant conditioning, studies of generalization and discrimination have played a pivotal role in attempts to understand how complex cognitive tasks are conquered. Two opposing positions have dominated research in this area. One is that these cognitive tasks represent unique ways of dealing with the world that cannot be understood in terms of simpler mechanisms. The other is that these complex tasks can be understood in terms of operant conditioning phenomena.

Some experiments conducted with pigeons lend support to the second position. Pigeons were trained to discriminate slides containing a target object from ones not containing that object. The pigeons demonstrated what appeared to be quite complex concepts, learning to discriminate photographs containing trees from those not containing trees and those containing humans from those not. The pigeons appeared not only to learn each slide as a separate stimulus but also to develop a "rule" for categorizing the target objects which they could then apply successfully to slides they had never seen before.

Using generalization and discrimination techniques similar to those used to teach language skills to retarded and autistic children, apes have been taught to communicate in American Sign Language. Some researchers argue that the apes have learned nothing more than simple imitation, while others maintain that they have learned genuine language skills.

Bibliography

Baldwin, John D., and Janice I. Baldwin. *Behavior Principles in Everyday Life*. 2d ed. Englewood Cliffs, N.J.: Prentice-Hall, 1986. Uses hundreds of examples from ordinary human behavior to illustrate the basic principles of conditioning, including special considerations of generalization and discrimination. Detailed, yet easy to follow, this is one of the best introductions available.

Herrnstein, Richard J. "Objects, Categories, and Discriminative Stimuli." In *Animal Cognition*, edited by H. L. Roitblat, T. G. Bever, and H. S. Terrace. Hillsdale, N.J.: Lawrence Erlbaum, 1984. A review of some of the work of Herrnstein and others on operant discrimination, including concept learning. Highly recommended for serious students of operant behavior.

Liddell, Howard S. "Conditioning and Emotions." *Scientific American* 190 (January, 1954): 48-57. Liddell describes his research with conditioned neurosis in goats and sheep and discusses behavioral as well as physiological effects of this procedure. The implications for human behavior are made clear in this fascinating article.

Mackintosh, N. J., ed. *Animal Learning and Cognition*. San Diego, Calif.: Academic Press, 1994.

Martin, Garry, and Joseph Pear. *Behavior Modification: What It Is and How to Do It*. 3d ed. Englewood Cliffs, N.J.: Prentice-Hall, 1988. This introduction to behavior modification offers clear explanations of the principles underlying operant behavior change, including changes based on generalization and discrimination. Discusses techniques for intentionally producing generalization and discrimination in human beings.

Miller, L. Keith. *Principles of Everyday Behavior Analysis*. 2d ed. Monterey, Calif.: Brooks/Cole, 1980. An excellent introduction to behavior analysis for the high school or college student. Material is presented in a modified programmed-instruction format. There are chapters dealing specifically with generalization and discrimination.

Sarafino, Edward P. *Principles of Behavior Change: Understanding Behavior Modification Techniques*. New York: John Wiley & Sons, 1996.

Skinner, B. F. "How to Teach Animals." *Scientific American* 185 (December, 1951): 26-29. Describes operant conditioning, including the conditioning of discrimination, in clear and readable terms accessible to a wide audience.

Verhave, Thom. "The Pigeon as a Quality Control Inspector." *American Psychologist* 21 (1966): 109-115. In this fascinating report, Verhave describes his research on using pigeons trained to discriminate good from defective pills as quality control agents. The article is lively and easy to read, as it is written largely in a nontechnical style.

Linda J. Palm

See also:

Avoidance Learning, 93; Habituation and Sensitization, 266; Imprinting and Learning, 290; Instrumental Conditioning: Acquisition and Extinction, 309; Learned Helplessness, 359; Learning, 364; Pavlovian Conditioning, 433.

LOGIC AND REASONING

Type of psychology: Cognition
Fields of study: Cognitive processes; thought

Logic and reasoning are essential elements of the human mind and underlie many daily activities. Although humans may not follow the prescriptions of formal logic precisely, human reasoning is nevertheless often systematic. Study of the structures and processes involved in the use of logic and reasoning provides insight into both the human mind and the possible creation of intelligent machines.

Principal terms

ATMOSPHERE HYPOTHESIS: a hypothesis that states that when the quantifiers in the conclusion of a syllogism match the quantifiers in the premises, people are more likely to accept that syllogism as valid

AVAILABILITY: a heuristic in which an estimate of the frequency of a class of events is based on how easily different examples or instances of that class can be brought to mind

BELIEF-BIAS EFFECT: the phenomenon that when a valid conclusion is unbelievable, people are less likely to accept it as valid; when an invalid conclusion is believable, people are more likely to accept it as valid

CONFIRMATION BIAS: the tendency to seek confirming evidence but not to seek disconfirming evidence

DEDUCTIVE REASONING: reasoning in which the truth of the conclusion follows with certainty from the truth of the premises if a valid rule of inference has been applied

GAMBLER'S FALLACY: the belief that if a small sample is drawn from an infinite and randomly distributed population, that sample must also appear randomly distributed

HEURISTIC: an informal "rule-of-thumb" method for solving problems that often yields an approximately correct answer

INDUCTIVE REASONING: reasoning in which the truth of the premises offers support for the truth of the conclusion, but in which the truth of the conclusion cannot be known with certainty

REPRESENTATIVENESS: a heuristic in which an estimate of the probability of an event or sample is determined by the degree to which it resembles the originating process or population

SYLLOGISM: a logical argument constructed of a major premise, a minor premise, and a conclusion, the validity of which is determined by rules of inference

Overview

Logical and reasoning tasks are typically classified as either deductive or inductive. In deductive reasoning, if the premises are true and a valid rule of inference is used, the conclusion must be true. In inductive reasoning, in contrast, the conclusion can be false even if the premises are true. In many cases, deductive reasoning also involves moving from general principles to specific conclusions, while inductive reasoning involves moving from specific examples to general conclusions.

Cognitive psychologists study deductive reasoning by examining how people reason using syllogisms, logical arguments that comprise a major and a minor premise that lead to a conclusion. The premises are assumed to be true; the validity of the conclusion depends upon whether a proper rule of inference is used. The classic example of deduction is:

All men are mortal.
Socrates is a man.
Socrates is a mortal.

A more modern (and more controversial) example of deduction might be:

Abortion is murder.
Murder should be illegal.
Abortion should be illegal.

The second example prompts a distinction between "truth" and "validity." Even though the second syllogism is logically valid, it may or may not be true. Broadly speaking, truth refers to content (that is, applicability of the conclusion to the real world), and validity refers to form (that is, whether the conclusion is drawn logically). It is thus possible to have a valid argument that is nevertheless untrue. For a clearer example, consider this syllogism:

All dinosaurs are animals.
All animals are in zoos.
Therefore, all dinosaurs are in zoos.

The conclusion is valid but is not true, because one of the premises (all animals are in zoos) is not true. Even though a valid rule of inference was applied and a valid conclusion was drawn, the conclusion is not true. If a valid conclusion has been drawn from true premises, however, the argument is called "sound."

With inductive reasoning, the validity of the conclusion is less certain. The classic example of induction is:

Every crow I have seen in my life up to this time has been black.
All crows are black.

Other examples of induction include a child who begins to say "goed" (from "go") instead of "went," a detective piecing together evidence at the scene of a crime, and a stock analyst who, after observing that prices have fallen during the past two Septembers, urges clients to sell in August. In all these cases, a conclusion is drawn based on evidence observed prior to the conclusion. There remains the possibility, however, that additional evidence may render the conclusion incorrect. It does not matter how many positive instances (for example, black crows, September stock declines) have been observed; if one counterexample can be found (for example, a white crow, a September stock rise), the conclusion is incorrect.

The study of induction spans a variety of methods and topics. In this chapter, most of the consideration of induction involves cases in which people rely on heuristics in their reasoning. Heuristics involve "rules of thumb" that yield "ballpark" solutions that are approximately correct and can be applied across a wide range of problems.

One common heuristic is representativeness, which is invoked in answering the following questions: What is the probability that object A belongs to class B, event A originates from process B, or that process B will generate event A? The representativeness heuristic suggests that probabilities are evaluated by the degree to which A is representative of B; that is, by the degree to which A resembles B. If A is representative of B, the probability that A originates from B is judged to be high; if A does not resemble B or is not similar to B, the probability that A originates from B is judged to be low.

A second heuristic is availability, which is invoked in judgments of frequency; specifically, people assess the frequency of a class by the ease with which instances of that class can be brought to mind. Factors that influence the ability to think of instances of a class, such as recency, salience, number of associations, and so forth, influence availability in such a way that certain types of events (such as recent and salient) are more available. For example, if several people one knows have had car accidents recently, one's subjective probability of being in a car accident is increased.

Applications

Before examining how people reason deductively, two rules of inference must be considered: modus ponens (the "method of putting," which involves affirming a premise) and modus tollens (the "method of taking," which involves negating a premise). Considering P and Q as content-free abstract variables (much like algebraic variables), modus ponens states that given "P implies Q" and P, one can infer Q. In the following example, applying modus ponens to 1 and 2 (in which P is "it rained last night" and Q is "the game was canceled"), one can infer 3.

1. If it rained last night, then the game was canceled.
2. It rained last night.
3. The game was canceled.

Modus tollens states that given "P implies Q" and ~Q (read "not Q"; "~" is a symbol for negation), one can infer "~P." Applying modus tollens to 1 and 4, one can infer 5.

4. The game was not canceled.
5. It did not rain last night.

In general, people apply modus ponens properly but do not apply modus tollens properly. In one experiment, four cards showing the following letters or numbers were placed in front of subjects:

E   K   4   7

Subjects saw only one side of each card but were told that a letter appeared on one side and a number on the other side. Subjects judged the validity of the following rule by turning over only those cards that provided a valid test: If a card has a vowel on one side, then it has an even number on the other side. Turning over E is a correct application of modus ponens, and turning over 7 is a correct application of modus tollens (consider P as "vowel on one side" and Q as "even number on the other side"). Almost 80 percent of subjects turned over E only or E and 4, while only 4 percent of subjects chose the correct answer, turning over E and 7. While many subjects correctly applied modus ponens, far fewer correctly applied modus tollens. Additionally, many subjects turned over 4, an error called affirmation of the consequent.

When stimuli are concrete, reasoning improves. In an analogous experiment, four cards with the following information were placed before subjects:

beer   Coke   16   22

One side of each card showed a person's drink; the other side showed a person's age. Subjects evaluated this rule: If a person is drinking beer, that person must be at least nineteen. In this experiment, nearly 75 percent of the subjects made the correct selections, showing that in some contexts people are more likely to apply modus tollens properly.

When quantifiers such as "all," "some," and "none" are used within syllogisms, additional errors in reasoning occur. People are more likely to accept positive conclusions to positive premises and negative conclusions to negative premises, negative conclusions if premises are mixed, a universal conclusion if premises are universal (all or none), a particular conclusion if premises are particular (some), and a particular conclusion if one premise is general and the other is particular. These observations led to the atmosphere hypothesis, which suggests that the quantifiers within the premises create an "atmosphere" predisposing subjects to accept as valid conclusions that use the same quantifiers.

Prior knowledge or beliefs can influence reasoning if people neglect the form of the argument and concentrate on the content; this is referred to as the belief-bias effect. If a valid conclusion appears unbelievable, people reject it, while a conclusion that is invalid but appears believable is accepted as valid. Many people accept this syllogism as valid:

All oak trees have acorns.
This tree has acorns.
This tree is an oak tree.

Consider, however, this logically equivalent syllogism:

All oak trees have leaves.
This tree has leaves.
This tree is an oak tree.

In the first syllogism, people's knowledge that only oak trees have acorns leads them to accept the conclusion as valid. In the second syllogism, people's knowledge that many types of trees have leaves leads them to reject the conclusion as invalid.

A common bias in inductive reasoning is the confirmation bias, the tendency to seek confirming evidence and not to seek disconfirming evidence. In one study, subjects who were presented with the numbers (2, 4, 6) determined what rule (concept) would allow them to generate additional numbers in the series. In testing their hypotheses, many subjects produced series to confirm their hypotheses—for example, (20, 22, 24) or (100, 102, 104)—of "even numbers ascending by 2," but few produced series to disconfirm their hypotheses—for example, (1, 3, 5) or (20, 50, 187). In fact, any ascending series (such as 32, 69, 100005) would have satisfied the general rule, but because subjects did not seek to disconfirm their more specific rules, they did not discover the more general rule.

Heuristics also lead to biases in reasoning. In one study, subjects were told that bag A contained ten blue and twenty red chips, while bag B contained twenty blue and ten red chips. On each trial, the experimenter selected one bag; subjects knew that bag A would be selected on 80 percent of the trials. The subject drew three chips from the bag and reasoned whether A or B has been selected. When subjects drew two blues and one red, all were confident that B had been selected. If the probability for that sample is actually calculated, however, the odds are 2:1 that it comes from A. People chose B because the sample of chips resembles (represents) B more than A, and ignored the prior probability of 80 percent that the bag was A.

In another experiment, subjects were shown descriptions of "Linda" that made her appear to be a feminist. Subjects rated the probability that Linda was a bank teller and a feminist higher than the probability that Linda was a bank teller. Whenever there is a conjunction of events, however, the probability of both events is less than the probability of either event alone, so the probability that Linda was a bank teller and a feminist was actually lower than the probability that she was only a bank teller. Reliance on representativeness leads to overestimation of the probability of a conjunction of events.

Reliance on representativeness also leads to the "gambler's fallacy." Consider a chance event such as flipping a coin (H represents "heads," T represents "tails"). Which sequence is more probable: HTHTTH or HHHHHH? Subjects judge that the first sequence is more probable, but both are equally probable. The second sequence, HHHHHH, does not appear to be random, however, and so is believed to be less probable. After a long run of H, people judge T as more probable than H because the coin is "due" for T. A problem with the idea of "due," though, is that the coin itself has no memory of a run of H or T. As far as the coin is concerned, on the next toss there is .5 probability of H and .5 probability of T. The fallacy arises because subjects expect a small sample from an infinitely large random distribution to appear random. The same misconceptions are often extended beyond coin-flipping to all games of chance.

In fallacies of reasoning resulting from availability, subjects misestimate frequencies. When subjects estimated the proportion of English words beginning with R versus words with R as the third letter, they estimated that more words begin with R, but, in fact, more than three times as many words have R as their third letter. For another example, consider the following problem. Ten people are available and need to be organized into committees. Can more committees of two or more committees of eight be organized? Subjects claimed that more committees of two could be organized, probably because it is easier to visualize a larger number of committees of two, but equal numbers of committees could be made in both cases. In both examples, the class for which it is easier to generate examples is judged to be the most frequent or numerous. An additional aspect of availability involves causal scenarios (sometimes referred to as the simulation heuristic), stories or narratives in which one event causes another and which lead from an original situation to an outcome. If a causal scenario linking an original situation and outcome is easily available, that outcome is judged to be more likely.

Context

Until the twentieth century, deductive logic and the psychology of human thought were considered to be the same topic. The mathematician George Boole entitled his 1854 book on logical calculus *An Investigation of the Laws of Human Thought*. This book was designed "to investigate the fundamental laws of those operations of the mind by which reasoning is performed." Humans did not always seem to operate according to the prescriptions of logic, but such lapses were seen as the malfunctioning of the mental machinery. When the mental machinery functioned properly, humans were logical. Indeed, it is human rationality, the ability to think logically, that for many thinkers throughout time has separated humans from other animals (for example, Aristotle's man as rational animal) and defined the human essence (for example, René Descartes' "I think, therefore I am").

As a quintessential mental process, the study of reasoning is an integral part of modern cognitive psychology. Fifty years ago, however, when psychology was in the grip of the behaviorist movement, little attention was given to such "mentalistic" conceptions, with the exception of isolated works such as Frederick C. Bartlett's studies of memory and Jerome S. Bruner, Jacqueline J. Goodnow, and George A. Austin's landmark publication *A Study of Thinking* (1956), dealing with, among other topics, induction and concept formation. The development of the digital computer and the subsequent application of the computer as a metaphor for the human mind suggested new methods and vocabularies for investigating mental processes such as reasoning, and with the ascendency of the cognitive approach within experimental psychology and the emergence of cognitive science, research on human reasoning has become central in attempts both to understand the human mind and to build machines that are capable of independent, intelligent action.

In the latter part of the twentieth century, there have been attempts to simulate human reasoning with computers and to develop computers that are capable of humanlike reasoning. One notable attempt involves the work of Allan Newell and Herbert Simon, who provided human subjects with various sorts of problems to solve. Their human subjects would "think out loud," and transcripts of what they said became the basis of computer programs designed to mimic human problem solving and reasoning. Thus, the study of human logic and reasoning has not only furthered the understanding of human cognitive processes but also given guidance to those working in artificial intelligence. One caveat, however, is that even though such transcripts may serve as a model for computer intelligence, there remain important differences between human and machine "reasoning." For example, in humans, the correct application of some inference rules (for example, modus tollens) depends upon the context (for example, the atmosphere hypothesis or the belief-bias effect). Furthermore, not all human reasoning may be strictly verbalizable, and to the extent that human reasoning relies on nonlinguistic processes (such as imagery), it might not be possible to mimic or re-create it on a computer.

After being assumed to be logical or even being ignored by science, human reasoning is finally being studied for what it is. In solving logical problems, humans do not always comply with the dictates of logical theory; the solutions reached may be influenced by the context of the problem, previous knowledge or belief, and the particular heuristics utilized in reaching a solution. Discovery of the structures, processes, and strategies involved in reasoning promises to increase the understanding not only of how the human mind works but also of how to develop artificially intelligent machines.

Bibliography

Boden, Margaret A. *Computer Models of the Mind.* New York: Cambridge University Press, 1988. Examines attempts to simulate human cognition on computers and use humans as models for building intelligent machines. The author examines computer models in a wide range of areas, including vision, language, and reasoning.

Evans, Jonathan St. B. T., and David E. Over. *Rationality and Reasoning.* Hove, East Sussex, UK: Psychology Press, 1996.

Faye, Jan, Uwe Scheffler, and Max Urchs, eds. *Logic and Causal Reasoning*. Berlin: Akademie Verlag, 1994.

Garnham, Alan, and Jane Oakhill. *Thinking and Reasoning*. Cambridge, Mass.: Blackwell, 1994.

Halpern, Diane F. *Thought and Knowledge: An Introduction to Critical Thinking*. 2d ed. Hillsdale, N.J.: Lawrence Erlbaum, 1989. Presents a brief overview of memory and language, then presents data and theory on performance with different types of deductive arguments, analyzing arguments, fallacies, reasoning with probabilities, and hypothesis testing. The author provides numerous examples and exercises, and the text can be understood by high school or college students.

Holland, John H., et al. *Induction: Processes of Inference, Learning, and Discovery*. Cambridge, Mass.: MIT Press, 1986. Presents a broad cross-disciplinary account of induction and examines the role of inferential rules in induction, people's mental models of the world, concept formation, problem solving, and the role of induction in discovery. The authors provide an extensive bibliography of scholarly research on induction.

Johnson-Laird, Philip Nicholas. *Mental Models*. Cambridge, Mass.: Harvard University Press, 1983. Presents an extensive review of data and theory on syllogistic reasoning. The author presents a unified theory of the mind based on recursive procedures, propositional representations, and mental models. The text is very thorough and detailed, and many readers may find it daunting.

Kahneman, Daniel, Paul Slovic, and Amos Tversky, eds. *Judgment Under Uncertainty: Heuristics and Biases*. New York: Cambridge University Press, 1982. Presents a collection of many of the important papers on heuristics, including several papers each on representativeness, availability, causality and attribution, and corrective procedures. Many of the papers are thorough and present detailed information on experiments or theory.

Sternberg, Robert J., and Edward E. Smith, eds. *The Psychology of Human Thought*. New York: Cambridge University Press, 1988. Contains chapters on concepts and thought, induction, understanding causality, deduction, judgment, and decision making. Each chapter is written by an expert on the topic and contains an extensive bibliography.

Weizenbaum, Joseph. *Computer Power and Human Reason*. New York: W. H. Freeman, 1976. Provides many examples of "computer reason" and argues that some aspects of the mind cannot be explained in information-processing (computational) terms. Makes the case that computers should not be given tasks that demand human reason or wisdom. Written in a very accessible and easy-to-read style.

Timothy L. Hubbard

See also:

THEORIES OF MEMORY

Type of psychology: Memory
Field of study: Cognitive processes

Theories of memory attempt to identify the structures and explain the processes underlying the human memory system. These theories give coherence to an understanding of memory and suggest new research needed to extend knowledge about learning and memory.

Principal terms

LONG-TERM MEMORY: a memory system of unlimited capacity which consists of more or less permanent knowledge

MEMORY TRACE: the physiological changes thought to occur in the brain when it records information

NEURONS: the specialized nerve cells in the brain that transmit information

PARALLEL PROCESSING: the decomposing of information into different components for separate and simultaneous processing, either by the brain or by computers

REVERBERATING CIRCUIT: a set of brain cells firing repeatedly during learning

SCHEMAS: large clusters of interrelated concepts that organize and interpret information

SEMANTIC MEMORY: stored knowledge of words, meanings, and their interrelationships

SHORT-TERM MEMORY: a memory system of limited capacity which holds information for a very short period of time before it is forgotten

SYNAPSE: the area between neurons where communication occurs between the axon of one neuron and the dendrite of another

Overview

Human memory is among the most complex phenomena in the universe. A Russian newspaper reporter once flawlessly recalled a list of fifty unrelated words he had studied for only three minutes fifteen years before. On the other hand, as everyone knows from personal experience, the memory system is also capable of losing information presented only seconds in the past. Errors in memory create so many problems that it seems imperative to know all that is possible about human memory. For that, a theory is needed.

A scientific theory is a systematic way to understand complex phenomena which occur in nature. A theory is judged to be useful insofar as its claims can be supported by the findings of empirical tests, especially experimentation, and insofar as it leads to further research studies. A theory is not right or wrong; it is simply a tool to describe what is known and to suggest what needs further study.

Theories of memory have been important to psychology for a long time, often occupying the time and interest of researchers throughout their careers. Memory, which is always connected to learning, is defined as the mental process of preserving information acquired through the senses for later use. Such a concise definition does not, however, do justice to the complexity of memory. In a sense, memory is the record of the experiences of a lifetime. Without it, a person could not reexperience the past; everything at every moment would be brand-new. A person could not even recognize the face of a loved one or learn from any experience. A person would thus have a greatly reduced chance for survival and would have no sense of personal identity. Memory is, in short, critical to functioning as a human being.

The goal of a theory of memory is to explain the structures (hardware) and the processes (software) that make the system work. Explaining how such a complex system works is a massive undertaking. The attempts have taken the form of large-scale theories, which seek to deal with all major operations of the memory systems. The major theories of memory are associationism and theories from cognitive psychology and neuropsychology. The theories differ primarily in views of the retention and retrieval functions of memory. They also differ in terms of their conception of memory as active or passive.

Associationism, the oldest of the three, is the theory that memory relies on forming links or bonds between two unrelated things. This theory stems from the work of Hermann Ebbinghaus, who started the use of laboratory methods in the study of memory in the late nineteenth century. According to this theory, the ability to remember depends on establishing associations between stimuli and responses (S-R). Establishing associations depends on the frequency, recency, and saliency of their pairing. If these bonds become very strong, the subject is said to have developed a habit. Associationism also assumes the existence of internal stimuli that produce behavioral responses. These responses then become stimuli for other unobservable internal responses, thus forming chains. In this way, complex physical behaviors and mental associations can be achieved. Associationists tend to view the memory system as an essentially passive one, responding to environmental stimuli.

Cognitive theory emphasizes studying complex memory in the real world; it is concerned with the ecological validity of memory studies. Most of this work stems from the research of Sir Frederic C. Bartlett, who is not satisfied with laboratory emphasis on "artificial memory," but rather chose to study what he called meaningful memory. Meaningful memory, he said in his book *Remembering: A Study in Experimental and Social Psychology* (1932), is a person's effort to make sense of the world and to function effectively in it. Cognitive psychology recognizes subjective experiences as inescapably linked to human behavior. It centers on internal representation of past experiences and assumes that intentions, goals, and plans make a difference in what is remembered and how well it is remembered. The focus in memory research is on semantic memory—the knowledge of words, categories, concepts, and meanings located in long-term memory. People have highly complex networks of concepts, which helps account for their behavior in the real world. These networks are called schemas. New experiences and new information are viewed in light of old schemas so that they are easier to remember. Cognitive theory emphasizes how the individual processes information, and it uses the computer as its working model of memory.

Neuropsychology has contributed the third major theory of memory. Although psychology has always recognized the connection between its concerns and those of biology and medicine, the technology now available has made neuropsychological analysis of brain structure and functioning possible. Karl Lashley was an early researcher who sought to find the location of memory in the brain. He ran rats through mazes until they had learned the correct pathway. His subsequent surgical operations on experimental rats' brains failed to show localization of memory. The search for the memory trace, the physiological change that presumably occurs as a result of learning, continued with Donald Hebb, who had assisted Lashley. The brain consists of billions of nerve cells, which are connected to thousands of other neurons. Hebb measured the electrical activity of the brain during learning, and he discovered that nerve cells fire repeatedly. He was able to show that an incoming stimulus causes patterns of neurons to become active. These cell assemblies discovered by Hebb constitute structure for the reverberating circuits, a set of neurons firing repeatedly when information enters short-term memory. This firing seems to echo the information until it is consolidated in long-term memory. Other researchers have found chemical and physical changes associated with the synapses and in the neurons themselves during learning and when the learning is consolidated into long-term memory. The discovery of the memory trace, a dream of researchers for a long time, may become a reality. Neuropsychology sees memory as a neural function controlled by electrical and chemical activity.

Applications

Human memory is so important to daily life that any theory which could explain its structures and processes and thus potentially improve its functioning would be invaluable. Memory is inextricably tied to learning, planning, reasoning, and problem solving; it lies at the core of human intelligence.

None of the three theories is by itself sufficient to explain all the phenomena associated with memory. Over the years, a number of ideas have been developed in the attempt to improve memory functioning through passive means. Efforts to induce learning during sleep and to assess memory of patients for events taking place while under anesthesia have had mixed results, but on the whole have not succeeded. Memory enhancement through hypnosis has been attempted but has not been shown to be very effective or reliable. Pills to improve memory and thereby intelligence have been marketed but so far have not been shown to be the answer to memory problems. Research has begun on the possibility that certain drugs (such as tacrine) may interactively inhibit memory loss in people afflicted with certain kinds of dementia (for example, Alzheimer's disease). Work in neuropsychology has shown the influence of emotion-triggered hormonal changes in promoting the memory of exciting or shocking events (such as one's first kiss, or an earthquake). This has led to an understanding of state-dependent memory: Things learned in a particular physical or emotional state are more easily remembered when the person is in that same state again. This helps explain the difficulties in remembering events that took place when a person was intoxicated or depressed. In fact, heavy use of alcohol may result in significant memory loss. A person may not even remember having injured someone in a car accident. Although not fully researched yet, it may be that certain kinds of memory are mood-congruent. Perhaps memories of events that occurred when a person was in a certain mood may become available to the person only when that mood is again induced.

More active means for memory improvement have met with greater success. Associationist theory has demonstrated the value of the use of mnemonics—devices or procedures intentionally designed to facilitate encoding and subsequent recall. The use of rhymes, acronyms, pegwords, and the like enables people to recall factual information such as the number of days in each month ("Thirty days have September . . ."), the names of the Great Lakes (the acronym HOMES), and the colors of the visible spectrum (ROY G. BIV). Visual cues, such as tying a string around one's finger or knotting one's handkerchief, are traditional and effective ways to improve prospective memory. Cognitive psychology has demonstrated the importance of emotional factors—how and why something is learned—to the effectiveness of memory. It has provided the research base to demonstrate the effectiveness of study strategies such as the SQ3R (survey, question, read, recite, review) technique. Cognitive theory has also shown that metamemory, a person's knowledge about how his or her memory works, may be important for the improvement of memory.

In clinical settings, much research has been concerned with memory impairment as another means to test the applicability of theories of memory. Head injuries are a common cause of amnesia in which events immediately prior to an accident cannot be recalled. Damage to the hippocampus, a part of the brain that is vital to memory, breaks down the transfer of information from short-term to long-term memory. One dramatic case concerns "H. M.," a patient who had brain surgery to control epileptic seizures. After surgery, H. M.'s short-term memory was intact, but if he was momentarily distracted from a task, he could not remember anything about what he had just been doing. The information was never transferred to long-term memory. Such patients still remember information stored in long-term memory before their operation, but to them everyday experiences are always strangely new. They can read the same paragraph over and over, but each time the material will be brand-new. In H. M.'s case, it was discovered that his intelligence as measured by standardized tests actually improved, yet he was continually disoriented and unable to learn even the simplest new associations. Intelligence tests are made to measure general information, vocabulary, and grammatical associations; these things were stored in H. M.'s long-term memory and were apparently not affected by brain surgery. In cases less dramatic than H. M.'s, damage to particular areas of the brain can still have devastating effects on the memory. Damage can be caused by accidents, violent sports activity, strokes, tumors, and alcoholism. Alzheimer's disease is another area to which research findings on memory may be applied. In this fatal disease a patient's forgetfulness increases from normal forgetting to the point that the patient cannot remember how to communicate, cannot recognize loved ones, and cannot care for his or her own safety needs.

Associationism, cognitive psychology, and neuropsychology can each explain some of the structures and processes involved in these and other real-world problems, but it seems as though none of the theories is sufficient by itself. Memory is such a complex phenomenon that it takes all the large-scale theories and a number of smaller-scale ones to comprehend it. The truth probably is that the theories are not mutually exclusive, but rather are complementary to one another.

Context

Theories of learning and memory have been of great concern to philosophers and psychologists for a long time. They have formed a major part of the history of psychology. Each of the theories has been ascendant for a time, but the nature of theory building requires new conceptions to compensate for perceived weaknesses in currently accepted theories and models. Associationism was the principal theory of memory of stimulus-response psychology, which was dominant in the United States until the mid-1950's. Cognitive psychology evolved from Gestalt psychology, from Jean Piaget's work on developmental psychology, and from information-processing theory associated with the computer, and was extremely important during the 1970's and 1980's. Neuropsychology developed concurrently with advanced technology that permits microanalysis of brain functioning. It has resulted in an explosion of knowledge about how the brain and its systems operate.

An understanding of the nature of memory has been important in the field of psychology, but it is also important to the history and the future of humankind. Learning and remembering the alphabet and the multiplication tables are only two obvious examples of the importance of the associationist theory to human life. Associative learning also accounts for much of motor memory (for example, riding a bicycle). Things that need to be learned by rote show S-R connections most explicitly. Much of American schooling continues to be based on this theory of memory. Even though rote learning may be necessary and efficient for some things, there are many other things which are learned and remembered in other ways.

Cognitive psychologists advise taking account of schemas that the learner brings to the task. The principle is to connect the new learning to what already exists in the mind of the learner. In this way, learning is more meaningful and therefore more likely to be remembered in the future. Cognitive theory holds that a child learns language in this way. Discovery and insight learning, which have become very important to science and mathematics education, have their roots in cognitive psychology. Neuropsychology has explained much of what happens when the brain has been damaged by injury or disease. There is a possibility that drugs can be developed to enhance memory functioning, or that memories can be revived by brain surgery. There is hope that advances from the neuropsychological theory will ultimately provide treatments for amnesia.

The future probably holds a synthesis of the memory theories discussed. The three theories of memory are based on the assumption that humans operate in a rational, logical way. A more recent approach assumes that memory is active and constructive, and that it does not always follow rules of logic. The approach is called connectionism (also known as neural nets, or parallel distributed processing). The approach is an attempt to build a model that operates in the same manner as the human brain. Connectionist theorists are interested in accounting for the speed of processing, the evaluative nature of processing, the plasticity evident in the system, and the redundancy built into human memory. Research in cognitive psychology, computer science, and biochemistry seems to suggest that parallel processing may be the model of memory of the future.

Bibliography

Ashcraft, Mark H. *Human Memory and Cognition*. Glenview, Ill.: Scott, Foresman, 1989. This introductory textbook takes the reader on a delightful journey through the world of memory and cognition. Includes illustrations and suggestions for further reading on memory.

Baddeley, Alan D. *Human Memory: Theory and Practice*. Boston: Allyn & Bacon, 1990. One of the world's leading researchers on memory summarizes the history of research on memory and describes controversies in the field. This comprehensive treatment of memory research includes many practical examples.

Conway, Martin A., ed. *Cognitive Models of Memory*. Cambridge, Mass.: MIT Press, 1997.

Ellis, Henry Carlton, and R. Reed Hunt. *Fundamentals of Human Memory and Cognition*. 3d ed. Dubuque, Iowa: Wm. C. Brown, 1983. An excellent discussion of important topics in human memory from a cognitive psychology perspective. One strong feature is a list of multiple-choice questions with explanations of correct answers at the end of each chapter. Undergraduates will find the book very useful.

Fuster, Joaquin M. *Memory in the Cerebral Cortex: An Empirical Approach to Neural Networks in the Human and Nonhuman Primate*. Cambridge, Mass.: MIT Press, 1995.

Gregg, Vernon H. *Introduction to Human Memory*. London: Routledge & Kegan Paul, 1986. Explores the cognitive approach to memory, explaining sensory memory, encoding, and retrieval. Includes a very interesting treatment of amnesias. Has an extensive bibliography.

Higbee, Kenneth L. *Your Memory: How It Works and How to Improve It*. 2d ed. New York: Prentice-Hall, 1988. Practical suggestions on how to use research-based principles of memory in daily life. Applies results of laboratory studies to real-life problems. Useful for improving one's study habits and grades.

Neisser, Ulric. *Cognition and Reality: Principles and Implications of Cognitive Psychology*. San Francisco: W. H. Freeman, 1976. This book marked the acceptance of cognitive psychology as a major school of psychology. Neisser makes the case for studying real-world memory instead of the artificial memory of the laboratory. Discusses the major goals of cognitive psychology and implications for future research.

Norman, Donald A. *The Psychology of Everyday Things*. New York: Doubleday, 1988. An absolutely delightful book that addresses the use of human cognitive abilities in dealing with daily problems in living. Easily understandable by the general reader; will provoke much discussion.

R. G. Gaddis

See also:

Memory: Animal Research, 389; Memory: Long-Term Versus Short-Term, 394.

MEMORY
Animal Research

Type of psychology: Memory
Field of study: Cognitive learning

Memory research relies heavily on demonstrating learning in animals. Animals can be conditioned to respond to particular stimuli, but they also show problem-solving behaviors, cognitive-map memory, insight behavior, and language abilities. Animals learn these cognitive behaviors by observation and imitation, although some animals seem to have remarkably humanlike cognitive abilities.

Principal terms

CLASSICAL CONDITIONING: a type of learning in which two stimuli (such as bell and bone) are paired together so that the presence of one (bell) predicts the presence of the second (bone) and elicits the same response (salivation)
COGNITIVE MAP: a mental representation of an area
Homo sapiens: the modern species of humans
OPERANT CONDITIONING: a type of learning in which a response is repeatedly followed by a reinforcement or reward so that the animal learns that if it performs a particular response, it will obtain a reward
PHYLOGENY: the evolutionary history of a species

Overview

Learning is defined as a relatively permanent change in behavior attributable to some experience. Implied in that definition is the concept that learning and memory are much the same process. In humans, it is easier to demonstrate memory apart from learning. In animals, there is little research that looks at memory without also demonstrating learning. There is no doubt that animals can learn and retain memory of events. Even an earthworm can be taught by operant conditioning to trace a maze and receive a reward for its performance. Pets learn inadvertently through classical conditioning that the sound of the can opener means feeding time. These two types of conditioning predict that any animal can learn to perform a behavior very easily. There is also no doubt that behavior is remembered once it is learned.

Memory that involves more complex thinking processes is an area in which researchers have found some surprising results. This type of memory is referred to as cognitive learning, and it includes processes such as observational learning, problem solving, insight learning, cognitive maps, and even language. Sometimes these processes include conditioning principles, but they also may not. Observational learning is the acquisition of a behavior by observing someone (or something) else performing that behavior. Rats observing other rats running a complex maze will show fewer errors and improved running time than rats in a trial-and-error situation. Observational learning may also be performed immediately in the presence of the performer, a process known as imitation. In an observation study by W. H. Thorpe in 1963, Japanese macaque monkeys observed one female washing its food before eating and then imitated that behavior in food preparation.

Problem-solving behavior implies that memory from a past event is transferred to a new situation and used by the animal to overcome obstacles in the environment. Harry Harlow (1949) showed that monkeys given a set of practice problems had more correct responses in less trials on a later set of similar problems than during the original learning trials.

A similar situation involves insight learning, in which animals appear to study a situation and then use ordinary objects in novel ways to obtain their goals. In 1925, Wolfgang Köhler experimented with chimpanzees by placing food beyond their reach. The chimpanzees appeared to think the problem over and then, with great excitement, arrange boxes and sticks that were present in the cage to obtain the food. Similarly, even pigeons have demonstrated the ability to solve novel events by being taught the preliminary behaviors. For example, pigeons have been trained to climb onto and push boxes around in their cages. Later, a banana was hung above their cage; after hesitating, they pushed the box under the banana to obtain a snack. This implies that the birds not only used their memory of prior events but also combined cognitive processes in a creative manner.

Some of the most impressive research on animal memory involves that of cognitive maps. Many animals have been tested to see if they can remember particular locations of items in their environment. David Sherry (1984) researched the common chickadee in food-hoarding behavior. In this experiment, the birds hid sunflower seeds in storage sites. The seeds were removed to prevent smell or visual cues for the bird's memory. Twenty-four hours later, the birds were returned and their searching time for the hoard sites observed. The birds searched in the previous hoard sites 80 percent more of the time than in nonhoard sites, indicating that they remembered the particular location where they had previously stored food.

Other research showing that animals have cognitive maps has been done with chimpanzees. In this research, chimps have been carried around a large compound by the caretaker and allowed to watch as food was hidden at a number of random locations. Twenty-four hours later, the chimps were returned to the compound to see if they could remember the food sites. The chimps had no problems remembering the locations, and they recovered the food with 100 percent accuracy.

Another area of research which focuses on memory is language, which demands not only memory but also comprehension. Language requires using a signal as a symbol for something that is not necessarily present and using these symbols to give information to another being. Research which demonstrates that animals have language is concerned primarily with apes and monkeys. They do not have the same capabilities of producing verbal language that humans do. In fact, their vocal cords are much like those of a human infant, which are too immature to produce words. Thus, in the first experiments, apes were taught to use their hands to produce the language of the deaf, known as American Sign Language (ASL). More recently, Ann and David Premack (1978) and Sue Savage-Rumbaugh (1986) have used plastic symbols to represent words or concepts, and the animals respond either by placing the correct symbol on a magnetic board or by punching in the symbol on a computer keyboard. It seems quite possible that these chimpanzees, and more recently several other apes, are able to understand, remember, and produce some form of language, demonstrating that animals do possess a remarkable memory system.

Applications

Research into the memory processes of animals provides valuable information within itself. Not only are researchers allowed a glimpse into another species' world and mental processes, but also people are enabled to know their own pets, and other animals, better. Thus, people can train their pets more effectively, prevent damage to property and agriculture by wild animals, aid farm animals and farmers, and possibly use this information to prevent certain species of animals from becoming extinct. For example, study on the memory of geographical locations (such as cognitive maps) could aid in the relocation of animals when their habitat has been destroyed by fires or encroaching civilization.

The study of animal memory has also provided information that can be applied to humans. For example, in many ways a rat's physiological system is very similar to that of a human being. Thus, scientists can infer that if a rat is given a particular drug and reacts a certain way, that drug may affect a human in much the same way. Some research with rats and memory has, in fact, demonstrated that a rat trained to run a maze will forget the layout of the maze once it is given an injection of an amphetamine. This implies that amphetamines may also affect human memory.

The more that is known about the memory systems of animals, the more researchers can compare animal research and human research. This is particularly important in nonhuman primate research, as the apes (such as chimpanzees and gorillas) are the closest kin of humans. They possess memory processes of pattern recognition whereby they can recognize symbols, pictures, and even people after long periods of time. One particular anecdotal example concerns the memory that chimpanzees have for people they have known. One research chimp was separated from his trainer, Herbert Terrace, for a period of time after research funds ran out. Upon reunion, the ape shrieked an emotional cry of recognition and ran to his trainer with very humanlike hugs and signs of affection. Not only did the chimp remember his trainer, but also it displayed signs of emotional attachment. More scientific evidence of recognition memory in monkeys has been shown by Steven Sands (1981). A rhesus monkey was given a twenty-item list and later, out of 211 photographs, it correctly recognized more than 80 percent of the original items. In addition, the monkey exhibited a recall pattern exactly like that of humans, whereby the first and last items of a list are recalled best.

The greatest evidence of memory processes has been shown with the research concerning teaching language to apes. Allen and Beatrice Gardner trained a chimpanzee named Washoe to use his hands to communicate in American Sign Language. After four years, Washoe could remember about 130 signs. This is not as impressive as what a human child can learn in the same amount of time, but it is clear that the chimp comprehends the language.

Similarly, in a different type of testing of language for chimps, David Premack (1976) taught a young chimp named Sarah to use plastic cut-outs of arbitrary shapes to communicate. These shapes included symbols for objects (apple, chocolate), verbs (is, give), concepts (same, different, if-then), and adjectives (colors). Using the plastic symbols, Sarah acquired a reading and writing vocabulary of about 130 words, but she was also capable of comprehending concepts and propositional thought. For example, Premack showed Sarah an apple and a banana with a question mark in between. Sarah responded with a chip that meant "different." To ensure that Sarah and other subjects really understood what they were doing, Premack would show two objects that were exactly alike except that one of them had undergone some change. Sarah was to respond with an object that had caused the change.

For example, given two apples, one of which had been cut in half, Sarah would pick from three alternatives—a bowl of water, a knife, or a pencil—whichever of the three was the cause of the change in the apple. Given a sponge, one of which was dry and the other wet, Sarah would determine that the cause was a bowl of water. Sarah would correctly respond in all causality tests, indicating that she not only remembered the correct term but also understood the cause of events.

More recently, Savage-Rumbaugh taught two chimps, Sherman and Austin, to communicate via a computer-monitored board with geometrical shapes symbolizing words. The two chimps learned to request and to respond to each other's commands such that when Sherman requested a piece of bread, Austin correctly retrieved the item and passed it to his mate. Even this research, however, has been usurped by the remarkable acquisition of language by two "brother and sister" pygmy chimpanzees, Kanzi and Mulika, who share the same laboratory. Kanzi had never been explicitly taught to use the symbols but spontaneously, through imitating his mother, began to acquire language. Mulika, in observing Kanzi, acquired language in a remarkably short time and superceded the acquisition rate of her brother, Kanzi. Both learned to understand much spoken English from their trainer and could respond appropriately to spoken questions.

In the example of language learning in chimpanzees, many exciting results have emerged from these studies. Not only do researchers know much more about the memory and cognitive processes of nonhuman primates, but also they can study the language development of these chimp "children" to see whether it develops along the same lines as it does in human children. If so, this might tell something about the earliest days of humankind, when language was in its infancy, or offer some insight into humans who have language disorders and need special help. In fact, one serendipitous outcome of this research has been that certain tools and techniques that were used to study apes are now being revised and adapted to aid in teaching handicapped humans.

Context

In the broadest sense, research with animals began long before true science was formulated. Prehistoric humans focused on animal behavior to hunt and to protect the tribe from injury. Animals are the primary topic of the cave paintings of early humans. Even in the more modern history of *Homo sapiens*, categorization of animals can be traced back to Aristotle, who lived in the fourth century B.C.E. Aristotle was an astute observer of nature and recorded his many findings about animal species.

The scientist who had the most profound influence on animal research was Charles Darwin, who, in his *On the Origin of Species* (1859), theorized that humans had evolved from animal ancestors. Darwin made extensive observations of animals, which he recorded in his many writings; by his theorizing, he also made humans a part of the hierarchical classification of the animal kingdom. In order to study human phylogenetic origins, the study of animal behavior became crucial. Laboratory animal research began in the late 1800's when Ivan Pavlov, a Russian scientist, was studying the digestive reflex in dogs. While observing the salivation rate of a dog when it was in sight of a dog biscuit, he noticed that the dog had associated the sight of the white laboratory coat with the forthcoming presentation of the food and began salivating prior to the stimulus. This learning process became known as classical (or Pavlovian) conditioning, and it set off a long series of animal experiments in this and related areas.

Similarly, animals were made subjects for research in the American laboratory in the early 1900's by John B. Watson, followed by Edward L. Thorndike. Thorndike used cats in the laboratory to study thinking and reasoning processes. He was primarily interested in whether animals learn as humans do. Thorndike was the first person to compare the laboratory findings on animal behavior to human behavior. This comparative method, known as the animal model, is still used.

In terms of memory research, the tradition began with the study of humans because the topic for memory research typically is verbal learning. With the growth of cognitive psychology over the last fifty years, other areas of memory such as problem solving, cognitive maps, reasoning, insight learning, memory structures and characteristics are now being explored. With such improved and diverse methods to study human memory processes, it is expected that these methods will be extended to animal research in a more applied way. It will be important, given our shrinking planet, to understand how animals function and what other environments they could adapt to in the future. Thus, the study of animal research will grow in its own right instead of being used primarily as a model for human functions.

Bibliography

Griffin, Donald Redfield. *The Question of Animal Awareness*. New York: Rockefeller University Press, 1981. This book discusses animal communication, from the honeybee to the chimpanzee. Discusses issues of animal and insect awareness and the relationships between animal language and its human counterpart.

Halliday, T. R., and P. J. Slater. *Communication: Animal Behavior*. New York: W. H. Freeman, 1983. A very comprehensive text that includes an emphasis on social processes and groups, environmental influences, and evolutionary explanations. This is a clear introductory book that can be easily read by the novice. Informative and well written.

Herrmann, Douglas, et al., eds. *Theory in Context*. Vol. 1 in *Basic and Applied Memory Research*. Hillsdale, N.J.: Lawrence Erlbaum, 1996.

Krebs, J. R., and N. B. Davies. *An Introduction to Behavioral Ecology*. London: Blackwell Scientific Publications, 1987. An easily readable overview on all aspects of animal behavior. Although there is not a specific section on memory research, this book introduces the reader to the principles of animal research and its findings.

Mackintosh, N. J. *The Psychology of Animal Learning*. New York: Academic Press, 1974. This book reviews the principles of learning in animals in the context of classical and operant conditioning as well as more recent accounts of learning theories. Not suitable for light reading, but an excellent source for reference material.

Staddon, J. R. "Learning as Adaptation." In *Handbook of Learning and Cognitive Processes*, edited by W. K. Estes. Hillsdale, N.J.: Lawrence Erlbaum, 1975. This review of laboratory procedures focuses on learning studies with animals. It also is concerned with the natural habitat of the animal. Clear and precise; presents an informative psychological perspective.

Donna J. Frick

See also:

Memory, Theories of, 383; Memory: Long-Term Versus Short-Term, 394.

MEMORY
Long-Term Versus Short-Term

Type of psychology: Memory
Field of study: Cognitive processes

There appear to be two distinct types of memory, short-term and long-term; each of these systems is essential and each has its own characteristics. Short-term memory is very limited in both its capacity and its duration, whereas long-term memory seems to have an unlimited capacity and memory traces that can be lifelong.

Principal terms

DECAY: the disappearance of a memory trace
ENCODING: the process of learning new information and putting it into memory
LONG-TERM MEMORY: information that is retained for a long period of time, sometimes for most of one's life
RETRIEVAL: the recalling or remembering of previously learned information
SENSORY REGISTER: information that is received for only a very brief period of time, perhaps half a second to two seconds
SHORT-TERM MEMORY: information traces or data that rapidly fade; intense concentration is often needed to hold information in short-term memory

Overview

Memory is a major aspect of learning and hence of psychology. There are often thought to be two main systems of memory: short-term memory and long-term memory. Before information can enter either system, however, it must be encountered in the environment. When one first encounters information or a stimulus from the external world, it reaches the brain from the senses. Turning a light on, hearing a sound, or feeling heat or cold activates what is called the sensory register, or sensory memory. If one then pays close attention to the light, sound, or sensation, one activates one's short-term memory.

People do not pay close attention to most material in the sensory register; one does not often examine one's socks closely, count the leaves on a tree, or inspect the texture of a hamburger. Instead, people attend selectively to certain data. Selective attention is the mechanism whereby people choose to pay attention only to certain important items. If one has just had lunch and is driving through town, one will ignore the restaurants one passes; if one has not eaten for the last eight hours, however, one will very likely be paying close attention to those restaurants that might be open. Information that is not attended to decays (disappears) very quickly—within a second, and sometimes within a fraction of a second—from the sensory register.

Once information is selected, it may be encoded into short-term memory. Short-term memory has both a limited duration (fifteen to twenty seconds is often given as a range) and a limited capacity. Short-term memory decays rapidly if it is not rehearsed (repeated) several times or entered into long-term memory. An example of short-term memory would be remembering a number that one has just looked up in the telephone book. Perhaps a woman needs to call the dentist because of a toothache. She may look up the number in the kitchen, then walk to the living room to use the telephone, repeating the number as she walks. After she has placed the call and hung up, she would probably not remember the number an hour or two (perhaps even a few minutes) later. The number—the memory trace—has disappeared.

If, however, she were to repeat aloud or write her dentist's number a hundred times, she would probably remember it for the next several months at least: It would be put into long-term memory. Similarly, if she were to post it on the dashboard of her car and see it every day, she might learn it and be able to recall it at home.

Events can sometimes disrupt or interfere with the short-term memory process. If, as the woman was walking into the living room, her roommate asked her a question and she responded, she might have "lost" the number and had to look it up again. If she then wrote it down to avoid losing it again, she would be utilizing "external storage." Many people write down things they need to remember, from students taking notes to prepare for a test to people on the job who carry notepads to write things down so they will have the information later.

Within the short-term domain are different forms of memory, such as auditory and visual memory, one of which may be better developed than another. For example, if a man is verbally given a list of items to get from the store, he may remember them better than if he had read a list and left the list at home. The ability to read, then recall, information depends on visual memory. If a worker reads a list of procedures on a posted sign, then goes to perform the tasks, that person is relying on visual memory.

It is long-term memory that makes it possible to learn and develop one's intelligence. Long-term memory contains information that has been deeply learned and that a person may even remember all of his or her life. If one is thirty years old, one probably has one's social security number memorized quite well and can "retrieve" it from long-term memory very quickly. Retrieval refers to the process of getting information from one's brain and into words—either verbally or on paper. Tremendous amounts of information can be stored in long-term memory; it is uncertain exactly how much information the human memory can hold. It seems to be virtually impossible to measure scientifically, which has led some theorists to suggest that, for all intents and purposes, the capacity of long-term memory is infinite.

Endel Tulving has made a distinction between two types of long-term memory: semantic and episodic memory. Semantic memory is one's storehouse of facts, figures, names, dates, and more abstract concepts of objects and qualities. Episodic memory involves one's personal memories of events in one's own life, dating as far back as early childhood. Another suggested type of memory is procedural memory, sometimes defined as consisting of learned associations that relate a stimulus to a behavior; hearing the doorbell and automatically going to see who is there is said to occur via procedural memory. Procedural memory has also been defined as the memory system that deals with physical and physiological processes—one must "remember," for example, in order to play a game such as volleyball, use a typewriter, or even move one's legs to walk.

The differences in processing that allow some information to enter only short-term memory and some to be stored in long-term memory are not well understood. The amount of rehearsal (repetition) that one devotes to the information has an effect; the more the repetition, the more likely it will be stored in long-term memory. The type of rehearsal that is used also seems to have a strong effect. The more one considers the appearance, meaning, applications, or context of a piece of information, the more likely it is to be stored.

Applications

Although short-term memory has a limited capacity, a mental technique known as "chunking" provides a way to overcome this limitation somewhat. It is often said that short-term memory can only handle about seven bits of information at once (the number seems to range, in different people, from five to nine). Chunking, or combining bits of information into larger units, allows this memory system to handle more information than it otherwise could. For example, a telephone number, including the area code, includes ten digits; the mind, however, combines—chunks—some of them together into larger units. If the last four digits were 2245, short-term memory might handle them as "twenty-two forty-five," reducing four digits to two chunks. This process can be helpful when one is learning large amounts of material relatively quickly. Concentration is an obvious factor in the effectiveness of short-term memory. Some people are able to concentrate very well, whereas others are more susceptible to distractions. An extreme example of this is children suffering from hyperactivity (attention-deficit hyperactivity disorder); they often have very poor concentration skills and are readily distracted by outside stimuli.

There are many ways to enhance memory; overlearning, or repeating material to be learned many times, is one method. It can involve repeating information over and over or rehearsing complex actions, such as practicing a violin concerto. Repeating something many times appears to be one of the best ways to learn; however, it is easy to become bored or frustrated with this type of learning, sometimes known as rote learning.

Understanding also helps the memory process. Relating new material to older material can help a person remember better, and making a conscious effort to connect new information with old can be very beneficial—both in learning and in retrieving information later. Effects of this can be seen in the difficulties encountered in school by students who do not have the background of knowledge on which new material they are being taught is based. Proper diet and adequate amounts of sleep also help memory, although in cases of lack of sleep or poor nutrition it is not specifically the memory system that is defective, but the entire physiological system.

Aging seems to cause some deterioration of memory skills, but how much and at what point it begins are uncertain. Once people leave school or college, they may no longer work as hard at learning and remembering. Adults also become distracted by immediate concerns, such as the needs of their families and jobs. The use of alcohol and drugs can affect one's ability to learn and to use memory effectively. As people enter later adulthood and old age, memory often becomes unpredictable; an older person may remember detailed events from childhood but be unable to remember clearly what happened only a week ago. In general, memory traces often do decay over time. There is debate, however, as to whether the memory has truly disappeared or the cue needed to retrieve it has simply been lost.

Interference is one reason that certain things may not be remembered. Events that occur either before or after the event or information one is trying to remember can interfere with learning. Broadly speaking, any event—certainly an unexpected or overwhelming event—may cause interference. In trying to learn academic material, a common cause of interference is learning other material that is similar to it. Students trying to learn two languages at once or in close time frames find it easy to confuse the two. A student taking a history class at ten in the morning and a political science class at eleven may find they interfere with each other. Proactive interference is an event or learning that comes before specific learning; retroactive interference occurs after the learning.

Many people have experienced what is often called the "tip-of-the-tongue" phenomenon. They have learned something (a person's name, perhaps) but simply cannot recall the information. They may try concentrating, then associating, but cannot pull the information from long-term memory. This is referred to as "retrieval failure." Then, after a few minutes—or the next day—they suddenly recall the information they were seeking. What triggers the memory is not exactly clear, but some link has been made. Sometimes a person simply tries too hard to remember something and the anxiety this produces interferes with memory; relaxation later allows memory to work unhindered. Students may experience this when taking an examination; it is a part of what is known as test anxiety.

Context

As people are increasingly required to learn and remember more and more data in a technological society, memory will continue to be a major area of interest to psychologists and educators. People must learn how to be aware of their memories and use them effectively. Schools, including some colleges and universities, are attempting to teach memory strategies to enhance learning.

A number of theorists since 1970 have developed ideas about how people remember and recall information. Fergus Craik and Robert Lockhart, in 1972, postulated a levels-of-processing concept. In this view, people deliberately act on, or process, information either deeply or in a superficial manner, depending on the relative importance of the information to the individual. Later followers of this perspective have indicated that the degree of elaboration has much to do with the amount of material that one is able to recall. Some people mull over newly learned materials thoroughly and are thus able to remember them later. Other theorists have suggested that the number of decisions that one must make regarding materials to be learned may be important in one's ability to learn and recall the material. The idea of making material "distinctive" is another facet of the levels-of-processing perspective that has been found to apply to the ability to remember information.

One concept of memory holds that there are two large memory systems, declarative memory and procedural memory. Declarative memory contains the systems commonly called short-term and long-term memory. It contains all factual and episodic memories. Procedural memory contains physical and physiological memories; these are not usually considered when one thinks of one's memory, yet any time one ties one's shoes, uses a word processor, plays a sport, or learns to play an instrument, unconscious memories of how to accomplish these tasks are automatically used.

Bibliography

Craik, Fergus I., and Robert S. Lockhart. "Levels of Processing: A Framework for Memory Research." *Journal of Verbal Learning and Verbal Behavior* 11, no. 6 (1972): 671-684. This article revolutionized thinking about memory, how it works, and how people process information. Much subsequent work has been based on this perspective.

Delacour, J. *The Memory System of the Brain*. Teaneck, N.J.: World Scientific Publishing, 1994.

Gathercole, Susan E., ed. *Models of Short-Term Memory*. Hove, East Sussex, UK: Psychology Press, 1996.

Graham, Kenneth G., and H. Alan Robinson. *Study Skills Handbook*. Springfield, Mass.: International Reading Association, 1984. A straightforward text that includes many tricks for enhancing memory.

Healy, Alice F., and Lyle E. Bourne, Jr., eds. *Learning and Memory of Knowledge and Skills: Durability and Specificity*. Thousand Oaks, Calif.: Sage Publications, 1995.

Higbee, Kenneth L. *Your Memory: How It Works and How to Improve It*. Englewood Cliffs, N.J.: Prentice-Hall, 1977. An excellent source for people interested in understanding and improving their memory. The process of improving memory efficiency takes time, but the results can be significant.

Kail, Robert V. *The Development of Memory in Children*. 3d ed. New York: W. H. Freeman, 1990. Addresses the development of memory: how children develop memory strategies and the ways memory develops from infancy to childhood to adolescence.

Loftus, Geoffrey R., and Elizabeth F. Loftus. *Human Memory: The Processing of Information*. Hillsdale, N.J.: Lawrence Erlbaum, 1976. The Loftuses' work on memory, including the implications of memory's weaknesses for eyewitness testimony in the courts, has been very influential; this is an excellent and comprehensive book.

Lorayne, Harry, and Jerry Lucas. *The Memory Book*. New York: Stein & Day, 1974. A short paperback text designed to help people remember names, faces, dates, and so on; utilizes a variety of techniques and strategies. Well written and easy to read.

Stern, Leonard. *The Structures and Strategies of Human Memory*. Homewood, Ill.: Dorsey Press, 1985. A fairly sophisticated book that examines various aspects of memory and explores both how to encode and how to retrieve information.

Tulving, Endel. "Episodic and Semantic Memory." In *Organization of Memory*, edited by Endel Tulving and Wayne Donaldson. New York: Academic Press, 1972. This chapter outlines Tulving's conceptualization of these two forms of memory.

Michael F. Shaughnessy

See also:

Memory, Theories of, 383; Memory: Animal Research, 389.

MORAL DEVELOPMENT

Type of psychology: Developmental psychology
Fields of study: Infancy and childhood; social perception and cognition

Moral development is the process of internalizing society's rules and principles of right and wrong. In order to maintain a stable social order, the achievement of morality is necessary. Acquiring morals is a sequential process linked to a person's stage of moral reasoning and cognitive understanding.

Principal terms

COGNITIVE: the mental processes of thinking, reasoning, knowing, remembering, understanding, and problem solving
DEVELOPMENT: orderly changes in the life span of an organism, including physical, mental, social, and personality changes
EMPATHY: the capacity for experiencing the feelings and thoughts of other people
MORAL DEVELOPMENT: the onset and growth of an individual's ability to determine right from wrong, resulting in appropriate ethical behavior
MORAL RULES: obligatory social regulations based on the principles of justice and welfare for others
MORALITY: a system of rules handed down by cultural and/or societal consensus
SOCIAL ORDER: the way in which a society or culture functions, based on the rules, regulation, and standards that are held and taught by each member of the society

Overview

Morality is a set of standards that a person has about the rightness and wrongness of various kinds of behavior. Moral development is the way in which these sets of standards change over a period of time and experiences. Without moral rules, society would be chaotic and without order. Most societies, for example, agree that certain behaviors (such as murder and theft) are wrong, and most people follow these moral principles. Not everyone has the same way of reasoning about the morality of a situation, however; consider the following two scenarios from the work of psychologist Jean Piaget.

A little boy named John is in his room. He is called to dinner, and he goes into the dining room. Behind the door on a chair is a tray with fifteen cups on it. John does not know this; when he goes in, the door knocks against the tray, and all fifteen cups are broken. There is another boy, named Henry. One day when his mother is out he tries to get some jam from the cupboard. He climbs onto a chair but cannot reach it; he knocks over a cup. The cup falls down and breaks.

When asked which of the above two boys is more naughty, most adults would immediately reply that Henry is more guilty. Conversely, a child between six and ten years of age usually will say that John is more guilty. The differences between the two scenes consist of both the amount of damage done and the intentions of the two children. It is obvious that children and adults do not view the situations in the same way.

According to two developmental psychologists, Piaget and Lawrence Kohlberg, moral judgments are related to the stage of cognitive development from which a person is operating when making these judgments. According to Piaget's theory, the development of morality includes several stages. People cannot progress to higher stages of moral development until they have also progressed through higher stages of cognitive understanding. During the premoral stage (through five years of age), the child has little awareness of morals. As children grow, they learn about cooperative activity and equality among peers. This cognitive knowledge leads to a new respect for rights and wrongs. At this stage (age six to ten), children cannot judge that Henry is more guilty than John, because they are not capable of understanding the differences in the children's intentions. The only understanding is of the degree of damage done. Therefore, the number of cups broken is the basis for the judgment of the wrongness of the act, regardless of the actor's good or bad intentions.

Finally, as the child develops, the child learns that rules can be challenged and is able to consider other factors, such as a person's intentions and motivation. Once this shift in perception occurs, the child's moral development will progress to a higher stage.

Lawrence Kohlberg expanded Piaget's theory by investigating how people reasoned the rightness or wrongness of an act and not how people actually behaved. For example, Kohlberg proposed the following moral dilemma. A man named Heinz had a wife who was dying from a disease that could be cured with a drug manufactured by a local pharmacist. The drug was expensive to make, but the druggist was charging ten times the cost amount. Heinz could not afford the drug and pleaded with the man to discount the drug or let him pay a little at a time. The druggist refused, so Heinz broke into the pharmacy and stole the drug for his wife. Should Heinz have stolen the drug?

By listening to people's reasoning concerning Heinz's actions, Kohlberg proposed that there are three levels (of two stages each) of moral reasoning. The first level is called the preconventional level; in this stage, a person's feelings of right and wrong are based on an external set of rules that have been handed down by an authority figure such as a parent, teacher, or religious figure. These rules are obeyed in order to avoid punishment and/or to gain rewards. In other words, people at this stage of moral reasoning would not steal the drug—not because they believed that stealing was wrong, but rather because they had been told not to and would fear getting caught and punished for their action.

The second level of moral reasoning is the conventional level, at which judgments of right and wrong are based on other people's expectations. For example, at this level there are two substages. One is known as the "good boy–nice girl" orientation, in which morality is based on winning approval and avoiding disapproval by one's immediate group. In other words, people may or may not steal the drug based on what they believe their peers would think of them. The second substage is called the "law and order" orientation, under which moral behavior is thought of in terms of obedience to the authority figure and the established social order. The "laws" are usually obeyed without question, regardless of the circumstances, and are seen as the mechanism for the maintenance of social order. A person operating from this stage would say that Heinz should not steal the drug because it was against the law—and if he did steal the drug, he should go to jail for his crime.

The third level of moral reasoning is called the postconventional orientation. At this stage, the person is more concerned with a personal commitment to higher principles than with behavior dictated by society's rules. Disobeying the law would be in some instances far less immoral than obeying a law that is believed to be wrong, and being punished for the legal disobedience would be easier than the guilt and self-condemnation of disobeying the personal ethical principles held by that person. For example, many civil rights workers and Vietnam War conscientious objectors were jailed, beaten, and outcast from mainstream society, but those consequences were far less damaging to them than transgressing their own convictions would have been.

According to Kohlberg, the preconventional stage is characteristic of young children, while the conventional stage is more indicative of the general population. It has been estimated that only about 20 percent of the adult population reach the postconventional stage. Thus, the course of moral development is not the same for everyone. Even some adults operate at the preconventional level of moral reasoning. Education, parental affection, observation and imitation, and explanations of the consequences of behavior are factors in determining the course of moral development in a child.

Applications

As stated, moral development is a progression from one stage to a different, higher stage of reasoning. One cannot proceed to a higher stage of morality without the accompanying cognitive understanding. Thus, if a child thinks that John, who broke fifteen cups, is more guilty than Henry, who broke one cup, then merely telling the child that Henry's intentions were not as good as John's, and therefore John is not as guilty, is not going to change the child's perceptions. The child's understanding of the situation must be actively changed. One way of doing this is through role-playing. The child who thinks that John is more guilty can be told to act out the two scenes, playing each of the two boys. By asking the child questions about his or her feelings while going through each of the scenes, one can help the child gain empathy for each of the characters and gain a better understanding of intentions and actions. Once the child has the cognitive understanding of intentions, he or she is then able to reason at a higher level of moral development.

In other words, in trying to elevate someone's moral reasoning, the first goal is to elevate his or her cognitive understanding of the situation. This can also be done by citing similar examples within the person's own experience and chaining them to the event at hand. For example, if last week the child had accidentally broken something, then asking the child how he or she remembers feeling when that event happened will remind the child of the emotions experienced at the time of the event. The child must then associate the remembered emotions with the situation at hand. This can be accomplished by asking questions, such as "Do you think that John might have felt the same way as you did when you broke the vase?" or "How do you think John felt when the cups fell down? Have you ever felt the same?" If one merely tells the child that John felt bad, the child may or may not comprehend the connection, but if one asks the child to reason through the situation by having empathy for John, then the child is more likely to progress to the next stage of moral reasoning.

This type of empathetic role-playing can be very important in trying to change deviant behavior. If a child is stealing, then having the child imagine or play a role in a situation where he or she is the one being stolen from is the quickest way for the child to change his or her judgments of the rightness or wrongness of the situation. Punishment may deter the behavior but does not result in a change in cognitive understanding or moral reasoning.

In addition to changing moral reasoning powers, this type of role-playing is also more likely to aid the child from an understimulated home environment. The child whose social environment includes many incidents of undesirable behaviors or who lacks examples of positive behaviors must be stimulated in ways that appeal to current cognitive understanding but that show ways of thinking differently than current examples in his or her life.

Context

Human morality has been an issue in philosophy since the days of Aristotle; psychology primarily began to study the topic in the early twentieth century. At this time, both Jean Piaget and Sigmund Freud addressed the issue of children's moral development.

Freud proposed that children around four years of age assimilate the morals and standards of their same-sex parent, resulting in the onset of the child's superego, which is the storehouse for one's conscience. Thus, children have a rudimentary sense of right and wrong based on the morals of their parental figure. Since Freud's concept was based on his theory of psychosexual development, it was discredited by his European colleagues for most of his lifetime. Thus, his theory of moral acquisition has not generally been the basis of research on the development of morality.

Piaget began observing children when he was giving intelligence tests in the laboratory of Alfred Binet. He observed that children do not reason in the same way that adults do. Thus, by questioning Swiss schoolchildren about their rules in a game of marbles, Piaget adapted his theory of cognitive development to moral development. Kohlberg elaborated on Piaget's theory by studying children's as well as adults' reasoning concerning moral dilemmas. Kohlberg is still generally considered the leading theorist of moral development.

Other areas of psychological research are concerned with the topic of children's "social cognitions," which subsumes the topic of morals and considers other issues such as empathy, attribution, and motivations. One area that has come to light is the issue of the effect of the emotions on cognitions and their contribution to moral judgments. For example, it has been shown that when people are in a good mood they are more likely to help another person than when they are in a bad mood. Expanding on this premise, other research has demonstrated that even the way people perceive an object or situation is closely linked to their psychological or emotional state at the time. Even concrete perceptions can be changed by a person's state of being. One example is that people who are poor actually judge the size of a quarter to be larger than do people who are rich.

As cognitive theories begin to consider the interactive components that emotions have in cognitions, new methods of study and new theoretical predictions will change the way cognitive psychologists study such areas as problem solving, decision making, reasoning, and memory. Each of these areas is independently related to the study of moral development and should affect the way psychologists think about how people acquire and think about morality within society.

In addition, as society increases in sophistication and technology, new issues will emerge that will strain old theories. Issues that are particular to new generations will result in new ways of thinking about morality that were not faced by past generations. The direction that moral development goes is ultimately highly dependent on the problems of the current society.

Bibliography
Coles, Robert. *The Moral Intelligence of Children*. New York: Random House, 1997.

_____. *The Moral Lives of Children*. Boston: Atlantic Monthly Press, 1986. Gives a comprehensive overview of Freudian theory and moral development. Investigates issues such as motion pictures and morality, social classes, psychological events, and personality and moral development. This book is easily read more as a novel than a research text and could generally be enjoyed by high school students.

Duska, Ronald F., and Mariellen Whelan. *Moral Development: A Guide to Piaget and Kohlberg*. New York: Paulist Press, 1975. Presents Piaget's theory and its implications for Kohlberg's expansion into his own theory of moral development. All of the moral stories used by Piaget and Kohlberg in their research are replicated in this book. Also includes research findings and ways in which to apply these theories to everyday situations in teaching children. This book can easily be read by the high school or college student.

Rest, James R. *Moral Development: Advances in Research and Theory*. New York: Praeger, 1986. This book relates the cultural, educational, religious, and experiential influences on moral development. Shows the results of a moral dilemma test, which is available to the reader, and gives directions for gaining the manual for grading the test. Although generally the reading is too advanced for the beginning student, this book is recommended because of the availability of these tests.

Reuben, Steven Carr. *Raising Ethical Children: Ten Keys to Helping Your Children Become Moral and Caring*. Rocklin, Calif.: Prima Publishing, 1994.

Rich, John Martin, and Joseph L. DeVitis. *Theories of Moral Development*. Springfield, Ill.: Charles C Thomas, 1985. Presents a range of psychologists' theories on moral development, including Freud, Adler, Jung, and Sears. In addition, it places moral development within the framework of higher education and relates it to a life-span perspective. Certain sections of the book would be difficult for a novice student to follow; however, in terms of a summary review of theoretical positions, the book is a handy reference.

Shaffer, David Reed. "Moral Development." In *Social and Personality Development*. Monterey, Calif.: Brooks/Cole, 1979. Reviews aspects and theories of moral development. Each theoretical outlook is examined in depth, including research for and against the findings. This chapter includes the definitions of relevant terms and uses easy-to-read graphs and tables. Highly recommended as an elementary text.

Donna J. Frick

See also:

MOTIVATIONAL CONSTRUCTS

Type of psychology: Motivation
Field of study: Motivation theory

Motivational constructs attempt to explain why people and animals act, think, and feel as they do. These theoretical explanations, which usually focus on either internal or external motivating factors, have provided insight into such diverse areas of life as work, sports, and drug abuse.

Principal terms

AROUSAL: the general state of neurological alertness to stimulation

CONSTRUCT: a scientific model that attempts to explain relationships among diverse facts about phenomena

DRIVE: the tendency of a person or animal to engage in behaviors brought about by some change or condition inside that organism; often generated by deprivation or exposure to painful or other noxious stimuli

ECLECTIC APPROACH: an approach to explanation or understanding that uses findings from diverse facts, theories, or viewpoints; reliance is placed on multiple sources of information

EXTRINSIC ORIENTATION: a position that seeks to understand something by examining those factors outside the object of study

INTRINSIC ORIENTATION: a position that seeks to understand something by examining those factors inside the object of study

MOTIVATION: why people or animals do or do not originate, choose, strengthen, or persist in certain actions, feelings, or thoughts

NEED: any condition that a person or animal must have in order to remain alive or healthy

Overview

Motivational psychology is concerned with the "whys" of thinking, feeling, and behavior. Why do anorectics starve themselves, while the obese cannot stop eating? Why does one person strive relentlessly for excellent school grades while another seemingly does not care? Motivational psychologists have proposed many constructs to explain these and other questions. Most of these theoretical explanations can be broadly categorized either as those that focus on looking "inside" (intrinsic orientation) the person (or animal), such as biological or cognitive theories, or as those that take an "outside" perspective (extrinsic orientation), focusing on the environment, such as behavioral or social theories.

Biological theories assert that the primary motivational factors are built into the physiological constitution. One of the oldest psychological theories proposes that both lower animals and people are motivated by instincts: inborn, unlearned behavior patterns. At the beginning of the twentieth century, psychologists such as William James and William McDougall constructed lists of instincts, such as love, sympathy, and aggressiveness, in an attempt to explain human motivation. As the years passed, the list of instincts grew so long that the labels became meaningless. For example, does a supposed instinct "music-listening" adequately explain why someone listens to the radio? Although the instinct concept fell out of favor with most psychologists, emphasis on the biological roots of human motives has continued to be a central feature of several other important motivational theories.

In the 1930's, Clark Hull developed a drive-reduction theory, arguing that humans are motivated to reduce basic physiological drives such as hunger and thirst. In contrast, Donald Hebb proposed in the 1950's that people are motivated primarily to maintain a certain level of optimal arousal. Contemporary research has focused more on the optimal arousal approach to motivation. For example, according to a 1986 study by Frank Farley, some people need to maintain high levels of arousal and thus are more likely to seek out stimulating activities, such as riding a roller coaster. Others are motivated to maintain lower levels of arousal, finding a ride on the merry-go-round sufficiently stimulating.

A biological perspective that attempts to explain human motivation in terms of its evolutionary value and purpose was popularized in *Sociobiology: The New Synthesis* (1975), in which Edward O. Wilson described the sociobiological viewpoint. Sociobiologists claim that humans are socially motivated to engage in behaviors because they have survival value. For example, if humans are aggressive, it is because aggressiveness yields a greater survival advantage, making it more likely that more "aggressive genes" are passed on to the next generation.

Cognitive theories, like biological theories, look inside the person for motivational roots; however, the emphasis is placed on thinking, particularly the ability to acquire and use information and to make choices. In *Motivation and Personality* (1954), Abraham Maslow proposed one type of cognitive theory when he argued that humans are primarily motivated by the striving for self-actualization: the need to be what they are capable of becoming. His theory is called humanistic because it focuses on the conscious desire for personal growth. Expectancy-value theories, which represent another type of cognitive approach, propose that people are motivated by the expectation of reaching certain goals that have different values attached to them. Studying hard for good grades could be motivated by either the expectation that studying will lead to good grades or the high value placed on good grades, according to expectancy-value theorists such as Edward Tolman.

In contrast to the biological and cognitive theories, an extrinsic perspective is central to the propositions of the behavioral psychologists. B. F. Skinner, first writing in the 1930's, contended that humans are motivated to obtain positive consequences and to avoid negative consequences for their actions. Thus, according to Skinner, a worker is likely to try to continue those behaviors that will lead to promotion and to avoid those behaviors that may lead to being fired. Theories similar to Skinner's are often called incentive theories because they emphasize the role of incentives: external goals that can motivate behavior.

At the same time that Skinner was formulating his theory in the 1930's, Henry Murray was suggesting that much of human behavior is motivated by social needs. Three of Murray's twenty-seven social needs have been studied in great detail in succeeding years. In a 1984 study, Eugene Fodor found that people who are high in the need for power, the motivation to control or influence others, become more aroused when a social situation calls for leadership than those who are low in the need for power.

The need to maintain good social relations with others is called the affiliative need. People who are high in this need emphasize cooperative rather than competitive relationships with others, according to a 1975 study by David McClelland. The desire for significant accomplishment and mastery over things is called achievement motivation. In *Human Motivation* (1985), McClelland reported that people who are high in achievement motivation have greater success in their occupations.

Applications

No single theory of motivation appears to be adequate in explaining all the "whys" of animal and human motivation. Theories that work well for lower animals, such as the drive-reduction perspective, often fail to provide adequate explanation for complex human activities. Furthermore, theories that do provide seemingly plausible explanations for human activities often offer strongly divergent viewpoints. Instead of judging which theory is best, many psychologists take an eclectic perspective regarding motivational theories. In other words, psychologists pick from different theories those explanations that work best depending on what phenomenon is being studied. Thus, as can be seen in the following examples from the areas of work, sports, and drug abuse, different theories may offer good complementary explanations for some human activities, whereas for other activities one theory may offer a better explanation than another.

Motivational theories have probably been applied most frequently to the workplace: How can people be motivated to work more productively? Biological theories such as the instinctual and sociobiological approaches may reveal something about the instincts or genes that supposedly make good workers, but they fail, in a practical sense, to describe how to motivate different types of people to become good workers. Cognitive and behavioral approaches have met with much greater success in this area.

In *Motivation: Theories and Principles* (1990), Robert Beck describes how expectancy-value theories have provided useful explanations of worker motivation. Expectancy can be understood as the likelihood that a certain amount of effort will lead to a certain level of performance that will eventually lead to a certain goal (a raise or promotion) that has a particular value to a worker. If a person believes that a high level of work effort will lead to a performance level that will bring a valued goal, that person is more likely to work harder than a person who does not believe that either of those two conditions will be met.

A behavioral approach to increasing job performance would stress setting specific and attainable goals, designing the work environment in order to make productive behaviors more likely, and tying rewards to performance. Frank Landy, in *Psychology of Work Behavior* (1985), describes how the application of such a behavioral approach to the workplace has yielded greater job satisfaction, greater work effort, and better job performance.

The world of sports has also received much attention from motivational psychologists since 1898, when Norman Triplett postulated a "competitive instinct" as the reason that bicyclists rode faster when competing against others than when riding solo against the clock. Rather than focusing on supposed "athletic instincts," contemporary motivational psychologists tend to emphasize a more cognitive approach to athletic motivation. Robert Nideffer, in *Athletes' Guide to Mental Training* (1985), describes the relationship between mental concentration and maintaining an optimal level of arousal. "Psyching up" athletes to motivate them to achieve superior performance may help some athletes maintain a desired optimal level of arousal for a particular sport, but it may lead to arousal levels that are too high for other athletes, hindering their performances. Different athletes must learn the particular mental techniques that lead them to their optimal levels of arousal, if superior performance is to be gained.

The relationship between achievement motivation and sport has also been studied extensively. McClelland, in his 1985 book on motivation, relates that people who are high in achievement motivation seek goals that are realistically attainable but challenging. A basketball player with high achievement motivation would thus be more interested in making moderately difficult jump shots than in concentrating on too-easy layups or too-difficult half-court shots. Thus, athletes who are high in achievement motivation will seek athletic situations that are fair tests of their abilities.

Applications of social motives and the optimal arousal theory have also been made in the study of drug abuse. Few people are likely to report a lifelong goal of becoming addicted to drugs, which makes it difficult to determine the underlying motivational factors behind drug abuse. Psychologists have suggested that both the social need for power and individual differences in optimal arousal level are important factors in this regard.

David McClelland and his colleagues reported in a 1972 study that alcohol drinking often raises feelings of power, particularly in men. It was also found that the percentage of heavy drinkers was much higher among those people scoring high in the need for power than among those scoring low in that need. The role of the need for power in other forms of drug abuse has also been indicated.

Frank Farley proposed in the 1980's that individual differences in arousal level also play a role in drug abuse. Some people have naturally lower levels of arousal and are therefore inclined to seek out stimulating and novel experiences in order to raise their arousal levels to a more comfortable zone. These people, often called "thrill seekers" or "sensation seekers," have been found to be more likely to experiment with a wider range of drugs than people of more moderate arousal levels. Thus, the potential for drug abuse, given the need to change the existing level of arousal and the tendency to experiment more with drugs, is greater among the "thrill seekers" than among those who have more moderate levels of naturally occurring arousal.

Context

The philosophical roots of current motivational theories can be traced back directly to the *Republic*, Plato's book of the fourth century B.C. In that book, Plato describes a debate between Thrasymachus and Socrates. Thrasymachus argues that people are primarily motivated by self-interest in that they try to seek pleasure and avoid pain—a point of view called hedonism. External factors, environmental pains and pleasures, therefore play the key role in motivation. Socrates disagrees, contending that people are motivated to know what is true and right, depending on their reasoning abilities. Internal factors, in contrast to the view of Thrasymachus, are therefore the central factors in motivation. The history of motivational theories has seen swings in emphasis from these intrinsic and extrinsic orientations.

When psychology became a science in the 1870's, largely as a result of the work of Wilhelm Wundt in Germany and William James in America, the emphasis was on the study of the mind, an intrinsic orientation. Techniques such as introspection, however, which relied heavily on self-reports of questionable validity, and concepts such as instincts fell into disfavor, which led to a dramatic shift in orientation. In a 1913 paper, John B. Watson argued that psychology would advance further if it studied what people do—observable, external factors—rather than making judgments about what people are supposedly thinking: the intrinsic factors. Watson's view, called behaviorism, dominated psychology for nearly a half-century—until the 1960's. Motivational thinking, with some notable exceptions, particularly Sigmund Freud's theories about unconscious factors in motivation, overwhelmingly had an extrinsic orientation during this period.

In the 1960's, the influence of computers swayed many psychologists to rethink the heavy emphasis on external factors in motivation. Computers could do many things that the human mind could do—specifically, acquiring, modifying, and outputting information—and a powerful model for the human mind was born. The subject matter of psychology began to swing back to the study of mental factors. Many motivational theories also followed this trend, taking on a more intrinsic orientation.

Motivational theories in the last decades of the twentieth century have tended to emphasize internal rather than external factors in motivation. Although extrinsic orientations such as behavioral theories are still influential, intrinsic orientations, particularly the cognitive and biological approaches, are more popular. With the increasing sophistication of computers, it is likely that cognitive approaches to motivation will continue to gain in influence and popularity. Similarly, advances in genetics and the neurosciences bring increasing impetus and promise to biological theories of motivation.

Bibliography

Geen, Russell G. *Human Motivation: A Social Psychological Approach*. Pacific Grove, Calif.: Brooks/Cole, 1995.

McClelland, David Clarence. *Human Motivation*. Glenview, Ill.: Scott, Foresman, 1985. McClelland's textbook on human motivation primarily attempts to develop a theoretical synthesis of the author's own view on human motivation rather than to present a broad-based approach to motivation. Particular emphasis is placed on the social motives of achievement, power, affiliation, and avoidance. Such practical issues in motivation as motivational training and relationships to societal trends set this book apart from most motivational textbooks.

Maslow, Abraham Harold. *Motivation and Personality*. New York: Harper & Row, 1954. A classic book in which the foundations of humanistic psychology are presented. Important concepts such as self-actualization and Maslow's theory of the hierarchy of needs are described in an accessible, easily read style. The book relates an optimistic view of human nature.

Mook, Douglas G. *Motivation: The Organization of Action*. New York: W. W. Norton, 1987. This book provides a comprehensive look at motivation that effectively integrates animal research with an understanding of human motivation. Written primarily for a college audience. Strengths of the book include an evenhanded presentation of divergent theories and exceptional coverage of diverse research and disciplines.

Petri, Herbert L. *Motivation: Theory, Research, and Application*. 3d ed. Belmont, Calif.: Wadsworth, 1990. Divides the study of motivation into three sections: biological, behavioral, and cognitive approaches. Good coverage of various motivational perspectives in their historical context is presented. Shorter and easier reading than Mook's textbook, though not as comprehensive.

Skinner, B. F. *Beyond Freedom and Dignity*. New York: Alfred A. Knopf, 1971. A controversial, at times shocking, view of human nature from the most influential behaviorist of the twentieth century. Argues for the external control of humans and changing society through the techniques of behaviorism. As the title suggests, many of the cherished ideals of humanity are considered illusory and a hindrance to the improvement of society. Skinner's radical behaviorism is discussed in a style that is accessible to the general reader.

Sorrentino, Richard M., and E. Tony Higgins, eds. *The Interpersonal Context*. Vol. 3 in *Handbook of Motivation and Cognition*. New York: Guilford Press, 1996.

Wilson, Edward Osbourne. *Sociobiology: The New Synthesis*. Cambridge, Mass.: The Belknap Press of Harvard University Press, 1975. Wilson contends that genetic influences play the major role in human motivation. He goes so far as to conclude that the patterns of human social behavior, including altruism, conformity, homosexuality, and gender differences, are under genetic control. A lengthy integration of motivational and evolutionary theory that the casual reader may find difficult reading.

Paul J. Chara, Jr.

See also:

Achievement Motivation, 7; Affiliation and Friendship, 25; Behaviorism, 98; Drive Theory, 218; Homosexuality, 278; Instinct Theory, 303; Learning, 364; Psychoanalytic Psychology, 471.

MOTOR DEVELOPMENT

Type of psychology: Developmental psychology
Field of study: Infancy and childhood

Motor development refers to the development of voluntary control over one's body and its parts, as in crawling, walking, reaching, and grasping. Motor development parallels brain growth and development and is influenced by both biological and environmental factors.

Principal terms

CENTRAL NERVOUS SYSTEM: the nerve cells, fibers, and other tissues associated with the brain and spinal cord
CEPHALO-CAUDAL DEVELOPMENT: motor development that proceeds from head to toe
CEREBRAL CORTEX: the outer layer of the brain that controls complex voluntary functions such as thinking, reasoning, motor coordination, memory, and language
FINE MOTOR MOVEMENTS: small muscle movements such as those required in eye-hand coordination and eye movements
GROSS MOTOR MOVEMENTS: body movements that involve the large muscle masses such as in crawling, walking, running, and throwing
MASS-TO-SPECIFIC DEVELOPMENT: motor development that proceeds from gross, random body movements to more refined movements that involve specific body parts
MATURATION: development attributable to one's genetic timetable and not to experience
PROXIMO-DISTAL DEVELOPMENT: motor development that proceeds from the center of the body to its periphery

Overview

Motor development refers to the development of voluntary control over the body and its parts. "Gross" motor development refers to the development of skills or behaviors that involve the large muscle masses and large body movements (such as crawling, walking, running, and throwing), whereas "fine" motor development refers to the development of small muscle movements, usually in reference to the hands (as in grasping, writing, and buttoning buttons). Motor skills develop rapidly during the early years of life and follow a predictable sequence of stages.

Motor development proceeds according to three developmental principles: from head to toe ("cephalo-caudal" development), from the center of the body to the body's periphery ("proximo-distal" development), and from large to small muscle control, with actions becoming more refined and directed ("mass-to-specific" development). Cephalo-caudal development is illustrated by the fact that infants gain control over their head and shoulders before their legs. Proximo-distal development is shown by young children gaining control over their arms before their hands and fingers, and mass-to-specific development is illustrated by the fact that infants reach for an object with both arms before they can reach with one arm at a time.

The development of both gross and fine motor skills depends on the maturation of the nervous system. Voluntary movements develop as the cortex, which is the outer layer of the brain, matures. Whereas the cortex is barely functioning at birth, the "lower" parts of the brain—such as the brain stem and the midbrain—that control basic, nonthinking functions such as breathing, heartbeat, digestion, and reflexes are mature at birth. This is part of the reason that newborns have only reflexive, involuntary movements during the first few months of life. Voluntary control over the body develops gradually as connections between the muscles and the higher brain centers such as the cortex become established. The parts of the brain concerned with posture and balance also develop gradually over the first year of life; these contribute to infants being able to sit up, stand, and then walk.

Gross motor and fine motor skills follow a specific sequence of development. Gross motor (or locomotor) development eventually results in a young child being able to walk and run. To reach this point, a child must first develop control of his or her head, sit up, and then develop enough balance and strength to stand. By approximately two months of age, most infants can lift their heads, and by three to four months of age they are usually able to roll over. At five or six months they can sit up, and by seven to nine months they usually begin crawling. Infants may be able to stand while holding onto an object at six months, pull themselves to standing between eight and ten months, and walk independently at around twelve to fourteen months. By eighteen months of age, toddlers are usually able to run, walk backward, throw a ball, and climb stairs; between twenty-four to thirty-six months they may be able to ride a tricycle. From two to six years of age, children continue to refine their movements. For example, a two-year-old's awkward gait and poor balance change by three years of age to a more stable and balanced gait, allowing the child to hop, jump, and run back and forth. By four years of age, children's walking movements are similar to adults', allowing them to move easily up and down stairs and even to hop on one foot. By age five, children are well coordinated, have good balance, and are able to move skillfully and gracefully while walking, running, climbing, and throwing.

Fine motor development eventually results in refined eye-hand coordination, which will enable a child to write. To achieve this, children must first be able to reach, grasp, and manipulate objects voluntarily and possess refined finger (especially thumb-to-index-finger) control. At birth, no voluntary control exists. By three months of age, babies begin to make poorly directed "swiping" movements with their entire arms (fists closed). At around four months, infants use an open-handed, scooping movement with a slightly better aim; by five months, infants can reach and grasp objects with both hands, holding the object in the center of the palm by all fingers. Between nine and ten months, infants can hold objects by the palm and middle fingers in a "palmar grasp." The ability to use the thumb and index finger together ("pincer grasp") typically develops between nine and fifteen months. Infants who have developed this skill usually enjoy practicing it and will pick up tiny objects such as lint or bugs from the floor. By eighteen months of age, toddlers are able to hold crayons and to open drawers and cupboards; by twenty-four months, the development of full thumb-to-index-finger control makes it easier for them to turn doorknobs, unscrew lids, scribble, and feed themselves. By age three, children may be able to put some puzzle pieces together. They also have better control when using forks and can begin to dress themselves. (The ability to lace shoes, button buttons, and zip zippers, however, generally does not appear until age six or seven.) By age four or five, eye-hand coordination and fine motor skills improve. Children may be able at this time to print large letters that look "pieced together"; these are typically placed anywhere on a piece of paper. Many can print their first names and a few numbers by age five. From age six on, hand movements become more fluid and refined; writing is characterized by more continuous strokes and is less choppy.

Although the sequence of stages of motor development is uniform in normal individuals, there is wide variation among individuals in the ages at which certain skills are acquired. This normal variation is attributable to both biological and environmental factors, including maturation, heredity, neurological maturity, health, activity level, experience, and nutrition.

Applications

Learning to walk, achieving bowel and bladder control, and even learning to read and write are not physiologically possible until the child's nervous and motor systems are sufficiently developed. Although normal experience (such as that offered by an average home environment) appears to be necessary for normal motor development, biological maturation places limits on what can be achieved through experience or practice. In fact, efforts by parents or other adults to teach or push young children to learn particular skills before they are maturationally ready may actually be harmful to their development.

Learning to walk, for example, requires central nervous system maturity, postural balance, muscular and skeletal strength, and well-developed sight and hearing. Studies have suggested that "practicing" the early walking reflex in infants to "speed up" their learning to walk may actually be harmful, because it may interfere with the development of the "higher" (cortical) areas of the brain that gradually take over the control of mature, independent walking. Early walking movements, which are evident between birth and three months of age, are actually a reflex that is controlled by the "lower" parts of the brain that control involuntary behavior. In addition, other studies have found that using "walkers" (seats on frames with wheels) too early or too often may damage infants' hip sockets.

Toilet training is also dependent on nervous system maturation. The neurons (nerve cells) controlling bowel and bladder movements mature at about the same time that children generally achieve voluntary control, around eighteen to twenty-four months of age. Bowel control is achieved before bladder control, and girls typically achieve bowel and bladder control before boys.

Being able to ride a tricycle (which usually occurs around age three) or a bicycle (which typically occurs by age six or seven) also requires that a certain level of muscle strength, posture, and balance be achieved before these skills are possible. Catching a ball is usually too difficult and complex for four-year-olds because it requires timing, distance perception, quick reactions, and coordinated movements of the arms, hands, eyes, and body. A successful way of playing "catch" with children of this age is to roll the ball on the ground.

Fine motor skills (such as pouring juice from a pitcher, writing with a pencil, assembling a puzzle with many small pieces, cutting food with a knife and fork, or buttoning small buttons) develop more slowly than gross motor skills during infancy and early childhood and are therefore more difficult for young children to master. Children lack the motor control necessary to complete these tasks successfully because the central nervous system is not completely developed at this age—the parts of the brain governing fine motor coordination take years to mature fully.

Reading and writing also depend on maturational readiness. Reading requires focused attention, controlled coordination between the eye muscles and the brain, and a certain level of nervous system maturity. Children younger than six years of age usually are not physiologically capable of moving their eye muscles slowly and deliberately across lines of small letters. They also have a difficult time sustaining controlled and systematic focusing and are farsighted. Because reading depends on maturity of the nervous system, it is generally recommended that formal reading be delayed until age six or seven. Writing, on the other hand, depends on the eyes, brain, and small muscles of the fingers working together. As nervous system maturation progresses, greater fine motor control is achieved, and children's hand strokes become more fluid and continuous during the school-age years.

Finally, hand preference ("handedness") is also biologically based. Hand preference in reaching, grasping, and writing may be found even in infancy. Hand preference appears to be determined partly by heredity but also by the organization of the brain, with structural and functional differences between the left and right sides of the brain evident at birth. Most children develop hand preferences by age three or four, with the majority (85 to 90 percent) showing a right-hand preference. It may, however, take some children several years after this to solidify their hand preference. Forcing children to change their handedness may create a number of problems, including stuttering and other language problems, fine motor skill deficits, and emotional problems.

Context

Early interest in motor development focused primarily on outlining the sequence of stages of motor development, identifying approximate ages at which these milestones occur, and speculating about the relative contributions of biology and the environment to motor development. These themes mirror two principal concerns of developmental psychology: the sequence of stages of development and the influence of biology versus experience on development.

Interest in, and observations of, early motor development date back at least to the eighteenth century. The earliest accounts of children's development, known as "baby biographies," were detailed descriptions of the developmental sequence of behavior during the early years of life. A more methodical approach to outlining behavioral milestones began around the early 1900's, when "normative" studies (studies investigating the typical performance of children at different ages) were undertaken. In 1911, for example, Arnold Gesell founded the Yale Clinic of Child Development and constructed norms for such motor skills as grasping, crawling, swimming, standing, and walking. His norm charts were used throughout most of the twentieth century.

The general conclusion of Gesell and others during the 1930's and 1940's was that motor development is under biological control; however, studies have since shown that severe environmental deprivation can retard motor development and that environmental improvement by age two is necessary for infants to recover fully. Most researchers today believe that both maturation and experience play important roles in the course of motor development.

Although there was interest in motor development during the first half of the twentieth century, this interest declined somewhat from the 1950's until the 1980's. During this lull, however, motor development was still considered an integral part of Jean Piaget's well-known theory of cognitive development in young children. Whereas motor development was originally viewed as the gradual acquisition of isolated skills, motor skill acquisitions are currently viewed as parts of a complex, interrelated motor system that parallels brain growth and development. It is likely that future research will continue to examine these issues as well as the relationship of motor development to cognition, language acquisition, and social development.

The gradual acquisition of fine and gross motor skills has a number of important implications for a child's social, cognitive, and personality development. The development of fine motor skills allows infants to examine and experiment with objects, explore their environment, and even communicate with others by showing objects or by pointing. Gross motor milestones provide children with a new and progressively complex perspective of the world, more opportunities to explore and learn about the physical and social environment, and increasing degrees of independence—which have implications for children's developing sense of mastery and competence. These motor milestones in turn affect parents' interactions with, and treatment of, their increasingly independent children.

Bibliography

Amenta, Francesco, ed. *Aging of the Autonomic Nervous System*. Boca Raton, Fla.: CRC Press, 1993.

Bower, T. G. R. *Development in Infancy*. San Francisco: W. H. Freeman, 1982. A detailed overview of infancy that emphasizes motor skill development and motor perceptual development.

Crary, Michael A. *Developmental Motor Speech Disorders*. San Diego, Calif.: Singular Publishing Group, 1993.

Fitzgerald, Hiram E., et al. "The Organization of Lateralized Behavior During Infancy." In *Theory and Research in Behavioral Pediatrics*. Vol. 5, edited by Hiram E. Fitzgerald, B. Lester, and M. Yogman. New York: Plenum Press, 1991. A good overview on the lateralization of motor skills and behaviors in early development. Covers the influence of brain development on lateralized motor skills.

Gallahue, D. L. *Motor Development and Movement Experiences*. New York: John Wiley & Sons, 1976. A well-written resource on the theory, research, and practical applications of motor development and movement from age three to seven years.

Payne, V. G., and L. D. Isaacs. *Human Motor Development: A Lifespan Approach*. Mountain View, Calif.: Mayfield, 1987. This book is a comprehensive, in-depth overview of motor development from birth to maturity.

Rosenblith, Judy F., and Judith E. Sims-Knight. *In the Beginning*. Monterey, Calif.: Brooks-Cole, 1985. A very readable resource on early development that has excellent chapters on developmental milestones and the influence of the environment on development.

Santrock, John W., and Steven R. Yussen. *Child Development*. Dubuque, Iowa: Wm. C. Brown, 1987. A standard book on child development that has an excellent section on physical and motor development. Very readable for the high school or college student.

Streri, Arlette. *Seeing, Reading, Touching: The Relations Between Vision and Touch in Infancy*. Translated by Tim Pownall and Susan Kingerlee. Cambridge, Mass.: MIT Press, 1993.

Laura Kamptner

See also:

The Autonomic Nervous System, 88; The Central and Peripheral Nervous Systems, 115; Cognitive Development Theory: Jean Piaget, 135; Language: The Developmental Sequence, 346; Speech Disorders, 576.

NEURAL ANATOMY AND COGNITION

Type of psychology: Cognition
Fields of study: Biological influences on learning; cognitive development

Cognitive processes within vertebrate animals depend upon elaborate nervous systems which contain millions of neurons. These neurons grow together into networks which relay electrical nerve impulses throughout the organismal body, thereby coordinating information flow through the body and controlling most bodily processes. Thinking, intelligence, and memory hinge upon the plasticity and patterned growth of these networks.

Principal terms

ARTIFICIAL INTELLIGENCE: a term referring to computers, machines, and processes that exhibit properties of intelligence which are characteristic of living organisms

AXON: the extension of a neuron that transmits to another neuron or target body structure

CENTRAL NERVOUS SYSTEM: a large concentration of millions, even billions, of neurons within the cephalic (head) and back regions of vertebrate animals

DENDRITE: the receiving extension of a neuron, which relays electrical information from the axon of another neuron

NEUROGLIA: specialized, insulating nerve cells that wrap around neurons located within the central nervous systems of vertebrate animals

NEURON: the cell type within animal nervous systems that conducts electrical information; it receives information from another neuron and delivers it to still another neuron or target body tissue

NEUROTRANSMITTER: a protein hormone that relays electrical information from the axon of one neuron across a synapse to the dendrite of another neuron

PLASTICITY: the ability of neurons and neural networks to grow into specific patterns based partially upon the organism's genetics and partially upon the organism's learned experience

SCHWANN CELL: a type of insulating nerve cell that wraps around neurons located peripherally throughout the organism's body

SYNAPSE: a gap between two neurons, between the axon of one neuron and the dendrite of the other, across which neurotransmitter molecules will travel to continue the electrical transmission of information

Overview

Cognition, the process by which animals learn and acquire knowledge from their environment and experience, is a complex yet poorly understood phenomenon that is determined by a variety of factors. These influencing factors include the nervous system anatomy and physiology of the organism, the inherited genes which encode the proteins of this nervous system, and the environmental stimuli which influence the development of the organism's nervous system in conjunction with the organism's genetics. Genetics and environment are the ultimate determinants of an organism's cognitive abilities, although it is the organism's neural anatomy through which such cognition is actively expressed.

Nervous systems are information-processing and transmitting phenomena of animals, both invertebrates and vertebrates. The fundamental unit of nervous systems is the neuron, a cell which is capable of conducting electricity. Compared to most body cells, the neuron has no distinct shape. It may assume all manner of twisted and distorted configurations, often involving extensions or protrusions of its cytoplasm pushing against the neuron cell membrane. Extensions of a neuron that receive electrical information from other neurons or from various bodily stimuli are called dendrites. Extensions of a neuron that transmit electrical information to the dendrites of other neurons or to target body tissues are called axons. A typical neuron may contain one or several dendrites; similarly, a neuron may contain one or several axons. The numbers of dendrites and axons per neuron depend upon the number of crosslinks, or information junctions, which the neuron must make with other neurons and nerve pathways. The complexity of such neuronal crosslinks increases with the complexity of the animal, as well as with the animal's intelligence.

The method of electrical transmission along a neuron involves the exchange of ions across the neuronal cell membrane. The continuation of an electrical wave front along the dendrite, cell body, or axon of a neuron requires the influx of sodium ions across the cell membrane into the neuron cell cytoplasm and the efflux of potassium ions across the cell membrane to the outside of the cell. Such an ion exchange across neuronal cell membranes occurs extremely rapidly, usually requiring only a few milliseconds (thousandths of one second). The electrical impulse, initially triggered by a chemical or physical stimulus within or outside the body, flows along a receiving dendrite through the cell body of a neuron to its axon. Upon reaching the termination of the neuronal axon, the electrical impulse must "jump" the synapse, or gap, separating the axon from the dendrite of the next neuron.

The electrical impulse does not actually cross the synapse. Instead, the neuron releases special protein hormones called neurotransmitters, which cross the synapse and trigger the continuation of the same electrical impulse (sodium influx, potassium efflux) having the same electrical intensity, or voltage. An electrical impulse can traverse hundreds of neurons in less than one second. Every muscle in the human body is controlled by electrical impulses which are transmitted by neurons. In order for one to snap one's fingers, thousands of neurons must be involved. Complex networks of hundreds of neurons within the cerebrum must relay electrical information as a human contemplates snapping her or his fingers. Then, many more neurons must relay the electrical command from the cerebrum to the brain stem to the spinal cord to the peripheral nerves to forearm and wrist muscles, which contract and snap the fingers together with perfect coordination and timing. Such a simple act is extremely complicated.

Three principal types of neurons exist in animal nervous systems: sensory, internuncial, and motor. Sensory neurons, which are located throughout the body and especially on the skin, detect stimuli and relay the stimulus along other sensory neurons toward the central nervous system (the brain and spinal cord). Within the complex neural arrangements of the central nervous system, internuncial neurons connect sensory neurons with motor neurons. Motor neurons transmit commands from the central nervous system to various target body tissues. Other types of nerve cells include the neuroglia in the central nervous system and the Schwann cells in the peripheral nervous system; both of these nerve types insulate neurons by wrapping around them and enhancing electrical conductivity.

The central nervous system is most developed in the mammals, which evolved from reptiles more than 200 million years ago. The entire nervous systems of two mammalian groups, the primates (humans, chimpanzees, gorillas, and orangutans) and cetaceans (dolphins and whales), contain several trillion neurons per individual. Furthermore, the brain of such individuals alone contains approximately 100 billion neurons arranged in complex, interconnected neural networks and pathways. The traditional, anatomical division of the mammalian brain consists of the more ancient brain stem, pons, and medulla oblongata for controlling essential bodily processes such as heartbeat and respiration, the cerebellum for balance and coordination, and the evolutionarily recent cerebrum for memory and intelligence.

The cerebrum is very pronounced in mammals, especially in the primates and cetaceans. The most amazing feature of the cerebrum is the networking between the tens of billions of cerebral neurons. The intricate interconnections between all these neurons enable humans, other primates, and cetaceans to think, remember, reason, and communicate at a level far above any other group of animals. The number of cerebral neurons in these species is important; however, the patterning of these neurons during the organism's growth, experience, and development is also very important.

The high cognitive abilities of cetaceans and primates is attributable to tens of billions of cerebral neurons, intricate cross-linking between networks of cerebral neurons, and high neuronal plasticity. Plasticity refers to the ability of neurons to change shape and to grow in specific patterns based upon environmental stimuli. Cerebral neurons are highly plastic in mammalian species. Cognitive scientists believe that learning and memory require high neuronal plasticity. As an animal is exposed to environmental stimuli and personal experiences, the neurons of the cerebral cortex (the outer cerebrum) grow in patterns that are much like a crystal. Once growth is completed, the neuronal network becomes fixed, and memory is established. In mammals, the periods of highest neural plasticity and learning both occur during youth. Cognitive abilities and plasticity both decline with increasing age.

The plasticity of the networks of thousands of neurons is determined by an individual's genetic makeup. Plasticity is then molded by an individual's learning experiences caused by environmental exposure. Therefore, differences in plasticity among different individuals of a single species will be normal. Individuals will vary in their respective intelligence levels because of varying levels of neuronal plasticity within their central nervous systems. Most individuals will fall close to the mean value for the species, although there will be exceptional individuals having very high or very low neuronal plasticity. Neuronal plasticity is highest among humans, but it is also very high for dolphins. Various debilitating inherited diseases of the central nervous system, such as Alzheimer's disease and parkinsonism, erode the neuronal networks established by plasticity in humans. Certain plasticities may yield abnormal human behaviors. Research is aimed at understanding the role of neural networking and plasticity in cerebral functioning and learning.

Applications

The deciphering of human neuroanatomy and the mechanisms of neurophysiology are of critical concern to medical science in terms of understanding how the human brain functions, how brain damage can be treated, and how abnormal behaviors and learning disabilities can be amended. The problem of neural networking patterns is a task that will challenge researchers for many decades. The plastic nature of neurons is beyond question; however, the precise growth patterns and the exact coordination of neurons to form ideas, memories, language, visual images, and so on are not well understood.

Studies of mammalian brain function indicate that an excess of neurons exists in the early development of an individual. The excess neurons serve as a mesh to absorb external stimuli and begin the formation of specific patterns. Some neurons become parts of established neural networks. Others serve as extras in order to construct future neural networks or the continuance of existing networks. Still other neurons remain unused and die. The preponderance of cerebral neurons is a phenomenon of hunting mammals, those animals which had to seek and capture food; the cerebrum, for the most part, is an elaborate outgrowth of the olfactory (smell) apparatus, an equally important structure for hunting. The excess neurons and high plasticity enabled the evolution of intelligence, language, and strong social bonding in the higher mammals.

The neurophysiological mechanisms by which ideas and images are formed are very poorly understood. Nevertheless, many scientists believe that neural networks within the human cerebrum coordinate concepts by pattern. Such a phenomenon is indicated from visual patterning studies in humans and in a variety of other mammalian species. An excess of neurons would be essential for the processing of such events.

Rapid eye movement (REM) sleep, the deepest stage of the mammalian sleep cycle, is a time during which dreaming occurs. It also appears to be an event during the normal circadian (approximately twenty-four-hour) rhythm of a mammal during which the cerebral cortex processes information and during which neuronal networks are probably encoded as to their specific growth patterns. REM sleep is essential for proper functioning of the body; failure to achieve REM sleep during only a few days can lead to hallucinations and other bodily disturbances.

The genetic and chemical control of neuronal plasticity and patterning could be of tremendous value in enhancing human intelligence and in the treatment of numerous learning disorders. Advances in biotechnology and the cloning of specific organismal genes could lead to major breakthroughs in the control of neural growth, leading to the use of isolated hormones to increase an individual's capacity and speed at learning. Of equal importance is the identification of key stages in an individual's life during which plasticity and, therefore, learning are optimal. The understanding of optimal plasticity periods could be extremely useful for educators.

Learning disabilities invariably involve the improper production of certain important cerebral neuronal hormones or the improper growth of neuronal networks. Dyslexia and autism probably involve neural networking problems. Certain forms of mental retardation may involve more drastic alterations in neural networks. Some of these disorders are genetic; others are environmentally induced and are therefore more amenable to treatment. Some disorders are partially genetic and partially environmental. Breakdowns in neural networks are associated with degenerative diseases of the central nervous system such as Alzheimer's disease and parkinsonism. With the increasing life expectancy of Americans, the occurrence of these disorders will become more widespread. Nursing homes will be crowded with disoriented patients who are suffering from these disorders. Medical research is focused upon the genetic, physical, and chemical causes of these age-related diseases.

At the same time, other biologists are studying how such neural networks function in other intelligent species. Scientists such as Beatrice Gardner, R. Allen Gardner, and Roger Fouts have taught American Sign Language (ASL) to chimpanzees, who subsequently have taught it to their offspring. Others have concentrated upon the seagoing mammals, the dolphins and whales. John Lilly, a neurophysiologist with the Human Dolphin Foundation in Redwood City, California, maintains that dolphins are more intelligent than humans. He bases his conclusions upon studies of their communication patterns and behaviors, and on the fact that their cerebral cortex is larger than that of humans. Their elaborate means of communication has yet to be decoded.

Other researchers are experimenting with artificial intelligence, the design and construction of computers and machines that think. One of the original pioneers of the computer, John von Neumann, attempted to design computer programs which would mimic the human brain, although he was unsuccessful prior to his untimely death. Supercomputers have been constructed which can perform or control millions of operations per second, much faster than the human brain. The best computers so far have one major problem, however: Their information flow is linear. The human nervous system consists of a seemingly infinite series of neural patterns that allow omnidirectional flow of information, so that many seemingly unrelated areas can communicate in an instant. The best computers are faster, but they are woefully inefficient at the cross-connection of information at many different levels. Nevertheless, artificial intelligence researchers are beginning to achieve success with computer programs that mirror the human nervous system, with its patterns of functions. Besides intelligent machines, such research has important medical applications in the construction of devices for overcoming paralysis in paraplegic and quadriplegic individuals—individuals who have no control over their legs, and both arms and legs, respectively.

Context

The study of human neural anatomy and cognition has tremendous potential within psychological, medical, educational, and computer sciences. The process of learning and knowledge acquisition is a distinguishing feature of higher mammals, especially of humans. The biological basis of human cognitive capacity and potential lies with the human central nervous system.

The control center for human consciousness, knowledge, intelligence, memory, and language is within the cerebral cortex—a complex, folded system of millions of neural networks containing tens of billions of neurons that conduct, transmit, and relay electrical information throughout the brain and through the rest of the body. Most of the cognitive regions of neural networks lie within the frontal cerebral lobe behind the forehead. This structure has evolved in higher mammals such as primates and cetaceans from the more primitive cerebral olfactory apparatus for purposes of hunting and acquiring food.

Extensive biological research is aimed at understanding the incredibly complex patterns of neural networks within the cerebral cortex, the plasticity of these neurons, the synthesis of several dozen different information-carrying neurotransmitter molecules, and the patterning of information for storage within the cerebral cortex. This work is an enormous undertaking and will require decades to decipher the intricate methods of brain activity and patterning of knowledge storage.

So far, the principal cerebral regions of memory and intelligence have been isolated by surgical removal and/or stimulation of brain regions during brain surgery; however, the cell-to-cell information coordination is a mystery. Numerous models of knowledge acquisition and memory have been proposed and are being tested. Many of these models envisage the brain as consisting of interconnected neural networks which three-dimensionally process a pattern of information flow and plastic growth to record information. Such models are being investigated in psychological tests on humans, dolphins, whales, chimpanzees, and other mammals.

Intelligence in other species such as dolphins and chimpanzees is of intense interest to numerous animal behaviorists. Numerous researchers, including Jacques Cousteau, Jane Goodall, and Dian Fossey, have detailed the psychologies of dolphins and chimpanzees, in the process discovering remarkable similarities to many human behaviors. Other researchers have made considerable progress in communicating with apes and dolphins, although the "language" of the latter is intricately complicated. The cetacean species have larger cerebral cortices than humans and may be more intelligent, although they are handicapped in not possessing a grasping hand for the manipulation of tools, as a number of scientists have carefully stressed.

The field of artificial intelligence seeks to understand the human nervous system's method of logic and knowledge acquisition. Artificial intelligence research and the closely associated field of robotics seek to reproduce intelligence in machines. In so doing, these scientists may unravel the methods of human cognitive processes and even further human evolution via machines; the implications of intelligent machines are both promising and disquieting.

The connection between neural anatomy and cognitive processes will enable medical science to enhance learning, human potential, and human health. A variety of mental, physical, and learning disorders will be alleviated once researchers have a clear picture of how the cerebral cortex processes information. Cognitive science is in its infancy and offers tremendous promise in the future.

Bibliography

Calvin, William H. *The Cerebral Code: Thinking a Thought in the Mosaics of the Mind.* Cambridge, Mass.: MIT Press, 1996.

Crick, Francis H. C. "Thinking About the Brain." *Scientific American* 241 (September, 1979): 219-230. Crick, 1962 Nobel laureate in physiology or medicine for his codiscovery (with James D. Watson) of the structure of DNA, discusses in this survey article knowledge about brain functioning and techniques which are being used to decipher cognitive processes within the brain. He devotes considerable attention to neural plasticity and network patterning in the encoding of information.

Curtis, Helena. *Biology.* 3d ed. New York: Worth, 1979. Curtis' outstanding introductory biology text describes all aspects of life on Earth in very clear detail. The development of organisms is described in evolutionary sequence. Chapter 34, "Integration and Control," is a thorough but basic introduction to the mammalian nervous and endocrine systems. Other chapters demonstrate the interrelatedness of the nervous and endocrine systems with other body tissues.

Fichtelius, Karl Erik, and Sverre Sjolander. *Smarter than Man? Intelligence in Whales, Dolphins, and Humans.* Translated by Thomas Teal. New York: Pantheon Books, 1972.

Fichtelius, a Swedish physician, and Sjolander, a Swedish ethologist, examine the comparative intelligences of cetaceans and humans in this interesting, simple book. They argue that larger brain size and other behavioral characteristics indicate that whales and dolphins have higher intellectual potential than do humans. They also state the case for human conservation of nature, including the intelligent cetaceans.

Gray, Henry. *Gray's Anatomy: Descriptive and Surgical*. Edited by T. Pickering Pick and Robert Howden. New York: Bounty Books, 1977. This updated classic describes human anatomy and physiology, especially anatomy, in exquisite detail. Numerous diagrams and a clear, descriptive text make this book a tremendous reference for the student of medicine or anatomy. More than 200 pages are devoted to the structure and functioning of the human central and peripheral nervous systems.

Gutnick, Michael J., and Istvan Mody, eds. *The Cortical Neuron*. New York: Oxford University Press, 1995.

Lilly, John C. *Communication Between Man and Dolphin: The Possibilities of Talking with Other Species*. New York: Crown, 1978. Lilly, a controversial neurophysiologist and dolphin researcher, presents compelling evidence supporting the view that dolphins and other cetaceans may be more intelligent than humans. He bases his arguments upon the dolphin's larger cerebral cortex, dolphin behavior, and an elaborate dolphin communication system. Chapter 16, "The Possible Existence of Non-Human Languages," explores humans' naïveté in interpreting the behaviors of other creatures.

Llinas, Rodolfo R., and Patricia S. Churchland, eds. *The Mind-Brain Continuum: Sensory Processes*. Cambridge, Mass.: MIT Press, 1996.

Manning, Aubrey. *An Introduction to Animal Behavior*. 3d ed. Reading, Mass.: Addison-Wesley, 1979. Manning's excellent work is a short, but very thorough summary of animal behavior research for the beginning student. He addresses cognitive processes in animals in chapters 2, "The Development of Behaviour," and 6, "Evolution." Case studies and numerous references are provided to illustrate key theoretical models describing learning processes in animals.

Raven, Peter H., and George B. Johnson. *Biology*. St. Louis: Times Mirror/Mosby, 1989. Raven and Johnson's *Biology* is a beautifully illustrated and diagrammed introduction. Major topics in biology and evolution are discussed, including mammalian anatomy and physiology. Several chapters are devoted to the functioning of the human nervous and endocrine systems.

Rich, Elaine, and Kevin Knight. *Artificial Intelligence*. 2d ed. New York: McGraw-Hill, 1991. In this detailed introduction to the science of artificial intelligence, Rich and Knight describe models of intelligent behavior in humans and other species. They discuss neural networks and their functioning, logic, game playing, knowledge representation, understanding, and semantic analysis in a very thought-provoking work. Computer program simulations of artificial intelligence also are presented.

David Wason Hollar, Jr.

See also:

The Central and Peripheral Nervous Systems, 115; The Cerebral Cortex, 121; Logic and Reasoning, 376; Neuropsychology, 422; Thought: Study and Measurement, 621.

NEUROPSYCHOLOGY

Type of psychology: Origin and definition of psychology
Fields of study: Cognitive processes; organic disorders

Neuropsychology is the study of the relationship between the brain and behavior. It has provided insights into the workings of the normal brain as well as innovations for diagnosing and assisting individuals with an injury to or disease of the brain.

Principal terms

ALZHEIMER'S DISEASE: a type of premature senility resulting from brain deterioration
ASSESSMENT: the process of psychological testing and interviewing to ascertain which of the patient's cognitive abilities have been compromised by injury or disease
COGNITION: the process of perceiving, learning, thinking, or remembering
LESION: physical damage to an organ or tissue resulting in impairment of function
NORM: a representative standard or value for a given group
REHABILITATION: attempts to restore an individual's cognitive or psychological functioning to the level displayed prior to injury

Overview

Neuropsychology is the study of the relationships between the brain and behavior. More fully, it is the study of both human and animal cerebral organization as it relates to behavior. Considerable attention is directed toward investigating the workings of both healthy and damaged neural systems; specifically, there is interest in obtaining a more complete understanding of disorders of language, perception, and motor action. While the field of neuropsychology can be divided into a number of specialty areas, a discussion of experimental neuropsychology and clinical neuropsychology may be the most productive. While this distinction is not absolute, it serves to classify the types of work in which neuropsychologists are involved.

Clinical neuropsychology refers to the study of individuals who have lesions of the brain. These lesions are often produced by tumors, cerebral vascular accidents (strokes), or trauma (for example, an automobile accident). The clinical neuropsychologist is heavily involved in the assessment of cognitive deficits brought on by these brain lesions. By evaluating the patient's performance on a variety of paper-and-pencil tests, the neuropsychologist can make valuable diagnostic inferences. The clinician can begin to develop hypotheses concerning the location, extent, and severity of the lesion.

Similarly, an attempt is made to discern the functional significance of the brain lesion on the patient. Damage to the same part of the brain may affect two individuals very differently. Because of this fact, it is vital that the clinical neuropsychologist assess the effect of the lesion on the patient's daily functioning at work, home, and in social contexts as well as the relatively artificial environment of the testing room. Furthermore, it is important that evaluation consider the patient's current strengths in addition to weaknesses or impairments. Intact abilities can assist the patient in coping and compensating for the loss of some other function.

A comprehensive neuropsychological test battery should assess the integrity of the entire brain. To assure the thoroughness of the evaluation, the neuropsychologist generally gives a large number of diverse tests to the patient. The tests typically demand different mental or cognitive abilities, which are subserved by different regions of the brain. These different cognitive abilities are commonly referred to as cognitive domains, and include functions such as attention, memory, perception, movement, language, and problem solving. A number of comprehensive test batteries have been created to assess the various cognitive domains. The Halstead-Reitan and Luria-Nebraska are two such batteries that have been used to diagnose the location and severity of brain damage in neurological patients.

These batteries consist of a variety of subtests that are believed to tap into different cognitive abilities. For example, the Halstead-Reitan contains subtests that have proved to be helpful in localizing brain damage. This is done by first administering the Halstead-Reitan to a large number of patients with previously diagnosed brain damage. The researcher then looks at those patients with damage to a particular region of the brain (for example, right frontal) and observes which subtests gave them difficulty. By repeating this process on each patient group (left frontal, right posterior, and so on), the researcher can establish norms.

When a patient with suspected damage is tested with the battery, his or her scores can be compared to those in each patient group. Thus, if he or she performs similarly to the right-frontal norms, damage may be diagnosed to this region. While this is an oversimplification, it provides a general model of how test batteries are used in neuropsychology to evaluate patients with suspected brain damage.

Experimental neuropsychology focuses on answering theoretical questions rather than solving clinical or practical ones. Because of the invasive nature of these questions, experimental neuropsychologists often use animals rather than humans in their research. Typically, animals are used in the initial stages of a line of research. After the research procedure has been proved to be safe and effective, however, it is then confirmed on a human sample. Experimental neuropsychologists have shed light on a number of cognitive functions and the parts of the brain involved in those functions.

The methods that experimental neuropsychologists use to study cognitive abilities in humans can be quite creative. The tachistoscope is a device that projects a visual image to either the right or the left half of the visual field very quickly, so that the right or left hemisphere of the brain has preferential access to the visual image. Thus, the importance of the left or right hemisphere of the brain in a given task can be identified.

While the daily routines of clinical and experimental neuropsychologists are quite different, their work can be considerably intertwined. For example, the insights of experimental neuropsychologists often improve clinicians' ability to assess and treat individuals with neurological impairment. Similarly, clinicians' descriptions of interesting patients can often open the road for further theoretical investigation by experimental neuropsychologists.

Applications

The fields of clinical and experimental neuropsychology have been useful in solving a number of practical problems as well as more theoretical ones. For example, clinical neuropsychological procedures have been applied in the assessment and treatment of individuals suspected of having Alzheimer's disease. This disease is difficult to confirm unless a sample of brain is removed and inspected microscopically, a procedure that is quite invasive and is rarely attempted until after the patient's death. Neuropsychological test procedures have contributed dramatically to the accurate diagnosis of Alzheimer's disease without the use of invasive measures such as surgery.

Typically, a series of memory, language, perceptual, and problem-solving tasks are given to the individual when the disease is first suspected. The patient is then tested serially at six-month intervals, and the overall pattern of test scores across time is evaluated. If the patient tends to display a decremental pattern of performance across two or more cognitive domains (for example, memory, language), a diagnosis of dementia is supported.

Along with the measurement of various cognitive functions, neuropsychology also seems particularly equipped to investigate other aspects of the disease. While a patient's performance on a test battery is helpful, other features must be examined in diagnosing the disorder. For example, depression, hallucinations, delusions, and verbal or physical outbursts are often common with the disease. Conversely, the appearance of certain other signs or symptoms make a diagnosis of Alzheimer's disease unlikely. Because of this diverse collection of psychological and behavioral symptoms, clinical neuropsychology may be the best manager of services for these patients.

A second application of neuropsychological techniques concerns the recent surge in rehabilitation efforts with the brain-injured. Many individuals who have sustained an injury to or have a disease of the brain have great difficulty returning to their premorbid jobs or avocations. Neuropsychological rehabilitation attempts to assist these patients with ongoing cognitive difficulties as they reenter the work and home setting. Very often, people who have brain injuries do not have problems with all cognitive domains, but rather with a select few (for example, attention, language). Because of this selective impairment, clinical neuropsychologists can focus their efforts on improving an individual's attentional abilities, or his or her use of language.

A specific example of neuropsychological rehabilitation can be seen in the case of an individual who has been involved in a motor vehicle accident. These patients tend to sustain primary damage to the frontal aspects of the brain because it withstands the initial impact. Damage to the frontal regions normally produces individuals who are very unaware of their surroundings. Furthermore, they typically lack appropriate social skills as well as planning and organizational abilities. These abilities can be improved, however, if the patient works with a neuropsychologist who knows what to expect from each patient based on the exact area of damage.

Generally, rehabilitation involves intensive exposure to the problematic cognitive task. In the case of a patient with damage to the frontal area of the brain, this might entail placement in a group situation in which the patient practices social skills. Specific activities might include working on conversation skills, role-playing a job interview or asking for a date, or working on a group project. Individual sessions with the patient might be better suited for the treatment of the organizational and planning deficits experienced by frontal patients. Here, the neuropsychologist might teach the patient to use a diary to plan the week's activities and learn to solve problems to get things done.

While neuropsychologists often assist patients in acquiring compensation strategies to work around their particular difficulties, there are other rationales for rehabilitative efforts. Many researchers and psychologists believe that practicing the impaired function assists the repairing brain in doing that task. There appears to be a six- to twelve-month period immediately after a brain injury when the brain is developing pathways around the damaged tissue. Many believe that during this critical period, it is important to engage the patient in activities that were most compromised by the injury. Thus, if the injury took a major toll on memory abilities, the patient should be exposed to exercises and activities that demand he or she remember things.

In general, neuropsychology has tremendous applied value for persons who have sustained a neurological insult such as a stroke or brain injury. Furthermore, it is useful in the initial assessment and accurate diagnosis of a given neurological disorder, as well as in the continued care and treatment of individuals with known brain pathology.

Context

Neuropsychology rapidly emerged as a separate branch of the neurosciences throughout the 1970's and 1980's. During that time, there was an explosion of training programs for neuropsychologists and scientific research concerning the relationships between the brain and behavior. While the field has only recently evolved, however, the discipline's underpinnings can be traced back thousands of years. Egyptian writings dating back to 2500 B.C. describe trauma to the brain and the behavior of the patient sustaining this damage.

A second early milestone occurred with the anatomical studies and illustrations of the 1800's. In 1861, Paul Broca demonstrated that a lesion of the left frontal lobe of the brain caused a disruption of the production of speech. Soon after this revelation, researchers became quite consumed with localizing all cognitive functions to some discrete part of the brain.

Those who believed that each function could be neatly contained in a small region of the brain came to be known as localizationists. Those who believed that all areas of the brain were equally involved in all cognitive abilities were labeled equipotentialists. A third view, known as interactionist theory, suggests that more basic cognitive functions are relatively localized but interact to allow for more complex cognitive processes. This perspective was derived from the late nineteenth century work of Hughlings Jackson in his clinical work as a neurologist. In many ways, Jackson's ideas were quite advanced for his time and available research methodology.

The twentieth century witnessed a steady accumulation of knowledge concerning the relationships between the brain and behavior. These developments occurred primarily because of the need to assist soldiers who had sustained wartime brain injuries. In the process of treating these individuals, much was learned about the role of various brain regions in carrying out various behaviors. The systematic study of brain-injured persons by Aleksandr Luria has contributed tremendously to the process of assessing and localizing brain dysfunction.

This new awareness provided psychology with a better understanding of how the physical brain can produce very atypical behaviors. Before this time, it was believed that behavioral disturbance was universally caused by disruption of the nonphysical "mind." The new knowledge has given clinical psychologists much more sophisticated answers about how best to treat patients with behavioral difficulties. It has also served to remove some of the stigma attached to mental illness or dysfunction. The lay public seems more willing to tolerate atypical behavior from an individual with physical damage to the brain than from a patient labeled as being mentally ill.

The future of neuropsychology appears to be full of promise. It is expected that investigators will continue to conduct research that sheds light on the workings of the healthy brain as well as assisting those with neurological damage. Furthermore, it appears that neuropsychology will continue to advance the larger field of psychology by providing physiological explanations for behaviors and disorders that now have only hypothetical ones.

Bibliography

Beaumont, J. Graham. *Introduction to Neuropsychology*. New York: Guilford Press, 1983. A very accessible reference for the student who is new to the field. Particularly helpful in describing the methods used to investigate experimental neuropsychological phenomena.

Ellis, Andrew W., and Andrew W. Young. *Human Cognitive Neuropsychology*. Hove, England: Lawrence Erlbaum, 1988. Presents ideas and research from the mid-1980's on the integrated workings of the brain. Particularly helpful in establishing a theoretical framework that assists the student in integrating the often divergent research findings in a more holistic manner.

Kolb, Bryan, and Ian Q. Whishaw. *Fundamentals of Human Neuropsychology*. 3d ed. New York: W. H. Freeman, 1990. A very comprehensive textbook that fully covers the fields of clinical and experimental neuropsychology. Lengthy, but clear and well written. Best suited to the student who has previously read an introductory work in the field (for example, Beaumont).

Luria, Aleksandr Romanovich. *The Working Brain: An Introduction to Neuropsychology*. New York: Basic Books, 1973. Considered by many to be the seminal work in the field. Presents many of Luria's most dramatic insights about normal and damaged brains. Although the title suggests this is an introduction, the ideas presented in this source are often highly complex.

Restak, Richard W. *The Brain: The Last Frontier*. Garden City, N.Y.: Doubleday, 1979. Available in paperback. Entertaining as well as informative. Written for the lay public; it is a "kind" introduction to research in the field.

Sacks, Oliver. *The Man Who Mistook His Wife for a Hat*. New York: Summit Books, 1985. Sacks is a gifted writer as well as successful neurologist, and he displays the best of both these talents in this work. Reads more like a novel than a textbook. Based on actual neurological cases seen by Sacks.

Walsh, Kevin W. *Neuropsychology: A Clinical Approach*. 3d ed. New York: Churchill Livingston, 1994.

Zaidel, Dahlia W., ed. *Neuropsychology*. 2d ed. San Diego, Calif.: Academic Press, 1994.

Jeffery B. Allen

See also:

Behaviorism, 98; The Cerebral Cortex, 121; Cognitive Psychology, 146; Neural Anatomy and Cognition, 415; Psychoanalytic Psychology, 471.

OBSESSIONS AND COMPULSIONS

Type of psychology: Psychopathology
Field of study: Anxiety disorders

Obsessions and compulsions are the cardinal features of a chronic anxiety disorder known as obsessive-compulsive disorder. The identification of repetitive, anxiety-provoking thoughts known as obsessions and of associated compulsive, ritualistic behaviors is critical in the diagnosis and assessment of this debilitating condition.

Principal terms

ANXIETY: an affective state characterized by physiological arousal, motor tension, and disturbing thoughts

CHECKING RITUAL: a series of compulsive behaviors, usually associated with fear of personal harm or threat, that consists of checking pilot lights, door locks, and/or electrical appliances

CLEANING RITUAL: a series of compulsive behaviors, usually associated with the fear of contamination, that consists of the repetitive cleaning of hands, body, and/or objects such as doorknobs

CLOMIPRAMINE: an antidepressant medication that has been used in the treatment of obsessive-compulsive disorder

COMPULSIONS: ritualistic patterns of behavior that commonly follow obsessive thinking and that reduce the intensity of the anxiety-evoking thoughts

FEAR OF CONTAMINATION: an obsessive pattern of thinking in which the individual is preoccupied with bacteria and germs or tainted products

OBSESSIONS: intrusive, recurrent, anxiety-provoking thoughts, ideas, images, or impulses that interfere with an individual's daily functioning

OBSESSIVE-COMPULSIVE DISORDER: a chronic, debilitating anxiety disorder characterized by continuous obsessive thinking and frequent compulsive behaviors

RESPONSE PREVENTION: a behavioral treatment for obsessive-compulsive disorder which involves exposing the patient to the feared stimuli or thoughts and preventing the ritualistic behavior from occurring

Overview

Obsessive thinking and urges to engage in ritualistic compulsive behaviors are common phenomena that most individuals experience to some extent throughout their lives. It is not uncommon, for example, for a person to reexperience in his or her mind involuntary, anxiety-provoking images of circumstances surrounding a traumatic accident or embarrassing moment. Similarly, behaviors such as returning home to make sure the iron is turned off or refusing to eat from a spoon that falls on a clean floor represent mild compelling rituals in which many persons engage from time to time. It is only when these patterns of obsessive thinking and behaving become either too frequent or too intense that they may escalate into a distressing clinical condition known as obsessive-compulsive disorder.

According to the American Psychiatric Association's *Diagnostic and Statistical Manual of Mental Disorders* (rev. 3d ed., 1987, DSM-III-R), the primary feature of this disorder is the presence of distressing obsessions or severe compulsive behaviors that interfere significantly with a person's daily functioning. Although diagnosis requires only the presence of either obsessions or compulsions, they typically are both present in obsessive-compulsive disorder. In most cases, persons with this diagnosis spend more time on a daily basis experiencing obsessive thinking and engaging in ritualistic behaviors than other constructive activities, including those pertaining to occupational, social, and family responsibilities. Therefore, it is not uncommon for obsessive-compulsive patients also to experience severe vocational impairment and distraught interpersonal relationships.

The word "obsession" comes from the Latin word obsidere ("to besiege"), and can be defined as a recurrent thought, impulse, idea, or image that is intrusive, disturbing, and senseless. Among the most common types are themes of violence (for example, images of killing a loved one), contamination (for example, thoughts of catching a disease from a doorknob), and personal injury/harm (for example, impulses to leap from a bridge). Obsessional doubting is also characteristic of most patients with obsessive-compulsive disorder, which leads to indecisiveness in even the most simple matters such as selecting a shirt to wear or deciding what to order at a restaurant. The basic content of obsessive thinking distinguishes it from simple "worrying." Worrying involves thinking about an event or occurrence that may realistically result in discomfort, embarrassment, or harm and has a likely probability of occurring; obsessive thinking is typically recognized by the patient as being senseless and not likely to occur. An example of a worry is thinking about an event that possesses a strong likelihood of occurring, such as failing a test when one has not studied. Imagining that one might leap from the third-floor classroom during the exam, a highly unlikely event, is considered an obsession. Furthermore, because the obsessive-compulsive patient is aware that these intrusive thoughts are senseless and continuously attempts to rid the thought from his or her mind, obsessive thinking is not delusional or psychotic in nature. Although both delusional and obsessive patients may experience a similar thought (for example, that they have ingested tainted food), the obsessive patient recognizes that the thought is unlikely and is a product of his or her mind, and struggles to get rid of the thought. The delusional patient adheres to the belief with little to no struggle to test its validity.

Most obsessive-compulsive patients also exhibit a series of repetitive, intentional, stereotyped behaviors known as compulsions, which serve to reduce the anxiety experienced from severe obsessive thinking. The most common forms include counting (for example, tapping a pencil three times before laying it down), cleaning (for example, hand washing after shaking another person's hand), checking (for example, checking pilot lights several times a day), and ordering (for example, arranging pencils from longest to shortest before doing homework). Compulsions are different from simple habits in that attempts to resist urges to engage in them result in a substantial increase in anxiety, eventually forcing the patient to engage in the compelling behavior to reduce the tension. Urges to engage in simple habits, on the other hand, can often be resisted with minimal discomfort. Furthermore, most habits result in deriving some degree of pleasure from the activity (for example, shopping, gambling, drinking), while engaging in compulsive behaviors is rarely enjoyable for the patient. Compulsions must also be distinguished from superstitious behaviors, such as an athlete's warm-up ritual or wearing the same "lucky" shoes for each sporting event. In contrast to superstitious people, who employ their rituals to enhance confidence, obsessive-compulsive patients are never certain their rituals will result in anxiety reduction. This typically forces these patients continually to expand their repertoire of ritualistic behaviors, searching for new and better ways to eliminate the anxiety produced by obsessive thinking.

It is now estimated that approximately 2 percent of the adult population in the United States—a larger percentage than was once believed—has at some time experienced obsessive-compulsive symptoms severe enough to warrant diagnosis. Typically, obsessive-compulsive symptoms begin in adolescence or early adulthood, although most patients report symptoms of anxiety and nervousness as children. Regarding early developmental histories, many obsessive-compulsive patients report being reared in very strict, puritanical homes. The disorder occurs equally in males and females, although cleaning rituals occur more frequently among women. While the course of the disorder is chronic, the intensity of symptoms fluctuates throughout life and occasionally has been reported to remit spontaneously. Because of the unusual nature of the symptoms, obsessive-compulsive patients often keep their rituals hidden and become introverted and withdrawn; as a result, the clinical picture becomes complicated by a coexisting depressive disorder. It is typically the depression which forces the patient to seek psychological help.

Applications

Because of the distressing yet fascinating nature of the symptoms, several theoretical positions have attempted to explain how obsessive-compulsive disorder develops. From an applied perspective, each theoretical position has evolved into a treatment or intervention strategy for eliminating the problems caused by obsessions and compulsions. According to psychoanalytic theory, as outlined by Sigmund Freud in 1909, obsessive-compulsive rituals are the product of overly harsh toilet training which leaves the patient with considerable unconscious hostility, primarily directed toward an authoritarian caregiver. In a sense, as uncomfortable and disconcerting as the obsessions and compulsive behaviors are, they are preferable to experiencing the intense emotions left from these childhood incidents. Obsessions and compulsions then permit the patient to avoid experiencing these emotions. Furthermore, obsessive-compulsive symptoms force the patient to become preoccupied with anxiety-reduction strategies which prevent them from dealing with other hidden impulses, such as sexual urges and desires. Based upon the psychoanalytic formulation, treatment involves identifying the original unconscious thoughts, ideas, or impulses and allowing the patient to experience them consciously. In his classic case report of an obsessive patient, Freud analyzed a patient known as the "rat man," who was plagued by recurrent, horrifying images of a bucket of hungry rats strapped to the buttocks of his girlfriend and his father. Although periodic case reports of psychoanalytic treatments for obsessive-compulsive disorder exist, there is very little controlled empirical work suggesting the effectiveness of this treatment approach.

Behavioral theorists, differing with the psychoanalytic tradition, have proposed that obsessive-compulsive disorder represents a learned habit that is maintained by the reinforcing properties of the anxiety reduction that occurs following ritualistic behaviors. It is well established that behaviors that are reinforced occur more frequently in the future. In the case of compulsive behaviors, the ritual is always followed by a significant reduction in anxiety, therefore reinforcing the compulsive behavior as well as the preceding obsessive activity. Based upon the behavioral perspective, an intervention strategy called response prevention, or flooding, was developed to facilitate the interruption of this habitually reinforcing cycle. Response prevention involves exposing the patient to the feared stimulus (for example, a doorknob) or obsession (for example, an image of leaping from a bridge) in order to create anxiety. Rather than allowing the patient to engage in the subsequent compulsive activity, however, the therapist prevents the response (for example, the patient is not permitted to wash his or her hands). The patient endures a period of intense anxiety but eventually experiences habituation of the anxiety response. Although treatments of this nature are anxiety provoking for the patient, well-controlled investigations have reported significant reductions in obsessive thinking and ritualistic behavior following intervention. Some estimates of success rates with response prevention are as high as 80 percent, and treatment gains are maintained for several years.

Theories emphasizing the cognitive aspects of the obsessive-compulsive disorder have focused on information-processing impairments of the patient. Specifically, obsessive-compulsive patients tend to perceive harm (for example, contamination) when in fact it may not be present and to perceive a loss of control over their environment. While most individuals perceive a given situation as safe until proved harmful, the obsessive-compulsive patient perceives situations as harmful until proved safe. These perceptions of harm and lack of control lead to increased anxiety; the belief that the patient controls his or her life or the perception of safety leads to decreased anxiety. Accordingly, compulsive rituals represent a patient's efforts to gain control over his or her environment. Cognitive interventions then aim to increase the patient's perception of control over the environment and to evaluate realistically environmental threats of harm. While cognitive approaches may serve as a useful adjunct to behavioral treatments such as response prevention, evidence for their effectiveness when used in treating obsessions and compulsions is lacking.

Finally, biological models of obsessive-compulsive disorder have also been examined. There is some indication that brain electrical activity during information processing, particularly in the frontal lobes, is somewhat slower for obsessive-compulsive patients in comparison to other people. For example, metabolic activity of the frontal brain regions measured using positron emission tomography (PET) scans differentiates obsessive-compulsive patients from both normal people and depressive patients. Further, a deficiency in certain neurotransmitters (for example, serotonin, norepinephrine) has been implicated in the etiology of the disorder. Several interventions based upon the biological model have been employed as well. Pharmacotherapy, using antidepressant medications that primarily act to facilitate neurotransmitter functioning (for example, clomipramine), has been shown to be effective in treating from 20 to 50 percent of obsessive-compulsive patients. More drastic interventions such as frontal lobotomies have been reported in the most intractable cases, with very limited success.

Among the interventions employed to rid patients of troublesome obsessions and compulsions, response prevention holds the most promise. Because of the intensity of this treatment approach, however, the cost may be substantial, and many patients may not immediately respond. A number of predictors of poor treatment response to behavioral interventions (characteristic of those most refractory to treatment) have been identified. These include a coexisting depression, poor compliance with exposure/response-prevention instructions, the presence of fears that the patient views as realistic, and eccentric superstition. In these cases, alternative forms of treatment are typically considered (for example, pharmacotherapy).

Context

Obsessions and compulsions represent human phenomena that have been a topic of interest for several centuries; for example, William Shakespeare's characterization of the handwashing Lady Macbeth has entertained audiences for hundreds of years. Prior to the first therapeutic analysis of obsessive-compulsive disorder, then called a neurosis—Freud's description of the "rat man"—obsessive thoughts were commonly attributed to demoniac influence and treated with exorcism. Freud's major contribution was delivering the phenomenon from the spiritual into the psychological realm. Although initial case reports employing psychoanalysis were promising, subsequent developments using behavioral and pharmacological formulations have more rapidly advanced the understanding of the phenomenology and treatment of this unusual condition. In addition, with the public revelation that certain prominent individuals such as the aircraft designer and film producer Howard Hughes have suffered from this condition, the prevalence estimates of this disorder have steadily increased. Although a number of patients have sought help for this debilitating disorder since the time it was first clinically described, it has been confirmed that this problem is far more prevalent than initially thought. The increase is probably not related to an actual increase in incidence, but to individuals becoming more willing to seek help for the problem. Because of the increasing number of individuals requesting help for problems relating to obsessions and compulsions, it is becoming more and more important to foster the maturation of appropriate treatment strategies to deal with this disorder.

Further, it has become increasingly important to understand the manifestation of obsessions and compulsions from a biological, psychological, and socio-occupational level. Ongoing investigations are examining the biological makeup of the nervous systems peculiar to this disorder. Research examining the specific information-processing styles and cognitive vulnerabilities of obsessive-compulsive patients is also being conducted. Both response-prevention and biochemical-intervention strategies (for example, clomipramine) are deserving of continued research, primarily examining characteristics of obsessive-compulsive patients which predict treatment efficacy with either form of intervention. Finally, early markers for this condition, including childhood environments, early learning experiences, and biological predispositions, require further investigation so that prevention efforts can be provided for individuals who may be at risk for developing obsessive-compulsive disorder. With these advances, psychologists will be in a better position to reduce the chronic nature of obsessive-compulsive disorder and to prevent these distressing symptoms in forthcoming generations.

Bibliography

American Psychiatric Association. *Diagnostic and Statistical Manual of Mental Disorders.* Rev. 3d ed. Washington, D.C.: Author, 1987. The DSM-III-R provides specific criteria for making psychiatric diagnoses of obsessive-compulsive disorder and other anxiety disorders. Brief summaries of research findings regarding each condition are also provided.

Bellenir, Karen, ed. *Mental Health Disorders Sourcebook*. Detroit, Mich.: Omnigraphics, 1996.

Emmelkamp, Paul M. G. *Phobic and Obsessive Compulsive Disorders: Theory, Research, and Practice*. New York: Plenum Press, 1982. A somewhat dated but classic work outlining the importance of behavioral strategies in overcoming obsessive-compulsive, as well as phobic, conditions.

Jenike, Michael A., Lee Baer, and William E. Minichiello. *Obsessive-Compulsive Disorders: Theory and Management*. Littleton, Mass.: PSG, 1986. A comprehensive overview of the topic that does not burden the reader with intricate details of analysis. Readable by the layperson. Covers the topic thoroughly.

Kozak, M. J., E. B. Foa, and P. R. McCarthy. "Obsessive-Compulsive Disorder." In *Handbook of Anxiety Disorders*, edited by Cynthia Last and Michel Hersen. New York: Pergamon Press, 1988. Covers some intriguing research questions that are rarely mentioned elsewhere, those pertaining to cognitive styles and psychophysiological responses of obsessive-compulsive patients. Also presents data pertaining to biological theories of obsessive-compulsive disorder.

Mavissakalian, Matig, Samuel M. Turner, and Larry Michelson. *Obsessive-Compulsive Disorders: Psychological and Pharmacological Treatment*. New York: Plenum Press, 1985. An exceptionally well-written text based upon a symposium held at the University of Pittsburgh. Issues pertaining to etiology, assessment, diagnosis, and treatment are covered in detail.

Rachman, S. J. "Obsessional-Compulsive Disorders." In *International Handbook of Behavior Modification and Therapy*, edited by Alan S. Bellack, Michel Hersen, and Alan E. Kazdin. New York: Plenum Press, 1982. Rachman's work using behavioral strategies with obsessive-compulsive patients is unparalleled. No bibliography would be complete without a contribution from Rachman, one of the most respected authorities in the field.

Turner, S. M., and L. Michelson. "Obsessive-Compulsive Disorders." In *Behavioral Theories and Treatment of Anxiety*, edited by Samuel M. Turner. New York: Plenum Press, 1984. Summarizes information regarding diagnostic issues, assessment strategies, and treatment interventions for obsessive-compulsive disorder. Provides an excellent review of intervention efforts employing response prevention and clomipramine.

Kevin T. Larkin
Virginia L. Goetsch

See also:

Abnormality, 1; Anxiety Disorders, 65; Bipolar Disorder, 104; Depression: Theoretical Explanations, 200; Phobias, 459; Suicide, 610.

PAVLOVIAN CONDITIONING

Type of psychology: Learning
Field of study: Pavlovian conditioning

The processes of acquisition, extinction, and inhibition in Pavlovian conditioning explain how people learn to predict the relationship between events in their environment, including their own behavior. Forming positive and negative behavioral and emotional expectations is of great value, because such expectations allow people to adjust their behavior and emotional state for effective and efficient action.

Principal terms

ACQUISITION: the forming of an association between two stimuli, the first of which predicts an increased likelihood of the second; it is rapid at first, then subject to diminishing returns

CONDITIONED RESPONSE: the behavior and emotional quality that occurs when a conditioned stimulus is presented; related to but not the same as the unconditioned response

CONDITIONED STIMULUS: the event that predicts the likelihood of the unconditioned stimulus; greater than expected in excitatory conditioning, less than expected in inhibitory conditioning

CONTINGENCY: the relationship between the conditioned stimulus and the unconditioned stimulus when the likelihood of the latter is statistically correlated with the occurrence of the former

EXTINCTION: the reduction in strength, or elimination, of the conditioned response following repeated presentation of the conditioned stimulus without the unconditioned stimulus

INHIBITION: the effect of a conditioned stimulus that reduces or nullifies an excitatory conditioned response (or retards the formation of one) to the same unconditioned stimulus

UNCONDITIONED RESPONSE: the innate or previously conditioned behavior and emotion that follow presentation of the unconditioned stimulus

UNCONDITIONED STIMULUS: an event that is strong, noticed, and surprising, thereby producing behavior, emotion, and rehearsal that together support acquisition of a conditioned response

Overview

The great Russian physiologist Ivan Pavlov developed the original, highly physiological model of conditioning at the beginning of the twentieth century. The modern concept of Pavlovian conditioning is that it allows an organism to form associations between events as experienced in its mind. In order for conditioned associations to occur, there must be a predictive relationship between experienced events.

In Pavlov's most famous experiment, he conditioned dogs to salivate at the sound of a bell by the repeated process of ringing the bell and then giving the dog food. Research showed that each time the bell and food were paired (called a learning trial), the amount of saliva the dog produced increased. In fewer than twenty trials, there was as much saliva produced in response to the bell as would have normally been secreted in response to food. The increase in salivation was rapid for the early trials, but this increase became less and less for each successive trial until there was virtually no change. In this regard, the acquisition of a conditioned response is rapid at first but is then subject to diminishing returns. This characteristic change in the rate of acquisition is believed to be based on the progressive loss of both the conditioned stimulus' ability to attract the organism's attention and the unconditioned stimulus' ability to provide the emotional surprise thought to motivate mental rehearsal. As one acquires an expectation, one's attention becomes diverted to novel events and one's surprise at the increasingly expected unconditioned stimulus declines, causing the rate of acquisition to taper off. The increase, at a diminishing rate, of the conditioned response during acquisition is called the learning curve.

To use the standard terminology of Pavlovian conditioning, a conditioned stimulus (CS), such as the bell, predicts the likelihood of an unconditioned stimulus (US), such as food. This predictive relationship leads to the formation of a conditioned response (CR), in the example above the salivation to the bell. The conditioned response typically has much in common with the ordinary response to the unconditioned stimulus, called the unconditioned response, but can often differ significantly, sometimes being opposite in nature to the unconditioned response. Whatever the character of a conditioned response, it usually can be best understood by viewing it as part of the organism's preparation for the unconditioned stimulus.

As discussed above, the organism must attend to the conditioned stimulus, and the unconditioned stimulus must be strong, emotionalizing, and surprising (relatively unexpected). Typically, but not necessarily, the conditioned stimulus should come immediately before the unconditioned stimulus. Most important, the occurrence of the conditioned stimulus must inform the organism that the likelihood of the unconditioned stimulus occurring is different, either greater or less, than at other times in the organism's life without the occurrence of the conditioned stimulus. When this last condition is met, the occurrence of the unconditioned stimulus is said to be contingent upon the occurrence of the conditioned stimulus.

When a conditioned response has been acquired, it becomes a reliable part of the organism's behavior and is often found to have two parts: specific actions (such as a dog salivating) and general emotional changes, called conditioned emotional responses (as inferred from a dog's eagerness and tail wagging), both of which agree with the assumption, in the case of a dog, that it expects food.

Pavlov also found that when a conditioned stimulus is presented repeatedly without the unconditioned stimulus, the strength of the conditioned response declines, rapidly at first and then more gradually, until it finally stops occurring. This process thus appears to follow a time course that is the reverse of acquisition. Pavlov termed the phenomenon extinction and believed it to be the effect of inhibitory brain connections which were built up because the reinforcing power of the unconditioned stimulus was absent (by definition) in extinction trials. While it is no longer believed that excitatory or inhibitory brain processes directly explain acquisition, extinction, or other aspects of conditioning, the term inhibition is used to describe a specific effect of conditioning that can either reduce the size of a response caused by the "excitation" of another stimulus or make the formation of specific new conditioned responses more difficult. Although the issue is not entirely clear, it appears that during extinction trials the organism is learning a new expectation, reinforced by the unconditioned stimulus' surprising failure to occur as expected following the conditioned stimulus. Recall that extinction is defined by the presence of the conditioned stimulus only on trials in which the unconditioned stimulus is absent, or highly unlikely, compared to other times or in the memory of the organism. Because of this relationship, the organism comes to associate the presence of the conditioned stimulus with the non-occurrence of the unconditioned stimulus and behaves accordingly. Eventually, the new inhibitory association becomes strong enough to nullify the original excitatory conditioning.

There are many situations other than extinction in which inhibition also affects the size of a conditioned response. To evaluate inhibition, one normally uses an excitatory stimulus, the response to which serves as a "baseline" for measurement. Remember that "excitatory" only means that the conditioned stimulus is an effective predictor of something important, not necessarily something "good." If the expectation is for something beneficial, the organism makes appropriate approach responses and feels good; expectations of something aversive lead the organism to make escape responses and feel bad. One then can use another conditioned stimulus that has a negative predictive relationship to the same unconditioned stimulus, and can test to see that when the two are presented together, the second conditioned stimulus reduces the effect of the first, as if they algebraically summated. As mentioned above, one may also show that a particular conditioned stimulus is inhibitory if its presentation can be shown to retard the acquisition of an excitatory conditioned response to the same unconditioned stimulus.

Applications

Pavlovian conditioning is far from being a primitive form of learning relevant only to the behavior of lower animals. Because the human world is filled with regularities and contingencies between salient events, conditioning allows people's bodies to prepare for action. It also gives people the emotional incentives—desire or distaste—for most of their actions, and regulates their emotional tone in most of the situations they are in.

As Pavlov discovered, the digestive system becomes active in anticipation of food. When a person sits down to a meal, the cooking aromas and the appetizers stimulate the digestive system to prepare for the full meal to come. Think of how the stomach feels if a much-contemplated meal is unexpectedly interrupted. Indeed, rats injected with insulin in amounts close to but not sufficient to cause insulin shock and then fed an artificial sweetener often do succumb to the dose of insulin. Apparently, the sweet taste causes the pancreas to release insulin as a conditioned response; but without the expected sugar to metabolize, the endogenous (internally secreted) insulin together with the injected amount is enough to cause insulin shock.

Similarly, people unaccustomed to drinking diet sodas sometimes feel hungrier after consuming one, rather than satisfied. The insulin released in response to the sweet taste causes a reduction in the person's blood sugar. Someone who drinks large amounts of diet soda, however, associates the taste with the failure to ingest sugar, extinguishes the conditioned insulin release, and thus does not have this response.

The situation is far more serious when it comes to the potential for taking an overdose of an addictive drug such as heroin. If an addict injects heroin in a certain room or location, that place will become a conditioned stimulus for the physiological release of heroin (opioid) antagonists, which the body produces to defend itself against the drug effects. If the addict takes the same drug dose in a novel situation, these endogenous opioid antagonists will not be released and the person may overdose and die.

Just as a specific life situation can be a conditioned stimulus for the release of opioid antagonists, the release of endogenous opioids, called endorphins, can be triggered by conditioned stimuli. The euphoria experienced by some long-distance runners and joggers, called "runner's high," is thought to be caused by the release of these internal painkillers in response to the early cues that a stressful situation is beginning.

The acquisition of conditioned responses is not limited to physiological response. Many, but certainly not all, phobias (irrational fears) are thought to result from conditioned associations. One of the most famous experiments in psychology was conducted by behavioral psychologist John B. Watson and his associate Rosalie Raynor in 1920. They conditioned an infant, less than a year old, to fear a tame white rat by putting the rat in the crib (something to which the child looked forward) and then creating a loud and obviously frightening sound. The infant, referred to as "Little Albert," soon came to show crying and other signs of fear and distress whenever the rat was introduced. It might seem that all traumatic events could create phobic tendencies, but, fortunately, such is not the case. It is much easier for phobias to be conditioned if a person has a very sensitive and responsive emotional nervous system, and if the person is in other ways biologically prepared to attend and emotionally respond to the stimuli present during the potentially traumatic situation; this situation, however, is not fully understood.

The most important role of Pavlovian conditioning is in the acquisition, extinction, and inhibition of conditioned emotional responses that are not related to phobias. Every time an organism is positively or negatively reinforced, that organism's behavior changes. One reason for the behavior change is that the stimuli that preceded reinforcement, which include those caused by the behavior itself, become conditioned stimuli for the feeling which the reinforcement creates in the organism. People do the things they do because they anticipate rewards and feeling good. Similarly, if an organism anticipates something aversive and feels bad, that organism will engage in behavior that serves to remove it from the situation that has been conditioned to make it feel bad. Thus, if a person skips class or an important business meeting and later "pays the price," the next time he or she is in a similar situation, it will most likely be a conditioned stimulus for anxiety and fear of failure. These bad feelings will motivate a person to change the situation, often by engaging in the required behavior.

Inhibitory conditioning is a valuable process in the modification of conditioned emotional responses. Modern life has many unavoidable stressors and anxiety-producing situations. These conditions often lead to debilitating anxiety and panic attacks, as well as a host of psychosomatic symptoms. Specific stimuli can be conditioned to predict stressor-free periods in a person's life. The person can then use these cues as conditioned inhibitors during stressful periods. Relaxation training is one popular method: A busy executive can mentally create an image, such as a woodland stream, that was used during a relaxation training session in which nothing bad could ever happen every time he or she feels severe anxiety. This image then produces conditioned inhibition of the anxiety response. Indeed, even stimuli that merely let a person know when something bad but unavoidable will happen can serve to reduce stress. They do this by making the periods when these stimuli are absent predict "safe" periods in the person's life. In this way, the absence of the warning signal becomes a conditioned inhibitor of anxiety, a phenomenon called learned safety.

Context

Scientific psychology began as an attempt to explain how people come to know about the world. Although people are undoubtedly born with genetically encoded information about how to interact with their environment, early psychologists were heavily influenced by the notion of the seventeenth century English philosopher John Locke. Locke was the founder of British empiricism, a school of philosophy that held that the mind at birth was a "blank slate" (tabula rasa) upon which experience writes all knowledge. This emphasis on acquired rather than inborn knowledge dominated the development of psychology and was only recently called into serious question. Pavlovian conditioning is the model for the formation of acquired empirical associations or expectations.

It is ironic that Pavlov was a physiologist whose original theory was specifically intended to provide a completely reflex-based explanation of associative learning. Today, his research and terminology are used to describe how mental relationships between sensory events come about. The processes discussed in this article—acquisition, extinction, and inhibition—produce changes in human behavior. Yet these changes are often part of the way human understanding of the world has been changed: the way that emotion, meaning, and value are attached to previously neutral events. As such, these processes are important tools for education, psychotherapy, advertising, and even propaganda and thought control. Advertisements for tobacco products, for example, things without much intrinsic value, depend almost exclusively on irrational associations with powerful symbols of sex, attractiveness, and popularity in order to begin and strengthen people's addiction to them.

Excitatory and inhibitory conditioned responses may also be seen as the foundation of the much more complex associative processes that support semantic memory. Human concepts are rich associative combinations of experiences and expectations, some excitatory, some inhibitory. (For example, think of the range of meaning and emotion the word "mother" can evoke.) Modern psychology is moving away from inadequate models of the self characterized by a little executive person inside one's head who solves problems and generates action like a coach telling one's body what plays to run. Instead, the self is coming to be seen as the direct result of countless simultaneous conditioned expectations and relationships. While an understanding of Pavlovian processes can aid researchers in becoming more objective about the subjective quality of the self, the unique experience of life and what it is to be an individual may have to remain an irreducible summation of these processes.

Bibliography

Domjan, Michael, and Barbara Burkhard. *The Principles of Learning and Behavior.* 2d ed. Monterey, Calif.: Brooks/Cole, 1986. A particularly well-written text that manages to pack a stunning amount of important information, including very clear everyday examples, into a relatively small book. Primarily covers animal research but has numerous sections dealing with human applications.

Lutz, John. *Introduction to Learning and Memory.* Pacific Grove, Calif.: Brooks/Cole, 1994.

Mackintosh, N. J., ed. *Animal Learning and Cognition*. San Diego, Calif.: Academic Press, 1994.

Mackintosh, N. J., and M. M. Cotton. "Conditioned Inhibition from Reinforcement Reduction." In *Information Processing in Animals: Conditioned Inhibition*, edited by Ralph R. Miller and Norman E. Spear. Hillsdale, N.J.: Lawrence Erlbaum, 1985. Many of the chapters in this book are demanding for the nonspecialist, but Mackintosh presents a crucial alternative but complementary approach to conditioning to that of Rescorla. A full understanding of conditioning requires the effort this chapter demands.

Pavlov, Ivan Petrovich. *Conditioned Reflexes*. Oxford, England: Oxford University Press, 1927. Surprisingly, the original Pavlov monograph is readable by the patient nonspecialist. Much is of interest here, not the least of which is the quality of Pavlov's scientific dedication, brilliance, and personal humanity. It is revealing to compare Pavlov's philosophical commitment to brain theory with the contemporary emphasis on cognitive process.

Rescorla, R. A. "Conditioned Inhibition and Extinction." In *Mechanisms of Learning and Motivation*, edited by Anthony Dickinson and Robert A. Boakes. Hillsdale, N.J.: Lawrence Erlbaum, 1979. Although many of the articles in this collection are demanding for the nonspecialist, the Rescorla chapter is important enough to warrant the effort. There is information in this book that is difficult to find elsewhere.

Schwartz, Barry, and Dan Reisberg. *Learning and Memory*. New York: W. W. Norton, 1991. Verbose and occasionally rambling, yet one of the most down-to-earth but accurate descriptions of difficult material around. An important benefit of this text is that it relates conditioned to higher cognitive processes.

John Santelli

See also:

PERSON-CENTERED THERAPY

Type of psychology: Psychotherapy
Field of study: Humanistic therapies

Person-centered therapy is based on a philosophy that emphasizes an inherent human tendency for growth and self-actualization. Psychologist Carl Rogers developed and described person-centered therapy as a "way of being."

Principal terms

CONGRUENCE: the consistency or correspondence among thoughts, experience, and behavior

EMPATHY: the focusing of the therapist's attention on the needs and experience of the client; also refers to the therapist's ability to communicate an understanding of the client's emotional state

GENUINENESS: a characteristic in which the therapist does not act out a professional role but instead acts congruently with his or her own sensory and emotional experience

PHENOMENOLOGY: a method of exploration in which subjective and/or experiential data are accepted without any need for further analysis

SELF: an existing picture of oneself; perceptions of "I" or "me" either in relationships with others or by oneself

SELF-ACTUALIZATION: a biologically and culturally determined process involving a tendency toward growth and full realization of one's potential

UNCONDITIONAL POSITIVE REGARD: the attempt by a therapist to convey to a client that he or she genuinely cares for the client

Overview

Psychologist Carl R. Rogers (1902-1987) was the leading figure in the development of phenomenological therapy, and his name has been used synonymously ("Rogerian" therapy) with person-centered therapy. Phenomenological theory is a method of exploration that emphasizes all aspects of human experience. In particular, it highlights the importance of an individual's creative power, in addition to genetics and environment. Moreover, this theory focuses primarily on a person's subjective experience (opinions, viewpoints, and understandings) and defines therapy on the basis of a good human-to-human relationship.

Rogers remained primarily concerned with the conditions for personal growth rather than with the development of personality theory; he focused on personality functioning rather than on personality structures. He did, however, offer formal conceptions of personality. The central concepts and key formulations of person-centered therapy were published in Rogers' *Counseling and Psychotherapy: Newer Concepts in Practice* (1942), *On Becoming a Person* (1961), and his landmark book *Client-Centered Therapy* (1951). Rogers presented nineteen propositions about personality development. These propositions included the following concepts: Each individual exists in a continually changing world in which he or she is the center. Individuals react to the world as they experience and perceive it; thus, "reality" is defined by the person's phenomenal field. Behavior is basically the goal-directed attempt of the organism to satisfy its needs as experienced in the phenomenal field. Each individual has a unique perspective—his or her own private world—and to comprehend a person one must assume a frame of reference from the person's perspective. Emotion facilitates goal-directed behavior. The structure of the self is formed as a result of evaluative interactions with others; the self is an organized, fluid, yet consistent pattern of perceptions about oneself.

The phenomenal field refers to everything experienced by an individual at any given time. The term "internal frame of reference" refers to the process by which therapists attempt to perceive clients' experiences and "reality" as closely as they can. An individual's reality is essentially that which the person perceives. Moreover, it is the person's subjective experience and perceptions that shape the person's understanding of reality and guide behavior. Events are significant for an individual if the individual experiences them as meaningful. In treatment, therapists strive to understand clients by understanding their views of themselves and the environment in which they live.

A central concept within phenomenological theory is the "self"(a structure derived from experiences involving one's own body or resulting from one's own actions). The self (or self-concept), then, is a self-picture or self-awareness. It is a changing process that incorporates the individual's meaning when he or she refers to the characteristics of "I" or "me" in isolation or in relationships with others. The concept of self is also considered to be an organized, consistent, and learned attribute composed of thoughts about self. Rogers views the need for positive regard to be universal. The self-concept depends, in large part, on the "conditions of worth" that a child has learned through interactions with significant others. According to Rogers, the child's need to maintain the love of parents inevitably results in conflict with his or her own needs and desires. For example, as young children assert greater autonomy, a growing awareness of individuality and uniqueness follows. Quite often, the young child demonstrates a negativistic pattern wherein conflicts become more common as the child's needs are in conflict with parent desires.

Maladjustment occurs when there is a lack of consistency between one's concept of self and one's sensory and visceral experiences. If the self-concept is based on many conditions of worth and includes components of failure, imperfection, and weakness, then a lack of positive self-regard will be evident. When such incongruence occurs, individuals are viewed as being vulnerable to psychological problems. Of particular importance is self-esteem (feelings about self), which is often negative or problematic in clients. Poor self-esteem occurs when the phenomenal self is threatened. A threat for one person is not necessarily a threat for another. A person will experience threat whenever he or she perceives that the phenomenal self is in danger. For example, if a well-adjusted athlete misses the final shot at the buzzer in a close basketball game, he or she will not blame the referees or claim physical illness, but instead will examine this experience and perhaps revise his or her self-concept.

Other key principles that underlie person-centered theory involve the processes of self-direction and self-actualization. According to Rogers, humans have an innate tendency to maintain and enhance the self. In fact, all needs can be summarized as the urge to enhance the phenomenal self. Although the process of self-actualization may become disrupted by a variety of social, interpersonal, and cultural factors (determined in large part by the actions of parents, teachers, and peers), Rogers states that the positive growth tendency will ultimately prevail. This actualizing tendency is what produces the forward movement of life, the primary force upon which therapists rely heavily in therapy with clients. Self-actualization refers to the concept that unhampered individuals strive to actualize, enhance, and reach their full potential.

Via self-actualization, a person becomes a fully functioning individual. The qualities of a fully functioning person include being open to experience all feelings while being afraid of none; demonstrating creativity and individual expression; living in the present without preoccupation with past or future; being free to make choices and act on those choices spontaneously; trusting oneself and human nature; having an internal source of evaluation; demonstrating balance and realistic expressions of anger, aggression, and affection; exhibiting congruence between one's feelings and experience; and showing a willingness to continue to grow.

Congruence is the term used by Rogers and others to imply the correspondence between awareness and experience. If a client is able to communicate an awareness of feelings that he or she is currently experiencing, the behavior is said to be congruent or integrated. On the other hand, if an individual attempts to communicate a feeling (love, for example) to another person while experiencing incongruence (hostility toward that person), the recipient of that individual's expression of feelings may experience an awareness of miscommunication.

Person-centered theory and therapy have evolved since the 1940's. When Rogers published *Counseling and Psychotherapy* (1942), the predominant view among mental health professionals was that the therapist should act as an expert who directs the course of treatment. Rogers, however, described counseling as a relationship in which warmth, responsiveness, and freedom from coercion and pressure (including pressure from the therapist) are essential. Such an approach to treatment emphasized the client's ability to take positive steps toward personal growth. This phase, from 1940 to 1950, has been referred to as Rogers' nondirective period. The second phase, reflective psychotherapy, spanned the years from 1950 to 1957. During this period, Rogers changed the name of his approach to "client-centered counseling" and emphasized the importance of reflecting (paraphrasing, summarizing, and clarifying) the client's underlying feelings.

The third phase, experiential psychotherapy, has been described as lasting from 1957 to 1970. During this phase, Rogers focused on the conditions that would be necessary and sufficient for change to occur. Results of his studies demonstrated that the most successful clients were those who experienced the highest degree of accurate empathy, and that client ratings, rather than therapist ratings, of the quality of the therapeutic relationship were most closely associated with eventual success or failure. Also evident during this phase of development was Roger's de-emphasis of psychotherapy techniques, such as reflection. Instead, he focused more on the importance of basic therapist attitudes. By so doing, a wider range of therapist behaviors was encouraged in order to establish the essential relationship components of empathy, positive regard, and congruence. Therapists were encouraged to attend to their own experiences in the session and express their immediate feelings in the therapy relationship.

In 1974, Rogers changed the name of his approach to person-centered therapy. Rogers believed that person-centered therapy more appropriately described the human values that his approach incorporates. Since the 1970's, an additional phase of person-centered therapy, incorporating a more eclectic approach to treatment, has evolved. Specifically, person-centered therapists frequently employ strategies that focus on thoughts, feelings, and values from other schools of psychotherapy within the framework of a productive, accepting relationship. Person-centered approaches have been successfully incorporated into teaching and educational curricula, marriage programs, and international conflict-resolution situations.

Applications

Person-centered therapy aims to increase the congruence, or matching, between self-concept and organismic experience. As Rogers described it, psychotherapy serves to "free up" the already existing capacity in a potentially competent individual, rather than consisting of the expert manipulation of techniques designed to change personality. The primary mechanism for reintegration of self and experience is the interpersonal relationship between therapist and client. In fact, the therapeutic relationship is viewed as being of primary importance in promoting healing and growth. Thus, it is this relationship in and of itself that produces growth in the client. Rogers argues that the process of therapy is synonymous with the experiential relationship between client and therapist; change occurs primarily as a result of the interaction between them.

As described by N. J. Raskin and Rogers (1989), the most fundamental concept in person-centered therapy is trust—that is, trust in clients' growth tendency toward actualization, and trust in clients' ability to achieve their own goals and run their own lives. Similarly, it is important that the therapist be seen as a *person* in the relationship (not as a role), and that the therapist be appreciated and regarded with trust. Rogers stated that clients enter treatment in a state of incongruence, often resulting in vulnerability and anxiety. For treatment to be effective, he identified three necessary and sufficient ingredients for constructive change: The counselor experiences empathic understanding of the client's internal frame of reference, the counselor experiences unconditional positive regard for the client, and the counselor acts congruently with his or her own experience, becoming genuinely integrated into the relationship with the client. It is also essential to the therapy process that the counselor succeed in communicating unconditional positive regard, genuineness, and empathic understanding to the client.

Of particular importance is empathy. Empathy reflects an attitude of interest in the client's thoughts, feelings, and experiences. Moreover, Rogers describes empathy as "a way of being" that is powerfully curative because of its nonevaluative and accepting quality. In fact, the process of conveying accurate empathic understanding has been described as the most important aspect of the therapeutic endeavor. Therapists who convey this form of sensitivity to the needs, feelings, and circumstances of the client can in essence climb inside the client's subjective experience and attempt to understand the world as he or she does. Empathy facilitates a process through which clients assume a caring attitude toward themselves. Moreover, empathy allows clients to gain a greater understanding of their own organismic experiencing, which in turn, facilitates positive self-regard and a more accurate self-concept.

In perhaps all of their previous relationships, clients have learned that acceptance is conditional upon acting in an acceptable manner. For example, parents typically accept children if they do as they are told. In therapy, however, Rogers argued that no conditions of worth should be present. Acceptance of the client as a fallible yet essentially trustworthy individual is given without ulterior motives, hidden causes, or subtle disclaimers. The primary challenge of the therapist's unconditional positive regard comes with clients whose behavior and attitude run strongly counter to the therapist's beliefs. A sex offender, an abusive parent, or a lazy client can test a therapist's level of tolerance and acceptance. Rogers' position is that every individual is worthy of unconditional positive regard.

Genuineness refers to the characteristic of being congruent—the experience of therapists who appropriately express the behavior, feelings, and attitudes that the client stimulates in them. For example, a person does not laugh when sad or angry. Similarly, acting congruently with one's own emotional experience does not mean hiding behind a mask of calm when a client makes upsetting statements. Rogers believed that, in the long run, clients would respond best to a "real person" who is dedicated to the client's welfare and acts in an honest and congruent manner.

In person-centered treatment, sessions are usually scheduled once or twice a week. Additional sessions and telephone calls are typically discouraged in order to avoid dependency on the therapist that will stifle personal growth. Rogers has described the general process of therapy as involving a series of seven steps. Step one is an initial unwillingness to reveal self and an avoidance of feelings; close relationships may be perceived as threatening or dangerous. In step two, feelings are described briefly, but the person is still distant from his or her own personal experience and externalizes issues; the person begins to show recognition that conflicts and difficulties exist. In step three, describing past feelings becomes unacceptable; there is more self-disclosure and expression, and the client begins to question the validity of his or her constructs and beliefs.

Step four involves the description of personal feelings as owned by the self and a limited recognition that previously denied feelings may exist; there is an increasing expression of self-responsibility. Step five involves the free expression and acceptance of one's feelings, an awareness of previously denied feelings, a recognition of conflicts between intellectual and emotional processes, and a desire to be who one really is. In step six, there is an acceptance of feelings without the need for denial and a willingness to risk being oneself in relationships with others. In step seven, the person is comfortable with his or her self, is aware of new feelings and experiences, and experiences minimal incongruence.

Context

As Rogers began his career during the late 1930's, psychoanalysis was the primary approach to psychotherapy and the dominant model in personality theory. Though Rogers was subjected to traditional psychoanalytic influences, his perspective was nearly the exact opposite of Sigmund Freud's theory; Rogers tended to reject the notion of unconscious processes. Instead, he was strongly influenced by the therapeutic approach of psychoanalyst Otto Rank (and his followers at the University of Pennsylvania School of Social Work), the relationship therapy of social worker Jessie Taft, and the feeling-focused approach of social worker Elizabeth Davis. Rank believed that clients benefit from the opportunity to express themselves in session, exhibit creativity in treatment, and even dominate the therapist. Taft emphasized that there are key components to the therapeutic relationship (including a permissive therapeutic environment and a positive working relationship between the therapist and client) which are more important than psychoanalytic explanations of the client's problems. Davis focused almost exclusively on the feelings being expressed in treatment by her clients. From his association with Davis, Rogers developed the therapy component referred to as reflection of feelings. Rogers believed strongly that no individual has the right to run another person's life. Thus, his therapeutic approach was generally permissive and accepting, and he generally refused to give advice to clients.

Person-centered approaches have made major contributions to therapy, theory, and empirical research. In fact, Rogers was responsible for the first systematic investigations of the therapeutic process. He was the first to employ recordings of therapy sessions to study the interactive process and to investigate its effectiveness. Although the use of such recordings is now commonplace in most training programs, Rogers' willingness to open his approach to such scrutiny was unusual for its time.

Person-centered therapy has generated numerous research contributions. A 1971 review of research on "necessary and sufficient" conditions concluded that counselors who are accurately empathic, genuine, and nonpossessively warm tend to be effective with a broad spectrum of clients regardless of the counselors' training or theoretical orientation. The authors also concluded that clients receiving low levels of such conditions in treatment showed deterioration. Many researchers have questioned the "necessary and sufficient" argument proposed by Rogers, however; they suggest that the therapeutic conditions specified by Rogers are neither necessary nor sufficient, although such therapeutic approaches are facilitative.

Although Rogers' approach was developed primarily for counseling clients, the person-centered approach has found many other applications. Person-centered approaches are frequently used in human relations training, including paraprofessional counselors, YWCA/YMCA volunteers, crisis center volunteers, Peace Corps and VISTA workers, and charitable organization workers. Small group therapy programs and personal growth groups also make frequent use of person-centered approaches.

Bibliography

Farber, Barry A., Debora C. Brink, and Patricia M. Raskin, eds. *The Psychotherapy of Carl Rogers: Cases and Commentary*. Foreword by Maria Villas-Boas Bowen. New York: Guilford Press, 1996.

Raskin, N. J., and Carl R. Rogers. "Person-Centered Therapy." In *Current Psychotherapies*, edited by Raymond J. Corsini and Danny Wedding. 4th ed. Itasca, Ill.: F. E. Peacock, 1989. One of the last projects that Rogers worked on prior to his death in 1987. Raskin knew Rogers for forty-seven years, and in this chapter he summarizes many of the key principles and concepts associated with person-centered therapy.

Rogers, Carl R. *Client-Centered Therapy*. Boston: Houghton Mifflin, 1951. A landmark text wherein Rogers highlights many of the key components of his evolving approach. The book describes aspects of the therapeutic relationship and the process of therapy.

_____. *Counseling and Psychotherapy: Newer Concepts in Practice*. Boston: Houghton Mifflin, 1942. Rogers' first book-length description of his approach to therapy. This book is of historical significance because it presents a revised version of Rogers' address at the University of Minnesota on December 11, 1940, at which time client-centered therapy was "officially" born.

_____. *On Becoming a Person*. Boston: Houghton Mifflin, 1961. One of Rogers' best-known and most highly regarded books. Presents valuable insight into Rogers, his approach, and the uses of client-centered approaches in education, family life, and elsewhere.

_____. *A Way of Being*. Boston: Houghton Mifflin, 1980. Rogers wrote this book as a follow-up to *On Becoming a Person*, and in it he updates his theory and therapeutic approach. An excellent bibliography is also included.

Gregory L. Wilson

See also:

Analytical Psychotherapy, 54; Cognitive Behavior Therapy, 128; Cognitive Therapy, 153; Psychoanalysis: Classical Versus Modern, 465; Psychoanalytic Psychology, 471; Self: Definition and Assessment, 524; Self-Esteem, 530.

PERSONALITY
Psychophysiological Measures

Type of psychology: Personality
Field of study: Personality assessment

Psychophysiological studies comparing individuals with different personality traits have sought to determine the physical characteristics of particular behavioral characteristics. Such research can provide information that helps clarify the importance of various personality types with regard to risk of psychological and physical disorders.

Principal terms

ANXIETY SENSITIVITY: the tendency to fear sensations associated with anxiety because of beliefs that anxiety may cause illness, embarrassment, or additional anxiety

HARDINESS: a constellation of behaviors and perceptions thought to buffer the effects of stress; characterized by perceptions of control, commitment, and challenge

LOCUS OF CONTROL: individual perception of the world and evaluation of the amount of control the individual has over his or her own successes and failures

PERSONALITY: a relatively enduring set of behaviors that characterize the individual

PSYCHOPHYSIOLOGY: the scientific study of cognitive, emotional, and behavioral phenomena as related to and revealed through physiological principles and events

TYPE A BEHAVIOR PATTERN: a constellation of behaviors—competitiveness, time urgency, and hostility—thought to place the individual at risk for disease, particularly heart disease

Overview

A broad definition of personality typically includes the dimensions of stability, determinism, and uniqueness. That is, personality changes little over time, is determined by internal processes and external factors, and reflects an individual's distinctive qualities. Personality also can be thought of as unique, relatively stable patterns of behavior, multiply determined over the course of an individual's life. There are many theories for understanding the development of these patterns of behavior.

Twin studies have provided evidence that biological factors help to shape personality; such studies support Hans Eysenck's theory that personality is inherited. The psychodynamic perspective holds that personality is determined primarily by early childhood experiences. Some of the most influential contributions to this perspective came from Sigmund Freud. He argued that unconscious forces govern behavior and that childhood experiences strongly shape adult personality via coping strategies people use to deal with sexual urges. B. F. Skinner, founder of modern behavioral psychology, assumed that personality (or behavior) is determined solely by environmental factors. More specifically, he believed that consequences of behavior are instrumental in the development of unique, relatively stable patterns of behavior in individuals. According to Albert Bandura's social learning perspective, models have a great impact on personality development. That is, patterns of behavior in individuals are influenced by the observation of others. Finally, the humanistic perspective of Carl Rogers suggests that personality is largely determined by the individual's unique perception of reality in comparison to his or her self-concept.

Assessment of personality can be accomplished from three domains: subjective experience, behavior, and physiology. Traditional means for assessing personality have included objective and projective paper-and-pencil or interview measurements that tap the domain of subjective experience. Behavioral assessment techniques such as direct observation of behavior, self-monitoring (having the individual record occurrences of his or her own behavior), self-report questionnaires, role-play scenarios, and behavioral avoidance tests (systematic, controlled determination of how close an individual can approach a feared object or situation) tap the domains of subjective experience and objective behavior. These techniques have been used in clinical settings to aid in the diagnosis and treatment of deviant or abnormal behavior patterns.

Although psychophysiological measurement of personality has not gained popular use in clinical settings, it complements the techniques mentioned above and contributes to understanding the nature and development of psychological and physical disorders. Just as patterns of responding on traditional personality tests can indicate the possibility of aberrant behavior, so too can tests of physiological patterns. Typical measures taken during this type of assessment include heart rate, blood pressure, muscle tension (measured via electromyography), brain-wave activity (measured via electroencephalography), skin temperature, and palmar sweat gland or electrodermal activity. These measures of physiological activity are sensitive to "emotional" responses to various stimuli and have been instrumental in clarifying the nature of certain psychological and physical conditions. One of the fundamental assumptions of psychophysiology is that the responses of the body can help reveal the mechanisms underlying human behavior and personality.

Physiological responsivity can be assessed in a number of different ways. Two primary methodologies are used in the study of the relations between personality and physiology. The first method simply looks at resting or baseline differences of various physiological measures across individuals who either possess or do not possess the personality characteristic of interest. The second method also assesses individuals with or without the characteristic of interest, but does this under specific stimulus or situational conditions rather than during rest. This is often referred to as measuring reactivity to the stimulus or situational condition. Resting physiological measures are referred to as tonic activity (activity evident in the absence of any known stimulus event). It is postulated that tonic activity is relatively enduring and stable within the individual while at rest, although it can be influenced by external factors. It is both of interest in its own right and important in determining the magnitude of response to a stimulus. On the other hand, phasic activity is a discrete response to a specific stimulus. This type of activity is suspected to be influenced to a much greater extent by external factors and tends to be less stable than tonic activity. Both types of activity, tonic and phasic, are important in the study of personality and physiology.

Standard laboratory procedures are typically employed to investigate tonic activity and phasic responses to environmental stimuli. For example, a typical assessment incorporating both methodologies might include the following phases: a five-minute baseline to collect resting physiological measures, a five-minute presentation of a task or other stimulus suspected to differentiate individuals in each group based on their physiological response or change from baseline, and a five-minute recovery to assess the nature and rate of physiological recovery from the task or stimulus condition. Investigations focusing on the last phase attempt to understand variations in recovery as a response pattern in certain individuals. For example, highly anxious individuals tend to take much longer to recover physiologically from stimulus presentations that influence heart rate and electrodermal activity than individuals who report low levels of anxiety.

Studies of physiological habituation—the decline or disappearance of response to a discrete stimulus—also have been used to investigate personality differences. Physiological responses to a standard tone, for example, eventually disappear with repeated presentations of the tone. The rate at which they disappear varies across individuals; the disappearance generally takes longer in individuals who tend to be anxious. Thus, individuals who tend to have anxious traits may be more physiologically responsive, recover from the response less rapidly, and habituate to repeated stimulation more slowly than those who tend to be less anxious. Such physiological differences may be an important characteristic that determines anxious behavior and/or results from subjective feelings of anxiousness.

Applications

Research has demonstrated that there is considerable variability across individuals in their physiological response patterns, both at rest and in response to various situational stimuli or laboratory manipulations. Evidence indicates that part of this variability across individuals may in some cases be attributable to certain personality traits or characteristic patterns of behavior. Furthermore, research suggests that these personality traits may also be related to the development of psychological or physical disorders. Although the causal links are not well understood, a growing body of research points to relations among personality, physiological measures, and psychopathology/health.

Examples of these relationships are evident in the field of psychopathology, or the study of abnormal behavior. Hans Eysenck proposed that the general characteristics of introversion and extroversion lead individuals to interact very differently with their environment. Some psychophysiological studies support this notion and suggest that the behaviors characteristic of these traits may be driven by physiological differences. Anxiety sensitivity and locus of control are two personality traits that some suggest are related to the development of anxiety disorders and depression, respectively. To varying degrees, anxiety disorders and depression have been investigated in the psychophysiology laboratory and have been found to differentiate individuals with high and low levels of the personality trait, based on their physiological responses.

Introversion describes the tendency to minimize interaction with the environment; extroversion is characterized by the opposite behaviors, or the tendency to interact more with the environment. Eysenck has proposed that such traits reflect physiological differences that are genetically determined and reflected in the individual's physiology. Introverted individuals are thought to be chronically physiologically hyperaroused and thus to seek to minimize their arousal by minimizing external stimulation. Extroverted individuals are believed to be chronically physiologically underaroused and to seek a more optimal level of arousal through increased environmental stimulation. It should be easy to confirm or disprove such a theory with psychophysiological studies of resting physiological activity in introverts and extroverts. Electroencephalograph (EEG) studies have produced contradictory evidence about the validity of Eysenck's theory, however; problems in EEG methodology, experimental design, and measurement of the traits themselves have led to considerable confusion about whether the traits actually do have a physiological basis.

Anxiety sensitivity describes the tendency for individuals to fear sensations they associate with anxiety because of beliefs that anxiety may result in harmful consequences. Research in the development and assessment of this construct was pioneered by Steven Reiss and his associates in the late 1980's. They developed a sixteen-item questionnaire, the Anxiety Sensitivity Index (ASI), to measure anxiety sensitivity and found it to be both reliable and valid. Anxiety sensitivity has been most closely related to panic disorder, an anxiety disorder characterized by frequent, incapacitating episodes of extreme fear or discomfort. In fact, as a group, individuals with panic disorder score higher on the ASI than individuals with any other anxiety disorder. Furthermore, some researchers have demonstrated that individuals scoring high on the ASI are five times more likely to develop an anxiety disorder after a three-year follow-up.

Research investigating responses to arithmetic, caffeine, and hyperventilation challenge in the laboratory has demonstrated that individual differences in anxiety sensitivity levels are probably more closely related to the subjective experience of anxiousness than to actual physiological changes. Individuals high and low on anxiety sensitivity, however, have exhibited differential heart-rate reactivity to a mental arithmetic stressor. That is, individuals high on anxiety sensitivity show a greater acceleration in heart rate than individuals low on anxiety sensitivity when engaging in an arithmetic challenge. Individuals scoring high on the ASI also more accurately perceive actual changes in their physiology when compared with their low-scoring counterparts. Such heightened reactivity and sensitivity to physiological change may partially explain how anxiety sensitivity influences the development of anxiety disorders. Individuals high in anxiety sensitivity may be more reactive to environmental threat; therefore, their increased sensitivity may have a physiological basis. They also may be more likely to detect changes in their physiology, which they are then more likely to attribute to threat or danger.

On a more general note, cardiovascular and electrodermal measures can differentiate between anxiety patients and other people at rest. The differences become greater under conditions of stimulation. Delayed habituation rates in anxiety patients are also part of the pattern of physiological overarousal typically seen in individuals with heightened anxiety. Indeed, heightened physiological arousal is one of the hallmark characteristics of anxiety.

Locus of control, made popular by Julian Rotter in the 1960's, refers to individuals' perceptions of whether they have control over what happens to them across situations. This personality construct has been related to the development of depression. Specifically, it is believed that individuals who attribute failures to internal factors (self-blame) and successes to external factors (to other people or to luck) are more susceptible to developing feelings of helplessness, often followed by despair and depression. Locus of control also is hypothesized to have implications in the management of chronic health-related problems.

In oversimplified categorizations, individuals are labeled to have an "internal" or "external" locus of control. "External" individuals, who believe they have little control over what happens to them, are said to be more reactive to threat, more emotionally labile, more hostile, and lower in self-esteem and self-control. Psychophysiological assessment studies have revealed heart-rate acceleration and longer electrodermal habituation for "externals" in response to the presentation of tones under passive conditions. When faced with no-control conditions in stress situations such as inescapable shock, "internals" show elevated physiological arousal, while findings for "externals" are mixed. Thus, the locus of control has varying effects on physiology, depending on the circumstances. Such effects may play a role in psychological disorders such as depression and anxiety. Heightened physiological reactivity may also inhibit recovery from acute illness or affect the course of chronic health problems such as hypertension.

In addition to the relevance of personality to physiological reactivity and psychopathology, research has demonstrated that certain personality types may be risk factors or serve protective functions with regard to physical health. Type A behavior pattern and hardiness are two examples. Type A behavior pattern is characterized by competitiveness, time urgency, and hostility. It has been identified as a potential risk factor for the development of coronary heart disease. Psychophysiological studies have suggested that, under certain laboratory conditions, males who exhibit the Type A pattern are more cardiovascularly responsive. This reactivity is the proposed mechanism by which Type A behavior affects the heart. More recent research has suggested that not all components of the Type A pattern are significantly associated with heightened cardiovascular reactivity. Hostility seems to be the most critical factor in determining heightened reactivity. Males who respond to stress with hostility tend to show greater heart-rate and blood-pressure increases than individuals low in hostility. It is unclear whether hostility is a risk factor for heart disease in women.

In contrast to hostility, hardiness is proposed to buffer the effects of stress on physiology. Hardy individuals respond to stressors as challenges and believe that they have control over the impact of stressors. They also feel commitment to their life, including work and family. Psychophysiological studies have supported the buffering effect of hardiness. Individuals who are more hardy tend to be less physiologically responsive to stressors and to recover from stressors more rapidly. Again, the construct of hardiness seems to be more relevant for males, partially because males have been studied more often.

These studies show that various personality types can be distinguished to varying degrees by psychophysiological measurement. The implications of such findings include possible physiological contributions to the development of various psychological problems, and personality contributions to the development or course of physical disease.

Context

Although the sophisticated techniques and instruments that have enabled psychologists to study physiological events were not developed until the twentieth century, the notion that physiology and psychology (body and mind) are linked dates back as far as ancient Greece. Hippocrates, for example, described four bodily humors or fluids thought to influence various psychological states such as melancholy and mania. Although the link between mind and body has received varying degrees of importance in scientific thinking across the centuries, it regained prominence in the mid-1900's with the development of the field of psychosomatic medicine along with the widespread influence of Sigmund Freud's theories of personality. Psychosomatic medicine embraced the notion that personality and physiology are intertwined. Psychosomatic theorists believed that certain diseases, such as diabetes, asthma, and hypertension, were associated with particular personality characteristics. They suggested that personality influenced the development of specific diseases. Although much of this theorizing has been disproved, these theorists did return the focus to investigating the interactive nature of a person's psychological and physiological makeup.

Psychophysiologists acknowledge the influence of personality characteristics on physiology and vice versa, and they are working to characterize these relationships. Future work will better measure particular personality constructs and will clarify the interaction of gender with personality and physiology. Psychophysiologists also must be concerned with the external validity of the data they obtain in the laboratory. It has not been satisfactorily demonstrated that physiological responses measured in a given individual in the laboratory are at all related to that individual's response in the natural environment. Thus, in order to establish fully the usefulness of laboratory findings, psychophysiologists must also study individuals in their natural environments. Recent technological advances will enable ongoing physiological measurement, which should achieve this goal and further establish the relations among personality, physiology, and behavior.

Bibliography

Eysenck, Hans J. *The Biological Basis of Personality*. Springfield, Ill.: Charles C Thomas, 1967. This older book provides a thorough, in-depth discussion of Eysenck's theories of the relations between neuroticism, introversion, and extroversion with physiology.

Hugdahl, Kenneth. *Psychophysiology: The Mind-Body Perspective*. Cambridge, Mass.: Harvard University Press, 1995.

Pennebaker, James W. *The Psychology of Physical Symptoms*. New York: Springer-Verlag, 1982. Pennebaker discusses his theories about the influence of individual differences in the experience of health and illness. He also provides an overview of some of the research that supports his views.

Stern, Robert Morris, William J. Ray, and Christopher M. Davis. *Psychophysiological Recording*. New York: Oxford University Press, 1980. The authors provide an excellent, readable introduction to basic principles of psychophysiology. Part 2, the main body of the text, covers physiology of and recording procedures for the brain, muscles, eyes, respiratory system, gastrointestinal system, cardiovascular system, and skin. Illustrations depicting typical recordings and a glossary of psychophysiological terms are helpful additions.

Surwillo, Walter W. *Psychophysiology for Clinical Psychologists*. Norwood, N.J.: Ablex, 1990. This text provides basic knowledge of psychophysiology and highlights some areas of application. Surwillo also incorporates helpful diagrams and relevant references for research in the area.

Weiten, Wayne, Margaret A. Lloyd, and R. L. Lashley. "Theories of Personality." In *Psychology Applied to Modern Life: Adjustment in the 90's*. Pacific Grove, Calif.: Brooks/Cole, 1991. This text, written for undergraduate students, provides the reader with a very readable chapter on personality and theories of personality development. Other chapters highlight the dynamics of adjustment, interpersonal factors, developmental transitions, and the impact that personality and styles of coping can have on psychological and physical health.

Virginia L. Goetsch
Lois Veltum

See also:

Analytical Psychology: Carl G. Jung, 49; Ego Psychology: Erik Erikson, 223; Individual Psychology: Alfred Adler, 296; Personality Theory: Major Issues, 453; Psychoanalytic Psychology, 471; Psychoanalytic Psychology and Personality: Sigmund Freud, 478; Radical Behaviorism: B. F. Skinner, 501; Social Learning: Albert Bandura, 559; Social Psychological Models: Erich Fromm, 565; Social Psychological Models: Karen Horney, 571.

PERSONALITY THEORY
Major Issues

Type of psychology: Personality
Field of study: Personality theory

Personality theories seek to describe and explain the characteristics of thought, feeling, and behavior that differ among individuals, and the coherence of these characteristics within a single individual. Personality theories describe approaches to human nature, and provide the foundation for psychological therapies.

Principal terms

ATTRIBUTION THEORY: the study, in social psychology, of how people describe themselves and others and explain their behavior

HUMANISTIC THEORY: the approach to personality which emphasizes people's potential for personal growth and self-awareness; exemplified by the theories of Carl Rogers and Abraham Maslow

PERSONALITY TRAIT: an internal psychic organizing characteristic which serves to provide stability and consistency to the personality

PSYCHOANALYTIC THEORY: the approach to personality adopted by Sigmund Freud and his followers, emphasizing unconscious motivation, psychological conflict, and early childhood experiences

SOCIAL LEARNING THEORY: the approach to personality which emphasizes learning of behavior via observations and direct reward; exemplified by the theories of Albert Bandura, Walter Mischel, and Julian Rotter

Overview

Psychologists who study personality are interested in explaining both the coherence of an individual's behavior, attitudes, and emotions, and how that individual may change over time. To paraphrase Clyde Kluckhohn, personality theorists seek to describe and explain how each individual is unique, how groups of people meaningfully differ from one another, and how all people share some common attributes. In developing answers to the above questions, theorists use widely varying definitions of personality that may differ greatly from the way the term "personality" is used in everyday language. Indeed, if there is a single overriding basic issue in personality theory it is, What is personality?

Most theorists agree that people have an internal "essence" that determines who they are and that guides their behavior, but the nature of that essence differs from theory to theory. Psychoanalytic theories such as Sigmund Freud's see the essence of personality as arising from conflict among internal psychic processes. For Freud, the conflict is viewed as occurring among the urges for instinctual gratification (called the id), the urges for perfection (the superego), and the demands of reality (the ego). Humanistic theories such as those of Carl Rogers and Abraham Maslow also see people as often engaged in conflict. For these theorists, however, the conflicts are between an internal self which is striving for positive expression, and the constraints of a restrictive external social world. In general, the humanists have a much more optimistic outlook on human nature than do psychoanalytic theorists.

Still other theorists are more neutral with respect to human nature. George Kelly's cognitive personality theory, for example, views people as scientists, developing and testing hypotheses to understand themselves better and to predict events in their world. Social learning theorists such as Walter Mischel, Albert Bandura, and Julian Rotter see people as developing expectations and behavioral tendencies based on their histories of rewards and punishments, and their observations of others.

To some extent, the question of "essence" is also the question of motivation. Psychoanalytic theorists view people as trying to achieve a balance between instinctual urges and the demands of reality. In contrast, humanistic theorists view people as motivated toward personal growth rather than homeostatic balance. Social learning theorists view people as motivated to avoid punishments and obtain rewards.

Related to the question of the "essence" of personality is the notion of whether part, or all, of the personality can be hidden from the person him- or herself. Psychoanalytic theorists believe that the driving forces of the personality are in the unconscious and thus are not directly accessible to the person except under exceptional circumstances such as those which arise in therapy. Humanists are much more optimistic about the possibility of people coming to know their inner selves. According to Carl Rogers, parts of the self which were once hidden can, when the individual receives acceptance from others, become expressed and incorporated into self-awareness. Social learning theories do not place much weight on hidden personality dynamics. From the social learning perspective, people are viewed as unable to verbalize easily some of their expectations, but no special unconscious processes are hypothesized.

Theories also differ in the degree to which a person's personality is seen as changing over time. Most personality theories address the development of personality in childhood, and the possibility for change in adulthood. Psychoanalytic theorists believe that the most basic personality characteristics are established by the age of five or six, although there are some minor further developments in adolescence. While the person may change in adulthood in the course of psychotherapy, and become better able to cope with the conflicts and traumas experienced during the early years, major personality transformations are not expected. Again, humanists are more optimistic than psychoanalytic theorists about personality change, although humanists, too, see the childhood years as important. For example, Rogers suggests that during childhood the parents may communicate their approval of some of the child's feelings and their disapproval of others, leaving the child with a distorted self-concept. Yet, from the humanistic point of view, the person's true inner self will constantly strive for expression. Thus, positive personality change is always seen as possible. Social learning theorists also see personality as changeable. Behaviors learned in childhood may later be changed by direct training, by altering the environment, or by revising one's expectations.

A final issue is the relationship between personality and behavior. For social learning theorists, behaviors and related expectations are personality. A person's behaviors are taken as a sample of a full behavioral repertoire which forms who the person is. Both psychoanalytic and humanistic theorists view behavior as a symptom or sign of underlying, internal personality dynamics rather than a sample of the personality itself. According to this viewpoint, a person's behaviors reflect personality only when interpreted in the light of the underlying traits they reveal. Diverse behaviors may thus be related to a single internal characteristic.

Applications

The study of personality is a scientific discipline, with roots in empirical research; a philosophical discipline, seeking to understand the nature of people; and the foundation for the applied discipline of psychological therapy. While these three aspects of personality often support and enrich one another, there are also tensions as the field accommodates specialists in each of these three areas.

The approach which focuses on personality as a scientific discipline has produced an array of methods to measure personality characteristics. They range from projective tests, such as having people tell stories inspired by ambiguous pictures, to more standardized paper-and-pencil personality tests in which people respond on bipolar numerical or multiple-choice scales to questions about their attitudes or behaviors. Methodologically, personality testing is quite sophisticated; however, people's scores on personality tests often are rather poor predictors of behavior. The poor record of behavioral prediction based on personality traits, coupled with evidence that suggests that behavior does not have the cross-situational consistency that one might expect, has led Walter Mischel and many other personality specialists to question the utility of most traditional personality theories. Social learning approaches, which emphasize the power of the situation in determining a person's behavior, tend to fare better in these analyses.

Yet research has found circumstances under which people's behavior can be predicted from knowledge of their underlying personality characteristics. If one classifies personality characteristics and behaviors at a very general level, combining observations and predicting to a group of behaviors, prediction improves. For example, predictions would be more accurate if several measures of a person's conscientiousness were combined, and then used to predict an overall level of conscientious behavior in a variety of situations, than if one measured conscientiousness with a single scale, and then attempted to predict behavior in one specific situation. Prediction on the basis of personality traits also improves when the situations in which one seeks to predict behaviors allow for individual variation as opposed to being highly constrained by social norms. Five basic personality traits often emerge in investigations: extroversion, agreeableness, conscientiousness, emotional stability, and culture (high scores on culture reflect characteristics such as intelligence and refinement). Some researchers view these trait terms as accurately describing consistent personality differences among people, while others view them as reflecting the "eye of the beholder" more than the core of personality.

Ultimately, people's personality traits and situations interact to produce behavior. Situations may often determine behavior, but people choose to place themselves in specific situations that elicit their traits. A child with a predisposition to aggression may provoke others and thus set the stage for the expression of aggression; one who is highly sociable may seek out others in cooperative situations. The relation between personality and behavior is very complex, and it is difficult to describe fully using standard research methods.

Research is highly unlikely to answer philosophical questions concerning human nature; however, considering people from the different points of view offered by various theories can be an enriching experience in itself. For example, a Freudian perspective on former U.S. president Lyndon Johnson might see his leadership during the Vietnam conflict as guided by aggressive instincts or even sublimated sexual instincts. On the other hand, a humanist might look at Johnson's presidency and find his decisions to be guided by the need for self-fulfillment, perhaps citing his vision of himself as the leader of the "Great Society" as an example of self-actualization. Social learning theorists would view Johnson's actions as president as determined by the rewards, punishments, and observational learning of his personal learning history, including growing up relatively poor in Texas and accruing power and respect during his years in the U.S. Senate, as well as by the reinforcements and punishments Johnson perceived to be available in the situations in which he found himself during his presidency. In the final analysis, none of these interpretations could be shown to be blatantly false or absolutely true. Historians, biographers, and others might find each to be an enriching viewpoint from which to consider this complex individual.

Multiple points of view also characterize the therapies derived from theories of personality. Most therapists take an eclectic approach, sampling from the ideas of various theories to tailor their treatment to a specific client. Each therapist, however, also may have her or his own biases, based on a particular theoretical orientation. For example, a client who often feels anxious and seeks help from a psychoanalytic therapist may find that the therapist encourages the client to explore memories of childhood experiences to discover the unconscious roots of the anxiety. Slips of the tongue, dreams, and difficulty remembering or accepting therapeutic interpretations would be viewed as important clues to unconscious processes. The same client seeking treatment from a humanistic therapist would have a different experience. There, the emphasis would be on current experiences, with the therapist providing a warm and supportive atmosphere for the client to explore feelings. A behavioral therapist, from the social learning orientation, would help the client pinpoint situations in which anxiety occurs, and teach the client alternative responses to those situations. Again, no one form of therapy is superior for all clients. Successes or failures in therapy depend on the combination of client, therapist, and mode of treatment.

Context

While people have long speculated on the causes and types of individual differences in personality, the theory of Sigmund Freud was the first and most influential psychological personality theory. All subsequent theories have directly or indirectly addressed the central concerns of motivation, development, and personality organization first proposed by Freud. Psychoanalytic theorists such as Carl G. Jung and Alfred Adler, while trained by Freud, disagreed with Freud's emphasis on sexual instincts and developed their own theories, emphasizing different motivations. Similarly, Karen Horney, Erich Fromm, and others developed theories placing greater emphasis on the ego and its interaction with society than did Freud's.

Psychoanalytic theory has had somewhat less of an influence in the United States than it did in Europe. Personality psychology in the United States is relatively more research-oriented, practical, and optimistic. In the United States, Gordon Allport developed one of the first trait approaches to personality. The humanistic theories of Carl Rogers and Abraham Maslow, social learning theories of Albert Bandura and Julian Rotter, and cognitive theory of George Kelly flourished in the 1950's and 1960's, and continue to have their advocates.

Modern personality psychologists, however, are much more likely to confine themselves to personality measurement and research than to propose broad theories of personality.

Many have questioned personality's status as a scientific subdiscipline of psychology. In 1968, Walter Mischel's *Personality and Assessment*, arguing that the consistency and behavior-prediction assumptions inherent in all personality theories are unsupported by the evidence, was published. At the same time, attribution theories in social psychology were suggesting that personality traits are largely in the "eye of the beholder" rather than in the person being observed. For example, Edward Jones and Richard Nisbett argued that people are more inclined to see others as possessing personality traits than they are to attribute traits to themselves. The continued existence of personality as a subdiscipline of scientific psychology was debated.

The result has been a refined approach to measurement and personality analysis. Current research on personality does not boldly assert the influence of internal personality characteristics on behavior. There are no new theories purporting to explain all of personality or the nature of all people. Rather, attention is paid to careful assessment of personality, and to the complex interactions of persons and situations. For example, research on loneliness has found that people who describe themselves as lonely often lack social skills and avoid interactions with others, thus perpetuating their feelings of loneliness. All personality characteristics, including loneliness, are most meaningfully seen as the product of a complex interrelationship between the person and the environment.

Bibliography

Hall, Calvin Springer, and Gardner Lindzey. *Theories of Personality.* 3d ed. New York: John Wiley & Sons, 1978. A classic textbook describing personality theories. Personality research is mentioned, but not discussed in detail. Includes particularly readable, thorough, and accurate descriptions of psychoanalytic theories. Chapter 1 introduces the topic of personality theories, and describes many dimensions upon which theories can be contrasted.

Hampden-Turner, Charles. *Maps of the Mind.* New York: Macmillan, 1981. Presents brief descriptions and pictorial representations (termed "maps") of basic psychological and philosophical concepts. The organization and presentation are a bit idiosyncratic; the summaries are very good, and the diagrams helpful in synthesizing complex information. Descriptions and maps relevant to the theories of Sigmund Freud, Carl Jung, Erich Fromm, Rollo May, Hans Eysenck, Carl Rogers, Harry Stack Sullivan, and Erik Erikson are particularly relevant to basic issues in personality theory.

Mayer, F. Stephan, and Karen Sutton. *Personality: An Integrative Approach.* Upper Saddle River, N.J.: Prentice Hall, 1996.

Mischel, Walter. *Introduction to Personality.* 4th ed. New York: Holt, Rinehart and Winston, 1986. A college-level personality textbook with an emphasis on contemporary issues and research. Each major orientation to personality—psychodynamic, trait, phenomenological (humanistic), and behavioral—is presented with thorough discussions of measurement and research. The reader may find that this text alone is incomplete in its description of personality theories per se, but it makes an excellent companion reading to Hall and Lindzey's *Theories of Personality.* Mischel's own approach to social learning theory is presented.

_____. *Personality and Assessment*. New York: John Wiley & Sons, 1968. The text that inspired debate about the utility of traditional personality theories. Readable but detailed; primarily of historical importance. Contemporary summaries of this issue can be found in Mischel's *Introduction to Personality* and in the *Handbook of Personality: Theory and Research*, edited by Pervin.

Pervin, Lawrence A., ed. *Handbook of Personality: Theory and Research*. New York: Guilford Press, 1990. A compilation of personality theory and research for the sophisticated reader. Chapters by Walter Mischel ("Personality Dispositions Revisited and Revised: A View After Three Decades"), David Magnusson ("Personality Development from an Interactional Perspective"), and Bernard Weiner ("Attribution in Personality Psychology") may be of particular interest.

_____. *The Science of Personality*. New York: John Wiley & Sons, 1995.

Storr, Anthony. *Churchill's Black Dog, Kafka's Mice, and Other Phenomena of the Human Mind*. New York: Grove Press, 1988. This fascinating book demonstrates how personality theories can be used to interpret lives. Storr describes the creative process in general, and the lives of Churchill, Kafka, and others in particular, from his psychological point of view, primarily psychoanalytic in orientation. The perspectives of Freud, Jung, and Erikson are featured.

Susan E. Beers

See also:

Analytical Psychology: Carl G. Jung, 49; Dream Analysis, 206; Ego Psychology: Erik Erikson, 223; Individual Psychology: Alfred Adler, 296; Personality: Psychophysiological Measures, 446; Psychoanalytic Psychology, 471; Psychoanalytic Psychology and Personality: Sigmund Freud, 478; Radical Behaviorism: B. F. Skinner, 501; Social Learning: Albert Bandura, 559; Social Psychological Models: Erich Fromm, 565; Social Psychological Models: Karen Horney, 571.

PHOBIAS

Type of psychology: Psychopathology
Field of study: Anxiety disorders

Phobias are exaggerated, unjustified fears of everyday objects or situations, such as fear of certain types of animals or fear of doing things in front of other people. Though many people experience irrational fears or phobias, few seek treatment; as a result, they suffer emotional pain and may find their lives limited by their phobias.

Principal terms

AGORAPHOBIA: a fear of situations in which escape is perceived to be difficult or assistance unavailable; these situations can include crowds, elevators, open spaces, or public places such as malls

CONDITIONED RESPONSE (CR): a behavior elicited by a conditioned stimulus (CS); related to the original unconditioned response (UR)

CONDITIONED STIMULUS (CS): a previously neutral stimulus (a sight, sound, touch, or smell) which, after Pavlovian conditioning, will elicit the conditioned response (CR)

INSTRUMENTAL CONDITIONING: the use of consequences (reward or punishment) to strengthen or weaken a behavior

OBSERVATIONAL LEARNING: the acquiring of new behavior by watching others

PAVLOVIAN CONDITIONING: the repeated presentation of a neutral stimulus just prior to an unconditioned stimulus, causing the neutral stimulus to become a conditioned stimulus and elicit the conditioned response

REINFORCER: a stimulus which strengthens the behavior occurring just before it

UNCONDITIONED RESPONSE (UR): an innate or unlearned behavior which occurs automatically following some stimulus; a reflex

UNCONDITIONED STIMULUS (US): a stimulus which produces a specific, unconditioned response (UR)

Overview

Phobias are a type of anxiety disorder characterized by a persistent, exaggerated, irrational fear of certain objects or situations and by efforts to avoid the object or situation. In many cases, the distress and the avoidance efforts significantly interfere with an individual's daily life. Phobias are common in the general population; approximately one person in ten suffers from mild phobias, and severe, disabling phobias are found in one person in five hundred.

The three major types of phobias are agoraphobia, social phobias, and specific (or "simple") phobias. In social phobias, being observed by others may elicit anxiety and the desire to avoid such situations. The person fears doing something which will lead to embarrassment or humiliation, such as being unable to speak or showing nervousness through trembling hands or other signs. Persons with specific phobias avoid a certain type of object or situation or suffer extreme anxiety when in the presence of these objects or situations. Some examples of common specific phobias are acrophobia, fear of heights; arachnophobia, fear of spiders; claustrophobia, fear of being in small, enclosed spaces;

pathophobia, fear of diseases and germs; and xenophobia, fear of strangers.

In the presence of the feared object or situation, the severely phobic person's experience and reaction differ dramatically from the average person's. Physiologically, changes in the body cause an increase in heart rate and blood pressure, tensing of muscles, and feelings of fear. In many cases, a panic state develops, characterized by muscular trembling and shaking, rapid, shallow breathing, and feelings of unbearable anxiety and dizziness. Behaviorally, the person will stop or redirect whatever activity in which he or she is engaged, then try to escape from or avoid the phobic object or situation. Cognitively, a phobic person at a distance from the object or situation can recognize it as posing little actual danger; but upon approaching it, fear rises, and the estimation of risk increases.

The many theories which attempt to explain how phobias develop can be grouped under three general headings: those which stress unconscious emotional conflicts, those which explain phobias based on the principles of learning, and those which consider biological factors. For Sigmund Freud, phobias represented the external manifestation of unconscious internal emotional conflicts which had their origin in early childhood. These conflicts typically involved the inhibition of primitive sexual feelings.

Learning-theory explanations of phobias are based on Pavlovian conditioning, instrumental conditioning, and social learning theory. According to a Pavlovian conditioning model, phobias result when a neutral stimulus—a dog, for example—is paired with an unconditioned stimulus (US), for example, a painful bite to the leg. After this event, the sight of the dog has become a conditioned stimulus (CS) which elicits a conditioned response (CR), fear; thus, a dog phobia has been learned. Instrumental conditioning (the modification of behavior as a result of its consequences) has been combined with Pavlovian conditioning in the two-factor model of phobias. After the establishment of the phobia by Pavlovian conditioning, as above, a person will attempt to escape from or avoid the phobic object or situation whenever it is encountered. When this is successful, the fear subsides. The reduction in fear is a desirable consequence which increases the likelihood of escape/avoidance behavior in the future (that is, the escape/avoidance behavior is reinforced). The two-factor model thus accounts for both the development and maintenance of phobias. Social learning theory suggests that human learning is based primarily on the observation and imitation of others; thus, fears and phobias would be acquired by observing others who show fearful behavior toward certain objects or situations. This learning occurs primarily during childhood, when children learn many behaviors and attitudes by modeling those of others.

Two theories suggest that inherited biological factors contribute to the development of phobias. The preparedness theory suggests that those stimuli which are most easily conditioned are objects or situations which may have posed a particular threat to humans' early ancestors, such as spiders, heights, small spaces, thunder, and strangers. Thus, people are genetically prepared to acquire fear of them quickly. Similarly, people vary in susceptibility to phobias, and this is also thought to be based at least partly on an inherited predisposition. A phobia-prone person may be physiologically highly arousable; thus, many more events would reach a threshold of fear necessary for conditioning.

Stressful life situations, including extreme conflict or frustration, may also predispose a person to develop a phobia or exacerbate an existing phobia. Further, a sense of powerlessness or lack of control over one's situation may increase susceptibility; this may partly explain why phobias are more common in women, as these feelings are reported more often by women than by men. Once initiated, phobias tend to persist and even worsen over time, and the fear may spread to other, similar objects or situations. Even phobias which have been successfully treated may recur if the person is exposed to the original US, or even to another US which produces extreme anxiety. Thus, many factors—unconscious, learned, and biological—may be involved in the onset and maintenance of phobias. As every person is unique in terms of biology and life experience, each phobia is also unique and represents a particular interaction of the factors above and possibly other, unknown factors.

Applications
The following two case studies of phobias illustrate their onset, development, and the various treatment approaches typically used. These studies are fictionalized composites of the experiences of actual clients.

Ellen P. entered an anxiety disorders clinic requesting large amounts of tranquilizers. She revealed that she wanted them to enable her to fly on airplanes; if she could not fly, she would probably lose her job as a sales representative for her company. Ellen described an eight-year history of a fear of flying during which she had simply avoided all airplane flights and had driven or taken a train to distant sales appointments. She would sometimes drive through the night, keep her appointments during the day, then again drive through the night back to the home office. As these trips occurred more often, she became increasingly exhausted, and her work performance began to decline noticeably.

A review of major childhood and adolescent experiences revealed only that Ellen was a chronic worrier. She also reported flying comfortably on many occasions prior to the onset of her phobia, but remembered her last flight in vivid detail. She was flying to meet her husband for a honeymoon cruise, but the plane was far behind schedule because of poor weather. She began to worry that she would miss the boat and that her honeymoon, and possibly her marriage, would be ruined. The plane then encountered some minor turbulence, and brief images of a crash raced through Ellen's mind. She rapidly became increasingly anxious, tense, and uncomfortable. She grasped her seat cushion; her heart seemed to be pounding in her throat; she felt dizzy and was beginning to perspire. Hoping no one would notice her distress, she closed her eyes, pretending to sleep for the remainder of the flight. After returning from the cruise, she convinced her husband to cancel their plane reservations, and thus began her eight years of avoiding flying.

Ellen's psychologist began exposure therapy for her phobia. First she was trained to relax deeply. Then she was gradually exposed to her feared stimuli, progressing from visiting an airport to sitting on a taxiing plane to weekly flights of increasing length in a small plane. After ten weeks of therapy and practice at home and the airport, Ellen was able to fly on a commercial airliner. Two years after the conclusion of therapy, Ellen met her psychologist by chance and informed her that she now had her own pilot's license.

In the second case, Steve R. was a high school junior who was referred by his father because of his refusal to attend school. Steve was described as a loner who avoided other people and suffered fears of storms, cats, and now, apparently, school. He was of above-average intelligence and was pressured by his father to outperform his classmates and attend a prestigious college. Steve's mother was described as being shy like Steve. Steve was her only child, and she doted on him, claiming she knew what it felt like to be in his situation.

When interviewed, Steve sat rigidly in his chair, spoke in clipped sentences, and offered answers only to direct questions. Questioning revealed that Steve's refusal to attend school was based on a fear of ridicule by his classmates. He would not eat or do any written work in front of them for fear he was being watched and would do something clumsy, thus embarrassing himself. He never volunteered answers to teachers' questions, but in one class, the teacher had begun to call on Steve regularly for the correct answer whenever other students had missed the question. Steve would sit in a near-panic state, fearing he would be called on. After two weeks of this, he refused to return to school.

Steve was diagnosed as having a severe social phobia. His therapy included a contract with his teachers in which it was agreed that he would not be called upon in class until therapy had made it possible for him to answer with only moderate anxiety. In return, he was expected to attend all his classes. To help make this transition, a psychiatrist prescribed an antianxiety drug to help reduce the panic symptoms. A psychologist began relaxation training for use in exposure therapy, which would include Steve volunteering answers in class and seeking social interactions with his peers. Steve finished high school, though he left the state university at the end of his first semester because of a worsening of his phobias. His therapy was resumed, and he was graduated from a local community college, though his phobias continued to recur during stressful periods in his life.

These cases illustrate many of the concepts related to the study of phobias. In both cases, it is possible that a high emotional reactivity predisposed the person to a phobia. In Ellen's case, the onset of the phobia was sudden and appeared to be the result of Pavlovian conditioning, whereas in Steve's case, the phobia likely developed over time and involved social learning: modeling of his mother's behavior. Steve's phobia may also have been inadvertently reinforced by his mother's attention; thus, instrumental conditioning may have been involved as well. Ellen's phobia could be seen to involve a sense of lack of control, combined with a possibly inherited predisposition to fear enclosed spaces. Steve's phobia illustrated both a spreading of the phobia and recurrence of the phobia under stress.

Context

As comprehensive psychological theories of human behavior began to emerge in the early 1900's, each was faced with the challenge of explaining the distinct symptoms, but apparently irrational nature, of phobias. For example, in 1909, Sigmund Freud published his account of the case of "Little Hans," a young boy with a horse phobia. Freud hypothesized that Hans had an unconscious fear of his father which was transferred to a more appropriate object: the horse. Freud's treatment of phobias involved analyzing the unconscious conflicts (through psychoanalysis) and giving patients insight into the "true" nature of their fears.

An alternative explanation of phobias based on the principles of Pavlovian conditioning was proposed by John B. Watson and Rosalie Rayner in 1920. They conditioned a fear of a white rat in an infant nicknamed "Little Albert" by pairing presentation of the rat with a frightening noise (an unconditioned stimulus). After a few such trials, simply presenting the rat (now a conditioned stimulus) produced fear and crying (the conditioned response).

As B. F. Skinner's laboratory discoveries of the principles of instrumental conditioning began to be applied to humans in the 1940's and 1950's, experimental models of phobias in animals were developed. In the 1950's, Joseph Wolpe created phobialike responses in cats by shocking them in experimental cages. He was later able to decrease their fear by feeding them in the cages where they had previously been shocked. Based on this countercondition-ing model, Wolpe developed the therapy procedure of systematic desensitization, which paired mental images of the feared stimulus with bodily relaxation.

Social learning theory as advanced by Albert Bandura in the 1960's was also applied to phobias. Bandura conducted experiments showing that someone might develop a phobia by observing another person behaving fearfully. It was later demonstrated that some phobias could be treated by having the patient observe and imitate a nonfearful model. Cognitive approaches to phobias were also developed in the 1970's and 1980's by therapists such as Albert Ellis and Aaron T. Beck. These theories focus on the role of disturbing thoughts in creating bodily arousal and associated fear. Therapy then consists of altering these thought patterns.

Phobias can thus be seen as providing a testing ground for the major theories of psychology. Whether the theorist adopts a psychodynamic, learning/behavioral, or cognitive perspective, some account of the development and treatment of phobias must be made. No one theory has been shown to be completely adequate, so research continues in each area. The study of phobias also illustrates the importance to psychology of animal research in helping psychologists to understand and treat human problems. For example, Susan Mineka has used monkeys to demonstrate the relative importance of social learning versus biology in the development of phobias. Future research will also likely consider the interactions among the various models of phobias and the conditions that might predict which models would be most effective in explaining and treating specific cases of phobias. As the models mature and are integrated into a comprehensive theory of phobias, this knowledge can then be applied to the prevention of phobias.

Bibliography

Beck, Aaron T., and Gary Emery. *Anxiety Disorders and Phobias: A Cognitive Perspective.* New York: Basic Books, 1985. Though cognitive explanations and treatments for phobias are stressed, this book considers other perspectives as well, and it could serve as an introduction to the topic for the interested high school or college student.

Bourne, Edmund. *The Anxiety and Phobia Workbook.* Oakland, Calif.: New Harbinger Publications, 1990. An excellent self-help book for the general reader who suffers from an anxiety disorder. Also an accessible introduction to the causes and treatments of phobias for high school and college students. Contains self-diagnostic and therapy exercises, as well as other resources for the phobia sufferer.

Gold, Mark S. *The Good News About Panic, Anxiety, and Phobias.* New York: Random House, 1989. For a general audience. Outlines many biological factors which may be associated with phobias. Presents a one-sided approach, heavily promoting a biopsychiatric view of phobias and their treatment.

Magee, William J. "Agoraphobia, Simple Phobia, and Social Phobia in the National Comorbidity Survey." *The Journal of the American Medical Association* 275 (April 10, 1996): 1064L.

Marks, Issac Meyer. *Fears, Phobias, and Rituals.* New York: Oxford University Press, 1987. With more than five hundred pages and a bibliography with more than two thousand references, this text provides comprehensive coverage of all aspects of phobias. Written for the professional and researcher, but accessible to college students who are interested in pursuing some aspect of phobias in detail.

Mineka, Susan. "Animal Models of Anxiety-Based Disorders: Their Usefulness and Limitations." In *Anxiety and the Anxiety Disorders*, edited by A. Hussain Tuma and Jack Maser. Hillsdale, N.J.: Lawrence Erlbaum, 1985. The phobia portion of this chapter reviews the major experiments done with animals which demonstrate the many similarities between human phobias and experimental phobias in animals. Clearly illustrates the relevance of animal research to human behavior. Difficult, yet indispensable for a thorough understanding of phobias.

Rauch, Scott L. "A Positron Emission Tomographic Study of Simple Phobic Symptom Provocation." *The Journal of the American Medical Association* 273 (March 1, 1995): 682B.

Wilson, R. Reid. *Breaking the Panic Cycle: Self-Help for People with Phobias*. Rockville, Md.: Anxiety Disorders Association of America, 1987. A publication of a nonprofit organization which is dedicated to disseminating information and providing help to phobia sufferers. The ADAA also publishes the *National Treatment Directory*, which lists treatment programs throughout the country.

David S. McDougal

See also:

Abnormality, 1; Anxiety Disorders, 65; Obsessions and Compulsions, 427; Psychoanalytic Psychology, 471.

PSYCHOANALYSIS
Classical Versus Modern

Type of psychology: Psychotherapy

Fields of study: Classic analytic themes and issues; evaluating psychotherapy; psychodynamic therapies

Classical psychoanalysis, developed by Sigmund Freud, was first used to treat people with symptoms (such as hysterical paralyses) lacking an organic cause. Modern psychoanalysis is more widely applicable, including to those whom Freud considered untreatable by psychoanalysis, those who are particularly resistant to treatment, and those who have had disappointing experiences with previous therapy.

Principal terms

CLASSICAL PSYCHOANALYSIS: the method of treatment of psychological disorders that was developed by Sigmund Freud

COUNTERTRANSFERENCE: errors therapists make in response to the errors their clients make; clients may assume that the therapist is omniscient and omnipotent, for example, and therapists may see themselves as infallible

DEVELOPMENT: the course of change and growth that an individual follows throughout life

PSYCHOANALYST: a person who has completed psychoanalytic training, a specialized and comprehensive form of psychotherapeutic training

PSYCHOTHERAPIST: a person who may have had a range of psychotherapeutic training (much or little); a general term for practitioners of various types of therapy

TRANSFERENCE: the errors clients make when they view therapists; one example would be believing that therapists will be as punitive toward them as their original caregivers were

Overview

Psychoanalysis, a method of treating psychological disorders and a way of investigating why people do what they do, was formulated by Sigmund Freud around the beginning of the twentieth century. When psychoanalysts and others in the mental health field investigate the reasons individuals act in specific ways (for example, avoiding contact with others), they are exploring human motivations. People who have completed psychoanalytic training are called psychoanalysts. Psychoanalysis was originally the province of psychiatry because Freud was a physician (by definition, a licensed psychiatrist is also a licensed physician). Since then, however, the specialty has broadened to include psychologists, social workers, the clergy, nurses, teachers, administrators, artists, and scientists.

Classical psychoanalysis is intended to assist individuals who have entered treatment. Those people most in need, however, usually do not elect treatment; those who enter appear to be better off than those who avoid saying "I need help." The ways in which help is rendered derive from the concept of excavating: Psychoanalysts "dig" for motivations of which clients may be unaware or less than fully aware; self-defeating patterns of thinking, feeling, or acting; and blocks to optimal functioning. Modern analysts share such conceptualizations. Both classical and modern analysts employ views of awareness ranging from conscious awareness through what Freud termed "preconscious" (accessible to awareness under the right conditions of preparation or growth) to "unconscious." Freud's is a tripartite schema, but what exists is a continuum between the polar extremes of full awareness and complete unawareness.

Freud developed the theory and technique that became classical psychoanalysis. It includes free association and the concepts of transference and resistance. Free association means that people in psychoanalytic treatment say whatever occurs to them, no matter how illogical, bizarre, or embarrassing their utterances may be. Free association has been called the "fundamental rule" of classical psychoanalysis. Transference constitutes the mistaken assumptions that a client makes about the analyst. For example, hope or magical thinking may generate the view that the analyst can and will fix everything without the person in therapy having to undertake any responsibilities for the treatment or for personal growth outside it. Pessimism (stemming, for example, from previous mistreatment) may be responsible for mistrust of the analyst or for an expectation that the analyst will be as condemnatory as others were.

Resistance refers to the many ways clients disregard requests to free-associate, refuse to observe other rules of treatment, or sabotage their own progress toward health. Resistance shows the analyst that the client is avoiding something that is difficult to confront and therefore important.

The person in analysis is not the only one who misperceives the other. The analyst is also a human being and is therefore vulnerable to countertransference. Analysts may find themselves succumbing to acting on these feelings, thereby helping the client to sabotage progress and avoid change. Experienced and talented psychoanalysts, however, can use countertransference to understand and help their clients.

Freud learned that the analyst must resist certain temptations in order for therapy to be most effective. When the client is free-associating, the analyst should resist the impulse to offer interpretations immediately (interpretations are explanations such as "The reason you are experiencing inappropriate fear is that the dread of your father, instilled in you when he treated you harshly, has generalized to include others who resemble your father in their authority over you"). The technique of interpretation was conceived as the principal manner in which the insights deduced by the psychoanalyst were to be imparted to the patient. The analyst's task is to listen carefully and respectfully, enabling the client to broaden and deepen transferential distortions or denials of reality, before offering interpretations.

Modern psychoanalysis evolved for several reasons. First, clients who are especially vulnerable, only marginally functional, or clearly at risk display tremendous fears and intractable resistances. Until such time as substitute behaviors become available to them and they are able to relax and ultimately discard their defenses, their resistances (defenses manifested during sessions) should be respected, understood, and used by their therapists. Modern psychoanalysis attempts to do so. Second, vulnerable clients demonstrate exquisite sensitivity to attempts to direct their activities or even to provide suggestions. They have received insufficient practice in running their lives and need more autonomy, not less. They have received too many orders and need fewer directives. Modern analysts try to minimize directions or suggestions (even when these are requested or demanded), to limit what they say to the briefest and fewest interventions, to avoid confrontations if possible, and to refrain from providing interpretations until clients give evidence of having achieved the maturity to accept and profit from them. Many practitioners believe that when clients are able to use interpretations, the clients themselves are more likely to originate them.

Applications

The essential distinction between psychoanalysis (both classical and modern) and other modalities of psychotherapy (including psychoanalytically oriented ones) rests not upon frequency of sessions or whether the client uses the couch rather than sitting face-to-face with the therapist but upon whether the treatment employs free association, transference, and resistance (embracing the preconscious and unconscious) and is an ego-maturational process. Analytic clients are assisted in becoming aware of alternatives, including new ways of viewing life events. Psychoanalysis tries to determine the ways clients avoid seeing and doing the things of which they are capable. Other therapies tend to be problem-oriented.

Modern psychoanalysis deals with a much wider spectrum of client pathologies than classical psychoanalysis and is prepared to work with clients whom current classical psychoanalysts regard as unsuitable for treatment. Modern analysts modify the fundamental rule of free association and ask clients to say whatever they wish, rather than demanding that they say everything. The objective of enabling clients to be able to say everything, however, remains the same. When the ego strength of clients permits, modern analysts say more, but they prefer asking questions to answering them or making statements.

Making statements tends to be regarded as objectionable either because unsolicited statements are interpreted by the client as being lectures (which is often true) or because they derive from the therapist's own insecurities. Self-initiated requests for help are considered evidence of progress. Questions asked by clients frequently conceal other questions they may have. Answering the original question makes it less likely that the other, more important questions will be unearthed.

Modern analysts attempt to reverse the direction of clients' self-injurious acts. Attacking oneself is conceptualized as the "narcissistic defense" intended to protect "the object" (Freud's term for the "other," the most typical example of which is the first object of the infant's rage, the nurturer). Anger is precipitated by frustration, unmodulated rage by abuse or neglect. Modern analysts offer themselves as legitimate objects of criticism. All communications of disapproval are accepted. Acts are discouraged, although intentions are unobjectionable and may be explored if the client can tolerate exploration. It is all right to *want* to destroy or hurt, but it is not all right to *do* either. Clients may be assisted to see such acceptable alternatives to destructive actions as hostile thoughts, negative feelings, and destructive fantasies. Clients are seen as engaging in the most harmful behaviors when they damage themselves—physically, psychologically (destroying their minds and requiring institutionalization), or both. Progress is demonstrated when clients start attacking others and diminish self-attacks. Further progress consists of their proceeding toward verbalization of their feelings, concerns, and wishes; diminishing ego-oriented attacks upon others even if expressed in words; and attempting to confine attacks solely to the analyst, who is expected to deal more constructively with them than laypersons are.

Attacks are difficult, even for professionals, especially when taken personally. Therapeutic work is made more tolerable, and even challenging, by personal analysis and supervision that enable practitioners to view the attacks as part of transference, a generalized phenomenon and a component of desirable progress. Analysts view *abuse* of themselves by clients, however (as opposed to verbal attacks), as harmful to both parties and as treatment-destructive. When one injures another, one injures oneself. Analysts insist that both they and their client or clients (partners in a dyad, or members of a family) be treated respectfully.

One significant difference between classical and modern psychoanalysis concerns the attitude toward, and use of, countertransference. Both classical and modern analysts recognize the inevitability and importance of countertransference. Freud, recognizing its perils, urged that it be obliterated as completely as possible; this was unrealistic. Moreover, countertransference can be used productively. Modern analysts, in fact, regard countertransference as the most valuable source of information about their clients and as the key to the most effective treatment. The comprehension of objective countertransference (feelings induced in the analyst by a client's problems) permits the analyst to understand more fully what the client is experiencing and formulate a treatment strategy. The recognition and correction of subjective countertransference (preexisting personal problems) via personal analysis and supervision afford measures to prevent analysts' blindnesses, vulnerabilities, and irrational expectations from interfering with their responsibilities for the welfare of their clients.

Classical psychoanalysts tend to agree with Freud that persons with particular kinds of mental illness (such as schizophrenia or narcissistic disorders) are not analyzable. They also regard interpretations as one of the foundations of treatment. In contrast, modern analysts regard no one with a psychologically reversible disorder as untreatable. In treating more vulnerable and remote clients, they have learned that interpretations can be viewed as attacks by such clients. They refrain from employing such feedback until they are sure that interpretations can be tolerated by the client.

Modern psychoanalysts are aware that thoughts and feelings play important roles in causing, exacerbating, ameliorating, treating, and curing somatic (that is, physical or bodily) conditions. Modern analysts have sought ways of treating organic disease (such as cancer) psychoanalytically—in effect considering such conditions psychologically reversible disorders rather than disease entities that are unchangeable.

Modern analysts are aware that a client's failure to make progress with a certain analyst does not necessarily mean that the individual will never have success in therapy. It may simply mean that the client does not have a proper "fit" with the analyst. Working with a different analyst, the client may have quite a different experience. Again, the effects of countertransference are important; in a curative relationship, the analyst should be able to experience feelings induced by the client and return to the client the necessary therapeutic feelings—appropriately spaced and in correct dosages—that lead to progress and eventual recovery.

In both classical and modern psychoanalysis, the intensity of treatment (the number of sessions per week) is often the result of a number of variables. These may include the particular benefits the client hopes to receive, how rapidly progress is desired, the ability of the client to afford the practitioner's fees, and the time available to both. One exception to this rule would be that modern analysts prefer limiting sessions to once a week at the beginning of therapy in order to assess whether the ego strength of the client is adequate to cope with the more intense and unsettling regression that occurs with more frequent sessions. Fees, like session frequency and treatment length, vary considerably. Professionals often employ a "sliding scale" of fees to accommodate people's varying abilities to afford treatment.

Context

Before Freud developed his theory at the beginning of the twentieth century, methods of dealing with psychological interferences with functioning (what are now called neuroses, character disorders, borderline conditions, and even some schizophrenias) as well as with more severe conditions (such as psychoses, narcissistic disorders, and chronic schizophrenias) lacked coherence and effectiveness. Functional impairment was perceived as being physiologically caused, even if a precise cause could not be located; it was therefore seen as requiring physiological treatment. Impairments that were psychological went untreated, often even undetected. The care of the more serious mental illnesses was at best ineffectual and at worst cruel and inhumane.

Freud confronted people with the concept that, in the psychic realm, they are not masters but servants of hidden drives and desires. Irrationality was suddenly seen as a universal condition. Freud's patients were upper-middle-class people who came for treatment of such conditions as "hysteria," in which psychic conflict is converted into a curtailment of functioning, such as blindness or an inability to perform particular motor skills. Other conditions he treated included autonomous episodes (such as sleepwalking) and anatomic anomalies. (One anatomic anomaly, for example, is glove anesthesia, in which a patient has no sense of feeling in an area roughly corresponding to that covered by a glove; since no local injury could cause such a loss of feeling, it is a symptom of a functional disorder, most likely hysteria.) All of these lacked an organic explanation. Freud provided a blueprint for such mental disorders: the psychodynamic method of explaining them and the psychoanalytic method of treating them. He also furnished concepts of development (of both individuals and groups—even civilizations) and personality, as well as two explanations of why dreams occur. His work ultimately led to countless other ways of explaining people, the events in which they participate (history), and the artifacts they create (literature, art, and music).

Freud has had many critics, and for good reason. His view of females, for example, was clearly flawed; it reflected the male-dominated society of his day that subordinated women and underestimated their potentials for accomplishment and creativity. Nevertheless, Freud's impact has been substantial and pervasive, and most of his contributions are incorporated into theory and practice.

Bibliography

Berger, Milton M., ed. *Women Beyond Freud: New Concepts of Feminine Psychology*. New York: Brunner/Mazel, 1994.

Dufresne, Todd, and Paul Roazen. *Freud Under Analysis: Psychoanalytic Theories, Psychoanalytic Movements*. Northvale, N.J.: Jason Aronson, 1997.

Forrester, John. *Dispatches from the Freud Wars: Psychoanalysis and Its Passions*. Cambridge, Mass.: Harvard University Press, 1997.

Freeman, Lucy. *The Story of Anna O*. New York: Walker, 1972. A popularly written examination of the psychoanalysis of the first analytic patient, with a description of her subsequent life (which was fascinating) and achievements; she became the first social worker in Germany and was responsible for many advances in the care of unwed mothers and their children. A particularly important accompaniment to the Freud and Breuer work.

Freud, Sigmund, and Josef Breuer. *Studies on Hysteria.* 1895. Reprint. New York: Avon Books, 1966. Contains not only the original source for the theory of psychoanalysis ("Anna O.," the only case conducted by Josef Breuer) but also the other analyses Freud conducted and about which he wrote. The germinative work in psychoanalysis.

Kearns, Katherine. *Psychoanalysis, Historiography, and Feminist Theory: The Search for Critical Method.* New York: Cambridge University Press, 1997.

Spotnitz, Hyman. *Modern Psychoanalysis of the Schizophrenic Patient.* 2d ed. New York: Human Sciences Press, 1985. The seminal work in modern psychoanalysis. More comprehensible than the first edition, it is still difficult reading because it requires some familiarity with the theory and (particularly) practice of modern psychoanalytic treatment.

_____. *Psychotherapy of Preoedipal Conditions: Schizophrenia and Severe Character Disorders.* New York: Jason Aronson, 1976. Considerably easier reading than the other Spotnitz book. While it does not contain as much theory or as many practice issues, it presents them more clearly and enjoyably.

Spotnitz, Hyman, and Phyllis W. Meadow. *Treatment of the Narcissistic Neuroses.* New York: Manhattan Center for Advanced Psychoanalytic Studies, 1976. A sound and important collaborative effort between the founder of modern psychoanalysis and the person (Phyllis W. Meadow) who spearheaded the movement's appearance and started, with others, the institution founded to advance the philosophy and techniques of modern psychoanalysis.

Elliott P. Schuman

See also:

Analytical Psychotherapy, 54; Cognitive Behavior Therapy, 128; Cognitive Therapy, 153; Dream Analysis, 206; Person-Centered Therapy, 439; Personality Theory: Major Issues, 453; Psychoanalytic Psychology, 471; Psychoanalytic Psychology and Personality: Sigmund Freud, 478; Psychosurgery, 490.

PSYCHOANALYTIC PSYCHOLOGY

Type of psychology: Origin and definition of psychology
Fields of study: Psychodynamic and neoanalytic models; psychodynamic therapies

Psychoanalytic and neoanalytic schools of thought provide explanations of human and neurotic behavior. Each of these models contributes to the understanding of personality development and psychological conflict by presenting unique theoretical conceptualizations, assessment techniques, research methodologies, and psychotherapeutic strategies for personality change.

Principal terms

ANALYTIC PSYCHOLOGY: a school of psychology founded by Carl Jung which views the human mind as the result of prior experiences and the preparation of future goals; deemphasizes the role of sexuality in psychological disorders

DYNAMIC CULTURAL SCHOOLS OF PSYCHOANALYSIS: two branches of psychoanalysis, represented in the schools of Karen Horney and Harry Stack Sullivan, both emphasizing cultural, environmental, and social factors

INDIVIDUAL PSYCHOLOGY: a school of psychology founded by Alfred Alder which stresses the unity of the person and his or her striving for superiority in order to compensate for feelings of inferiority

NEOANALYTIC PSYCHOLOGY: schools of psychology that extended and revised the ideas proposed by Freud; included are the theories of Adler, Jung, Horney, Sullivan, and Erikson

PSYCHOANALYTIC PSYCHOLOGY: a school of psychology founded by Sigmund Freud, which provides a theory concerning mental disorders, a procedure for examining mental processes, and the therapeutic technique of psychoanalysis

PSYCHOSOCIAL THEORY: an eight-stage model of human growth and psychosocial development proposed by Erik Erikson, emphasizing the role played by social and cultural forces

Overview

One grand theory in psychology that dramatically revolutionized the way in which personality and its formation were viewed is psychoanalysis. Orthodox psychoanalysis and later versions of this model offer several unique perspectives of personality development, assessment, and change.

The genius of Sigmund Freud (1856-1939), the founder of psychoanalysis, is revealed in the magnitude of his achievements and the monumental scope of his works. Over the course of his lifetime, Freud developed a theory of personality and psychopathology, a method for probing the realm of the unconscious mind, and a therapy for dealing with personality disorders. He posited that an individual is motivated by unconscious forces that are instinctual in nature. The two major instinctual forces are the life instincts, or Eros, and the death instinct, or Thanatos. Their source is biological tension whose aim is tension reduction through a variety of objects. Freud viewed personality as a closed system composed of three structures: the id, ego, and superego. The irrational id consists of the biological drives and libido, or psychic energy. It operates according to the pleasure principle, which seeks the immediate gratification of needs. The rational ego serves as the executive component of personality and the mediator between the demands of the id, superego, and environment. Governed by the reality principle, it seeks to postpone the gratification of needs. The superego, or moral arm of personality, consists of the conscience (internalized values) and ego ideal (that which the person aspires to be).

According to Freud, the origins of personality are embedded in the first seven years of life. Personality develops through a sequence of psychosexual stages which focus upon an area of the body (erogenous zone) that gives pleasure to the individual; these are the oral, anal, phallic, latency, and genital stages. The frustration or overindulgence of needs contributes to a fixation, or arrest in development at a particular stage.

Clinically speaking, Freud also developed a therapy for treating individuals experiencing personality disturbances. Psychoanalysis has shown how physical disorders have psychological roots, how unbearable anxiety generates conflict, and how problems in adulthood result from early childhood experiences. In therapy, Freud surmounted his challenge to reveal the hidden nature of the unconscious by exposing the resistances and transferences of his patients. His method for probing a patient's unconscious thoughts, motives, and feelings was based upon the use of many clinical techniques. Free association, dream interpretation, analyses of slips of the tongue, misplaced objects, and humor enabled him to discover the contents of an individual's unconscious mind and open the doors to a new and grand psychology of personality.

Erik Erikson's (1902-1994) theory of psychosocial development occupies a position between orthodox psychoanalysis and neoanalytic schools of thought. His theory builds upon the basic concepts and tenets of Freudian psychology by illustrating the influential role of social and cultural forces in personality development. Erikson's observations of infants and investigations of the parent-child relationship in various societies contributed to his development of the model of the eight stages of human development. He proposes that personality unfolds over the entire life cycle according to a predetermined plan. As an individual moves through this series of stages, he or she encounters periods of vulnerability that require him or her to resolve crises of a social nature and develop new abilities and patterns of behavior. Erikson's eight psychosocial stages not only parallel Freud's psychosexual ones but, more important, have contributed immensely to contemporary thought in developmental psychology.

Several other schools of thought arose in opposition to Freudian orthodoxy. Among the proponents of these new psychoanalytic models were Carl Gustav Jung (1875-1961), Alfred Adler (1870-1937), Karen Horney (1885-1952), and Harry Stack Sullivan (1892-1949). These theorists advocated revised versions of Freud's psychoanalytic model and became known as the neo-analysts.

Jung's analytical psychology stresses the complex interaction of opposing forces within the total personality (psyche) and the manner in which these inner conflicts influence development. Personality is driven by general life process energy, called libido. It operates according to the principle of opposites, for example, a contrast between conscious and unconscious. An individual's behavior is seen as a means to some end, whose goal is to create a balance between these polar opposites through a process of self-realization. Personality is composed of several regions, including the ego (a unifying force at the center of consciousness), the personal unconscious (experiences blocked from consciousness), and the collective unconscious (inherited predispositions of ancestral experiences). The major focus of Jung's theory is the collective unconscious, with its archetypes (primordial thoughts and images), persona (public self), anima/animus (feminine and masculine components), shadow (repulsive side of the personality), and self (an archetype reflecting a person's striving for personality integration). Jung further proposed two psychological attitudes the personality could use in relating to the world: introversion and extroversion. He also identified four functions of thought: sensing, thinking, feeling, and intuiting. Eight different personality types emerge when one combines these attitudes and functions. Like Freud, Jung proposed developmental stages: childhood, young adulthood, and middle age. Through the process of individuation, a person seeks to create an inner harmony that results in self-realization. In conjunction with dream analysis, Jung used painting therapy and a word association test to disclose underlying conflicts in patients. Therapy helped patients to reconcile the conflicting sides of their personalities and experience self-realization.

The individual psychology of Adler illustrates the significance of social variables in personality development and the uniqueness of the individual. Adler proposed that an individual seeks to compensate for inborn feelings of inferiority by striving for superiority. It is a person's lifestyle that helps a person achieve future goals, ideals, and superiority. Adler extended this theme of perfection to society by using the concept of social interest to depict the human tendency to create a productive society. He maintained that early childhood experiences play a crucial role in the development of a person's unique lifestyle. An individual lacking in social interest develops a mistaken lifestyle (for example, an inferiority complex). Physical inferiority as well as spoiling or pampering and neglecting children contributes to the development of faulty lifestyles. Adler examined dreams, birth order, and first memories to trace the origins of lifestyle and goals. These data were used in psychotherapy to help the person create a new social-interest-oriented lifestyle.

Horney's social and cultural psychoanalysis considers the influence of social and cultural forces upon the development and maintenance of neurosis. Her theory focuses upon disturbed human relationships, especially between parents and children. She discussed several negative factors, such as parental indifference, erratic behavior, and unkept promises, which contributed to basic anxiety in children. This basic anxiety led to certain defenses or neurotic needs. Horney proposed ten neurotic needs that are used to reestablish safety. She further summarized these needs into three categories that depicted the individual's adjustment to others: moving toward people (compliant person), moving against people (aggressive person), and moving away from people (detached person). Horney believed that neurosis occurs when an individual lives according to his or her ideal rather than real self. She also wrote a number of articles on feminine psychology that stressed the importance of cultural rather than biological factors in personality formation. Like Freud, she used the techniques of transference, dream analysis, and free association in her psychotherapy; however, the goal of therapy was to help an individual overcome his or her idealized neurotic self and become more real as he or she experienced self-realization.

Sullivan's interpersonal theory examines personality from the perspective of the interpersonal relationships that have influenced it, especially the mother-infant relationship. Sullivan believed that this relationship contributed to an individual's development of a "good me," "bad me," or "not me" personification of self. He also proposed six stages of development: infancy, childhood, juvenile epoch, preadolescence, early adolescence, and late adolescence. These stages illustrate an individual's experiences and need for intimacy with significant others. Overall, his theory emphasizes the importance of interpersonal relations, the appraisals of others toward an individual, and the need to achieve interpersonal security and avoid anxiety.

Applications

Psychoanalytic psychology and its later versions have been used to explain normal and abnormal personality development. Regardless of their perspectives, psychologists in all these schools have relied upon the case study method to communicate their theoretical insights and discoveries.

The theoretical roots of orthodox psychoanalysis may be traced to the famous case of "Anna O.," a patient under the care of Josef Breuer, Freud's friend and colleague. Fascinated with the hysterical symptoms of this young girl and with Breuer's success in using catharsis (the talking cure) with her, Freud asked Breuer to collaborate on a work entitled *Studien über Hysterie* (1895; *Studies in Hysteria* 1950) and discuss his findings. It was the world's first book on psychoanalysis, containing information on the unconscious, defenses, sexual cause of neurosis, resistance, and transference. Freud's own self-analysis and analyses of family members and other patients further contributed to the changing nature of his theory. Among his great case histories are "Dora" (hysteria), "Little Hans" (phobia), the "Rat Man" (obsessional neurosis), the "Schreiber" case (paranoia), and the "Wolf Man" (infantile neurosis). His method of treatment, psychoanalysis, is also well documented in contemporary cases such as the one described in the book *Sybil* (1974).

In his classic work *Childhood and Society* (1950), Erikson discussed the applicability of the clinical method of psychoanalysis and the case-history technique to normal development in children. His case analyses of the Sioux and Yurok Indians and his observations of children led to the creation of a psychosocial theory of development that emphasized the significant role played by one's culture. Moreover, Erikson's psychohistorical accounts, *Young Man Luther: A Study in Psychoanalysis and History* (1958) and *Gandhi's Truth on the Origins of Militant Nonviolence* (1969), illustrated the applications of clinical analyses to historical and biographical research so prominent today.

The founders of other psychoanalytic schools of thought have similarly shown that their theories can best be understood in the context of the therapeutic situations and in the writings of case histories. Harold Greenwald's *Great Cases in Psychoanalysis* (1959) is an excellent source of original case histories written by Freud, Jung, Adler, Horney, and Sullivan. Jung's case of "The Anxious Young Woman and the Retired Business Man" clarifies the differences and similarities between his theory and Freud's psychoanalytic model. In "The Drive for Superiority," Adler uses material from several cases to illustrate the themes of lifestyle, feelings of inferiority, and striving for superiority. Horney's case of "The Ever Tired Editor" portrays her use of the character analysis method; that is, she concentrates upon the way in which a patient characteristically functions. Sullivan's case of "The Inefficient Wife" sheds some light on the manner in which professional advice may be given to another (student) practitioner. In retrospect, all these prominent theorists have exposed their independent schools of though through case histories. Even today, this method continues to be used to explain human behavior and to enhance understanding of personality functioning.

Context

Historically, the evolution of psychoanalytic psychology originated with Freud's clinical observations of the work conducted by the famous French neurologist Jean Martin Charcot and his collaborations on the treatment of hysteria neurosis with Breuer. The publication of *Studies in Hysteria* marked the birth of psychoanalysis since it illustrated a theory of hysteria, a therapy of catharsis, and an analysis of unconscious motivation. Between 1900 and 1920, Freud made innumerable contributions to the field. His major clinical discoveries were contained in the publications *Die Traumdeutung* (1900; *The Interpretation of Dreams,* 1913) and *Drei Abhandlungen zur Sexualtheorie* (1905; *Three Contributions to the Sexual Theory,* 1910; also translated as *Three Essays on the Theory of Sexuality* in 1949) as well as in various papers on therapy, case histories, and applications to everyday life. During this time, Freud began his international correspondence with people such as Jung. He also invited a select group of individuals to his home for evening discussions; these meetings were known as the psychological Wednesday society. Eventually, these meetings led to the establishment of the Vienna Psychoanalytical Society, with Adler as its president, and the First International Psychoanalytical Congress, with Jung as its president. In 1909, Freud, Jung, and others were invited by President G. Stanley Hall of Clark University to come to the United States to deliver a series of introductory lectures on psychoanalysis. This momentous occasion acknowledged Freud's achievements and gave him international recognition. In subsequent years, Freud reformulated his theory and demonstrated how psychoanalysis could be applied to larger social issues.

Trained in psychoanalysis by Anna Freud, Erikson followed in Freud's footsteps by supporting and extending his psychosexual theory of development with eight stages of psychosocial identity. Among the members of the original psychoanalytic group, Adler was the first to defect from the Freudian school, in 1911. Protesting Freud's Oedipus complex, Adler founded his own individual psychology. Two years later (in 1913), Jung parted company with Freud to establish his analytical psychology; he objected to Freud's belief that all human behavior stems from sex. With Horney's publications *New Ways in Psycho-analysis* (1939) and *Our Inner Conflicts: A Constructive Theory of Neurosis* (1945), it became quite clear that her ideas remotely resembled Freud's. Objecting to a number of Freud's major tenets, she attributed the development of neurosis and the psychology of being feminine to social, cultural, and interpersonal influences. Similarly, Sullivan extended psychoanalytic psychology to interpersonal phenomena, arguing that the foundations of human nature and development are not biological but rather cultural and social.

The accomplishments of Freud and his followers are truly remarkable. The creative genius of each theorist spans a lifetime of effort and work. The magnitude of their achievements is shown in their efforts to provide new perspectives on personality development and psychopathology, theories of motivation, psychotherapeutic methods of treatment, and methods for describing the nature of human behavior. Clearly, these independent schools of thought have had a profound influence not only upon the field of psychology, but also upon art, religion, anthropology, sociology, and literature. Undoubtedly, they will continue to serve as the cornerstone of personality theory and provide the foundation for new and challenging theories of tomorrow—theories that seek to discover the true nature of what it means to be human.

Bibliography

Adler, Alfred. *Social Interest, a Challenge to Mankind.* New York: Capricorn Books, 1964. An excellent summary of Adler's theories of human nature and social education, incorporating his ideas on lifestyle, inferiority/superiority complex, neurosis, childhood memories, and social feelings. Also contains a chapter on the consultant and patient relationship, and a questionnaire for understanding and treating difficult children.

Dufresne, Todd, and Paul Roazen. *Freud Under Analysis: Psychoanalytic Theories, Psychoanalytic Movements.* Northvale, N.J.: Jason Aronson, 1997.

Erikson, Erik Homburger. *Identity, Youth, and Crisis.* New York: W. W. Norton, 1968. An impressive summation of Erikson's theories of human nature and development and the importance of societal forces. Erikson discusses his clinical observations, the life cycle and the formation of identity, and case histories to illustrate identity confusion and other relevant issues. This book carries forward concepts expressed in *Childhood and Society* (1963).

Forrester, John. *Dispatches from the Freud Wars: Psychoanalysis and Its Passions.* Cambridge, Mass.: Harvard University Press, 1997.

Freud, Sigmund. *A General Introduction to Psychoanalysis.* New York: W. W. Norton, 1977. An easy-to-read account of Freud's complete theory of psychoanalysis. Freud presents twenty-eight lectures to reveal major aspects of his theory, essential details in his method of psychoanalysis, and the results of his work. He also examines the psychology of errors, dream analysis technique, and general theory of neurosis.

Greenwald, Harold, ed. *Great Cases in Psychoanalysis.* New York: Ballantine, 1959. An outstanding source of case histories written by the theorists themselves. Greenwald uses these case histories to portray the historical context of the psychoanalytic movement. These original case studies provide insight into therapeutic methods used by these great analysts as well as their assessments. Included are Freud, Adler, Jung, Horney, and Sullivan.

Horney, Karen. *The Neurotic Personality of Our Time.* New York: W. W. Norton, 1937. This classic work contains Horney's portrayal of the neurotic personality and the relevance of cultural forces in the etiology of psychological disturbances. This post-Freudian document examines Horney's theoretical conceptualizations, including basic anxiety, neurotic trends, methods of adjustment, and the role played by culture.

Sullivan, Harry Stack. *The Interpersonal Theory of Psychiatry.* New York: W. W. Norton, 1953. A classic work on human development from an interpersonal perspective. Sullivan provides a comprehensive overview of his theory by describing his key concepts and developmental stages. He further illustrates the application of his theory by focusing upon inappropriate interpersonal relationships.

Joan Bartczak Cannon

See also:

Analytical Psychology: Carl G. Jung, 49; Dream Analysis, 206; Ego Psychology: Erik Erikson, 223; Individual Psychology: Alfred Adler, 296; Personality: Psychophysiological

PSYCHOANALYTIC PSYCHOLOGY AND PERSONALITY
Sigmund Freud

Type of psychology: Personality
Fields of study: Classic analytic themes and issues; personality theory; psychodynamic and neoanalytic models

Sigmund Freud's theory of personality, emphasizing unconscious motivation, sexual instincts, and psychological conflict, is one of the most profound and unique contributions in psychology. Freud described both the normal and abnormal personality, and he proposed a therapy for the treatment of mental problems.

Principal terms

ANAL STAGE: the second psychosexual stage of development, approximately from ages two to four; sexual energy is focused on the anus, and conflicts center on toilet training

EGO: the part of the personality responsible for perceiving reality and thinking; mediates between the demands of the id, supergo, and reality

GENITAL STAGE: the fourth psychosexual stage, beginning at adolescence; sexual excitation from the oral and anal zones is integrated into mature, genital sexuality

ID: the most primitive part of the personality, composed of the instincts

INSTINCTS: psychological representations of biological needs, they are the source of all psychological energy; the sexual instincts are the most important in Freudian theory

LATENCY: the period between approximately age six and adolescence, when sexual instincts are not strongly manifested; strictly speaking, not a psychosexual stage

OEDIPAL CONFLICT: sexual attraction for the parent of the opposite sex, and jealousy of and fear of retribution from the parent of the same sex; first manifested in phallic stage (in girls, sometimes called the "Electra complex")

ORAL STAGE: the first stage of psychosexual development, from birth to approximately age two; sexual energy focuses on the mouth, and conflicts may arise over feeding

PHALLIC STAGE: the third stage of psychosexual development, from approximately age four to six; sexual energy focuses on the genitals

SUPEREGO: the part of the personality internally representing the ideals and punishments of society, as transmitted by one's caregivers; it strives for moral perfection

Overview

Sigmund Freud saw people as engaged in a personal struggle between their instinctual urges and the requirements of society. This conflict often takes place outside one's awareness, in the unconscious, and affects all aspects of people's lives. The instinctual energy which fuels the mind has its source in the unconscious. It is highly mobile, and once engaged must achieve expression, however disguised the expression might be.

Freud likened the mind to an iceberg in that most of the mind is below the level of awareness—in the unconscious—as most of the mass of an iceberg is below the surface of the water. The id, the most primitive structure in the mind, is in the unconscious. The id is composed of the instincts, including the sexual and other life instincts and the aggressive and other death instincts. For Freud, the sexual instincts were particularly important. They take a long time to develop, and society has a large investment in their regulation.

The instincts press for gratification, but the id itself cannot satisfy them, because it has no contact with reality. Therefore, the ego, which contacts the id in the unconscious, but also is partly conscious, develops. The ego can perceive reality and direct behavior to satisfy the id's urges. To the extent that the ego can satisfy the id's instincts, it gains strength, which it can then use to energize its own processes, perceiving and thinking. It is important that the ego can also use its energy to restrict or delay the expression of the id. The ego uses psychological defense mechanisms to protect the individual from awareness of threatening events and to regulate the expression of the instincts. For example, a strong ego can use the defense mechanism of sublimation to direct some sexual energy into productive work rather than sexual activity itself.

In the course of development, the superego develops from the ego. The ego attaches energy to the significant people in the child's world—the caregivers—and their values are then adopted as the child's own ideal and conscience. This process becomes particularly significant during the phallic stage, between the ages of four and six. At that time, the child becomes sexually attracted to the opposite-sex parent. In giving up that passion, the child adopts the characteristics of the same-sex parent; this process shapes the child's superego. The superego is mostly unconscious, and it strives for perfection. Throughout life, the id will strive for instinctual gratification, and the superego will strive for perfection. It is the task of the ego to mediate between the two, when necessary, and to chart a realistic life course.

Freud considered the childhood years particularly significant, not only because during these years the ego and superego develop from energy captured from the id, but also because during this time the sexual instincts manifest themselves in a variety of forms. The sexual instincts become focused on particular erogenous zones of the child's body in a set order. This produces a series of psychosexual stages, each characterized by instinctual urges, societal response, conflict, and resolution. During the course of this process, lasting person-ality traits and defenses develop. At first, the sexual energy is focused on the mouth. In this, the oral stage, conflicts may surround feeding. At approximately age two, the anal stage begins. The sexual instincts focus on the anus, and conflicts may occur around toilet training. The phallic stage, in which the child is attracted to the opposite-sex parent, follows. According to Freud, for boys this Oedipal conflict can be severe, as they fear castration from their father in retribution for their attraction to their mother. For girls, the conflict is somewhat less severe; in Freudian psychology, this less-severe conflict means that in adulthood women will have less mature personalities than men. At approximately age six, the sexual instincts go into abeyance, and the child enters a period of latency. In adolescence, the sexual instincts again come to the fore, in the genital stage, and the adolescent has the task of integrating the impulses from all the erogenous zones into mature genital sexuality.

Psychological problems occur when the psychosexual stages have left the instinctual urges strongly overgratified or undergratified, when the instincts are overly strong, when the superego is overly tyrannical, or when the ego has dealt with childhood traumas by severe repression of its experiences into the unconscious. Undergratification or overgratification of the instincts during childhood can result in fixations, incomplete resolutions of childhood conflicts. For example, a person who is severely toilet trained can develop an "anal character," becoming either excessively neat, miserly, or otherwise "holding things inside." If the id urges are too strong, they may overwhelm the ego, resulting in psychosis. An overly strong superego can lead to excessive guilt. If the ego represses childhood trauma, relegating it to the unconscious, that trauma will persist, outside awareness, in affecting a person's thoughts and behaviors.

Freud believed that no one could escape the conflicts inherent in the mind but that one could gain greater familiarity with one's unconscious and learn to direct instinctual energies in socially appropriate ways. This was the task of psychoanalysis, a form of therapy in which a client's unconscious conflicts are explored to allow the individual to develop better ways of coping.

Applications

Freud's theory has had a dramatic impact on Western society, strongly influencing the ways people view themselves and their interactions with others. Terms such as "Freudian slip," "Oedipal complex," and "unconscious" are a part of everyday language. Emotions may be seen as "buried deep," and emotional expression may be called therapeutic. Assumptions about the unconscious influence both popular and professional conceptions of mental life.

The assumption that the expression of emotion is healthy and the repression of emotion is unhealthy may be traced to Freud. To some extent, this idea has received support from research which suggests that unresolved anger may contribute to physical health problems. Unfortunately, the release of anger in verbal or physical aggression may cause those aggressive behaviors to increase rather than decrease. The vicarious experience of aggression via watching television or films may also teach aggression rather than reduce the urge to aggress.

Freud believed that dreams were one vehicle of unconscious expression. He viewed dreams as expressing the fulfillment of a wish, generally of a sexual nature. During sleep, the ego relaxes its restrictions on the id; instinctual wishes from the id, or repressed material from the unconscious, may be manifested in a dream. The bizarre sense of time and the confusing combinations of people and odd incidents in dreams reflect that the unconscious is without a sense of time, logic, or morality.

In dreams, the ego transforms material from the id to make it less threatening. Once one awakens, the ego disguises the true meaning of the dream further. Important points will be repressed and forgotten, and distortions will occur as the dream is remembered or told. For this reason, it is virtually impossible, according to Freud, to interpret one's own dreams accurately. A psychoanalyst interprets dreams by asking a patient to free associate—to say whatever comes to mind—about the dream content. In this fashion, the censoring of the ego may be relaxed, and the true meaning will be revealed to the therapist.

Revealing unconscious material is at the center of Freudian psychotherapy. Since Freud, many have viewed psychological problems as the result of childhood conflicts or traumas. Once the source is revealed, the patient is expected to improve. The nature of treatment is considerably more complicated than this might suggest, because the patient's ego may actively defend against acknowledging painful unconscious material. One of the few cases that Freud reported in detail was that of "Dora." Dora was referred to Freud because of a persistent cough that was assumed to be of psychological origin. According to Freud, such physical symptoms often are the result of childhood sexual conflict. Dora's cough and other psychosomatic complaints were found to be rooted in her sexual attraction to her father and to other men who were seen as resembling him—including a family friend, and even Freud himself. Her attraction was accompanied by jealousy of her mother and the family friend's wife. The situation was complicated, because Dora's father was having an affair with the family friend's wife, to whom Dora was also attracted, and the family friend had expressed his attraction for Dora.

All this and more is revealed in two dreams of Dora's that Freud analyzes in detail. The first is a dream of being awakened by her father, dressing quickly, and escaping a house that is on fire. The dream does its work by equating her father with the family friend, who once really was beside her bed as she awoke from a nap. This caused her to decide to "dress quickly" in the mornings, lest the friend come upon her unclothed. Her unconscious attraction for the friend, however, is belied by the symbol of fire, which might be likened to consuming passion. In her second dream, Dora dreamed that her father was dead and that a man said "Two and a half hours more." The dream symbolizes both Dora's turning away from her father as an object of her sexual interest and her intention (not evident to Freud at the time) of leaving therapy after two more sessions.

If Dora had not stopped therapy prematurely, Freud would have continued to bring his interpretation of her unconscious conflicts to the fore. In particular, he would have used her transference of childhood emotions to Freud himself as a vehicle for making the material revealed by her dreams, free associations, and behaviors evident to consciousness. The use of such transference is a key element of psychoanalysis. While this would not have completely resolved Dora's strong instinctual urges, it would have allowed her to come to terms with them in more mature ways, perhaps by choosing an appropriate marriage partner. Indeed, Freud reveals at the end of his report of this case that Dora married a young man she mentioned near the end of her time in therapy.

Context

Freud was a unique, seminal thinker. His theory was controversial from its inception; at the same time, however, it is such a powerful theory that, while many have criticized it, no subsequent personality theorist has been able to ignore the ideas Freud advanced. Psycho-analytic theory has also provided an interpretive framework for literary critics, historians, philosophers, and others.

Freud's theory was a product of his personal history, his training in science and medicine, and the Viennese culture in which he lived. Freud's early training was as a neurologist. As he turned from neurology to psychology, he continued to apply the skills of careful observation to this new discipline and to assume that the human mind followed natural laws that could be discovered. Viennese society at the time of Freud was one of restrictive social attitudes, particularly for women, and of covert practices that fell far short of public ideals. Thus it was relatively easy to see the psychological problems of the middle-class Viennese women who often were Freud's patients as being attributable to sexual conflicts.

Although Freud himself was dedicated to developing a science of mental life, his methods are open to criticism on scientific grounds. His theory is based upon his experiences as a therapist and his own self-analysis. His conclusions may therefore be restricted to the particular people or time his work encompassed. He did not seek to corroborate what his patients told him by checking with others outside the therapy room. Freud was not interested in the external "truth" of a report as much as its inner psychological meaning. He did not make details of his cases available to scrutiny, perhaps because of confidentiality. Although he wrote extensively about his theory, only five case histories were published. In all, these difficulties make the assessment of Freudian theory in terms of traditional scientific criteria problematic.

Freud's theory has had strong adherents as well as critics. Although theorists such as Alfred Adler and Carl Jung eventually broke with Freud, arguing against the primacy of the sexual instincts, his influence can be seen in their theories. Similarly, the important work of Erik Erikson describing human development through the life span has its roots in psychoanalytic theory. Many contemporary psychoanalytic theorists place a greater emphasis on the ego than did Freud, seeing it as commanding its own source of energy, independent of and equal to the id. Much contemporary literature and social criticism also possess a Freudian flavor.

Bibliography

Berger, Milton M., ed. *Women Beyond Freud: New Concepts of Feminine Psychology*. New York: Brunner/Mazel, 1994.

Dufresne, Todd, and Paul Roazen. *Freud Under Analysis: Psychoanalytic Theories, Psychoanalytic Movements*. Northvale, N.J.: Jason Aronson, 1997.

Forrester, John. *Dispatches from the Freud Wars: Psychoanalysis and Its Passions*. Cambridge, Mass.: Harvard University Press, 1997.

Freud, Sigmund. *An Outline of Psychoanalysis*. Translated by James Strachey. New York: W. W. Norton, 1949. A brief introduction to Freudian theory. Beginning students of Freud may find the tone too didactic and the treatment too abbreviated; however, it is valuable when read in conjunction with a good summary of Freud from a secondary source.

Gay, Peter. *Freud: A Life for Our Time*. New York: W. W. Norton, 1988. A very well-written biography of Freud. Places Freud's work in historical and psychological context. Accessible to the reader who may only have a passing familiarity with Freudian theory.

_____, ed. *The Freud Reader*. New York: W. W. Norton, 1989. A well-edited volume of selections of Freud's work. *The Interpretation of Dreams, Fragment of an Analysis of a Case of Hysteria ("Dora")*, and *Three Essays on the Theory of Sexuality* are particularly important in defining the basics of Freud's theory.

Hall, Calvin Springer, and Gardner Lindzey. "Freud's Classical Psychoanalytical Theory." In *Theories of Personality*. 3d ed. New York: John Wiley & Sons, 1978. This chapter is the classic textbook summary of Freud's theory. Very readable, thorough, and accurate. Also presents a brief discussion of psychoanalytic research methods and criticisms of the theory.

Jones, Ernest. *The Life and Work of Sigmund Freud*. Edited and abridged by Lionel Trilling and Steven Marcus. New York: Basic Books, 1961. This is an abridged edition of Jones's three-volume biography of Freud. Jones was a confidant of Freud, and his official biographer. Interesting as an "insider's" account of Freud's life.

Kardiner, Abram. *My Analysis with Freud.* New York: W. W. Norton, 1977. Kardiner is a well-known analyst. This brief volume is a personal account of his own analysis, with Freud as the therapist. A fascinating "insider's" account of Freudian analysis and the forces that shaped the psychoanalytic movement.

Susan E. Beers

See also:

Analytical Psychology: Carl G. Jung, 49; Dream Analysis, 206; Ego Psychology: Erik Erikson, 223; Individual Psychology: Alfred Adler, 296; Personality Theory: Major Issues, 453; Psychoanalysis: Classical Versus Modern, 465; Psychoanalytic Psychology, 471; Social Psychological Models: Erich Fromm, 565; Social Psychological Models: Karen Horney, 571.

Psychological Experimentation
Variables

Type of psychology: Psychological methodologies
Fields of study: Experimental methodologies; methodological issues

The scientific method involves the testing of hypotheses through the objective collection of data. The experiment is an important method of data collection in which the researcher systematically controls multiple factors in order to determine the extent to which changes in one variable cause changes in another variable. Only the experimental method can reveal cause-effect relationships between the variables of interest.

Principal terms

CONTROL GROUP: a group of subjects that are like subjects of the experimental groups in all ways except that they do not experience the independent variable

CONTROL VARIABLES: extraneous factors that might influence the dependent variable, making it difficult to evaluate the effect of the independent variable

DEPENDENT VARIABLE: the behavior of interest to the experimenter; it is measured to determine the effect of changes in the independent variable

ECOLOGICAL VALIDITY: the extent to which the results of a study reveal something about "real-life" phenomena

EXPERIMENT: one of several data collection methods; requires systematically manipulating the levels of an independent variable under controlled conditions in order to measure its impact on a dependent variable

FIELD EXPERIMENT: an experiment conducted outside the laboratory in a naturalistic setting

HYPOTHESIS: an educated guess or prediction that is to be tested by research

INDEPENDENT VARIABLE: the fact manipulated by the experimenter in order to assess its impact on the dependent variable

RANDOM ASSIGNMENT: a technique for creating groups of subjects across which individual differences will be evenly dispersed

Overview

Psychology is typically defined as the science of behavior and cognition and is considered a research-oriented discipline not unlike biology, chemistry, and physics. To appreciate the role of experimentation in psychology, it is useful to view it in the context of the general scientific method employed by psychologists in conducting their research. This scientific method may be described as a four-step sequence starting with identifying a problem and forming a hypothesis. The problem must be one suitable for scientific inquiry—that is, questions concerning values, such as whether rural life is "better" than city life, are more appropriate for philosophical debate than scientific investigation. Questions better suited to the scientific method are those that can be answered through the objective collection of facts—for example, "Are children who are neglected by their parents more likely to do poorly in school than children who are well treated?" The hypothesis is the tentative guess, or the prediction regarding the question's answer, and is based upon other relevant research and existing theory. The second step, and the one with which this article is primarily concerned, is the collection of data (facts) in order to test the accuracy of the hypothesis. Any one of a number of methods might be employed, including simple observation, survey, or experimentation. The third step is to make sense of the facts that have been accumulated by subjecting them to careful analysis; the fourth step is to share any significant findings with the scientific community.

In considering step two, the collection of data, it seems that people often mistakenly use the words "research" and "experiment" interchangeably. A student might ask whether an experiment has been done on a particular topic when, in fact, the student really wants to know if *any* kind of research has been conducted in that area. All experiments are examples of research, but not all research is experimental. Research that is nonexperimental in nature might be either descriptive or correlational.

Descriptive research is nearly self-explanatory; it occurs when the researcher wants merely to characterize the behaviors of an individual or, more likely, a group. For example, one might want to survey the students of a high school to ascertain the level of alcohol use (alcohol use might be described in terms of average ounces consumed per student per week). One might also spend considerable time observing individuals suffering from, for example, infantile autism. A thorough description of the typical behaviors could be useful for someone investigating the cause of this disorder. Descriptive research can be extremely valuable, but it is not useful when researchers want to investigate the relationship between two or more variables (things that vary, or quantities that may have different values).

In a correlational study, the researcher measures how strongly the variables are related, or the degree to which one variable predicts another variable. Suppose a researcher is interested in the relationship between exposure to violence on television (variable one) and aggressive behavior (variable two) in a group of elementary school children. She could administer a survey asking the children how much violent television they view and then rank the subjects from high to low levels of this variable. The researcher could similarly interview the school staff and rank the children according to their aggressive behavior. A statistic called a correlation coefficient might then be computed, revealing how the two variables are related and the strength of that relationship.

Correlational studies are not uncommon in psychological research. Often, however, a researcher wants even more specific information about the relationships among variables—in particular, about whether one variable *causes* a change in another variable. In such a situation, experimental research is warranted. This drawback of the correlational approach—its inability to establish causal relationships—is worth considering for a moment. In the hypothetical study described above, the researcher may find that viewing considerable television violence predicts high levels of aggressive behavior, yet she cannot conclude that these viewing habits cause the aggressiveness. After all, it is entirely possible that aggressiveness, caused by some unknown factor, prompts a preference for violent television. That is, the causal direction is unknown; viewing television violence may cause aggressiveness, but the inverse (that aggressiveness causes the watching of violent television programs) is also feasible. As this is a crucial point, one final illustration is warranted. What if, at a certain

Rocky Mountain university, a correlational study has established that high levels of snowfall predict low examination scores? One should not conclude that something about the chemical composition of snow impairs the learning process. The correlation may be real and highly predictive, but the causal culprit may be some other factor. Perhaps, as snowfall increases, so does the incidence of illness, and it is this variable that is causally related to exam scores. Maybe, as snowfall increases, the likelihood of students using their study time for skiing also increases.

Experimentation is a powerful research method because it alone can reveal cause-effect relationships. In an experiment, the researcher does not merely measure the naturally occurring relationships between variables for the purpose of predicting one from the other; rather, he or she systematically manipulates the values of one variable and measures the effect, if any, that is produced in a second variable. The variable that is manipulated is known as the independent variable; the other variable, the behavior in question, is called the dependent variable (any change in it depends upon the manipulation of the independent variable). Experimental research is characterized by a desire for control on the part of the researcher. Control of the independent variable and control over extraneous variables are both wanted. That is, there is a desire to eliminate or hold constant the factors (control variables) other than the independent variable that might influence the dependent variable. If adequate control is achieved, the researcher may be confident that it was, in fact, the manipulation of the independent variable that produced the change in the dependent variable.

Applications
Returning to the relationship between television viewing habits and aggressive behavior in children, suppose that correlational evidence indicates that high levels of the former variable predict high levels of the latter. Now the researcher wants to test the hypothesis that there is a cause-effect relationship between the two variables. She decides to manipulate exposure to television violence (the independent variable) to see what effect might be produced in the aggressiveness of her subjects (the dependent variable). She might choose two levels of the independent variable and have twenty children watch fifteen minutes of a violent detective show while another twenty children are subjected to thirty minutes of the same show. If an objective rating of playground aggressiveness later reveals more hostility in the thirty-minute group than in the fifteen-minute group, she still cannot be confident that higher levels of television violence cause higher levels of aggressive behavior. More information is needed, especially with regard to issues of control. To begin with, how does the researcher know that it is the violent content of the program that is promoting aggressiveness? Perhaps it is the case that the more time they spend watching television, regardless of subject matter, the more aggressive children become. This study needs a control group: a group of subjects identical to the experimental subjects with the exception that they do not experience the independent variable. In fact, two control groups might be employed, one that watches fifteen minutes and another that watches thirty minutes of nonviolent programming. The control groups serve as a basis against which the behavior of the experimental groups can be compared. If it is found that the two control groups aggress to the same extent, and to a lesser extent than the experimental groups, the researcher can be more confident that violent programming promotes relatively higher levels of aggressiveness.

The experimenter also needs to be sure that the children in the thirty-minute experimental group were not naturally more aggressive to begin with. One need not be too concerned with this possibility if one randomly assigns subjects to the experimental and control groups. There are certainly individual differences among subjects in factors such as personality and intelligence, but with random assignment one can be reasonably sure that those individual differences are evenly dispersed among the experimental and control groups.

The experimenter might want to control or hold constant other variables. Perhaps she suspects that age, social class, ethnicity, and gender could also influence the children's aggressiveness. She might want to make sure that these subject variables are eliminated by either choosing subjects who are alike in these ways or by making sure that the groups are balanced for these factors (for example, equal numbers of boys and girls in each group). There are numerous other extraneous variables that might concern the researcher, including the time of day when the children participate, the length of time between television viewing and the assessment of aggressiveness, the children's diets, the children's family structures (single versus dual parent, siblings versus only child), and the disciplinary styles used in the homes. Resource limitations prevent every extraneous variable from being controlled, yet the more control, the more confident the experimenter can be of the cause-effect relationship between the independent and dependent variables.

One more example of experimental research, this one nonhypothetical, will further illustrate the application of this methodology. In 1973, Mark Lepper, David Greene, and Richard Nisbett tested the hypothesis that when people are offered external rewards for performing activities that are naturally enjoyable, their interest in these activities declines. The participants in the study were nursery school children who had already demonstrated a fondness for coloring with marking pens; this was their preferred activity when given an opportunity for free play. The children were randomly assigned to one of three groups. The first group was told previously that they would receive a "good player award" if they would play with the pens when later given the opportunity. Group two received the same reward but without advance notice; they were surprised by the reward. The last group of children was the control group; they were neither rewarded nor told to expect a reward.

The researchers reasoned that the group one children, having played with the pens in order to receive a reward, would now perceive their natural interest in this activity as lower than before the study. Indeed, when all groups were later allowed a free play opportunity, it was observed that the "expected reward" group spent significantly less time than the other groups in this previously enjoyable activity. Lepper and his colleagues, then, experimentally supported their hypothesis and reported evidence that reward causes interest to decline in a previously pleasurable behavior. This research has implications for instructors; they should carefully consider the kinds of behavior they reward (with gold stars, lavish praise, high grades, and so on) as they may, ironically, be producing less of the desired behavior. An academic activity that is enjoyable play for a child may become tedious work when a reward system is attached to it.

Context

While most would agree that the birth of psychology as a science took place in Leipzig, Germany, in 1879, when Wilhelm Wundt established the first laboratory for studying psychological phenomena, there is no clear record of the first use of experimentation.

Regardless, there is no disputing the attraction that many psychologists have had for this method of research in the twentieth century. Psychologists clearly recognize the usefulness of the experiment in investigating potential causal relationships between variables. Hence, experimentation is employed widely across the subfields of psychology, including developmental, cognitive, physiological, clinical, industrial, and social psychology.

This is not to say that all psychologists are completely satisfied with experimental research. It has been argued that an insidious "catch-22" exists in some experimental research that limits the usefulness of that research. The argument goes like this: Experimenters are motivated to control rigorously the conditions of their studies and the relevant extraneous variables. To gain such control, they often conduct experiments in a laboratory setting. Therefore, subjects are often observed in an artificial environment, engaged in behaviors that are so controlled as to be unnatural, and they clearly know they are being observed—which may further alter their behavior. Such research is said to be lacking in ecological validity or applicability to "real-life" behavior. It may show how subjects behave in a unique laboratory procedure, but it tells little about psychological phenomena as displayed in everyday life. The catch-22, then, is that experimenters desire control in order to establish that the independent variable is producing a change in the dependent variable, and the more such control, the better; however, the more control, the more risk that the research may be ecologically invalid.

Most psychologists are sensitive to issues of ecological validity and take pains to make their laboratory procedures as naturalistic as possible. Additionally, much research is conducted outside the laboratory in what are known as field experiments. In such studies, the subjects are unobtrusively observed (perhaps by a confederate of the researcher who would not attract their notice) in natural settings such as classroom, playground, or workplace. Field experiments, then, represent a compromise in that there is bound to be less control than is obtainable in a laboratory, yet the behaviors observed are likely to be natural. Such naturalistic experimentation is likely to continue to increase in the future.

Although experimentation is only one of many methods available to psychologists, it fills a particular need and that need is not likely to decline in the foreseeable future. In trying to understand the complex relationships among the many variables that affect the way people think and act, experimentation makes a valuable contribution: It is the one methodology available that can reveal unambiguous cause-effect relationships.

Bibliography

Barber, Theodore Xenophon. _Pitfalls in Human Research_. New York: Pergamon Press, 1976. It is useful to learn from the mistakes of others, and Barber provides the opportunity by describing ten categories of likely errors in designing and conducting research. This is not a long book (117 pages), and it is enjoyable reading, especially the specific accounts of flawed research.

Carlson, Neil R. _Psychology: The Science of Behavior_. 3d ed. Boston: Allyn & Bacon, 1990. The second chapter of this introductory psychology text may be the most reader-friendly reference in this bibliography. Entitled "The Ways and Means of Psychology," it provides a brief introductory overview of the scientific method, experimental and correlational research, and basic statistics; it is well suited for the novice. Colorful graphics, a concluding summary, and a list of key terms are all helpful.

Hearst, Eliot, ed. *The First Century of Experimental Psychology.* Hillsdale, N.J.: Lawrence Erlbaum, 1979. Primarily for the student interested in the history of experimental psychology. This is a 693-page book; while most of the fourteen chapters are devoted to specific topics in psychology such as emotion, development, and psychopathology, the final chapter by William Estes provides an excellent overview of experimental psychology and considers some broad, profound issues.

Leary, Mark R. *Introduction to Behavioral Research Methods.* 2d ed. Pacific Grove, Calif.: Brooks/Cole, 1995.

Shaughnessy, John J., and Eugene B. Zechmeister. *Research Methods in Psychology.* 2d ed. New York: McGraw-Hill, 1990. This is one of a number of textbooks that discusses psychological research in the light of the scientific method. It is fairly accessible, has a thorough and competent description of experimentation, and, as a bonus, considers some ethical issues. Glossary, index, and references are all provided.

Stern, Paul C. *Evaluating Social Science Research.* New York: Oxford University Press, 1979. This is a clearly written, nonthreatening book for the early to middle-level college student. The focus of the author is on encouraging the critical analysis of research; to this end, case-research examples are presented for examination. End-of-chapter exercises are included to aid the student in integrating information.

Mark B. Alcorn

See also:

Animal Experimentation, 59; Case-Study Methodologies, 110; Survey Research: Questionnaires and Interviews, 615.

PSYCHOSURGERY

Type of psychology: Psychotherapy
Field of study: Biological treatments

Psychosurgery is a method for treating certain mental disorders by performing surgical operations on the brain, either by severing the connections between different parts of the brain or by destroying brain tissue in specific areas. Psychosurgery was popular from about 1935 to 1960; it has now largely been replaced by drugs. It remains a highly controversial procedure.

Principal terms

BIOETHICS: includes the study of the moral, ethical, and social issues posed by treating mental disorders by biological means, especially psychosurgery

BIOLOGICAL DETERMINISM: the belief that behavior is determined or caused by a corresponding set of conditions within the brain

BIOMEDICAL MODEL: the belief, similar to biological determinism, that mental illness is the result of dysfunction in certain areas of the brain

BIOMEDICAL TREATMENT: a therapy for mental disorders that is based on altering brain function; includes drugs, electroconvulsive shock, and psychosurgery

LOBOTOMY: the archetypical psychosurgical technique for destroying brain tissue; although it is but one of several methods, it was the first and most commonly performed and remains the most notorious

Overview

Psychosurgery, also referred to as psychiatric surgery, psychiatric neurosurgery, or functional neurosurgery, is a medical procedure intended to alleviate certain mental illnesses by destroying brain tissue in selected areas of the brain. Psychosurgery is based on the biomedical model of mental illness, which posits that mental states and ensuing behavior are the result of activity in the nervous system. That is, at the most fundamental level, human thoughts and actions are biologically determined by the functioning nervous system. Therefore, mental illness and abnormal behavior are caused by abnormalities in the nervous system: by the release of certain neurotransmitters and/or by abnormalities in brain structure. If it is assumed that the basis of a mental illness is an abnormality of the nervous system, the appropriate therapy is biomedical: The nervous system is treated directly to alleviate the problem. Biomedical treatments include psychosurgery, electroconvulsive shock, and drugs.

Contemporary psychosurgery was founded in 1935 by the Portuguese neurosurgeon António Egas Moniz. Egas Moniz attended a symposium in August, 1935, at which Carlyle Jacobsen reported anecdotally a marked change in the level of emotionality of a chimpanzee following destruction of a large part of the frontal lobe of the cerebral cortex. Formerly, the chimpanzee had been highly emotional and obstinate; following the operation, the chimpanzee appeared calm and cooperative. Egas Moniz inquired of Jacobsen whether the technique could be used to relieve anxiety states in humans; less than three months later, in November, 1935, Egas Moniz performed his first operation.

In these operations, two holes were drilled into the skull of mental patients. Initially, alcohol was injected through the holes directly into the frontal lobes. Commencing with the eighth operation, however, a scalpel-like instrument was inserted through the hole into the frontal lobes, and a wire loop was then extended from the scalpel and rotated, destroying whatever nerve tissues it contacted. Egas Moniz coined the term "psychosurgery" to describe this kind of treatment. He referred to his particular technique as prefrontal leucotomy (from the Greek *leuco,* meaning "white matter," or nerve fibers, and *tome,* meaning "knife"). The instrument he used was called a leucotome.

Egas Moniz's claims of success in alleviating extreme states of emotionality with this procedure stimulated worldwide interest, excitement, and practice. About thirty-five thousand operations were performed in the United States from 1936 through 1978, with perhaps double that number worldwide. Psychosurgery was seen as a quick and effective method for alleviating certain commonly occurring mental illnesses which could not be treated rapidly and effectively by any other means, as well as providing a partial solution to the problem of overcrowding in mental hospitals.

As other psychosurgeons began performing psychosurgery, new techniques were developed that were believed to be improvements. Egas Moniz's prefrontal leucotomy, which did not permit precise location of the area to be cut, was superseded by the prefrontal lobotomy, developed by the Americans Walter Freeman and James Watts in 1937. Larger holes were drilled into both sides of the skull, and a leucotome was inserted and precisely moved in a sweeping motion through the frontal lobe. In 1948, Freeman introduced the transorbital lobotomy. This procedure involved inserting an ice-picklike knife through the top of the eye socket into the brain and then swinging it back and forth. This procedure was quick and efficient and could be performed as an office procedure. Freeman said that he could perform fifty operations in a day.

The lobotomy was handicapped, however, by two important limitations. Destruction of the frontal lobe usually produced a number of serious side effects. Although the lobotomy was perhaps more precise than the leucotomy, the psychosurgeon still could not know with certainty exactly what part of the brain was being excised. A considerable risk of damaging other areas of the brain or of inducing hemorrhaging was present.

Later technological innovations and increased understanding of the structure of the nervous system permitted more precise and less invasive surgical procedures. An apparatus called the stereotaxis allowed precise mapping of the brain. Using this instrument, Ernest Spiegel and Henry Wycis inserted electrodes into previously inaccessible parts of the brain and destroyed a small area of tissue with electricity. This procedure initiated surgery on small and precisely located areas of the brain other than the frontal lobes, thus minimizing side effects. Nevertheless, over its more than fifty-year history, the vast majority of psychosurgical operations have been lobotomies.

Applications

As John Kleinig observes in *Ethical Issues in Psychosurgery* (1985), nearly every brain structure has at some point been subject to a psychosurgical procedure. Psychosurgery involving various brain structures has been performed in the belief that specific abnormal mental states and behaviors that are unaffected by other treatments can be alleviated through psychosurgery. According to Kleinig, psychosurgery has been used to treat many disorders.

Psychosurgery has not in general produced favorable results with schizophrenia. Drugs are the preferred biomedical procedure. Schizophrenia is still occasionally treated by psychosurgery, but only in those cases with a high emotional component—that is, with affective behaviors or mood states. Psychosurgery has been most commonly used with cases characterized by severe and disabling depression, obsessive-compulsive disorders, and acute tension and anxiety. The purpose is to even or level out the patient's feelings and emotions. As with schizophrenia, drugs are the preferred mode of treatment for these disorders; however, psychosurgery may be a consideration for those patients who do not respond appropriately to drugs and whose dysfunction is extremely severe.

Anorexia nervosa is the chronic refusal to eat sufficient food to maintain normal health. It has been viewed by some as an extreme compulsion which may be related to a disorder of the limbic system. Psychosurgery has been performed in extreme cases. Hyperactive syndrome, or attention-deficit hyperactivity disorder, in children has been viewed by some as a disorder that is a genetically based brain dysfunction, and psychosurgery has been performed when other treatments have failed. Uncontrollable rage and/or aggression is believed to be regulated by the amygdaloid body in the limbic system. Moderately favorable results have been reported with amygdalectomies performed on both adults and children.

Substance abuse and addictions can be viewed as analogues to compulsions. The purpose of psychosurgery is to reduce the strength of the desire of the addiction's object. Data indicate favorable outcomes for certain groups of alcoholics and drug addicts, but the efficacy of the procedure with obesity and compulsive gambling is lacking.

Psychosurgery has been performed on pedophiliacs (child molesters) and others who have engaged in violent sexual offenses, in order to remove the desire to perform such acts. The operation has focused on the hypothalamus, a structure in the limbic system. In some cases, the operation has succeeded, probably by producing a reduction of sexual desire in general.

The anterior angulate region of the limbic system, which is believed to be involved with the perception of pain, has been subjected to psychosurgery. Some favorable results have been obtained, which some believe are the result of the alleviation of depression or obsessive behaviors associated with intractable pain. Some pain specialists believe that psychosurgery is not appropriate in any instance.

It is apparent from this survey that psychosurgery has been employed for a wide variety of disorders and performed upon a wide variety of patient populations. With its introduction by Egas Moniz in the 1930's, and its vigorous advocacy by Egas Moniz in Europe and by Freeman and Watts in the United States, psychosurgery was received with great hope and expectation. It was seen as providing a fast, easy, and inexpensive way of treating certain mental illnesses that were unresponsive to any alternative treatments available at the time. In addition, if institutionalized patients could be successfully treated by psychosurgery, they could be released, thus simultaneously alleviating the abysmal overcrowding and intolerable conditions of mental institutions and returning the patients to a productive life in society. In fact, Egas Moniz won the Nobel Prize in Physiology or Medicine in 1949 in recognition of his work. The citation states: "Frontal leucotomy, despite certain limitations of the operative method, must be considered one of the most important discoveries ever made in psychiatric therapy, because through its use a great number of suffering people and total invalids have recovered and have been socially rehabilitated."

Context

Egas Moniz's Nobel citation may be contrasted with David L. Rosenhan and Martin E. P. Seligman's assessment of lobotomy in the second edition of their book *Abnormal Psychology* (1989): "There is the danger that physicians and patients may become overzealous in their search for a quick neurological cure. . . . [T]he disastrous history of frontal lobotomies . . . should serve as a warning."

Although the biomedical model is a sound theory, and biological treatments have proved to be valuable and worthwhile, in retrospect, Rosenhan and Seligman were correct. Lobotomies were, in general, "disastrous," and their sorry history provides a textbook example of how not to bring a new medical procedure on-line. Irreversible destruction of brain tissue and side effects were produced by procedures of highly questionable effectiveness.

The goals and desires of the early psychosurgeons may have been laudable, but their methods were not. Within three months of hearing Jacobsen's anecdotal account, Egas Moniz was performing lobotomies, despite the lack of clear evidence from prior animal experimentation that might at least support the irreversible destruction of the brain tissue. Egas Moniz performed no animal experimentation himself. He declared the frontal lobes to be the area of the brain responsible for the mental disorders to be treated by psychosurgery. His reading of the scientific literature to support his beliefs, however, was spotty and selective, and contradictory evidence was ignored. Furthermore, there was present a large animal and human literature clearly demonstrating a range of serious side effects and deficits produced by lesions of the frontal lobes, such as apathy, retarded movement, loss of initiative, and mutism. Yet, with no supporting evidence, Egas Moniz insisted these side effects were only temporary. In fact, they could be permanent. Egas Moniz's initial report on twenty patients claimed a cure for seven, lessening of symptoms in six, and no effect on six. An impartial review of these cases by Stanley Cobb, however, concluded that only one of the twenty cases provided enough information to allow a judgment.

Mercifully, the introduction of psychoactive drugs and growing criticism of lobotomies effectively brought them to an end by the late 1950's. Psychosurgery is still occasionally performed; its advocates argue that newer techniques are used that avoid the frontal lobes, that the procedure is based upon a good understanding of how the nervous system functions, that side effects are minimal, that its use is much more strictly monitored and regulated, and that it is viewed only as a treatment of last resort. Nevertheless, psychosurgery still remains highly controversial. Many practitioners and scientists are skeptical about its effectiveness, arguing that destruction of any brain tissue can produce unavoidable side effects; psychosurgery is believed by these individuals to be an ethically and morally unacceptable procedure of dubious value.

Bibliography

Kleinig, John. *Ethical Issues in Psychosurgery*. London: Allen & Unwin, 1985. This informative book focuses on the bioethical problems raised by psychosurgery. Discusses psychiatric diagnosis, the use of experimental therapies, criteria for success, informed consent, medical priorities, safeguards, and the relation between personality and the brain.

Lader, Malcolm Harold, and Reginald Herrington. *Biological Treatments in Psychiatry*. 2d ed. New York: Oxford University Press, 1996.

Marsh, Frank H., and Janet Katz, eds. *Biology, Crime, and Ethics*. Cincinnati: Anderson, 1984. Explores the relationship between biological factors (genetics, physiology) and criminal and aggressive behavior. Contains a section on psychosurgery and its appropriateness in treating violent and aggressive behavior.

Rodgers, Joann Ellison. *Psychosurgery: Damaging the Brain to Save the Mind*. New York: HarperCollins, 1992.

Shuman, Samuel I. *Psychosurgery and the Medical Control of Violence*. Detroit: Wayne State University Press, 1977. This wide-ranging book focuses on the public concern over psychosurgery, its legitimacy as a scientific technique, and possible erosion of legal rights. Individual chapters examine landmark legal cases, the difficulties involved in deciding when psychosurgery is a viable option, and constitutional threats posed by psychosurgery.

Smith, J. Sydney, and L. G. Kiloh, eds. *Psychosurgery and Society*. New York: Pergamon Press, 1977. Presents a number of articles on various aspects of psychosurgery. Based upon a symposium held in Australia in 1974. Presentations include discussions of traditional psychosurgery, social apprehensions concerning psychosurgery, and potential safeguards to protect patients.

Valenstein, Elliot S. *Great and Desperate Cures*. New York: Basic Books, 1986. Highly recommended. A very interesting and readable treatment of psychosurgery and other extreme treatments for mental illness. Concentrates on psychosurgery and presents a thorough consideration of its history from its inception to the 1980's. Filled with many interesting photographs and anecdotes that collectively provide an intimate insider's view on psychosurgery.

_____, ed. *The Psychosurgery Debate*. San Francisco: W. H. Freeman, 1980. A wide-ranging discussion of various aspects of psychosurgery. Presentations include the rationale for psychosurgery, selection of patients, postoperative evaluation, techniques, evaluation, legal issues, and ethical issues.

Laurence Miller

See also:

Analytical Psychotherapy, 54; Psychoanalysis: Classical Versus Modern, 465; Psychoanalytic Psychology, 471.

RACE AND INTELLIGENCE

Type of psychology: Intelligence and intelligence testing
Fields of study: General issues in intelligence; intelligence assessment

The relationship between race and intelligence has long been the subject of heated debate among social scientists. At issue is whether intelligence is an inherited trait or is primarily attributable to environmental influences.

Principal terms

CORRELATION: the situation that results when changes in one factor are associated with changes in another factor

CULTURE: the shared attitudes, values, customs, symbols, art, experiences, and rules of a given people

ENVIRONMENT: all the conditions, circumstances, and influences surrounding and affecting a person or group of individuals; may be physical, social, political, and/or psychological in nature

HEREDITY: the transmission of characteristics from parent to offspring through genes in the chromosomes

HERITABILITY: the extent to which a given characteristic, such as intelligence, is inherited

INTELLIGENCE: the ability to learn, solve problems, and direct conduct effectively; mental ability

INTELLIGENCE QUOTIENT (IQ): a score received on an intelligence test

NATURE VERSUS NURTURE: the controversy over whether intelligence is solely or primarily inherited (nature) or is attributable to environmental factors (nurture)

RACE: commonly defined as a group of people distinguishable from another group of people on the basis of physical characteristics or inherited features

Overview

In 1969, educational psychologist Arthur Jensen published an article in the *Harvard Educational Review* entitled "How Much Can We Boost I.Q. and Scholastic Achievement?" He attempted to explain the consistent finding that whites, on the average, outperform blacks by about 15 points on intelligence quotient (IQ) tests. His major conclusion was that racial differences in intelligence are primarily attributable to heredity and that whites, as a racial group, are born with abilities superior to those of blacks.

Jensen, as well as William Shockley, presents the hereditarian hypothesis of intelligence. It argues that some people are born smarter than others and that this fact cannot be changed with training, education, or any alteration in the environment. Because they believe that African Americans as a group are not as smart as Caucasians, they suggest that special programs, such as Head Start, which are designed to help disadvantaged children improve in school achievement, are doomed to fail.

In contrast to the hereditarians, Urie Bronfenbrenner and Ashley Montagu can be described as environmentalists. They believe that although intelligence has some genetic component, as do all human characteristics, the expression of intelligent behavior is defined, determined, and developed within a specific cultural context. Therefore, what people choose to call intelligence is primarily caused by the interaction of genetics with environmental influences. Environmentalists believe that a person can improve in his or her intellectual functioning with sufficient changes in environment.

Much of the hereditarian argument is based on two types of studies: those comparing IQ test performance of twins, and studies of adopted children. Because identical twins have the same genetic endowment, it is thought that any differences observed between them should be attributable to the effects of the environment. Hereditarians also suggest that one should observe more similarities in the IQs of parents and their biological children (because they share genes) than between parents and adopted children (who are biologically unrelated, and therefore, share no genes).

Statistical formulas are applied to comparisons between family members' IQs to determine the relative contributions of heredity and environment. Using this method, Sir Cyril Burt in 1958 reported a heritability estimate of .93. This means that 93 percent of the variability in intelligence could be explained genetically. People have also interpreted this to mean that 93 percent of the intelligence level is inherited. Jensen has more recently reported heritability estimates of .80 and .67, depending on what formula is used. Hereditarians have also pointed out that when they compare African Americans and Caucasians from similar environments (the same educational level, income level, or occupation), the reported IQ differences remain. This, they argue, supports their view that heredity is more important in determining intelligence.

For environmentalists, it is not so much the reported IQ differences between different racial groups that are in question. Of more concern are the basic assumptions made by the hereditarians and the reasons they give for the reported differences. Not surprisingly, environmentalists challenge the hereditarian arguments on several levels. First, they point out that there is no evidence of the existence of an "intelligence" gene or set of genes. They say that scientists have been unsuccessful in distinguishing the genetic from the environmental contributions to intelligence.

Environmentalists also refute the assumption that IQ tests adequately measure intelligence. Although IQ has been noted to be a good predictor of success in school, it turns out to have little relationship to economic success in life. S. E. Luria reports an analysis that shows that the son of a Caucasian businessman with an IQ of 90 has a greater chance of success than an African-American boy with an IQ of 120. This example calls into question what actually is being assessed. It is not at all clear that "intelligence" is being measured—especially since there is no generally accepted definition among social scientists about what intelligence is.

The definition of race is also problematic. Although most people may identify several racial groups (such as African, or black; Caucasian, or white; and so on), Ashley Montagu and many other social scientists agree that race is a pseudoscientific concept, used as a social or political category to assign social status and to subordinate nonwhite populations. Because of the intermingling among different cultural groups, it is also difficult to identify strict biological boundaries for race, which in turn makes genetic interpretations of racial comparisons of IQ differences much less meaningful.

In addition to questioning what IQ tests measure, many psychologists have criticized IQ tests as being biased against individuals who are culturally different from the mainstream group (Caucasians) and who have not assimilated the white middle-class norms upon which the tests were based. Tests developed in one culture may not adequately measure the abilities and aptitude of people from another culture, especially if the two cultures emphasize different skills, ways of solving problems, and ways of understanding the world.

Environmentalists have also criticized the research and statistical techniques used by the hereditarians. It is now widely acknowledged that the data reported by Burt, upon which Jensen heavily relied, were false. In many different studies, he came up with the same figures (to the third decimal point) for the similarities between IQ scores for twins. This is statistically impossible. He also did not take into account how other variables, such as age and gender, might have produced higher IQ values in the twins he studied. Rather, he assumed that they shared genes for intelligence.

It is also charged that the concept of heritability is misunderstood by the hereditarians. This is a statistic that applies to groups, not to individuals. If one states that the heritability estimate of a group of IQ scores is .80, that does not mean that 80 percent of each IQ score is attributable to genetics, but that 80 percent of the difference in the group of scores can be attributed to genetic variation. Therefore, according to the enviromentalists, it is incorrect for hereditarians to establish heritability within one group (such as Caucasian children) and then apply that figure to a different racial group (such as African-American children).

Applications

Several examples may help clarify the relationships between heredity, environment, and characteristics such as IQ. The first example involves a highly heritable characteristic, height. Suppose a farmer had two fields, one rich in nutrients (field A) and the other barren (field B). The farmer takes seed from a bag that has considerable genetic variety and plants them in the two fields. She cares for the two fields of crops equally well. After several weeks, the plants are measured. The farmer would find that within field A, some plants would be taller than others in the same field. Since all these plants had the same growing environment, the variation could be attributed to the genetic differences in the seeds planted. The same would be the case with the plants in field B.

The farmer would also find differences between the two fields. The plants in field A would be taller than the plants in field B, because of the richer soil in which they grew. The difference in the average heights of the plants would be attributable to the quality of the growing environment, even though the genetic variation (heritability) within field A may be the same as that within field B. This same principle applies to IQ scores of different human groups.

Taking the example further, the farmer might call a chemist to test the soil. If the chemist was able to determine all the essential missing nutrients, the farmer could add them to the soil in field B for the next season. She would find that the second batch of plants would grow larger, with the average height being similar to the average height of plants in field A. Similarly, if one is comparing African Americans and Caucasians, or any number of racial groups, on a characteristic such as IQ test scores, it is important to understand that unless the groups have equivalent growing environments (social, political, economic, educational, and so on), differences between the groups cannot be easily traced to heredity.

As another example, suppose one took a set of identical twins who were born in Chicago, separated them at birth, and placed one of the twins in the !Kung desert community in Africa.

The life experiences of the twin in Africa would differ significantly from those of his Chicago counterpart because of the differences in diet, climate, and other relevant factors required for existence and survival in the two environments. The twin in Africa would have a different language and number system; drawing and writing would likely not be an important part of daily life. Therefore, if one were to use existing IQ tests, one would have to translate them from English to the !Kung language so that they could be understood. The translation might not truly capture the meaning of all the questions and tasks, which might interfere with the !Kung twin's understanding of what was being asked of him. More problems would arise when the !Kung twin is asked to interpret drawings or to copy figures, since he would not be very familiar with these activities.

It is likely that the !Kung twin would perform poorly on the translated IQ test, because it does not reflect what is emphasized and valued in his society. Rather, it is based on the schooling in society in which the Chicago twin lives. This does not mean that the !Kung twin is less intelligent than his Chicago twin. Similarly, the Chicago twin would do poorly on a test developed from the experience of !Kung culture, because the !Kung test would emphasize skills such as building shelter, finding water, and other activities that are not important for survival in Chicago. In this case, the !Kung test would not adequately measure the ability of the Chicago twin.

Studies done by psychologist Sandra Scarr show that evidence for a genetic basis for racial differences in IQ is far from clear. She looked at the IQ scores of African-American children who were born into working-class families but were adopted and reared by white middle-class families. The IQ scores of these children were close to the national average and were almost 10 to 20 points higher than would have been expected had they remained in their birth homes.

Change in children's environments seems to be a critical factor in enhancing their ability to perform on the IQ tests, as seen in the research done by Scarr. Bronfenbrenner found similar results. He examined a dozen studies that looked at early intervention in children's lives; he found that whenever it was possible to change the environment positively, children's scores on IQ tests increased.

Context

The notion of inherited differences is an ancient one; however, the concept of racial classifications is more recent. According to psychologist Wade Nobles, the Western idea of race emerged during the sixteenth century as Europeans began to colonize other parts of the world. As they came into contact with people who looked different from them, many Europeans developed the notion that some races were superior to others. This belief often was given as a justification for slavery and other oppressive activities.

Charles Darwin's theory of evolution was critical in promoting the belief that human differences were a result of heredity and genetics. His notion of "the survival of the fittest" led psychologists to research racial differences in intelligence in order to understand the successes and failures of different human groups. Francis Galton, Darwin's cousin, was instrumental in furthering the hereditarian perspective in psychology. In his book *Hereditary Genius: An Inquiry into Its Laws and Consequences* (1869), he attempted to illustrate that genius and prominence follow family lines. He also began the eugenics movement, which supported the use of selective mating and forced sterilization to improve racial stock.

Following Galton's lead, many psychologists embraced the notions of inherited racial differences in intelligence. G. Stanley Hall, the founder of the American Psychological Association, believed that African people were at a lower evolutionary stage than Caucasians. By the beginning of the 1900's, psychological testing was widely being used to support the view that intelligence was hereditary and was little influenced by the environment. More recently, Burt, R. J. Herrnstein, and Jensen have argued in favor of an overriding genetic factor in intelligence.

There were also early efforts to challenge the hereditarian perspective in psychology. During the 1920's and 1930's, Herman Canady and Howard Long, two of the first African Americans to receive graduate degrees in psychology, produced evidence showing the importance of environmental influences on IQ test performance. They were concerned about the increasing scientific justifications for the inequality and injustice experienced by African Americans, Native Americans, and other groups. Fighting racism was a major reason Leon Kamin became involved in the debate about race and intelligence. He gathered the original information that had been reported by scientists and reexamined it; Kamin was responsible for discovering that Burt had reported false information. He also noted that many hereditarians misused and misinterpreted their statistics.

Hereditarians maintain that racial differences in IQ test scores are primarily caused by genetics and that these scores do reflect differences in intelligence; environmentalists say no. It has not been proved definitively that IQ tests measure intelligence; however, the evidence does suggest that performance on IQ tests is determined by the interaction between genetic and environmental influences. The quality of the environment will determine how well people will reach their potential. In a society where the history of certain groups includes oppression, discrimination, and exclusion from opportunity, it is difficult to explain differences in achievement as being primarily inherited. Instead, it would seem to be a more important goal to eliminate injustices and to change the conditions of life so that all people could do well.

Bibliography

Fancher, Raymond E. *The Intelligence Men: Makers of the IQ Controversy*. New York: W. W. Norton, 1985. Examines the historical contexts of the IQ controversy. The life experiences of the major hereditarians and environmentalists and how these experiences influenced their perspectives are emphasized. This book is easy to read and does an excellent job of making complex statistics understandable.

Fraser, Steven, ed. *The Bell Curve Wars: Race, Intelligence, and the Future of America*. New York: Basic Books, 1995.

Goldsby, Richard. *Race and Races*. New York: Macmillan, 1971. Provides straightforward and accurate information about issues of race, racial differences, and racism. There is a balanced discussion of both the hereditarian and environmentalist perspectives of the IQ controversy. Enjoyable and easy to read for high school and college students alike.

Guthrie, Robert V. *Even the Rat Was White*. New York: Harper & Row, 1976. Provides an excellent historical view of how psychology has dealt with race as an issue. The first section of the book focuses on methods of study, early psychological testing, and the development of racism in the profession of psychology.

Herrnstein, Richard J., and Charles Murray. *The Bell Curve: Intelligence and Class Struc-*

ture in American Life. New York: Free Press, 1994.

Jensen, Arthur R. *Bias in Mental Testing.* New York: Free Press, 1980. An attempt to deal comprehensively with the issues of IQ testing and bias. Jensen challenges the criticisms against IQ tests and offers research to support his view that group differences in IQ test scores are not attributable to bias.

Kamin, Leon J. *The Science and Politics of IQ.* New York: Halstead Press, 1974. Discusses the political nature of the role psychologists have played in support of IQ testing. The role of psychologists in the eugenics movement and in education is discussed. Includes strong critiques of the work done by Burt and Jensen.

Montagu, Ashley, ed. *Race and IQ.* New York: Oxford University Press, 1975. Written to challenge the interpretations offered by the hereditarians. Most of the articles were previously published in professional journals or popular magazines. Some of the chapters contain very technical material; however, the authors generally do an effective job translating this into more understandable language.

Seligman, Daniel. *A Question of Intelligence: The IQ Debate in America.* New York: Carol Publishing Group, 1994.

Derise E. Tolliver

See also:

Creativity and Intelligence, 176; Intelligence: Definition and Theoretical Models, 321; Intelligence: Giftedness and Retardation, 327; Intelligence Tests, 333.

Radical Behaviorism
B. F. Skinner

Type of psychology: Personality
Fields of study: Behavioral and cognitive models; instrumental conditioning

Radical behaviorism describes the views of B. F. Skinner, an influential figure in American psychology since the 1930's. Skinner argued that most behavior is controlled by its consequences; he invented an apparatus for observing the effects of consequences, advocated a technology of behavior control, and believed that everyday views about the causes of behavior were an obstacle to a true understanding of it.

Principal terms

CONTINGENCY OF REINFORCEMENT: the dependent relationship between a response and a reinforcer
DISCRIMINATIVE STIMULUS: any stimulus in the presence of which a response is reinforced
EXPERIMENTAL ANALYSIS OF BEHAVIOR: a demonstration of the causes of behavior by controlling the behavior of an individual organism
MENTALISM: the view that an organism's actions are caused by ideas or feelings that arise in the mind
OPERANT: a class of responses defined by their common effect
PRIVATE EVENTS: events to which only the individual has access; for example, the pain of a toothache
RULE-GOVERNED BEHAVIOR: behavior under the discriminative control of formulized contingencies
SHAPING: the inducing of a response by reinforcing successive approximations

Overview

According to B. F. Skinner (1904-1990), the behavior of an organism is a product of current and past environmental consequences and genetic endowment. Since little can be done, at least by psychology, about genetic endowment, Skinner focused on those things that could be changed or controlled: the immediate consequences of behavior. By consequences, Skinner meant the results or effects that a particular behavior (a class of responses, or "operant") produce. There are many ways to open a door, for example, but since each one allows a person to walk to the next room, one would speak of a "door-opening" operant. The consequences not only define the class of responses but also determine how often members of the class are likely to occur in the future. This was termed the law of effect by early twentieth century American psychologist Edward L. Thorndike, whose work Skinner refined.

There are several kinds of consequences, or effects. Events that follow behavior and produce an increase in the rate or frequency of the behavior are termed reinforcers. In ordinary language, they might be called rewards, but Skinner avoided this expression because he defined reinforcing events in terms of the effects they produced (an increased rate) rather than the alleged feelings they induced (for example, pleasure). To attribute the increase in rate of response produced by reinforcement to feelings of pleasure would be regarded by Skinner as an instance of mentalism—the attribution of behavior to a feeling rather than an event occurring in the environment. Other consequences which follow a behavior produce a decrease in the rate of behavior. These are termed punishers. Skinner strongly objected to the use of punishment as a means to control behavior because it elicited aggression and produced dysfunctional emotional responses such as striking back and crying in a small child. Notice that consequences (reinforcers and punishers) may be presented following a behavior (twenty dollars for building a doghouse, for example, or an electric shock for touching an exposed wire) or taken away (a fine for speeding, the ending of a headache by the taking of an aspirin). Consequences may be natural (tomatoes to eat after a season of careful planting and watering) or contrived (receiving a dollar for earning an A on a test).

Reinforcing and punishing consequences are one example of controlling variables. Events that precede behaviors are also controlling variables and determine under what circumstances certain behaviors are likely to appear. Events occurring before a response occurs are called discriminative stimuli because they come to discriminate in favor of a particular piece of behavior. They set the occasion for the behavior and make it more likely to occur. For example, persons trying to control their eating are told to keep away from the kitchen except at meal times. Being in the kitchen makes it more likely that the person will eat something, not simply because that is where the food is kept but also because being in the kitchen is one of the events which has preceded previous eating and therefore makes eating more likely to occur. This is true even when the person does not intend to eat but goes to the kitchen for other reasons. Being in the kitchen raises the probability of eating. It is a discriminative stimulus for eating, as are the table, the refrigerator, or a candy bar on the counter. Any event or stimulus which occurs immediately before a response is reinforced gets reinforced with the response and makes the response more likely to occur again if the discriminative stimulus occurs again. The discriminative stimulus comes to gain some control over the behavior.

Discriminative stimuli and reinforcing stimuli are the controlling variables Skinner used to analyze behavior. These events constitute a chain of behavior called a contingency of reinforcement. It is a contingency because reinforcement does not occur unless the response is made in the presence of the discriminative stimuli. Contingencies of reinforcement are encountered every day. For example, a soda drink is purchased from a machine. The machine is brightly colored to act as a discriminative stimulus for dropping coins in a slot, which in turn yields a can or bottle of soft drink. The machine comes to control a small portion of a person's behavior. If the machine malfunctions, a person may push the selector button several times repeatedly, perhaps even putting in more coins, and still later, strike the machine. By carefully scheduling how many times an organism must respond before reinforcement occurs, the rate of response can be controlled as is done in slot or video machines, or gambling devices in general. Responses are made several hundred or thousand times for very little reinforcement—a near win or a small payoff. Schedules of reinforcement are another important set of controlling variables which Skinner explored.

Contingencies are relationships among controlling variables. Some of the relationships become abstracted and formulized, that is, put in the form of rules. When behavior is under the control of a rule, it is termed rule-governed behavior, as opposed to contingency-shaped behavior. As a person first learns any skill, much of his or her behavior is rule governed, either through written instructions or by the person's repeating the rule to him- or herself. For example, a novice golfer might review the rules for a good swing, even repeating them aloud. Eventually, though, swing becomes automatic; it seems to become "natural." The verbal discriminative stimuli have shifted to the very subtle and covert stimuli associated with swing without the golfer's thinking about it, and the natural consequences of a successful swing take over.

Skinner analyzed behavior by examining the antecedents and consequences which control any specific class of responses in the individual organism. From this view, he elaborated a psychology that encompassed all aspects of animal and human behavior, including language. By the late 1970's, historians of psychology ranked Skinner's work as the second most significant development in psychology since World War II; the general growth of the field was ranked first. Three journals arose to publish work in the Skinnerian tradition: *Journal of the Experimental Analysis of Behavior, Journal of Applied Behavior Analysis,* and *Behaviorism.* Moreover, an international organization, the Association for Behavior Analysis, was formed, with its own journal.

Applications

The operant chamber is a small experimental space or cage that Skinner invented to observe the effects that consequences have on behavior. A food-deprived organism (Skinner first used rats and later switched to pigeons) is placed in the chamber containing a lever that, when depressed, releases a small piece of food into a cup from which the organism eats. The first bar-press response is produced through the process of shaping, or reinforcing approximations to bar pressing (for example, being near the bar, having a paw above the bar, resting a paw on the bar, nearly depressing the bar) until bar pressing is regularly occurring. Once the operant of bar pressing is established, an experimental analysis of the variables which influence it can be done. The schedule of reinforcement can be changed, for example, from one reinforcer for each response to five responses required for each reinforcer. Changes in the rate of response can be observed on a device Skinner invented, a cumulative record, which automatically displays the rate at which the operant is occurring. A discriminative stimulus can be introduced in the form of a small light mounted on the wall of the chamber. If bar presses are reinforced only when the light is turned on, the light will come to have some control over the operant. Turning the light on and off will literally turn bar pressing on and off in a food-deprived rat.

Skinner controlled his own behavior in the same fashion that he had learned to control the behavior of laboratory organisms. He arranged a "writing environment," a desk used only for that purpose; wrote at a set time each day; and would keep careful records of time spent writing. Other examples of self-management may be found in Skinner's book *Walden Two* (1948). In this fictionalized account, children learn self-control through a set of exercises that teach ways to tolerate increasing delays of reinforcement.

Skinner also performed a behavior analysis of language (see his *Verbal Behavior,* 1957). For example, a behavioral analysis of the word "want," "believe," or "love," an operational definition in Skinner's sense, would be all those circumstances and situations which control the use of the word, that is, the discriminative stimuli for the verbal response. Skinner tried to show in *Verbal Behavior* that speaking and writing could be explained with the same principle he had used to explain animal behavior. Many of Skinner's works, and much of his private notebooks, are taken up with the recording of how words are used. His purpose was to de-mentalize them, to show that what controls their use is some aspect of the environment, or some behavioral practice on the part of the verbal community, rather than some internal or mental event. The earliest uses of the word "to know," for example, referred to action, something the individual could do, rather than something he or she possessed or had stored inside the mind.

Context

So much has been written about Skinner, some of it misleading or false, that it is important to clarify what he did not do. He did not rear either of his daughters in a "Skinner box." His youngest daughter was reared during her infancy with the aid of an "aircrib," a special enclosed crib Skinner built that allowed control of air temperature and humidity, and in which the infant could sleep and play without the burden of clothes. "Aircribs" were later available commercially. Skinner did not limit his analysis of behavior only to publicly observable events, as did the methodological behaviorists. Part of what made Skinner's behaviorism radical was his insistence that a science of behavior should be able to account for those private events to which only the individual has access. He described how the community teaches its members to describe covert events such as toothaches and headaches. He did not regard such events as anything other than behavior. That is, he did not give them a special status by calling them "mental events."

Skinner did not argue that reinforcement explains everything. He allowed, especially in his later works, that genetic endowment plays a role in the determination of behavior, as do rules and antecedent events. He did not reject physiological explanations of behavior, when actual physiology was involved. He did object to the use of physiological terms in psychological accounts, unless the physiological mechanisms were known. For Skinner, physiology was one subject matter, and behavior was another. Finally, he did not ignore complex behavior. Many of his works, particularly *Verbal Behavior* and *The Technology of Teaching* (1968), offered behaviorist analyses of what in other psychologies would be termed cognitive phenomena, such as talking, reading, thinking, problem solving, and remembering.

Skinner made many contributions to twentieth century psychology. Among them was his invention of the operant chamber and its associated methodology. Operant equipment and procedures are employed by animal and human experimental psychologists in laboratories around the world. Most of these psychologists do not adhere to Skinner's radical behaviorism, or to all the features of his science of behavior. They have, however, found the techniques that he developed to be productive in exploring a wide variety of problems, ranging from the fields of psychopharmacology to learning in children and adults to experimental economics. Skinner and his followers developed a technology of behavior that included techniques for working with the developmentally disabled, children in elementary classrooms, and persons with rehabilitation or health care problems; they also considered approaches to public safety, employee motivation and production, and any other field which involved the management of behavior. Although the technology developments never reached the vision described in *Walden Two*, the efforts are ongoing.

Skinner may have exhausted the law of effect. The idea that consequences influence behavior can be found in many forms in the literature of psychology and philosophy, especially since the middle of the nineteenth century, but it is only in the work of B. F. Skinner that one sees how much of human and animal behavior can be brought within its purview. Because Skinner took behavior as his subject matter, he greatly expanded what could be regarded as of interest to psychologists. Behavior was everywhere, in the classroom, at the office, in the factory. Nearly any aspect of human activity could become the legitimate object of study by a Skinnerian psychologist, a point well illustrated in Skinner's description of a utopian community which takes an experimental attitude toward its cultural practices and designs a culture based on a science of behavior (*Walden Two*). Finally, Skinner conceptualized an epistemology, a way of understanding what it means for humans to know something, that may be a lasting contribution to twentieth century philosophy.

In placing the radical behaviorism of B. F. Skinner in historical context, two nineteenth century doctrines are often called on. One view, shared by Skinner, is that operant psychology represents an extension of the principle of natural selection which Charles Darwin described at the level of the species. Natural selection explained the origin of species; contingencies of reinforcement and punishment explain the origin of classes of responses. The environment selects in both cases. In operant psychology, the role of the environment is to reinforce differentially and thereby select from among a pool of responses which the organism is making. The final effect is some one particular operant which has survival or adaptive value for the individual organism. Skinner has suggested that cultural evolution occurs in a similar fashion.

It is also observed that Skinner's psychology resembles nineteenth century pragmatism. The pragmatists held that beliefs are formed by their outcome, or practical effect. To explain why someone does something by reference to a belief would be regarded as mentalism by Skinner; he would substitute behavior for beliefs. Yet he comes to the same doctrine: one in which environmental consequences act in a Darwinian fashion. Finally, Skinner's philosophy shows the influence of the nineteenth century positivism of physicist Ernst Mach. Skinner desired a description of behavior and its causes, while avoiding mental states or other cognitive or personality entities that intervene between behavior and the environment.

Bibliography

Modgil, Sohan, and Celia Modgil, eds. *B.F. Skinner: Consensus and Controversy*. New York: Falmer Press, 1987. A collection of essays by psychologists and philosophers. Each topic has a pro and contrary opinion, with replies and rebuttals. Although written at a professional level, this is an excellent volume for a global view of Skinner's ideas and for the clearest understanding of what is "radical" about Skinner's behaviorism.

Nye, Robert D. *What Is B. F. Skinner Really Saying?* Englewood Cliffs, N.J.: Prentice-Hall, 1979. The best introductory-level secondary account of Skinner's psychology and philosophy.

Reynolds, George Stanley. *A Primer of Operant Conditioning*. Rev. ed. Glenview, Ill.: Scott, Foresman, 1975. This introductory-level book describes the basic processes and methods of operant psychology, explaining shaping, reinforcers and punishers, discrimination, and schedules of reinforcement.

Richelle, Marc N. *B. F. Skinner: A Reappraisal*. Hillsdale, N.J.: Lawrence Erlbaum, 1993.

Skinner, B. F. *About Behaviorism*. New York: Alfred A. Knopf, 1974. In this work, Skinner argues for his radical behaviorism by contrasting it with methodological behaviorism and by illustrating how it treats topics such as perception, memory, verbal behavior, private events, and thinking.

_____. *Particulars of My Life*. New York: Alfred A. Knopf, 1976.

_____. *The Shaping of a Behaviorist*. New York: Alfred A. Knopf, 1979.

_____. *A Matter of Consequences*. New York: Alfred A. Knopf, 1983. Skinner published his autobiography in these three separate volumes. The first describes his life from birth, through his college years as an English major, to his entering Harvard University for graduate study in psychology. *The Shaping of a Behaviorist* presents his years at Harvard and his rise to national prominence. *A Matter of Consequences* begins with his return to Harvard as a professor in the late 1940's.

_____. *Science and Human Behavior*. New York: Macmillan, 1953. A fine introduction to Skinner's thought. The principles of operant psychology are described, with numerous examples of the applicability to an individual's life and the major institutions of society. The chapter on private events illustrates one important way in which Skinner's radical behaviorism differs from methodological behaviorism.

_____. *Walden Two*. New York: Macmillan, 1948. A description of a fictional community based upon experimental practices and behavioral principles. The book was the source of inspiration for several communes and illustrates how all aspects of culture can be submitted to a behavioral analysis. Contains a lengthy criticism of democracy as a form of government.

Staats, Arthur W. *Behavior and Personality: Psychological Behaviorism*. New York: Springer Publishing, 1996.

Todd, James T., and Edward K. Morris, eds. *Modern Perspectives on B. F. Skinner and Contemporary Behaviorism*. Foreword by Ernest R. Hilgard. Westport, Conn.: Greenwood Press, 1995.

Vargas, Julie S. "B. F. Skinner, Father, Grandfather, Behavior Modifier." In *About Human Nature: Journeys in Psychological Thought,* edited by Terry J. Knapp and Charles T. Rasmussen. Dubuque, Iowa: Kendall/Hunt, 1987. An intimate description of Skinner by his eldest daughter, who is herself a psychologist. Skinner's home, study, and the activities occurring over a Thanksgiving weekend are described.

Terry J. Knapp

See also:

REFLEXES

Type of psychology: Biological bases of behavior
Field of study: Nervous system

A reflex is one of the most basic types of behavior that can be elicited; over the years, psychologists and physiologists have studied the behavioral and biological processes associated with reflex production in the hope of understanding principles and processes involved in generating both simple behaviors and a variety of more complex behaviors such as learning, memory, and voluntary movement.

Principal terms

CLASSICAL (PAVLOVIAN) CONDITIONING: a simple conditioning procedure, used to study behavioral and biological processes involved in learning, that generally involves pairing two stimuli in time—a neutral stimulus followed by a stimulus that reliably elicits a reflexive response

INFANTILE REFLEXES: a set of innate reflexes that are present for the first few months of life; they disappear as the central nervous system matures

MONOSYNAPTIC REFLEX: a reflex system that consists of only one synapse, the synapse between the sensory input and motor output

POLYSYNAPTIC REFLEX: a reflex system that consists of more than one synapse; these systems typically contain three elements—a sensory element, a motor element, and a central processing element

REFLEX: a highly stereotyped, unlearned response that is elicited by an external stimulus

SPINAL REFLEX: a set of simple reflexes that can be elicited by providing appropriate input to the spinal cord; these reflexes can be generated in the spinal cord even after it has been surgically isolated from the rest of the nervous system

Overview

The reflex is undoubtedly the simplest form of behavior that has been studied widely by psychologists and neuroscientists. Reflexes involve two separate yet highly related events: the occurrence of an eliciting stimulus and the production of a specific response. Most organisms are capable of displaying a variety of complex behaviors; however, because these behaviors are complex, it has been very difficult, if not impossible, to understand biological or psychological processes involved in generating or modifying the variety of complex behaviors that most organisms can display. In attempts to study these complex behaviors, a number of researchers have adopted a strategy of studying simpler behaviors, such as reflexes, that are thought to make up, contribute to, or serve as a model of the more complex behavior.

A number of reflexes can be generated in the mammalian spinal cord even after it has been surgically isolated from the brain. The stretch reflex is an example of a spinal reflex. When a muscle is stretched, such as when a tendon is tapped or when an attempt is made to reach for an object, sensory "detectors" or receptors within the muscle are activated to signal the muscle stretch. These receptors are at the end of very long nerve fibers that travel from the muscle receptor to the spinal cord, where they activate spinal motor neurons. The motor neurons control the same muscle on which the stretch receptor that initiated the stretch signal is located. When activated, the spinal motor neurons signal the muscle, causing it to contract. In this manner, when a muscle stretch is detected, the stretch reflex ensures that a contraction is generated in the muscle to counteract and balance the stretch. This type of reflex is referred to as a "monosynaptic reflex" because it involves only one synapse; the synapse between the sensory receptor neuron and the motor neuron (where a synapse is the junction between two neurons).

Another example of a spinal reflex is the flexion or withdrawal reflex. Anyone who has accidentally touched a hot stove has encountered this reflex. Touching a hot stove or applying any aversive stimulus to the skin activates pain receptors in the skin. These receptors are at the end of long sensory fibers that project to neurons in the spinal cord. The spinal neurons that receive input from the sensory fibers are not motor neurons, as in the stretch reflex, but rather very small neurons called spinal interneurons. The interneurons make synaptic contact on other interneurons as well as on motor neurons that innervate flexor muscles. When activated, the flexor muscles typically cause limb withdrawal. The flexor reflex ensures that a relatively rapid withdrawal of one's hand from a hot stove will occur if it is accidentally touched. The flexor reflex is an example of a "polysynaptic reflex" because there are two or more synapses involved in the reflex (the presence of at least one synapse between a sensory neuron and an interneuron and a second synapse between the interneuron and a motor neuron).

One functional difference between monosynaptic and polysynaptic reflexes is the amount of information processing that can take place in the two reflex systems. The monosynaptic reflex is somewhat limited, because information flow involves only the synapse between the sensory and motor neurons. This type of reflex is ideal for quick adjustments that must be made in muscle tension. Conversely, polysynaptic reflexes typically involve a number of levels of interneurons. Hence, convergence and divergence of information can occur as information flows from sensory to motor elements. In essence, the polysynaptic system, in addition to having afferent and efferent components, has a "processor" of sorts between the sensory and motor elements. In intact organisms, the integration that takes place within the processor allows information to be shared by other regions of the nervous system. For example, some of the interneurons send information upward to the brain. When a hot stove is touched, the brain is informed. This sensory experience is likely to be evaluated and stored by the brain, therefore making it less likely that the hot stove will be touched a second time.

Reflexes are not limited to the spinal cord. Responses involving the musculature of the face and neck can also be reflexive in nature. For example, a puff of air that strikes the cornea of the human eye elicits a brisk, short-latency eyelid closure. Like the polysynaptic spinal reflexes, this eyeblink reflex appears to involve three elements: a sensory nerve, called the trigeminal nerve, that carries information from receptors in the cornea of the eye to the trigeminal nucleus (a cranial nerve nucleus); interneurons that connect the trigeminal nucleus with several other brain-stem neurons; and a motor nerve that originates from brain-stem motor neurons and contracts the muscles surrounding the eye to produce the eyeblink. This reflex is defensive in nature because it ensures that the eyeball is protected from further stimulation if a stimulus strikes the cornea. Not all reflexes involve activation of skeletal muscles. For example, control of the urinary bladder involves a spinal reflex that activates smooth muscles. Also, temperature regulation is partially the product of a reflexive response to changes in external or internal environments. Many of these types of reflexes engage the autonomic nervous system, a division of the nervous system that is involved in regulating and maintaining the function of internal organs.

Not all reflexes involve simple, local, short-latency responses. The maintenance of posture when standing upright is a generally automatic, reflexive system that one does not think about. This system includes neurons in the spinal cord and brain stem. The body's equilibrium system (the vestibular or balance system) involves receptors in the middle ear, brain-stem structures, and spinal motor neurons, while locomotion requires the patterned activation of several reflex systems. Finally, a number of behavioral situations require a rapid response that integrates the motor system with one of the special senses (such as quickly applying the car brakes when a road hazard is seen). These are generally referred to as reaction-time situations and require considerable nervous system processing, including the involvement of the cerebral cortex, when engaged. Nevertheless, these responses are considered reflexive in nature because they involve an eliciting stimulus and a well-defined, consistent response.

Applications

During the late nineteenth century and early twentieth century, Sir Charles Sherrington, a British physiologist, conducted an extensive series of studies concerned with spinal reflexes. He showed that a number of skin stimulations, such as pinching or brushing, produced simple responses even when a spinal transection separated the spinal cord from the rest of the nervous system. From these experiments, he argued that the basic unit of movement was the reflex, which he defined as a highly stereotyped, unlearned response to external stimuli. This work created a flurry of activity among physiologists and psychologists, who tried to trace reflexes throughout the nervous system and assemble them into more complex behaviors.

Reflexes have also been widely studied by psychologists and biologists interested in learning and memory. Russian physiologists Ivan Sechenov and Ivan Pavlov have generally been credited with the first attempts to study systematically how reflexes could be used to examine relationships between behavior and physiology. Pavlov in particular had a huge influence on the study of behavior. Most students are familiar with the story of Pavlov and his successful demonstration of conditioned salivation in dogs produced by pairing a bell with meat powder. Over the years, the Pavlovian conditioning procedure (also known as classical conditioning) has often been used to study the behavioral principles and neural substrates of learning. The conditioning of a variety of reflexes has been observed, including skeletal muscle responses such as forelimb flexion, hindlimb flexion, and eyelid closure, as well as autonomic responses such as respiration, heart rate, and sweat gland activity.

One of the most widely studied classical conditioning procedures is classical eyelid conditioning. This reflex conditioning procedure has been studied in a variety of species, including rabbits, rats, cats, dogs, and humans. Mostly because of the research efforts of Isadore Gormezano and her colleagues, which began in the early 1960's, much is known about behavioral aspects of classical eyelid conditioning in rabbits. In this paradigm, a mild electric shock or air puff is presented to elicit reliably a reflexive blink from the rabbit. The blink is typically measured by means of devices that are attached to the nictitating membrane, a third eyelid that is present in a variety of species, including the rabbit. During training sessions, a neutral stimulus such as a tone or light is delivered 0.3 to 1.0 second prior to the air puff. After about one hundred of these tone and air-puff pairings, the rabbit learns to blink when the tone or light is presented (the rabbit begins to use the tone to signal the impending air-puff presentation). This preparation has yielded a wealth of data concerning the parameters of behavioral training that produce the fastest or slowest learning rates (such as stimuli intensities, time between stimuli, and number of trials per day). Furthermore, this simple reflexive learning situation has been used to study how the brain codes simple forms of learning and memory. A number of researchers (most notably, Richard F. Thompson) have studied the activity of a variety of brain structures during learning and performance of the classically conditioned eyelid response. These studies have shown that discrete brain regions such as the cerebellum and hippocampus alter their activity to generate or modify the conditioned response. In brief, these researchers have used the conditioning of a very simple reflex to advance the understanding of how the brain might code more complex learning and memory processes.

The study of reflexes has not been limited to learning and memory. Developmental psychologists have studied a variety of innate reflexes that are generated by newborn infants. Sucking is a very prominent reflex that is readily observed in newborns. Also related to feeding is the "rooting reflex," which can be elicited when the cheek of an infant is stroked softly. The skin stimulation causes the infant to open his or her mouth and turn toward the point of stimulation. This reflex has obvious applications in helping the infant locate food. The infant's ability to hold on to objects is, in part, attributable to the presence of the "grasp reflex." When an object touches the palm of a newborn's hand, the newborn's fist will close immediately around the object, thus allowing the infant to hold the object for a short period of time. The infantile reflexes disappear within a few months after birth and are replaced by voluntary responses. Most developmental researchers believe that the infantile reflexes are temporary substitutes for the voluntary responses. Apparently, the voluntary responses are not present during the first few months of life because various parts of the infant nervous system, including the cerebral cortex, have not matured sufficiently to support the behavior. Therefore, the disappearance of the infantile reflexes serves as an important marker of neural and behavioral development.

Context

The study of reflexes has played a prominent role in shaping the field of psychology. Early in the twentieth century, many psychologists and physiologists, among them Sherrington and Pavlov, adopted the reflex as the basic unit of behavior to study, in part because of the relative simplicity of the behavior and in part because of the ease with which the behavior could be reliably elicited by applying external stimuli. Based on his research, Sherrington believed that complex behaviors were produced by chaining together simple reflexes in some temporal order. This basic idea provided the framework for much of the physiological and behavioral work completed early in the twentieth century. Sechenov and Pavlov also believed that the concept of the reflex could explain more complex behaviors. Pavlov, for example, showed that not all reflexes were innate; rather, new reflexes could be established by associating a "neutral" stimulus (a stimulus that did not initially produce a reflex) with a stimulus that reliably elicited a reflex. As a result of this demonstration, Pavlov proposed an elaborate theory of reflex learning that involved forming associations between stimuli in the cerebral cortex.

In the latter half of the twentieth century, many psychologists interested in studying overt behavior and physiologists interested in studying nervous system function adopted the study of reflexes as a means of simplifying behavior or nervous system activity. Psychologists such as Gormezano, Robert Rescorla, and Allan Wagner, who have studied classical conditioning phenomena, hope to develop a comprehensive understanding of the learning process that occurs when simple paradigms such as classical conditioning are used. Behavioral neuroscientists and neurobiologists (such as Thompson and Eric Kandel) who study nervous system function have used reflexes as the basic unit of behavior in hope of catching a glimpse of nervous system function when a fairly simple behavioral response is being generated and modified by learning experiences. In both cases, a major reason for using the reflex as the unit of behavior is to simplify the experimental situation. Indeed, researchers are not likely to understand complex behavioral processes without first understanding how simpler behaviors and nervous system functions are generated, modified, and maintained. The study of reflexes, from both a behavioral and biological standpoint, has provided and should continue to provide a valuable approach for understanding human behavior as well as understanding how the nervous system generates activity to produce the behavior.

Bibliography

Domjan, Michael, and Barbara Burkhard. *The Principles of Learning and Behavior.* 2d ed. Monterey, Calif.: Brooks/Cole, 1986. This text is widely used by students interested in learning and behavior. The sections on the history of the reflex and its use in the learning research field is particularly applicable to the present discussion.

Fancher, Raymond E. *Pioneers of Psychology.* New York: W. W. Norton, 1979. This book provides biographies of several prominent psychologists who have had an impact on the field. Included is a chapter detailing the experiments and theories of Ivan Pavlov. Valuable for understanding how the study of the reflex fits into the history of psychology.

Gleitman, Henry. *Psychology.* 2d ed. New York: W. W. Norton, 1981. This text provides broad coverage of the field of psychology. The chapters on development, learning, and memory should provide the reader with additional information concerning reflexes and other simple behaviors.

Rosenzweig, Mark R., and Arnold L. Leiman. *Physiological Psychology.* 2d ed. New York: Random House, 1989. This textbook is filled with information concerning a variety of topics within the field of physiological psychology. The sections on motor systems are particularly useful in understanding how reflexes are generated and executed at the neural and muscular level.

Thompson, Richard F. *The Brain: An Introduction to Neuroscience.* New York: W. H. Freeman, 1985. Thompson's book was written to be accessible to individuals who have no background in science. Includes information about spinal reflexes and the neural substrates of learning and memory.

Joseph E. Steinmetz

See also:

The Autonomic Nervous System, 88; The Central and Peripheral Nervous Systems, 115; The Cerebral Cortex, 121; The Endocrine System, 248; Motor Development, 410.

SCHIZOPHRENIA
Background, Types, and Symptoms

Type of psychology: Psychopathology
Field of study: Schizophrenias

Schizophrenia is a severe mental illness that interferes with the patient's ability to think and communicate. Researchers have studied the illness for decades, but the causes are still unknown.

Principal terms

ANTIPSYCHOTIC DRUGS: medications, including a group called the phenothiazines, that reduce psychotic symptoms
ETIOLOGY: the study of the causes of disease
PROGNOSIS: the expected course and outcome of a disorder
PSYCHOTIC SYMPTOMS: symptoms of major mental disorder that involve a loss of contact with reality, such as delusions or hallucinations
SOMATIC TREATMENTS: physical treatments of the body, including drugs and surgery

Overview

Schizophrenia affects approximately one out of every hundred individuals. It is considered to be one of the most severe mental illnesses, because its symptoms can have a devastating impact on the life of the patient. The patient's thought processes, communication abilities, and emotional expressions are disturbed. As a result, many patients with schizophrenia are dependent on others for assistance with daily life activities.

Schizophrenia is often confused, by the layperson, with multiple personality disorder. The latter is an illness which is defined as two or more distinct personalities existing within the person. The personalities tend to be intact, and each is associated with its own style of perceiving the world and relating to others. Schizophrenia, in contrast, does not involve the existence of two or more personalities; rather, it is the presence of psychotic symptoms that defines schizophrenia.

The diagnostic criteria for schizophrenia have changed over the years; however, certain key symptoms, including disturbances in thought, perception, and emotional experiences, have remained as defining features. The most widely used criteria for diagnosing schizophrenia are those listed in the *Diagnostic and Statistical Manual of Mental Disorders* (rev. 3d ed., 1987, DSM-III-R). This manual is published by the American Psychiatric Association and is periodically revised to incorporate changes in diagnostic criteria.

The DSM-III-R contains the following symptoms for diagnosing schizophrenia: delusions, hallucinations, flat or inappropriate affect, and incoherence or loosening of associations. No single specific symptom is required for a person to receive a diagnosis of schizophrenia. Further, each of the above symptoms can take a variety of forms. Delusions are defined as false beliefs based on incorrect inference about external reality. Delusions are classified based on the nature of their content. For example, grandiose delusions involve false beliefs about one's importance, power, or knowledge. The patient might express the belief that he or she is the most intelligent person in the world but that these special intellectual powers have gone unrecognized. As another example, persecutory delusions involve beliefs of being persecuted or conspired against by others. The patient might claim, for example, that there is a government plot to poison him or her.

Hallucinations are sensory experiences that occur in the absence of a real stimulus. In the case of auditory hallucinations, the patient may hear voices calling or conversing when there is no one in physical proximity. Visual hallucinations may involve seeing people who are deceased or seeing inanimate objects move on their own accord.

The term "affect" is used to refer to observable behaviors that are the expression of an emotion. Affect is predominantly displayed in facial expressions. When affect is inappropriate, facial expressions are not consistent with the content of a patient's speech or thoughts. For example, the patient might laugh when discussing the death of a loved one. "Flat" affect describes a severe reduction in the intensity of emotional expressions, both positive and negative. Patients with flat affect may show no observable sign of emotion, even when experiencing a very joyful or sad event.

Among the symptoms of schizophrenia, abnormalities in the expression of thoughts are a central feature. When speech is incoherent, it is difficult for the listener to comprehend because it is illogical or incomplete. As an example, in response to the question "Where do you live?" one patient replied, "Yes, live! I haven't had much time in this or that. It is an area. In the same area. Mrs. Smith! If the time comes for a temporary space now or whatever." The term "loose associations" is applied to speech in which ideas shift from one subject to another subject that is completely unrelated. If the loosening of associations is severe, speech may be incoherent. As an illustration of loose associations, in describing her daily schedule at home, one patient said, "It starts out pretty easy, but things always become more complicated. I discussed this with my son, but he doesn't understand. Of course, he is an accountant, and his wife recently had a baby. I thought I would enjoy being a grandmother, but now I'm not sure."

With regard to speech, a variety of other abnormalities are sometimes shown by patients. They may use "neologisms," which are new words invented by the patient to convey a special meaning. Some show "clang associations," which involve the use of rhyming words in conversation: "Live and let live, that's my motto. You live and give and live-give." Abnormalities in the intonation and pace of speech are also common.

In addition to these symptoms, some patients manifest bizarre behaviors, such as odd, repetitive movements or unusual postures. Odd or inappropriate styles of dressing, such as wearing winter coats in the summer, may also occur in some patients. More deteriorated patients frequently show poor hygiene. In order to meet the diagnostic criteria for schizophrenia, the individual must show signs of disturbance for at least six months. Further, the presence of other disorders, such as drug reactions or organic brain disorders associated with aging, must be ruled out. Thus, the diagnosis of schizophrenia typically involves a thorough physical and mental assessment.

Applications

Because no one symptom is necessary for a diagnosis of schizophrenia, patients vary in the numbers and intensity of their symptoms. Four subtypes of schizophrenia are recognized;

the differentiation among them is based upon the symptom profile, and the criteria are clearly described in DSM-III-R.

Catatonic schizophrenia is predominantly characterized by abnormal motor behavior. The patient may be in a "catatonic stupor," which means that he or she shows a marked reduction in movement and is sometimes mute. Other catatonic schizophrenic patients adopt a rigid posture (catatonic rigidity), which they will maintain despite efforts to move them. In disorganized schizophrenia, the primary symptoms are incoherence, loose associations, and flat or inappropriate affect. In paranoid schizophrenia, the predominant symptom is a preoccupation with a systematized delusion, in the absence of incoherence, loose associations, or abnormal affect. The label undifferentiated schizophrenia is applied to cases that do not meet the specific criteria for catatonic, disorganized, or paranoid schizophrenia, but do show prominent delusions, hallucinations, incoherence, or disorganized behavior.

In his writings, Eugen Bleuler often used the phrase "the group of schizophrenias," because he believed the disorder could be caused by a variety of factors. In other words, he believed that schizophrenia may not be a single disease entity. Today, many researchers and clinicians who work in the field take the same position. They believe that the differences among patients in symptom patterns and the course of the illness are attributable to differences in etiology. Despite the widespread assumption that there are different subtypes of schizophrenia, however, each with its own etiology, there is no definitive evidence to support this. In fact, the four subtypes listed in DSM-III-R show similar courses and receive the same medications and psychotherapeutic treatments. Thus the distinctions among them are purely descriptive at this point.

Because schizophrenic symptoms have such a devastating impact on the individual's ability to function, family members often respond to the onset of symptoms by seeking immediate treatment. Clinicians, in turn, often respond by recommending hospitalization so that tests can be conducted and an appropriate treatment can be determined. Consequently, almost all patients who are diagnosed with schizophrenia are hospitalized at least once in their life. The majority experience several hospitalizations. Typically, the first hospitalization corresponds to the first manifestation of symptoms.

Research on the long-term outcome of schizophrenia indicates that the illness is highly variable in its course. A minority of patients have only one episode of illness, then go into remission and experience no further symptoms. Unfortunately, however, the majority of patients have recurring episodes that require periodic rehospitalizations. The most severely ill never experience remission, but instead show a chronic course of symptomatology. For these reasons, schizophrenia is viewed as having the poorest prognosis of all the major mental illnesses.

Prior to the 1950's, patients with schizophrenia were hospitalized for extended periods of time and frequently became "institutionalized." There were only a few available somatic treatments, and those proved to be of little efficacy. Included among them were insulin coma therapy (the administration of large doses of insulin in order to induce coma), electroconvulsive therapy (the application of electrical current to the temples in order to induce a seizure), and prefrontal lobotomy (a surgical procedure in which the tracts connecting the frontal lobes to other areas of the brain are severed).

In the 1950's, a class of drugs referred to as antipsychotic medications were discovered to be effective in treating schizophrenia. Antipsychotic drugs significantly reduce schizophrenic symptoms in many patients. As a result, the number of hospitalized patients has declined dramatically since the 1950's. Antipsychotic medications have freed many patients from confinement in hospitals and have enhanced their chances for functioning in the community.

Another factor that has contributed to the decline in the number of hospitalized patients with schizophrenia is the nationwide policy of deinstitutionalization. This policy, which has been adopted and promoted by most state governments in the years since 1970, emphasizes short-term hospitalizations, and it has involved the release of some patients who had been in institutions for many years. Unfortunately, the support services that were needed to facilitate the transition from hospital to community living were never put in place. Consequently, the number of homeless schizophrenic patients has increased dramatically. Some of these are patients whose family members have died or have simply lost touch with them. Other patients have withdrawn from contact with their families, despite efforts by concerned relatives to provide assistance. The plight of the homeless mentally ill is of great concern to mental health professionals.

Context

Writing in the late 1800's, an eminent physician named Emil Kraepelin was among the first to document the symptoms and course of this illness, referring to it as "dementia praecox" (dementia of early life). Subsequently, Eugen Bleuler applied the term "schizophrenia," meaning splitting of the mind, to the disorder. Both Kraepelin and Bleuler assumed that organic factors are involved in schizophrenia. Contemporary research, discussed below, has confirmed this assumption; brain scans reveal that a significant proportion of schizophrenia patients do have abnormalities. The precise nature and cause of these abnormalities remain unknown.

In the majority of cases, the onset of schizophrenic symptoms occurs in late adolescence or early adulthood. The major risk period is between twenty and twenty-five years of age. For some patients, there are no readily apparent abnormalities prior to this period. For others, however, the onset of schizophrenia is preceded by impairments in social, academic, or occupational functioning. Some are described by their families as having had adjustment problems in childhood. Childhood schizophrenia is relatively rare. It is estimated to occur in about one out of every ten thousand children. When schizophrenia is diagnosed in childhood, the same diagnostic criteria and treatments are applied. Children who receive the diagnosis are usually placed in special classrooms for the emotionally disturbed.

Schizophrenia shows no clear pattern in terms of its distribution in the population. It occurs in both males and females, although it tends to have a slightly earlier onset in males than in females. The illness strikes individuals of all social, economic, and ethnic backgrounds. Some patients manifest high levels of intelligence and had been excellent students prior to becoming ill; others showed poor academic performance and signs of learning disability.

Schizophrenia is an illness that has been recognized by medicine for more than a hundred years. During this time, only modest progress has been made in research on its etiology. Some significant advances have been achieved in treatment, however, and the prognosis for schizophrenia is better now than ever before. Moreover, there is reason to believe that the availability of new technologies for studying the central nervous system will speed the pace of further discovery.

Bibliography

Bellenir, Karen, ed. *Mental Health Disorders Sourcebook*. Detroit, Mich.: Omnigraphics, 1996.

Bleuler, Eugen. *Dementia Praecox: Or, The Group of Schizophrenias*. Translated by Joseph Zinkin. New York: International Universities Press, 1950. Original German first published in 1911. A classic book in the field, this provides excellent descriptions of the symptoms and very interesting discussions of possible causal factors.

Brunello, N., et al., eds. *Critical Issues in the Treatment of Schizophrenia*. Farmington, Conn.: S. Karger, 1996.

Herz, Marvin I., Samuel J. Keith, and John P. Docherty. *Psychosocial Treatment of Schizophrenia*. New York: Elsevier, 1990. This book, vol. 4 in the Handbook of Schizophrenia series, examines psychosocial causes of schizophrenia and psychosocial treatment approaches. Discusses early intervention. Behavior therapy and supportive living arrangements are covered; results of long-term outcome studies are also reviewed.

Hirsch, Steven, and Daniel Weinberger, eds. *Schizophrenia*. Oxford, England: Blackwell Science, 1995.

Kraepelin, Emil. *Clinical Psychiatry*. Translated by A. Ross Diefendorf. Delmar, N.Y.: Scholars' Facsimiles & Reprints, 1981. A facsimile reprint of the seventh (1907) edition of Kraepelin's classic text. Reveals the origins of contemporary thinking about schizophrenia and other mental disorders.

Neale, John M., and Thomas F. Oltmanns. *Schizophrenia*. New York: John Wiley & Sons, 1980. This book provides a comprehensive overview of the illness and examines many of the research methods for exploring its causes.

Walker, Elaine F., ed. *Schizophrenia: A Life-Span Developmental Perspective*. San Diego: Academic Press, 1991. The entire life-course of schizophrenic patients is addressed in this book, from early childhood precursors to geriatric outcome.

Elaine F. Walker

See also:

Abnormality, 1; Neuropsychology, 422; Psychosurgery, 490; Schizophrenia: Theoretical Explanations, 517.

SCHIZOPHRENIA
Theoretical Explanations

Type of psychology: Psychopathology
Fields of study: Models of abnormality; schizophrenias

Schizophrenia is one of the most bizarre and potentially devastating of all psychological disorders. Although it was thoroughly described in the late nineteenth century, the disorder's causes are not yet definitely known. Theoretical explanations, sometimes poorly supported by direct experimental evidence, abound; many of these theories have, however, been abandoned by researchers, most of whom now accept that schizophrenia is primarily an organic disorder.

Principal terms

ANTIPSYCHOTIC DRUGS: drugs that alleviate the symptoms of schizophrenia; chlorpromazine, haloperidol, clozapine, and thioridazine are examples

DOPAMINE: a neurotransmitter; a chemical that is released from one nerve cell and stimulates receptors on another, thus transferring a message between them

NEGATIVE SYMPTOMS: the absence of normal thoughts, feelings, or behaviors that should be present but are not; examples are lack of normal emotional responsiveness, thought blocking, inadequate social behavior, and inadequate self-care or personal-hygiene behaviors

POSITIVE SYMPTOMS: abnormal thoughts, feelings, or behaviors that are present but should not be present; delusions, hallucinations, strange mannerisms, and inappropriate emotions are examples

POSITRON EMISSION TOMOGRAPHY (PET) SCANNING: a brain-imaging technique that allows blood flow, energy metabolism, and chemical activity to be visualized in the living human brain

PSYCHOTOGEN: something that causes, or generates, psychosis; related adjectives are "psychotogenic" and "schizophrenogenic"

RETICULAR FORMATION: a system in the brain responsible for controlling arousal and attention, sleeping and waking, perceptual filtering, and other important functions

Overview

Schizophrenia, an illness that strikes 1 percent of adults, involves changes in all aspects of psychological functioning. Thinking disorders, perceptual distortions and hallucinations, delusions, and emotional changes are the most prominent of such changes. Although some people recover completely, in many others the illness is chronic and deteriorative. The cause of schizophrenia is not known. Theories about schizophrenia can be classified into four types: psychodynamic, family interaction, learning/attention, and organic.

Psychodynamic theories originated with Sigmund Freud, who believed that schizophrenia results when a child fails to develop an attachment to his or her parent of the opposite sex. This causes a powerful conflict (called an Oedipal conflict in males) in which unconscious homosexual desires threaten to overwhelm the conscious self. To prevent these desires from generating thoughts and feelings that cause painful guilt or behaviors that would be punished, the ego defends itself by regressing to a state in which awareness of the self as a distinct entity is lost. Thus, the person's behavior becomes socially inappropriate; the person mistakes fantasies for reality and experiences hallucinations and delusions.

Harry Stack Sullivan, a follower of Freud, believed that failure of maternal attachment creates excessive anxiety and sets the pattern for all future relationships. Unable to cope in a world seen as socially dangerous, the individual retreats into fantasy. Having done so, the individual cannot grow socially or develop a sense of trust in or belonging with others. By late adolescence or early adulthood, the person's situation has become so hopeless that all pretense of normality collapses and he or she withdraws totally and finally into a world of fantasy and delusion.

Family interaction theories dwell even more intensely on parent-child, especially mother-child, relationships. Theodore Lidz and coworkers, after conducting studies on families with a schizophrenic member, concluded that one or both parents of a future schizophrenic are likely to be nearly, if not overtly, psychotic. They proposed that the psychotogenic influence of these parents on a psychologically vulnerable child is most likely the cause of schizophrenia.

Gregory Bateson and colleagues proposed a family interaction theory called the double-bind theory. Bateson suggested that schizophrenia results when parents expose a child to a family atmosphere in which they never effectively communicate their expectations, and therefore the child is unable to discover which behaviors will win approval. Scolded for disobeying, for example, the child changes his or her behavior only to be scolded for being "too obedient." Subjected to such no-win situations constantly, the child cannot develop an attachment to the family, and this failure generalizes to all subsequent relationships.

Learning theories propose that failure of operant conditioning causes the bizarre behavior of schizophrenia. In one version, conditioning fails because mechanisms in the brain that support operant learning, such as reinforcement and attention, are faulty, thus preventing the learning of appropriate, adaptive behaviors.

For example, a person who is unable to focus attention on relevant stimuli would be unable to learn the stimulus associations and discriminations necessary for successful day-to-day behavior. Such an individual's behavior would eventually become chaotic. This learning/attention theory proposes a defect in perceptual filtering, a function of the brain's reticular formation. This system filters out the innumerable stimuli that impinge upon one's senses every moment but are unimportant. In schizophrenia, the theory proposes, this filtering system fails, and the individual is overwhelmed by a welter of trivial stimuli. Unable to cope with this confusing overstimulation, the person withdraws, becomes preoccupied with sorting out his or her thoughts, and becomes unable to distinguish internally generated stimuli from external ones.

Organic theories of schizophrenia are influenced by the knowledge that conditions known to have organic causes often produce psychological symptoms that mimic schizophrenia. Among these are vitamin-deficiency diseases, viral encephalitis, temporal-lobe epilepsy, and neurodegenerative disease such as Huntington's disease and Wilson's disease. Furthermore, evidence suggests that schizophrenia involves a genetic disorder, which presumably manifests itself as some organic brain abnormality. In the stress-diathesis model, such a genetic defect is necessary for the development of chronic schizophrenia but is not sufficient to produce it. Stressful life events must also be present. The genetic abnormality then leaves the person unable to cope with life stresses, the result being psychosis.

Many brain abnormalities have been proposed as causes of schizophrenia. One suggestion is that schizophrenia results from generalized brain pathology. For example, some researchers suggest that widespread brain deterioration caused by either environmental poisoning or infection by a virus causes schizophrenia.

Alternatively, some biochemical abnormality may be at fault. The endogenous psychotogen theory proposes that abnormal production of a chemical substance either inside or outside the brain produces psychotic symptoms by affecting the brain in a druglike fashion. Substances similar to the hallucinogenic drugs lysergic acid diethylamide (LSD) and mescaline are popular candidates for the endogenous psychotogen. The dopamine theory, however, proposes that schizophrenia results when a chemical neurotransmitter system in the brain called the dopamine system becomes abnormally overactive or when dopamine receptors in the brain become abnormally sensitive to normal amounts of dopamine.

Applications

Theories of schizophrenia are instrumental in generating experiments that provide definite knowledge of the condition. Experimental support for psychodynamic theories has not been forthcoming. Therefore, most researchers regard psychodynamic theories of schizophrenia as having little scientific merit. Family interaction theories also have not been supported by subsequent experiments. Although studies have found disturbed family relationships, the evidence suggests that these are the result of, not the cause of, having a schizophrenic individual in the family. Studies consistently fail to find that parent-child interactions are psychotogenic, and the once-popular notion of the schizophrenogenic parent has been discarded. Only learning/attention and organic theories are strongly supported by experimental evidence. The evidence for attentional or learning deficits resulting from a fault in the reticular formation is strong, and it stems from electrophysiological and behavioral studies.

The electroencephalogram (EEG) is often found to be abnormal in schizophrenic patients, showing excessive activation that indicates overarousal. Furthermore, studies of evoked potentials, electrical events recorded from the cortex of the brain in response to specific sensory stimuli, often find abnormalities. Significantly, these occur late in the evoked potential, indicating abnormality in the brain's interpretation of sensory stimuli rather than in initial reception and conduction.

Behavioral studies show that schizophrenic patients often overreact to low-intensity stimuli, which corresponds to their complaints that lights are too bright or sounds are too loud. In addition, patients are often unusually distractible—unable to focus attention on the most relevant stimuli. Orienting responses to novel stimuli are deficient in about half of schizophrenic patients. Patient self-reports also indicate that, subjectively, the individual feels overwhelmed by sensory stimulation.

Thus, considerable evidence suggests that, at least in many patients, there is an abnormality in the sensory/perceptual functioning in the brain, perhaps in the perceptual filtering mechanism of the reticular formation.

Franz J. Kallmann's twin studies of the 1940's provided convincing evidence of a genetic factor in schizophrenia. He found that genetically identical monozygotic twins are much more likely to be concordant for schizophrenia (that is, both twins are much more likely to be psychotic) than are dizygotic twins, who are not genetically identical. Studies using genealogical techniques also showed that schizophrenia runs in families.

The criticism of these studies was that twins not only are genetically similar but also are exposed to the same family environment, and therefore genetic and environmental factors were confounded. Seymour Kety and colleagues, working with adoption records in Denmark, effectively answered this criticism by showing that adopted children are more likely to become schizophrenic when their biological parents suffer from the illness than when their adoptive parents are stricken. These studies showed that schizophrenia is more closely associated with genetic relatedness than with family environment.

Presumably, this genetic predisposition works by producing some organic change. Studies using advanced brain-imaging techniques indicate that, in many patients, there is nonlocalized brain degeneration, which is revealed by the increased size of the ventricles, fluid-filled spaces within the brain. What causes this degeneration is unknown, but some researchers suggest that it is caused by a virus and that a genetic factor increases susceptibility to infection and the subsequent damaging effects of a viral disease. Although direct evidence of a virus has been found in a minority of patients, the viral theory is still considered speculative and unproved. There is no evidence that schizophrenia is contagious.

Experimental evidence of biochemical abnormalities in the brain's dopamine neurotransmitter systems is, however, impressive. Antipsychotic drugs are effective in relieving the symptoms of schizophrenia, especially positive symptoms such as hallucinations and delusions. These drugs block dopamine receptors in the brain. Furthermore, the more powerfully the drugs bind to and block dopamine receptors, the smaller the effective dose that is necessary to produce a therapeutic result.

Further evidence comes from a condition called amphetamine psychosis, which occurs in people who abuse amphetamine and similar stimulants such as cocaine. Amphetamine psychosis so closely mimics some forms of schizophrenia that misdiagnoses have been common. Furthermore, amphetamine psychosis is not an artifact of disturbed personality; experiments show that normal control subjects will develop the condition if they are given high doses of amphetamines every few hours for several days. Amphetamine psychosis, which is believed to result from the overactivation of dopamine systems in the brain, is treated with antipsychotic drugs such as chlorpromazine.

Direct evidence of abnormality in the dopamine systems comes from studies using advanced techniques such as positron emission tomography (PET) scanning. These studies show that the brains of schizophrenic patients, even those who have never been treated with antipsychotic medications, may have abnormally large numbers of dopamine receptors in an area called the limbic system, which is responsible for emotional regulation.

Dopamine-blocking drugs, however, help only a subset of patients. Studies show that those most likely to benefit from medication are patients who display primarily positive symptoms. Patients who show negative symptoms—such as withdrawal, thought blocking, and catatonia—are less likely to be helped by medication. These are precisely the patients, however, who are likely to show nonlocalized brain deterioration. Many researchers believe that there are two types of schizophrenia: one that is characterized by negative symptoms, has a poor prognosis, and is perhaps caused by generalized brain pathology; and a second, which is characterized by positive symptoms, responds well to medication, and is perhaps caused by biochemical abnormality in the dopamine systems of the brain. Attentional deficits may be related to this second type of schizophrenia, since the dopamine pathways originate in the reticular formation of the brain and play a critical role in learning and selective attention.

Context

The disorders that are now called schizophrenia were first characterized in the nineteenth century. Emil Kraepelin first grouped these disorders, referring to them by the collective name dementia praecox in 1893.

Many early neurologists and psychiatrists thought these dementias were organic conditions. This view changed, however, after Swiss psychiatrist Eugen Bleuler published his classic work on the disorder in 1911. Bleuler proposed that the primary characteristic of the condition was a splitting of intellect from emotions. He introduced the term "schizophrenia" (literally, "split mind"). Bleuler, influenced by the psychodynamic theories of Freud, believed that the bizarre content of schizophrenic thoughts and perceptions represented a breaking away from an external reality that was too painful or frightening. His ideas became especially influential in the United States.

Attempts to treat schizophrenia with traditional psychotherapies were, however, unsuccessful. Success rates rarely surpassed the rate of spontaneous recovery, the rate at which patients recover without treatment. Because medical interventions such as lobotomy, insulin shock therapy, and electroconvulsive therapy were also ineffective, psychiatric hospitals were filled with patients for whom little could be done.

The discovery of antipsychotic drugs in the 1950's changed things dramatically. Hospital populations declined. The surprising effectiveness of these medications, in concert with the discovery of amphetamine psychosis in the 1930's and the genetic studies of the 1940's, renewed the belief that schizophrenia is an organic condition.

Two problems impeded further understanding. First, techniques available for investigating the brain were primitive compared with modern techniques. Therefore, reports of organic changes in schizophrenia, although common, were difficult to confirm. Second, since the routinely administered medications powerfully influenced brain functioning, it became a problem to distinguish organic changes that were important in causing the disorder from those that were merely secondary to the action of antipsychotic drugs in the brain.

Indeed, it became "common wisdom" among many psychologists that organic factors identified by researchers were not primary to the disorder but were, rather, side effects of medication. Soft neurological signs such as eye-movement dysfunctions, abnormal orienting responses, and unusual movements were considered drug related even though Kraepelin and others had described them decades before the drugs were discovered. The drugs came to be called "major tranquilizers," implying that medication allowed patients to function more effectively by relieving the over-whelming anxiety that accompanied the disorder but that the drugs did not influence the schizophrenic process itself.

The fact that antipsychotic drugs have little usefulness as antianxiety agents in nonschizophrenics did not shake this opinion. The discovery of more powerful anti-anxiety agents such as Librium (chlordiazepoxide) and Valium (diazepam) did not either, even after they were shown to be almost useless in treating schizophrenia.

The next dramatic change in understanding schizophrenia came in the 1960's with the discovery of monoamine neurotransmitters, including dopamine, and the discovery that these chemical systems in the brain are strongly affected in opposite ways by psychotogenic drugs, such as cocaine and amphetamine, and antipsychotic drugs, such as chlorpromazine. With the advent of powerful imaging techniques such as PET scanning, research into schizophrenia surged ahead again. Perhaps these techniques will bring about a more complete understanding of, and possibly a cure for, this most devastating of psychological disorders.

Bibliography

Bowers, Malcolm B. *Retreat from Sanity: The Structure of Emerging Psychosis*. New York: Human Sciences Press, 1974. A fascinating description, often in the words of patients, of the experiences many people have in the very early stages of psychosis. Especially interesting are descriptions of "peak" and "psychedelic" experiences resulting from sensory alterations during the onset of the disorder.

Brunello, N., et al., eds. *Critical Issues in the Treatment of Schizophrenia*. Farmington, Conn.: S. Karger, 1996.

Gottesman, Irving I. *Schizophrenia Genesis: The Origins of Madness*. New York: W. H. Freeman, 1991. An excellent, well-written book that is easily accessible to the general reader. Highly recommended.

Gottesman, Irving I., James Shields, and Daniel R. Hanson. *Schizophrenia: The Epigenetic Puzzle*. Cambridge, England: Cambridge University Press, 1982. More technical than *Schizophrenia Genesis* but still accessible to anyone with a solid background in genetics of the type obtained in a good general biology course. Concentrates on genetic studies and gives complete references to original technical articles.

Helmchen, Hanfried, and Fritz A. Henn, eds. *Biological Perspectives of Schizophrenia*. Chichester, England: John Wiley & Sons, 1987. A collection of papers by experts in the field, this is a valuable reference source for readers who are interested in the state of knowledge about schizophrenia in the late 1980's. Many of the papers are quite technical, but the background supplied by other sources in this bibliography should help readers understand them.

Lidz, Theodore, Stephen Fleck, and Alice R. Cornelison. *Schizophrenia and the Family*. New York: International Universities Press, 1965. A collection of papers detailing studies of seventeen families that have a schizophrenic member. Selection of subject families was highly biased, and no appropriate matched control families were studied. Nevertheless, this work was extremely influential among mental health workers. The authors' conclusions are not supported, however, by more recent, more carefully controlled studies.

Mednick, Sarnoff A., and J. Meggin Hollister, eds. *Neural Development and Schizophrenia: Theory and Research*. New York: Plenum Publishing, 1995.

Snyder, Solomon H. *Madness and the Brain*. New York: McGraw-Hill, 1974. Written in a lively, breezy style, this short volume deals with biomedical factors in many psychological disorders, including schizophrenia. Especially interesting is Snyder's discussion of drug effects, neurotransmitters, and schizophrenia.

Sullivan, Harry Stack. *Schizophrenia as a Human Process*. New York: W. W. Norton, 1962. Perhaps the most available of Sullivan's writings, this book is actually a collection of articles written by him between 1924 and 1935. Once widely popular, Sullivan's theories have not been supported experimentally and are no longer accepted by most psychologists.

Torrey, Edwin Fuller. *Surviving Schizophrenia: A Family Manual*. Rev. ed. New York: Perennial Library, 1988. One of the best books available for the general reader on schizophrenia. Intended primarily for members of families that have a schizophrenic family member, this book should be read by everyone who is interested in the disorder, including every mental health worker. Torrey writes wonderfully and pulls no punches when dealing with outmoded theories and poorly done experiments. Many libraries have only the first edition; read the revised edition if possible.

William B. King

See also:

SELF
Definition and Assessment

Type of psychology: Social psychology
Fields of study: Personality assessment; personality theory; social perception and cognition

The self is a complex and multifaceted entity that is a combination of what an individual would like to be, what an individual is currently like, and what others would like the individual to be; because the self is created through, and has implications for, an individual's interactions with others, it is critical that its social nature be studied.

Principal terms

ACTUAL SELF: the self as the person sees himself or herself at the present time; large discrepancies between the actual and ideal selves can lower self-esteem

CONDITIONAL LOVE: love and praise that is given to another person with the expectation that the person will do something for the individual giving the love

IDEAL SELF: the self as the individual would like to be if the individual could be perfect in his or her own eyes

LOOKING-GLASS SELF: a sense of self that is created by imagining how others see the individual in comparison with how the individual would like to be seen

SELF-CONCEPT: the sum total of the attributes, abilities, attitudes, and values that an individual believes defines who he or she is

SELF-ESTEEM: a relatively permanent positive or negative feeling about self that may become more positive or negative as the individual encounters successes and failures in daily life

SELF-IMAGE: a specific attribute, ability, attitude, or value that a person believes makes up part of his or her self; self-image combines to create the self-concept

SPONTANEOUS SELF-CONCEPT: how individuals would automatically describe themselves at a particular moment; situations and other people influence how an individual views his or her self at a given time

TRAITS: relatively enduring tendencies that make people behave in particular ways

UNCONDITIONAL LOVE: love that is given with no expectations attached; when a baby cries, for example, a parent gives him or her food without asking for anything in return

Overview

The concept of self has been researched in depth since psychologist William James first discussed it in 1892. James believed that the self involves two basic factors that blend to determine the person. First, there is the "I," which represents the simple fact that a person realizes that he or she is separate and different from others. Second, there is the "me," which represents all that the person associates with his or her self. James believed that there are three aspects to the "me" that determine how an individual describes and feels about his or her self: the "material me," the "social me," and the "spiritual me."

The material me represents all the worldly goods and possessions that a person uses to define who he or she is. The social me represents all the interactions and relationships with others that are an important part of how a person views himself or herself. The spiritual me involves the more metaphysical nature of self that centers on one's quest for knowledge and growth. It represents one's sensations, emotions, thoughts, and inner states.

To avoid some of the confusion caused by James's use of the terms "I" and "me," current theorists of the self tend to distinguish between the total self, called the self-concept; a particular aspect of self, called the self-image; and the feelings one has about the self, called self-esteem. Numerous theorists, most notably Harry Stack Sullivan and Charles Horton Cooley, discussed the implications that other people have for an individual's conception of his or her own self.

Sullivan believed that a child comes to develop a sense of self when the mother figure begins to give conditional love. When babies are very young, parents unconditionally love them and meet their needs. As children grow older, they are taught that parents expect certain things from their children and that their love and praise may depend on the child's ability to do what they want. In this way, the child sees that the mother can be good ("she gives me what I want") or bad ("she does not give me what I want"). Along with this realization comes the knowledge that how the child acts often influences whether it is good mother or bad mother who responds. This teaches the child that his or her self includes both the good me (things that I do well) and the bad me (things that I do wrong).

Cooley agrees that the way others respond to the individual has a profound impact on how he or she views his or her self; Cooley refers to what he calls the "looking-glass self." According to this concept, the way people believe that others perceive them determines how they feel about themselves. People "reflect" on how they appear to others, and then try to modify their selves in a direction that they believe will make others see them as they want to be seen.

By using reflections in this way, the individual tries to project a particular self-image, then interprets how he or she thinks others are responding to that image. If the person thinks others are responding the way he or she had intended ("I wanted to be seen as honest and they agree"), then that image is likely to become part of the self-concept. If the person believes that others are responding negatively ("I wanted to be seen as suave, but she thinks I'm a jerk"), then the person is likely to question his or her ability to maintain that particular self-image.

Each person is born with, or quickly develops, a particular temperament (he or she likes certain things more than others, tends to be in a certain mood more than others, and gets upset by certain things more than others). Each person is also born with obvious characteristics that will determine, to some degree, how others will act toward him or her. Unchangeable characteristics, such as race and gender, are often used by others to categorize what people will be like. The way one is treated by these other individuals helps one to negotiate a sense of self. A person tries to convince others of what he or she is like, watches to see how others react to that, and then tries to fine-tune the image of self he or she is creating by using that feedback. Over time, these factors create a self-concept.

Once a person has a fairly stable idea of who he or she is and what he or she can do, that idea influences the situations in which that person finds him- or herself. For example, if a woman believes she is a good tennis player, then she is likely to put herself into a situation in which playing good tennis is important. Then, after she behaves, she asks, "Is my behavior consistent with the image of self I have?" If the answer to that question is "yes," then it feeds the self-concept, and the woman becomes even more certain of who she is. If, however, the answer is "no," then it loops back and causes the woman to question who she is. In this manner, a self-concept is created and continually tested in everyday life.

Applications

There are many life experiences that can be explained by understanding the concept of self. To develop a sense of self fully, an individual must go through a lengthy and complicated negotiation process in which he or she tries on different selves and observes how others react. Adolescence is probably the most striking example of this negotiation process. Individuals such as parents, teachers, and other authority figures tell the child what is right or wrong or what he or she can and cannot do. Suddenly, peers become an important part of this negotiation process: The adolescent tries to balance the desires of the parents and authority figures with the demands being put on him or her by friends and peers while trying to show the world what kind of self he or she would like to have.

The health of the self-concept depends on the adolescent's ability to complete the balancing act successfully and create a sense of self that blends societal demands with what the individual most wants to be. The teenager is experiencing a storm of bodily changes, an increase in expected responsibilities, pressure from peers to do the "in" thing, and an internal need to know "Who am I?" and "What am I meant to do in this world?" What career a person seeks, what schools a person attends, and what friends a person chooses to be with all depend on how a person comes to view his or her self and who the person thinks he or she is as a person at the end of this negotiation process.

For years psychologists have tried to create questionnaires to measure the self-concept. Answering prewritten questions is an imperfect method, at best, for measuring an individual's self-concept. When someone answers on a scale that he or she is "very aggressive," it does not necessarily mean that he or she is an aggressive person. Perhaps he or she just hurt someone accidentally before walking into the room and is feeling bad about it. Besides the survey, then, how can psychologists measure self-concept?

The answer lies with a less structured technique made popular by psychologist William McGuire. This technique, called the "spontaneous self-concept measure," asks subjects to write down the first twenty words or phrases they think of when they are asked, "Who are you?" This is a particularly useful method because the test does not suggest which characteristics are important. The subjects decide for themselves whether to mention "aggressive" as a word that describes them. Psychologists can then look at the kinds of descriptors individuals are using and gain some insight as to what characteristics make up their self-concept, how they feel about themselves, and how certain they are of themselves. If an individual mentions on line 4 that he or she is "shy" and then mentions on line 13 that he or she is "outgoing," this may signal to professionals that the person is uncertain of his or her self-image on the shy-outgoing dimension.

More often than not, the cause of an uncertain self lies in the negotiation process. If an individual hears from one group of people that he or she is "great" and "really smart" but constantly hears from others that he or she is "worthless" and "stupid," developing a stable sense of self will be very difficult. If an individual has continuously received conflicting messages about who he or she is, how can the process be turned around to stabilize the person's sense of self?

The answer, unfortunately, is not an easy one. It would be helpful to discover exactly what the individual considers to be important and unimportant about his or her self. It is often the case that a person has unrealistic standards because of the conflicting messages the person has received about his or her worth and abilities. It is entirely possible that the person has decided that the most important thing about his or her self is the ability to please everyone. Then the person will go through life constantly putting on a different face and acting like a different person.

A person may act intelligent around people who think being smart is important, and unintelligent around people who think it is not important. It is even possible that the individual will experiment with drugs and alcohol even if he or she does not like them or disapproves of their use, solely because someone who is important to him or her thinks that doing such things is important. In this manner, the individual may be overly influenced by the important people in his or her life and may never come to have a sense of self that is stable, secure, and positive.

To stabilize his or her sense of self, such a person must be convinced that it is perfectly all right not to be everything to everyone. The person will have to be convinced that true friends will accept the person for who he or she is rather than for who he or she can pretend to be. When a person projects a secure and satisfied sense of self to others, then others are more likely to accept that person.

Context

The study of the "self" grew out of early attempts by the Greek philosophers to understand what makes each human being different from, yet similar to, all other human beings. There was a need to understand how the environment in which one is reared, the challenges one is presented, and the people one encounters all work together to create a self that will influence one for the rest of one's life. Only when one understands how the development of self occurs normally can one do anything to help those individuals whose self-concepts are unstable or negative.

Intense attempts to study the self did not come about until the late 1800's and the early 1900's. Study of the self has played a large role in the history of psychological inquiry, and twentieth century views on self suggest that the influence of this topic will not diminish. As the world becomes increasingly complex, the multitude of factors that will influence a child's development of self-concept will continue to increase. Many demands are placed on individuals to be different people at different times. A tug-of-war such as this is bound to have a dramatic impact on how people view and feel about their selves.

Studying the self has been important in psychology because what people do in a social setting touches others. Kurt Lewin's research in the late 1940's provided the first empirical support to suggest to the science of psychology that the other individuals with whom a person comes in contact will have a profound impact on who the person becomes. Lewin argued that "behavior is a function of the person and the environment." Whenever someone behaves, to understand that behavior one must understand something about his or her personality or his or her self and something about the environment in which the person has interacted. Lewin did not believe that the term "environment" meant solely the physical environment. Other individuals are a significant part of one's environment. If the argument is carried to its logical conclusion, one's self-concept is a construction of one's own attributes, abilities, attitudes, and the values of the significant others with whom one has interacted and continues to interact.

In the late 1970's, research began to address the development of the self. Perhaps the most comprehensive attempt to systematize the developmental processes that create the self has been made by Mark Snyder. Snyder attempts to describe how an individual develops an identity that focuses on internal characteristics of self versus external characteristics. If an individual is constantly concerned with how he or she is doing in a situation—asking him- or herself, "Do I fit in?" or "Do my clothes look good?"—then he or she may be considered a "high self-monitor." An individual, however, called a "low self-monitor" is more concerned with whether he or she is behaving according to his or her internal standards, asking him-or herself, "Am I doing this because someone else wants me to or because I want to?" The aspect of self the person monitors (the inside or the outside) in a social situation will have a profound impact on how others will view, and act toward, the person. Given the importance of other persons in the development of one's self-concepts, clearly internal/external difference can drastically influence self-concept development.

The aspect of self that a person is monitoring or controlling (the internal or the external) indicates how that person will behave, what other people this person will choose to be with, what kinds of things this person will want to do, and even which products this person may want to buy. Psychology has as its goal a concern with trying to predict how different people will behave in different situations. Study of the nature and development of self has moved professionals a long way toward being able to predict such behavior. In this sense, the study of the self, in general, and the development of particular kinds of selves, more specifically, has been of great importance to the field of psychology.

Bibliography

Blakeslee, Thomas R. *Beyond the Conscious Mind: Unlocking the Secrets of the Self*. New York: Plenum Press, 1996.

Burn, Shawn Meghan. *The Social Psychology of Gender*. New York: McGraw-Hill, 1996.

Buss, Arnold. *Self-Consciousness and Social Anxiety*. San Francisco: W. H. Freeman, 1980. Very clearly written, this book tracks the development of internal and external awareness of self as well as some of the developmental causes of shyness and social anxiety.

Cooley, Charles H. *Human Nature and the Social Order*. New York: Charles Scribner's Sons, 1902. This is an early, but thorough, account of self-concept development. This was the first work to stress clearly that other individuals have a profound impact on the development of the self-concept.

Goffman, Erving. *The Presentation of Self in Everyday Life*. Garden City, N.Y.: Doubleday, 1959. A short book that is extremely fun to read and easy to understand, this is a contemporary look at the way people alter themselves to get by in everyday life.

Scheibe, Karl E. *Self Studies: The Psychology of Self and Identity*. Westport, Conn.: Praeger, 1995.

Snyder, Mark. *Public Appearances, Private Realities: The Psychology of Self-Monitoring*. New York: W. H. Freeman, 1987. Snyder tracks the development of the self-monitoring construct and systematically tells the reader how an internal or external monitoring of self affects people's behavior. It is easy to understand, clearly written, and thoroughly enjoyable.

Williams, Robert, and James D. Long. *Manage Your Life*. Boston: Houghton Mifflin, 1991. This book is intended to serve as a guide for personal growth in a variety of areas. The most significant chapters deal with changing the aspects of the self-concept with which a person is dissatisfied. It is a very readable book that uses real-life examples to help convey the main points.

Randall E. Osborne

See also:

Affiliation and Friendship, 25; Attraction Theories, 77; Cognitive Dissonance Theory, 141; Crowd Behavior, 182; Self-Esteem, 530.

SELF-ESTEEM

Type of psychology: Social psychology
Fields of study: Childhood and adolescent disorders; cognitive development; social perception and cognition

Self-esteem research examines how individuals come to feel as they do about themselves. Psychologists seek to understand how self-esteem develops and what can be done to change negative views of the self once they have been established.

Principal terms

ATTRIBUTIONS: assumptions about the causes for behavior, made on three levels: internal/external, stable/temporary, and specific/global

IDENTITY NEGOTIATION: the attempt to create the type of self one would like to have; conflicts arise if people view themselves differently from the way others see them

IMMUTABLE CHARACTERISTICS: physical attributes (such as gender) that are present at birth and that others assume give them information as to the kind of person they are seeing

INHERITABLE TRAITS: personality characteristics (such as aggressiveness) that may be inherited from parents and are presumed to influence the kind of person an individual becomes

SELF-CONCEPT: the sum total of the attributes, abilities, attitudes, and values that an individual believes define who he or she is

SELF-EFFICACY: the beginning realization experienced by the individual during infancy that he or she is a self capable of actions and that these actions have consequences

SELF-ESTEEM: a relatively permanent positive or negative feeling about the self that may become more positive or negative as a person encounters success and failure in daily life

Overview

Self-esteem is a term with which almost everyone is familiar, yet it is not necessarily easily understood. Psychologist William James gave the first clear definition in 1892 when he said that self-esteem equals success divided by pretensions. In other words, feelings of self-worth come from the successes an individual achieves tempered by what the person had expected to achieve. If the person expected to do extremely well on an exam (his or her pretensions are quite high) and scores an A, then his or her self-esteem should be high. If, however, the person expected to do well and then scored a D, his or her self-esteem should be low.

This important but simplistic view of self-esteem started a movement toward a better understanding of the complex series of factors that come together to create the positive or negative feelings individuals have about who they are. Once a person has developed a self-concept (a global idea of all the things that define who and what a person is), that person is likely to exhibit behaviors that are consistent with that self-concept. If a young woman believes that she is a good tennis player, then she is likely to put herself in situations in which that factor is important. Once she behaves (in this case, plays her game of tennis), she is likely to receive feedback from others as to how she did. This feedback determines how she will feel about her tennis-playing ability. Over time, these specific instances of positive or negative feedback about tennis-playing ability will come together to create the more global feelings of positivity or negativity a person has about the self in general.

Even though an individual may believe that she is good at tennis, her ability may not live up to those expectations, and she may receive feedback telling her so (for example, losing in the early rounds of a tournament). In this case, the individual may come to feel somewhat negative about her tennis ability. If this continues to happen, she will adjust her view of her ability and come to believe that she is not a good tennis player after all. To the extent that the person truly wanted to be good, this realization can cause her to feel quite negative about all aspects of her self. When this happens, the person is said to have developed low self-esteem.

The reality of how self-esteem develops, however, is more complicated than this example demonstrates. People do not always accept the feedback that others offer, and they may believe that their failure means nothing more than having an off day. In order to understand the impact that success and failure will have on self-esteem, it is important to understand the kinds of attributions people make for their successes and failures. When a person succeeds or fails, there are three levels of attributions that can be made for explaining the occurrence. First, the individual must decide if the event occurred because of something internal (something inside caused it to happen) or something external (something in the environment caused it to happen). Second, it must be decided whether the event occurred because of a stable factor (since it happened this time, it will happen again) or a temporary circumstance (it probably will not happen again). Finally, it must be decided whether the event occurred because of something specific (this failure resulted because of poor tennis ability) or something global (failure resulted at this undertaking because of lack of ability to do anything).

It is easy to see that the kinds of attributions individuals make for their successes and failures will have a profound impact on how a particular event influences their self-esteem. If a decision is made that a failure at tennis occurred because of something internal (lack of ability), stable (the ability will never be present), and global (lack of *any* ability), then a failure is going to damage self-esteem severely. Self-esteem is created through the blending of expectations for success, actual levels of success, and the kinds of attributions made for why success or failure occurred.

Once positive or negative self-esteem has developed, it will perpetuate itself in a cycle. If a person believes that he is a failure, he may put himself into situations in which he is destined to fail. If he does not think he can succeed, he may not put forth the amount of effort that success would require. Similarly, if a person believes that he is a success, he will not let one little failure cause him to change his entire opinion of his self. Self-esteem, once it is created, is very difficult to change. If a person dislikes who she is, yet someone else tries to tell her that she is wonderful, she probably will not believe that person. More likely, she will wonder what this person could possibly want from her that he or she is willing to lie and be so nice to get it. On the other hand, if the person feels positive about herself, a single instance of failure will be written off as bad luck, poor effort, or a simple fluke. A negative self-esteem cycle, once it gets started, is very difficult to change, and learning how to break this cycle is the single greatest challenge to self-esteem therapists.

Applications

Understanding self-esteem has considerable practical importance in daily life. If it is believed that all successes come from external sources (luck or someone's pity), then good things coming from others can be seen as an attempt to degrade the individual or offer a bribe. People feeling this way relate to others in a judgmental way and cause them to turn away. When others turn away, the person takes it as a signal that he or she was correct about his or her unworthiness, and the negative self-esteem level is perpetuated.

If this negative self-esteem cycle is to be broken, it is important to convince the person of the critical point made by George Herbert Mead. According to Mead, self-esteem is a product of people's interpretation of the feedback that they receive from others. A person with low self-esteem often misinterprets that feedback. If someone with low self-esteem is told, "You look really nice today," he or she is likely to misinterpret that to mean, "You usually look terrible; what did you do different today?"

Ralph Turner has said that the self is not fixed and that the person with low self-esteem must be convinced that he or she is not at the mercy of a self: He or she can be, and is, the creator of a self. It helps to put the person into a situation in which he or she can succeed with no possibility for the wrong attributions to be made. If a person cannot read, this failure will generalize to other situations and is likely to be considered a stable and global deficiency. If this person is taught to read, however, even a person with low self-esteem would find it difficult to argue that the success was situational. In this way, the person begins to see that he or she can take control and that failures need not be catastrophic for the other self-conceptions he or she might hold.

A person with negative self-esteem is extremely difficult to help. It takes more than the providing of positive feedback to assist such a person. Imagine a series of circles, one inside the other, each one getting smaller. Take that smallest, innermost circle and assign it a negative value. This represents an overall negative self-esteem. Then assign negative values to all the outer circles as well. These represent how the person feels about his or her specific attributes.

If positive messages are directed toward a person with negative values assigned to all these layers of self-esteem, they will not easily penetrate the negative layers; they will be much more likely to bounce off. Negative messages, on the other hand, will easily enter the circles and will strengthen the negativity. Penetration of all the negative layers can, however, sometimes be achieved by a long-term direction of positive and loving messages toward the person with low self-esteem. In effect, the innermost circle, that of global self-esteem, will eventually be exposed. Self-esteem can then be improved if enough positive, loving messages can be directed at the level of the person's global self-esteem. This is a difficult process, partly because as soon as the person's negative self-image comes into serious question, confusion about his or her identity results; living in self-hate, although often painful, is still more secure than suddenly living in doubt.

Once the negative signs have been replaced with positive ones, the new self-esteem level will be as impervious to change as the negative one was. Now, when the person enters a situation, he or she will have more realistic expectations as to what he or she can and cannot do. The person has been taught to make realistic attributions about success and failure. Most important, the individual has been taught that one need not succeed at everything to be a worthy person. William James suggested in 1892 that striving does as much to alleviate self-esteem problems as actual success. Once the individual is convinced that setting a goal and striving rather than not trying at all is all it takes to feel good about him- or herself, the person is truly on the way to having high self-esteem.

Context

An interest in self-esteem developed along with interest in psychological questions in general. Early psychologists such as Sigmund Freud, Carl G. Jung, William James, and others all realized that an important part of what makes individuals think and act the way they do is determined by the early experiences that create their sense of self and self-esteem. A very important aspect of psychological inquiry has been asking how and why people perceive and interpret the same event so differently. Self-esteem and self-concept play a big role in these interpretations. Knowing an individual's self-esteem level helps one to predict how others will be perceived, what kind of other individuals will be chosen for interaction, and the kinds of attitudes and beliefs the person may hold.

An understanding of childhood development and adolescence would be impossible without an understanding of the forces that combine to create a person's sense of self-esteem. Adolescence has often been described as a time of "storm and stress" because the teenager is trying to negotiate an identity (create a sense of self and self-esteem that he or she would like to have). Teenagers' own wishes and desires, however, are not the only things they must consider. They are receiving pressure from parents, peers, and society as a whole to be a certain kind of person and do certain kinds of things. Only when self-esteem development is fully understood will it be known how to alleviate some of the trials and tribulations of adolescence and ensure that teenagers develop a healthy and productive view of their worth.

The role of self-esteem will probably be even greater as psychological inquiry moves ahead. Contemporary society continues to tell people that if they want to succeed, they have to achieve more. Yet economic downturns and increasing competition to enter colleges and careers make it even more difficult for young people to live up to those expectations and feel good about who they are. The role that psychologists with experience in self-esteem enhancement training will play in the future cannot be overemphasized. In order for adults to lead healthy, productive, and satisfied lives, they must feel good about who they are and where they are going. This requires an intimate understanding of the factors that combine to create people's expectations for success and the likelihood that they will be able to achieve that level of success. Self-esteem development must be kept in mind in helping young people create for themselves a realistic set of expectations for success and an ability to make realistic attributions for why their successes and failures occur.

Bibliography

Bednar, Richard L., and Scott R. Peterson. *Self-Esteem: Paradoxes and Innovations in Clinical Theory and Practice*. 2d ed. Washington, D.C.: American Psychological Association, 1995.

Coopersmith, Stanley. *The Antecedents of Self-Esteem*. Palo Alto, Calif.: Consulting Psychologists Press, 1981. A very well-written and informative look at the background factors that influence the development of self-esteem. Includes statistics and figures but is fairly nontechnical, and the comprehensiveness of the book is well worth the effort.

Girodo, Michel. *Shy?* New York: Pocket Books, 1978. A delightful self-help book that is designed to help individuals overcome shyness. Helps the reader understand the connection between shyness and self-esteem. Appropriate for all age groups, from junior high school on.

Jones, Warren H., Jonathan M. Cheek, and Stephen R. Briggs. *Shyness: Perspectives on Research and Treatment.* New York: Plenum Press, 1986. Presents a thorough view of the development of shyness and the impact it has on social relationships. Many individuals with low self-esteem suffer from shyness, and it is difficult to understand one without the other. The writing is technical; appropriate for a college audience.

Mussen, Paul Henry, and Nancy Eisenberg-Berg. *Roots of Caring, Sharing, and Helping.* San Francisco: W. H. Freeman, 1977. Although this book is only partially related to self-esteem, it has a thorough discussion of how situations and other people influence children—influences which certainly cannot be ignored for their impact on self-esteem. Appropriate for most high school and college students.

Rosenberg, Morris. *Society and the Adolescent Self-Image.* Princeton, N.J.: Princeton University Press, 1972. Although written in the mid-1960's, this is still one of the best books available on self-esteem. Rosenberg's influence remains strong, and the self-esteem scale he included in this book is still widely used to measure self-esteem. Appropriate for both college and high school students.

Swann, William B., Jr. *Self-Traps: The Elusive Quest for Higher Self-Esteem.* New York: W. H. Freeman. 1996.

Randall E. Osborne

See also:

Affiliation and Friendship, 25; Attraction Theories, 77; Cognitive Dissonance Theory, 141; Crowd Behavior, 182; Self: Definition and Assessment, 524.

SENSATION AND PERCEPTION

Type of psychology: Sensation and perception
Fields of study: Auditory, chemical, cutaneous, and body senses; vision

The study of sensation and perception examines the relationship between input from the world and the manner in which people react to it. Through the process of sensation, the body receives various stimuli that are transformed into neural messages and transmitted to the brain. Perception is the meaning and interpretation given to these messages.

Principal terms

ABSOLUTE THRESHOLD: the smallest amount of stimulus that can be detected by the senses 50 percent of the time

ACUITY: the ability to detect minute details

ATTENTION: the ability to focus mentally

PERCEPTION: the organization and interpretation of sensory information, thus allowing people to recognize events and meaningful objects

SENSATION: the process by which the nervous system and sensory receptors receive and represent stimuli received from the environment

SENSORY DEPRIVATION: a condition in which an organism is deprived of sensory stimulation

SENSORY RECEPTORS: specialized body cells that convert physical energy, such as sound or light, into neural impulses

Overview

Although the distinction between sensation and perception is not always clear, psychologists attempt to distinguish between the two concepts. Sensation is generally viewed as the initial contact between organisms and their physical environment. It focuses on the interaction between various forms of sensory stimulation and how these sensations are registered by the senses (by the nose, skin, eyes, ears, and tongue). The process by which an individual then interprets and organizes this information to produce conscious experiences is known as perception.

The warmth of the sun, the distinctive sound of a jet airplane rumbling down the runway, the smell of freshly baked bread, and the taste of an ice-cream sundae all impact the body's sensory receptors. The signals received are transmitted to the brain via the nervous system; there, interpretation of the information is performed. The body's sensory receptors are capable of detecting very low levels of stimulation. Eugene Galanter's studies indicated that on a clear night, the eye is capable of viewing a candle at a distance of 30 miles (48 kilometers), while the ears can detect the ticking of a watch 20 feet (6 meters) away in a quiet room. He also demonstrated that the tongue can taste a teaspoon of sugar dissolved in 2 gallons (about 7.5 liters) of water, and people can feel a bee wing falling on the cheek and can smell a single drop of perfume in a three-bedroom apartment. Awareness of these faint stimuli demonstrates the absolute thresholds, defined as the minimum amount of stimulus that can be detected 50 percent of the time.

A person's ability to detect a weak stimulus, often called a signal, depends not only on the strength of the signal or stimulus but also on the person's psychological state. For example, a child remaining at home alone for the first time may be startled by an almost imperceptible noise. In a normal setting, with his or her parents at home, the same noise or signal would probably go unnoticed. Scientists who study signal detention seek to explain why people respond differently to a similar signal and why the same person's reactions vary as circumstances change. Studies have shown that people's reactions to signals depend on many factors, including the time of day and the type of signal.

Much controversy has arisen over the subject of subliminal signals—signals that one's body receives without one's conscious awareness. It has long been thought that these subliminal signals could influence a person's behaviors through persuasion. Many researchers believe that individuals do sense subliminal sensations; however, the chances that this information will somehow change an individual's behaviors is highly unlikely. Researchers Anthony Pratkanis and Anthony Greenwald suggest that in the area of advertising, subliminal procedures offer little or nothing of value to the marketing practitioner.

An individual's initial response to a stimulus may change over time. For example, when a swimmer first enters the cold ocean, the initial response may be to complain about the water's frigidity; however, after a few minutes, the water feels comfortable. This is an example of sensory adaptation—the body's ability to diminish sensitivity to stimuli that are unchanging. Sensory receptors are initially alert to the coldness of the water, but prolonged exposure reduces sensitivity. This is an important benefit to humans in that it allows an individual not to be distracted by constant stimuli that are uninformative. It would be very difficult to function daily if one's body were constantly aware of the fit of shoes and garments, the rumble of a heating system, or constant street noises.

The reception of sensory information by the senses, and the transmission of this information to the brain, is included under the term "sensation." Of equal importance is the process of perception: the way an individual selects information, organizes it, and makes an interpretation. In this manner, one achieves a grasp of one's surroundings. People cannot absorb and understand all the available sensory information received from the environment. Thus, they must selectively attend to certain information and disregard other material. Through the process of selective attention, people are able to maximize information gained from the object of focus, while at the same time ignoring irrelevant material. To some degree, people are capable of controlling the focus of their attention; in many instances, however, focus can be shifted undesirably. For example, while one is watching a television show, extraneous stimuli such as a car horn blaring may change one's focus.

The fundamental focus of the study of perception is how people come to comprehend the world around them through its objects and events. People are constantly giving meaning to a host of stimuli being received from all their senses. While research suggests that people prize visual stimuli above other forms, information from all other senses must also be processed. More difficult to understand is the concept of extrasensory perception (ESP). More researchers are becoming interested in the possible existence of extrasensory perception—perceptions that are not based on information from the sensory receptors. Often included under the heading of ESP are such questionable abilities as clairvoyance and telepathy. While psychologists generally remain skeptical as to the existence of ESP, some do not deny that evidence may someday be available supporting its existence.

Applications

Knowledge of the fields of sensation and perception assists people in understanding their environment. By understanding how and why people respond to various stimuli, scientists have been able to identify important factors which have proved useful in such fields as advertising, industry, and education.

Max Wertheimer discussed five laws of grouping that describe why certain elements seem to go together rather than remain independent. The laws include the law of similarity, which states that similar objects tend to be seen as a unit; the law of nearness, which indicates that objects near one another tend to be seen as a unit; the law of closure, which states that when a figure has a gap, the figure still tends to be seen as closed; the law of common fate, which states that when objects move in the same direction, they tend to be seen as a unit; and the law of good continuation, which states that objects organized in a straight line or a smooth curve tend to be seen as a unit. These laws are illustrated in the figure on the following page.

The laws of grouping are frequently utilized in the field of advertising. Advertisers attempt to associate their products with various stimuli. For example, Loudon and Della Bitta, after studying advertising dealing with menthol cigarettes, noted that the advertisers often show mentholated cigarettes in green, springlike settings to suggest freshness and taste. Similarly, summertime soft-drink advertisements include refreshing outdoor scenes depicting cool, fresh, clean running water, which is meant to be associated with the beverage. Also, advertisements for rugged four-wheel-drive vehicles utilize the laws of grouping by placing their vehicles in harsh, rugged climates. The viewer develops a perception of toughness and ruggedness.

The overall goal of the advertisers is to provide consumers with appropriate sensations that will cause them to perceive the products in a manner that the advertisers desire. By structuring the stimuli that reach the senses, advertisers can build a foundation for perceptions of products, making them seem durable, sensuous, refreshing, or desirable. By utilizing the results of numerous research studies pertaining to perception, subtle yet effective manipulation of the consumer is achieved.

Another area that has been researched extensively by industry deals with color. If one were in a restaurant ordering dinner and received an orange steak with purple French fries and a blue salad, the meal would be difficult to consume. People's individual perceptions of color are extremely important. Variations from these expectations can be very difficult to overcome. Researchers have found that people's perceptions of color also influence their beliefs about products. When reactions to laundry detergents were examined, detergent in a blue box was found to be too weak, while detergent in a yellow box was thought to be too strong. Consumers believed, based on coloration, that the ideal detergent came in a blue box with yellow accentuation. Similarly, when individuals were asked to judge the capsule color of drugs, findings suggested that orange capsules were frequently seen as stimulants, white capsules as having an analgesic action, and lavender capsules as having a hallucinogenic effect.

Studies have shown that various colors have proved more satisfactory than others for industrial application. Red has been shown typically to be perceived as a sign of danger and is used to warn individuals of hazardous situations. Yellow is also a sign of warning. It is frequently used on highway signs as a warning indicator because of its high degree of visibility in adverse weather conditions. Instrument panels in both automobiles and airplanes are frequently equipped with orange- and yellow-tipped instrument indicators, because research has demonstrated that these colors are easily distinguished from the dark background of the gauges. Finally, industry has not overlooked the fact that many colors have a calming and relaxing effect on people. Thus, soft pastels are often used in the workplace.

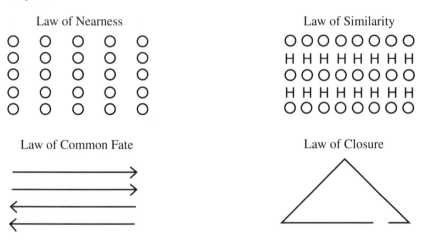

Law of Nearness   Law of Similarity

Law of Common Fate   Law of Closure

Law of Good Continuation

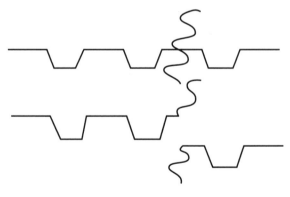

The field of education has also benefited from research in the areas of sensation and perception. Knowing how young children perceive educational materials is important in developing ways to increase their skills and motivation. Textbook publishers have found that materials need to be visually attractive to children in order to help them focus on activities. Graphics and illustrations help the young learner to understand written materials. Size of printed text is also important to accommodate the developmental level of the student. For example, primers and primary-level reading series typically have larger print to assist the student in focusing on the text. As the child's abilities to discriminate letters and numbers become more efficient with age, the print size diminishes to that of the size of characters in adult books. Similar techniques continue into high school and college; especially in intro-ductory courses, texts are designed utilizing extensive amounts of color, along with variation in page design. The reader's eyes are attracted by numerous stimuli to pictures, figures, definitions, and charts strategically placed on each page. This technique allows the author to highlight and accent essential points of information.

Context

The study of sensation and perception began more than two thousand years ago with the Greek philosophers and is one of the oldest fields in psychology. There are numerous theories, hypotheses, and facts dealing with how people obtain information about their world, what type of information they obtain, and what they do with this information once it has been obtained. None of this information has been sufficient to account for human perceptual experiences and perceptual behavior, so research in the area of sensation and perception continues.

The philosopher Thomas Reed made the original distinction between sensations and perceptions. He proposed that the crucial difference between them is that perceptions always refer to external objects, whereas sensations refer to the experiences within a person that are not linked to external objects. Many psychologists of the nineteenth century proposed that sensations are elementary building blocks of perceptions. According to their ideas, perceptions arise from the addition of numerous sensations. The sum of these sensations thus creates a perception. Other psychologists believed that making a distinction between sensations and perceptions was not useful.

The first psychologists saw the importance of perception when the realized that information from the senses was necessary in order to learn, think, and memorize. Thus, research pertaining to the senses was a central research component of all the psychological laboratories established in Europe and the United States during the late nineteenth and early twentieth centuries. By studying perceptions, researchers can identify potential environmental hazards that threaten the senses. Studying perception has also enabled people to develop devices that ensure optimal performance of the senses. For example, on a daily basis, one's senses rely on such manufactured objects as telephones, clocks, televisions, and computers. To be effective, these devices must be tailored to the human sensory systems.

The study of sensations and perceptions has also made it possible to build and develop prosthetic devices to aid individuals with impaired sensory function. For example, hearing aids amplify sound for hard-of-hearing individuals; however, when all sounds are amplified to the same degree it is often difficult for people to discriminate between sounds. From the work of Richard Gregory, a British psychologist, an instrument was developed that would only amplify speech sounds, thus allowing a person to attend more adequately to conversations and tune out background noise.

Another important application of research in the area of sensation and perception is consumer marketing. Companies carefully test the perceptual appeal of their products before marketing them. Taste, smell, and appearance have been modified to meet the appeal of the broadest possible population. Advertising also capitalizes on perception research by packaging and marketing products in a manner designed to draw the broadest possible consumer appeal. Finally, understanding perception is important for comprehending and appreciating the perceptual experience called art. When knowledge of perception is combined with the process of perceiving artistic works, this understanding adds an additional dimension to one's ability to view a work of art.

Bibliography

Coren, Stanley. *Sensation and Perception*. 4th ed. Forth Worth, Tex.: Harcourt Brace College Publishers, 1994.

Goldstein, Bruce E. *Sensation and Perception*. 4th ed. Monterey, Calif.: Brooks/Cole, 1996. An excellent overview of the field of sensation and perception. Chapters focus on typical subjects dealing with vision, hearing, and touch, but Goldstein also adds interesting chapters on perceived speech and the chemical senses.

Gregory, R. L. *Eye and Brain: The Psychology of Seeing*. 3d ed. New York: World University Library, 1978. A broad book on vision for the general reader. Beneficial for students in the areas of psychology, biology, and physiology. Includes many illustrations that help to explain complex matters in an understandable fashion.

Matlin, M. W. *Sensation and Perception*. 2d ed. Boston: Allyn & Bacon, 1988. Matlin's book is an introductory text covering all general areas of sensation and perception. Themes carried throughout the text are intended to provide additional structure for the material; these themes reflect the author's eclectic, theoretical orientation.

Rock, Irvin. *Perception*. New York: Scientific American Library, 1984. Rock deals particularly with perception and pays little attention to sensation other than vision. The text is designed to be an introductory work to motivate the reader to future studies. The book essentially explores the perception of the properties, distance, and motion of objects.

Schiff, William. *Perception: An Applied Approach*. Boston: Houghton Mifflin, 1980. Schiff's book is concerned with how people can, and do, use their senses to comprehend their world and their relation to it. Interesting chapters cover such topics as social-event perception, personal perception, and individual differences in perception.

Sekuler, Robert, and Robert R. Blake. *Perception*. New York: Alfred A. Knopf, 1985. Sekuler and Blake attempt to explain seeing, hearing, smelling, and tasting to students of perception. Extensive use of illustrations allows the reader to understand materials more fully. A series of short illustrations is also utilized by the authors to depict additional concepts.

Eugene R. Johnson

See also:

The Auditory System, 82; The Central and Peripheral Nervous Systems, 115; The Cerebral Cortex, 121; Smell and Taste, 553; Touch and Pressure, 627; Visual Development, 638; The Visual System, 643.

Sexual Variants and Paraphilias

Type of psychology: Psychopathology
Field of study: Sexual disorders

Sexual variations, or paraphilias, are unusual sexual activities, in that they deviate from what is considered normal at a particular time in a particular society; paraphilias include behaviors such as exhibitionism, voyeurism, and sadomasochism. It is when they become the prime means of gratification, displacing direct sexual contact with a consenting adult partner, that paraphilias are technically present.

Principal terms

EXHIBITIONISM: a behavior in which a person, who is usually a male, exposes the genitals to an involuntary observer

FETISHISM: a sexual behavior in which a person becomes aroused by focusing on an inanimate object or a part of the human body

FROTTEURISM: pressing or rubbing against a stranger in a public place for sexual gratification

SEXUAL MASOCHISM: the experiencing of sexual arousal by suffering physical or psychological pain

SEXUAL SADISM: the intentional infliction of pain on another person for sexual excitement

TRANSVESTISM: a behavior in which a person obtains sexual excitement from wearing clothing of the opposite gender

VOYEURISM: the derivation of sexual pleasure from looking at the naked bodies or sexual activities of others without their consent

ZOOPHILIA: sexual contact between humans and animals

Overview

Paraphilias are sexual behaviors that are considered a problem for the person who performs them and/or a problem for society because they differ from the society's norms. Psychologist John Money, who has studied sexual attitudes and behaviors extensively, claims to have identified about forty such behaviors.

Exhibitionism is commonly called "indecent exposure." The term refers to behavior in which an individual, usually a male, exposes the genitals to an involuntary observer, who is usually a female. The key point is that exhibitionistic behavior involves observers who are unwilling. After exposing, the exhibitionist often masturbates while fantasizing about the observer's reaction. Exhibitionists tend to be most aroused by shock and typically flee if the observer responds by laughing or attempts to approach the exhibitionist. Most people who exhibit themselves are males in their twenties or thirties. They tend to be shy, unassertive people who feel inadequate and afraid of being rejected by another person. People who make obscene telephone calls have similar characteristics to the people who engage in exhibitionism. Typically, they are sexually aroused when their victims react in a shocked manner. Many masturbate during or immediately after placing an obscene call.

Voyeurism is the derivation of sexual pleasure through the repetitive seeking of situations in which to look, or "peep," at unsuspecting people who are naked, undressing, or engaged in sexual intercourse. Most masturbate during the voyeuristic activity or immediately afterward in response to what they have seen. Further sexual contact with the unsuspecting stranger is rarely sought. Like exhibitionists, voyeurs are usually not physically dangerous. To a degree, voyeurism is socially acceptable, but it becomes atypical when the voyeuristic behavior is preferred to sexual relations with another person or when there is a high degree of risk. Most voyeurs are not attracted to nude beaches or other places where it is acceptable to look because they are most aroused when the risk of being discovered is high. Voyeurs tend to be men in their twenties with strong feelings of inadequacy.

Sadomasochistic behavior encompasses both sadism and masochism; it is often abbreviated "SM." The dynamics of the two behaviors are similar. It is thought that sadists are less common than masochists. Sadomasochistic behaviors have the potential to be physically dangerous, but most people involved in these behaviors participate in mild or symbolic acts with a partner they can trust. Most people who engage in SM activities are motivated by a desire for dominance or submission rather than pain. Interestingly, many nonhuman animals participate in pain-inflicting behavior before coitus. Some researchers think that the activity heightens the biological components of sexual arousal, such as blood pressure and muscle tension. It has been suggested that any resistance between partners enhances sex, and SM is a more extreme version of this behavior. It is also thought that SM offers people the temporary opportunity to take on roles that are the opposite of the controlled, restrictive roles they play in everyday life. The term "sadism" is derived from the Marquis de Sade, a French writer and army officer who was horribly cruel to people for his own erotic purposes. In masochism, sexual excitement is produced in a person by his or her own suffering. Preferred means of achieving gratification include verbal humiliation and being bound or whipped.

Fetishism is a type of sexual behavior in which a person becomes sexually aroused by focusing on an inanimate object or part of the human body. Many people are aroused by looking at undergarments, legs, or breasts, and it is often difficult to distinguish between normal activities and fetishistic ones. It is when a person becomes focused on the objects or body parts ("fetishes") to the exclusion of everything else that the term is most applicable. Fetishists are usually males. Common fetish objects include women's lingerie, high-heeled shoes, boots, stockings, leather, silk, and rubber goods. Common body parts involved in fetishism are hair, buttocks, breasts, and feet.

The term "pedophilia" is from the Greek language and means "love of children." It is characterized by a preference for sexual activity with children and is engaged in primarily by men. The activity varies in intensity and ranges from stroking the child's hair to holding the child while secretly masturbating, manipulating the child's genitals, encouraging the child to manipulate his or her own genitals, or, sometimes, engaging in sexual intercourse. Generally, the pedophile, or sexual abuser of children, is related to, or an acquaintance of, the child, rather than a stranger. Studies of imprisoned pedophiles have found that the men typically had poor relationships with their parents, drink heavily, show poor sexual adjustment, and were themselves sexually abused as children. Pedophiles tend to be older than people convicted of other sex offenses. The average age at first conviction is thirty-five.

Transvestism refers to dressing in clothing of the opposite sex to obtain sexual excitement. In the majority of cases, it is men who are attracted to transvestism. Several studies show that cross-dressing occurs primarily among married heterosexuals. The man usually achieves sexual satisfaction simply by putting on the clothing, but sometimes masturbation and intercourse are engaged in while the clothing is being worn.

Zoophilia involves sexual contact between humans and animals as the repeatedly preferred method of achieving sexual excitement. In this disorder, the animal is preferred despite other available sexual outlets. Necrophilia is a rare dysfunction in which a person obtains sexual gratification by looking at or having intercourse with a corpse. Frotteurism is a fairly common behavior involving a person, usually a male, who obtains sexual pleasure by pressing or rubbing against a fully clothed female in a crowded public place. Often it involves the clothed penis rubbing against the woman's buttocks or legs and appears accidental.

Applications

A problem in the definition and diagnosis of sexual variations is that it is difficult to draw the line between normal and abnormal behavior. Patterns of sexual behavior differ widely across history and within different cultures and communities. It is impossible to lay down the rules of normality; however, attempts are made in order to understand behavior that differs from the majority and in order to help people who find their own atypical behavior to be problematic, or to be problematic in the eyes of the law.

Unlike most therapeutic techniques in use by psychologists, many of the treatments for paraphilias are painful, and the degree of their effectiveness is questionable. Supposedly, the methods are not aimed at punishing the individual, but perhaps society's lack of tolerance toward sexual deviations can be seen in the nature of the available treatments. In general, all attempts to treat the paraphilias have been hindered by the lack of information available about them and their causes.

Traditional counseling and psychotherapy alone have not been very effective in the treatment of modifying the behavior of paraphiliacs, and it is unclear why the clients are resistant to treatment. Some researchers believe that the behavior might be important for the mental stability of paraphiliacs. If they did not have the paraphilia, they would experience mental deterioration. Another idea is that, although people are punished by society for being sexually deviant, they are also rewarded for it. For the paraphilias that put the person at risk for arrest, the danger of arrest often becomes as arousing and rewarding as the sexual activity itself. Difficulties in treating paraphiliacs may also be related to the emotionally impoverished environments that many of them experienced throughout childhood and adolescence. Convicted sex offenders report more physical and sexual abuse as children than do the people convicted of nonsexual crimes. It is difficult to undo the years of learning involved.

Surgical castration for therapeutic purposes involves removal of the testicles. Surgical castration for sexual offenders in North America is very uncommon, but the procedure is sometimes used in northern European countries. The reason castration is used as a treatment for sex offenders is the inaccurate belief that testosterone is necessary for sexual behavior. The hormone testosterone is produced by the testicles. Unfortunately, reducing the amount of testosterone in the blood system does not always change sexual behavior. Furthermore, contrary to the myth that a sex offender has an abnormally high sex drive, many sex offenders have a low sex drive or are sexually dysfunctional.

In the same vein as surgical castration, other treatments use the administration of chemicals to decrease desire in sex offenders without the removal of genitalia. Estrogens have been fairly effective in reducing the sex drive, but they sometimes make the male appear feminine by increasing breast size and stimulating other female characteristics. There are also drugs that block the action of testosterone and other androgens but do not feminize the body; these drugs are called antiandrogens. Used together with counseling, antiandrogens do benefit some sex offenders, especially those who are highly motivated to overcome the problem. More research on the effects of chemicals on sexual behavior is needed; the extent of the possible side effects, for example, needs further study.

Aversion therapy is another technique that has been used to eliminate inappropriate sexual arousal. In aversion therapy, the behavior that is to be decreased or eliminated is paired with an aversive, or unpleasant, experience. Most approaches use pictures of the object or situation that is problematic. Then the pictures are paired with something extremely unpleasant, such as an electric shock or a putrid smell, thereby reducing arousal to the problematic object or situation in the future. Aversion therapy has been found to be fairly effective but is under ethical questioning because of its drastic nature. For example, chemical aversion therapy involves the administration of a nausea- or vomit-inducing drug. Electrical aversion therapy involves the use of electric shock. An example of the use of electric shock would be to show a pedophile pictures of young children whom he finds sexually arousing and to give an electric shock immediately after showing the pictures, in an attempt to reverse the pedophile's tendency to be sexually aroused by children.

Other techniques have been developed to help clients learn more socially approved patterns of sexual interaction skills. In general, there has not been a rigorous testing of any of the techniques mentioned. Furthermore, most therapy is conducted while the offenders are imprisoned, providing a less than ideal setting.

Context

Beliefs regularly change with respect to what sexual activities are considered normal, so most therapists prefer to avoid terms such as "perversion," instead using "paraphilia." Basically, "paraphilia" means "love of the unusual." Aspects of paraphilias are commonly found within the scope of normal behavior; it is when they become the prime means of gratification, replacing direct sexual contact with a consenting adult partner, that paraphilias are technically said to exist. People who show atypical sexual patterns might also have emotional problems, but it is thought that most people who participate in paraphilias also participate in normal sexual behavior with adult partners, without complete reliance on paraphilic behaviors to produce sexual excitement. Many people who are arrested for paraphilic behaviors do not resort to the paraphilia because they lack a socially acceptable sex partner. Instead, they have an unusual opportunity, a desire to experiment, or perhaps an underlying psychological problem.

According to the approach of Kurt Freund and his colleagues, some paraphilias are better understood as disturbances in the sequence of courtship behaviors. Freund has described courtship as a sequence of four steps: location and appraisal of a potential partner; interaction that does not involve touch; interaction that does involve touch; and genital contact. Most people engage in behavior that is appropriate for each of these steps, but some do not. The ones who do not can be seen as having exaggerations or distortions in one or more of the steps. For example, Freud says that voyeurism is a disorder in the first step of courtship. The voyeur does not use an acceptable means to locate a potential partner. An exhibitionist and an obscene phone caller would have a problem with the second step: They have interaction with people that occurs before the stage of touch, but the talking and showing of exhibitionistic behaviors are not the normal courtship procedures. Frotteurism would be a disruption at the third step, because there is physical touching that is inappropriate. Finally, rape would be a deviation from the appropriate fourth step.

As a result of social and legal restrictions, reliable data on the frequency of paraphilic behaviors are limited. Most information about paraphilias comes from people who have been arrested or are in therapy. Because the majority of people who participate in paraphilias do not fall into these two categories, it is not possible to talk about the majority of paraphiliacs in the real world. It is known, however, that males are much more likely to engage in paraphilias than are females.

Bibliography

Allgeier, E. R., and A. R. Allgeier. "Atypical Sexual Activity." In *Sexual Interactions*. 3d ed. Lexington, Mass.: D. C. Heath, 1991. A highly readable description of sexual variations. Contains photographs, charts, and tables which help make the material understandable. Provides a multitude of references. The book itself is an excellent, thorough textbook.

Evans, David T. *Sexual Citizenship: The Material Construction of Sexualities*. New York: Routledge, 1993.

Gebhard, P. H., W. B. Pomeroy, B. Wardell, J. H. Gagnon, and C. V. Christenson. *Sex Offenders: An Analysis of Types*. New York: Harper & Row, 1965. Also available in paperback from Bantam Books, 1967, this book provides a detailed analysis of many types of atypical sexual behaviors that are against the law, with excellent information about the psychological and social factors that are involved in the development of these behaviors. The authors are well-respected researchers on other aspects of sexuality in addition to paraphilias.

Rosen, Ismond. *Sexual Deviation*. 3d ed. New York: Oxford University Press, 1996.

Rosen, Michael A. *Sexual Magic: The S/M Photographs*. San Francisco: Shaynew Press, 1986. Contains essays written by people who engage in sadomasochistic activities. Includes photographs of the people. In general, provides a personal, honest look into the lives of real people, using a case-study approach.

Stoller, Robert J. "Sexual Deviations." In *Human Sexuality in Four Perspectives,* edited by Frank A. Beach and Milton Diamond. Baltimore: The Johns Hopkins University Press, 1977. Provides a review of several common atypical sexual behaviors, along with several case studies. Concise and readable. Part of an interesting, well-rounded book on sexuality in general.

Weinberg, Thomas S., and G. W. Levi Kamel, eds. *S and M: Studies in Sadomasochism*. Buffalo, N.Y.: Prometheus Books, 1983. Composed of eighteen articles that provide thought-provoking information on a variety of issues relating to sadism and masochism.

Deborah R. McDonald

See also:

Abnormality, 1; Adolescence: Sexuality, 19; Cognitive Behavior Therapy, 128; Gender-Identity Formation, 254; Homosexuality, 278.

SLEEP
Stages and Functions

Type of psychology: Consciousness
Field of study: Sleep

The study of sleep stages and functions involves descriptions of the electrophysiological, cognitive, motor, and behavioral components of various sleep stages as well as the potential functions served by each. The sleep-wake cycle is one of several human circadian rhythms that regulate human attention, alertness, and performance.

Principal terms

CIRCADIAN RHYTHMS: human biological cycles that fluctuate on a daily basis, for example, the sleep-wake cycle, body temperature

DESYNCHRONIZED ELECTROENCEPHALOGRAM (EEG): an irregular brain-wave pattern that is caused by large groups of neurons firing at different times and rates in a given brain region

HYPNAGOGIC IMAGERY: dreamlike, fantasy images that occur in the borderline state between waking and sleeping

MYOCLONIA: brief, jerking movements of the skeletal muscles of the legs and arms

NONRAPID EYE MOVEMENT (NREM) SLEEP: four stages of sleep as measured by electrical changes in the brain, level of muscular activity, and eye movement patterns

PARADOXICAL SLEEP: another term for REM sleep, so named because it is paradoxical that elements of a waking electroencephalogram (EEG) are present in a sleeping state

RAPID EYE MOVEMENT (REM) SLEEP: a special stage of sleep that involves desynchronized electrical brain activity, muscle paralysis, rapid eye movements, and narrative dream recall

SYNCHRONIZED ELECTROENCEPHALOGRAM (EEG): a regular, repetitive brain-wave pattern that is caused by multitudes of neurons firing at the same time and same rate in a given brain region

Overview

Sleep, one of the most mysterious of human circadian rhythms, can be characterized as a naturally induced alteration in consciousness. Although the sleeper may appear to be unconscious, many complex cognitive, physiological, and behavioral processes occur during sleep. For example, parents may sleep through a nearby police siren yet easily awaken to their crying infant.

Efforts to understand sleep have focused on behavioral and electrical changes that occur each night. During every moment of a person's life, the brain, eyes, and muscles are generating electrical potentials that can be recorded by a polygraph. Minute electrical signals are conveyed through tiny disk electrodes attached to the scalp and face, which are recorded by the polygraph as wave patterns that can be described in terms of frequency, amplitude, and synchronization. Frequency is measured by the number of cycles that occur per second (cps), amplitude by the distance between the peaks and troughs of waves, and synchronization by the regular, repetitive nature of the waves.

Use of the polygraph has resulted in the identification of four stages of nonrapid eye movement (NREM) sleep, as well as a special stage referred to as rapid eye movement (REM) sleep. Each stage is described in terms of electrical changes in brain-wave patterns, speed and pattern of eye movements, and muscular activity in the body. Brain-wave activity is measured by the electroencephalogram (EEG), eye movement patterns with the electrooculogram (EOG), and muscle activity by the electromyogram (EMG).

Three EEG patterns can be described for NREM sleep. First, as a sleeper progresses from stages one through four, the waves increase in amplitude or voltage from approximately 50 to 100 microvolts in stage one to about 100 to 200 microvolts in stage four. Second, the frequency of the waves decreases gradually from 4 to 8 cps in stages one and two to 1 to 4 cps in stages three and four. Last, the waves become progressively more synchronized from stages one to four, so that by stage four, the waves assume a slow, regular pattern sometimes called S sleep, for slow-wave sleep or synchronized sleep. Each of these patterns is reflected in the type of brain-wave activity present, with stages one and two consisting predominantly of theta waves and stages three and four of delta waves.

In addition to the changes in brain electrical activity, the EMG records a gradual diminution of muscular activity as the sleeper progresses through each stage of NREM sleep. By the onset of stage four, the EMG is relatively flat, revealing a deep state of muscular relaxation. In fact, virtually all physiological activity is at its lowest during stage four, including respiration, heart rate, blood pressure, digestion, and so on. In this sense, stage four is considered to be the deepest stage of sleep.

As stated previously, the sleeper is not in an unconscious state, but is in a different level of consciousness. Cognitive activity is present in all stages of NREM sleep. Hypnagogic imagery, consisting of dreamlike images sometimes indistinguishable from REM dreams, is present in stage one. Subjects are easily awakened during this sleep stage, and regressions to a waking state are quite common. Often, these regressions occur because of myoclonias, which are brief jerking movements of the muscles. Since stage one is sometimes viewed as a transitional state between sleeping and waking, it should not be too surprising that sleep talking occurs primarily in this stage. Stage one sleep lasts for approximately fifteen minutes.

The sleeper is somewhat more difficult to arouse during stage two, and the cognitive activity present is more thoughtlike and fragmentary than in stage one. If the subject recalls any mental activity, it is rather sparse. Stage two also lasts for approximately fifteen minutes.

It was once assumed that dreams only occur in REM sleep, but it is now common knowledge that dreams of a different variety occur in stages three and four. These dreams are not of the narrative or storylike variety found in REM sleep; rather, they resemble nonsequential thoughts, images, sensations, or emotions. As might be expected in the deepest sleep stage, it is quite difficult to awaken the sleeper who is in stage four. Paradoxically, a subject awakened in stage four will often claim not to be sleeping. Finally, sleepwalking, night terrors, and bed-wetting, all of which are developmental disorders, occur predominantly in stage four. Stage three lasts approximately ten minutes, while the first episode of stage four usually lasts about fifty minutes.

Suddenly, about ninety minutes after falling asleep, the subject rapidly regresses back through the stages of NREM sleep to a special stage usually called stage one-REM sleep, or sometimes simply REM sleep. Three major changes occur in the electrical activity measured in this stage. First, the EEG pattern becomes highly desynchronized, resembling a combination of waking and stage one-NREM brain-wave activity. For this reason, REM sleep is sometimes called paradoxical sleep, because it is paradoxical that elements of a waking EEG should be present in a sleeping condition. Second, the EMG recordings become almost completely flat for most skeletal muscles, resembling paralysis. Finally, there is an onset of rapid eye movements, as measured by the EOG.

Cognitive activity, in the form of narrative or storylike dreams, is rich and varied in REM sleep—hence the term D sleep, for dreaming or desynchronized sleep. It is interesting to note that the rapid eye movements correspond closely with dream content. For example, if a person dreams of something running from left to right, the direction of rapid eye movements will also be left to right.

Throughout the remainder of the evening, a cycle of approximately ninety minutes will be established from one REM episode to the next. All together, the sleeper will experience four to five REM episodes in a typical eight-hour sleep period, with each one lasting for a longer interval than the previous one. The first REM episode may last only five to ten minutes, while the final one may be thirty to forty minutes or longer in duration. In contrast, S sleep episodes decrease in length throughout the evening, and will disappear completely after two to three episodes.

Applications

Although a description of sleep stages can be provided with relative ease, identifying a clear function for sleep is a more difficult proposition. Yet applications of sleep research are inextricably linked with the functions of sleep. For the typical layperson, the seemingly obvious function of sleep is to repair and restore the body after daily mental and physical exertion. This commonsense approach has been formalized by science as the repair and restoration theory. One of the most frequently used methods to assess this theory is to examine the mental and physical effects of sleep deprivation. If the primary function of sleep is to repair the body, then loss of sleep should disrupt cognitive, motor, and behavioral processes. Early laboratory research with animals seemed to support this position. If sleep deprivation persisted for a sufficient time, usually between three and twenty days, death ensued in laboratory animals. Unfortunately, to maintain sleep deprivation in animals, it is necessary to keep them active. Perhaps the continuous activity, rather than the sleep deprivation, killed the animals.

If it were possible to allow animals to rest and relax, but not sleep, would the sleep deprivation still prove fatal? This question was addressed by anecdotal accounts of human sleep deprivation during the Korean War. As a means of extracting confessions from American soldiers, Korean military intelligence operatives commonly subjected prisoners of war to sustained bouts of sleep deprivation. In the face of overwhelming exhaustion and clear signs of personality disintegration, American soldiers were often induced to sign confessions of their alleged war crimes. Yet Randy Gardner, a seventeen-year-old high school student, experienced sleep deprivation for 264 hours to get his name in the *Guinness Book of World Records* with no apparent permanent effects and no profound temporary deficits. Why would people respond in such radically different ways to sleep deprivation?

One hypothesis proposes that severe adverse effects arise as a function of stress and inability to rest and relax, rather than from the loss of sleep. Furthermore, laboratory investigations with volunteer subjects suggest that those individuals who exhibit severe reactions to sleep deprivation almost always have some predisposition to abnormal behavior. Sleep researchers would not deny that sleep serves to restore the body; however, rest and relaxation may serve the same restorative functions in the absence of sleep, which would suggest that repair and restoration is not the sole or even primary function of sleep.

To redress the shortcomings of the repair and restoration theory, an alternative theory of a need to sleep has been proposed. The adaptive or evolutionary theory postulates that the need to sleep arose in the course of biological evolution as an adaptive mechanism to conserve energy during the evening hours, when it would be inefficient to search for food and other resources. Sleep, according to this view, serves a function similar to the hibernation observed in several species of mammals. These animals reduce their metabolic processes to barely detectable levels during winter to conserve energy when food resources are scarce. To do otherwise would threaten the survival of these animals. It is important to note that the adaptive theory still considers sleep to be a real need; in essence, sleep is a remnant of the human evolutionary past when human forebears did not have the convenience of twenty-four-hour supermarkets to acquire their sustenance. Humans deprived of sleep will become just as irritable and ill-tempered as a groundhog prevented from hibernating.

Several predictions have been generated from the adaptive theory, most of which have been supported by scientific observations. First, the theory predicts that predators such as large cats and bears, which obtain most of their nutrients in one large meal per day, would sleep much more than grazing animals such as cattle and horses, who must eat frequently to survive. A second prediction of the theory is that predators such as wolves and mountain lions, which have few natural enemies, would sleep more than prey such as rabbits and guinea pigs, which are at risk if they fail to maintain constant vigilance. Finally, animals such as bats, which are well protected by the environment in which they live, would sleep for relatively long periods of time. These predictions are documented by scientific observations, which provide support for the adaptive or evolutionary theory of sleep.

The functions of sleep are extremely important in clinical applications. If the repair and restoration theory lacks strong scientific support, attempting to recover lost sleep time may serve no functional purpose. Indeed, most subjects expect to sleep for several hours longer than normal after staying awake for twenty-four hours, presumably because they believe sleep is required for repair and restoration of the body. In practice, however, most subjects report only four to six total hours of poor-quality sleep following such deprivation. Even after 264 hours of sleep deprivation, Randy Gardner slept for only fourteen hours and forty minutes the first evening, then resumed a normal nocturnal sleep pattern of eight hours per evening.

Knowledge of sleep stages may be especially valuable in diagnosing and treating sleep disorders, since the frequency, patterns, and symptoms of these disorders may be associated with specific stages of sleep. For example, knowledge of the muscular paralysis that accompanies REM sleep has been instrumental in diagnosing the cause of male impotence. Partial or total erections are present in about 95 percent of REM periods. Therefore, men who complain of impotence yet demonstrate normal REM erections can be diagnosed as suffering from psychologically based impotence. These patients may benefit from psychotherapy or sexual counseling. In contrast, men who do not achieve REM erections are diagnosed as suffering from organically based impotence and require hormone therapy or surgical implantations.

Nocturnal enuresis, or bed-wetting, is a stage four developmental disorder present in about four to five million children annually in the United States. The exact cause of this disorder is undetermined, although the extreme muscular relaxation during stage four sleep likely contributes to its occurrence. To prevent nocturnal enuresis, the patient must learn to associate a full bladder with waking up. Typically, a special apparatus is placed under the child, which sounds a loud buzzer when urine completes the circuit. Eventually, the child will learn to associate the feeling of a full bladder with waking up in the absence of the buzzer.

Context

Since sleep is a universal human experience, it is probably safe to conclude that it has interested people since the dawn of humanity; however, scientific inquiry into sleep is a relatively recent phenomenon. Early interest in sleep arose during the late nineteenth century from a need to isolate the brain structure responsible for lethargy syndromes. Similarly, the electrophysiological study of sleep originated with a discovery in 1875 by the English physiologist Richard Caton that the brain continually produces low-voltage waves. This discovery was largely ignored until 1929, when a German psychiatrist, Hans Berger, found that he could record from large groups of neurons by attaching electrodes to the scalp and the forehead. Berger's discovery marked the beginning of modern electroencephalography. With the advent of EEG recordings, it was not long before A. L. Loomis, E. N. Harvey, and G. A. Hobart found, in 1937, that EEG recordings could be used to differentiate stages of sleep. In 1952, Nathaniel Kleitman at the University of Chicago gave Eugene Aserinsky, one of his new graduate students, the assignment of watching the eye movements of sleeping subjects. Aserinsky quickly noted the rapid, darting nature of eye movements during certain times of the night, which differed from the usual slow, rolling eye movements observed at other times. William Dement later coined the term REM sleep; sleep in which slow, rolling eye movements predominate later came to be known as NREM sleep (for nonrapid eye movement sleep). Finally, in 1957, Dement and Kleitman presented the current system of four NREM sleep stages and stage REM.

As a naturally induced alteration in consciousness that can be studied objectively with electrophysiological recording equipment, sleep has assumed a prominent role in the psychology of consciousness. Electrophysiological recording techniques that were originally developed in sleep research are now widely used to study other aspects of consciousness, such as hemispheric asymmetries, meditation, sensory isolation, biofeedback, dreams, and drug effects on the brain and behavior. In addition, sleep is one of the few alterations in consciousness that plays a central role in several areas of psychological inquiry. For example, physiological psychologists are concerned with the neurobiological mechanisms underlying sleep, as well as the functions of sleep. From their perspective, sleep is simply one of many human behaviors and cognitive processes whose biological basis must be ascertained. Developmental psychologists are interested in age-related changes that occur in sleep, and attempt to develop applications of those findings for concerned parents of young children. Finally, physicians and clinical psychologists are often presented with patients who suffer from physical and/or psychological stress as a function of sleep disorders. These professionals are interested in developing effective drug and psychological therapies that can be used to treat sleep-disordered patients. Sleep is a concern in many areas of psychology.

Because sleep is universal in humans, it will continue to play a major role in consciousness studies and throughout the discipline of psychology. Future research will likely focus on applications of sleep research to industrial settings that employ shift workers. The emphasis will be on reducing fatigue and improving performance among employees by gradually adjusting them to shift work and by changing employee work schedules infrequently. In addition, research will seek ways to improve diagnostic procedures and treatments for a variety of sleep disorders, including insomnia, hypersomnia, sleep apnea, narcolepsy, and enuresis. The focus will be on developing effective drug and psychological therapies. Finally, pure research will continue to examine the functions of sleep, and to delineate more clearly the adverse effects of sleep, even those of a temporary nature.

Bibliography

Cohen, David B. *Sleep and Dreaming: Origins, Nature, and Functions*. New York: Pergamon Press, 1979. A comprehensive review of sleep and dreaming research, including sleep stages, functions, development, and disorders. Also includes findings on sex differences in the effects of REM sleep deprivation. Somewhat technical; recommended for advanced college students only.

Coleman, Richard M. *Wide Awake at 3:00 A.M.: By Choice or by Chance?* New York: W. H. Freeman, 1986. Reveals how a person's biological clock (or sleepwake cycle) works and how it controls periods of sleep, alertness, mood, and performance. Also examines sleep stages, functions, and sleep disorders. Highly readable; recommended for high school and college students, as well as other interested adults.

Coren, Stanley. *Sleep Thieves: An Eye-Opening Exploration into the Science and Mysteries of Sleep*. New York: Free Press, 1996.

Dement, William C. *Some Must Watch While Some Must Sleep*. San Francisco: San Francisco Book Company, 1976. William Dement, founder of the sleep disorders clinic at Stanford University, provides a nontechnical, personal report of sleep stages, dreams, and sleep disorders. Immensely readable and often humorous. Highly recommended for junior high school, high school, and college students, as well as other interested adults.

Hobson, J. Allan. *Sleep*. New York: Scientific American Library, 1989. A broad and interdisciplinary view of sleep research, combining knowledge drawn from neurology, psychology, and animal behavior studies. The nontechnical language and lavish illustrations are two major advantages of this book. Highly recommended for high school and college students.

Ogilvie, Robert D., and John R. Harsh, eds. *Sleep Onset: Normal and Abnormal Processes*. Washington, D.C.: American Psychological Association, 1994.

Webb, Wilse B. *Sleep: The Gentle Tyrant*. Englewood Cliffs, N.J.: Prentice-Hall, 1975. A nontechnical overview of sleep research, focusing particularly on behavioral components of sleep and sleep disorders. Somewhat dated, but perhaps the most comprehensive introductory book available on sleep that can be easily understood by most high school and college students.

Richard P. Atkinson

See also:

Consciousness, Functions of, 159; Consciousness, Levels of, 165; Dream Analysis, 206; Dreams, 212.

SMELL AND TASTE

Type of psychology: Sensation and perception
Fields of study: Auditory, chemical, cutaneous, and body senses

The senses of taste and smell, which are closely related, depend on sensory receptors known as chemoreceptors. These receptors detect molecules of various kinds and respond by generating nerve impulses. Chemoreception is believed to depend on proteins in receptor cell membranes that can recognize and combine with molecules from the environment.

Principal terms

ADAPTATION: a reduction in the number of nerve impulses generated by a receptor while a stimulus is held constant
ALKALOIDS: a group of organic substances, many of them toxic plant products, that have a strongly bitter taste
CHEMORECEPTORS: sensory receptor cells that generate nerve impulses on coming in contact with chemicals from the environment
OLFACTORY BULBS: two narrow extensions at the base of the brain to which extensions of olfactory cells make connections
OLFACTORY CELL: the chemoreceptor for the sense of smell
PAPILLA (pl. PAPILLAE): a moundlike outgrowth containing taste buds
TASTE BUD: a small bundle of taste receptor cells surrounded by supportive cells and communicating with the exterior through a small pore

Overview

The senses of taste and smell, which are closely related, depend on a type of sensory receptor cell known as a chemoreceptor. This receptor detects molecules of various kinds and responds on contact with them by generating nerve impulses. Although the basis for the detection is incompletely understood, chemoreceptor cells are believed to contain proteins in their surface membranes that are able to recognize and combine with various kinds of molecules. Combination with a recognized molecule causes the protein to open an ion channel in the surface membrane. The resulting ion flow creates an electrical change in the membrane that triggers generation of a nerve impulse by the chemoreceptor cell.

Chemoreceptors for taste occur primarily on the upper surface of the tongue. A comparatively few taste receptors are also located on the roof of the mouth, particularly on the soft palate, and in the throat. The taste receptors in these locations are parts of taste buds, which are small, pear-shaped bundles of cells. Molecules from the exterior environment reach the taste receptor cells through a small pore at the top of a taste bud. All together, there are about ten thousand taste buds on the tongue and throat. The taste buds of the tongue, which are only 30 to 40 micrometers in diameter and thus microscopic, are embedded in the surfaces of small, moundlike outgrowths called papillae. The papillae give the surface of the tongue its rough or furry texture.

Taste receptor cells occur in taste buds along with other cells that play a purely supportive structural role. Individual taste receptor cells are elongated and bear thin, fingerlike extensions at their tips that protrude through the pore of a taste bud. Combination with chemicals from the environment, which must dissolve in the saliva of the mouth to reach the taste buds, probably occurs in the membranes of the fingerlike processes at the tips of the taste receptor cells. The opposite end of the taste receptor cells makes connections with sensory nerves serving the taste buds.

Each taste receptor cell probably has membrane proteins that can combine with a variety of molecules from the environment; however, individual taste cells, depending on their location on the tongue, typically combine more readily with some molecular types than with others. Taste cells with a preponderance of membrane proteins recognizing and combining with organic molecules, such as carbohydrates, alcohols, and amino acids, are crowded near the tip of the tongue. Combination of these taste receptors with organic molecules gives rise to nerve impulses that are interpreted in the brain as a sweet taste. Just behind the tip of the tongue is a region containing taste receptor cells that combine most readily with inorganic salts; combination with these substances gives rise to nerve impulses that are interpreted in the brain as a salty taste.

Farther to the rear of the tongue, particularly along the sides, are taste receptor cells that combine most readily with the hydrogen (H^+) ions released by acids; this combination is perceived as a sour taste. The rear of the tongue contains taste receptor cells that combine most readily with a wide variety of organic and inorganic molecules, particularly long-chain organic molecules containing nitrogen and a group of organic substances called alkaloids. All the alkaloids, including molecules such as quinine, caffeine, morphine, and strychnine, give rise to a bitter taste. People tend to reject substances stimulating the bitter taste receptors at the rear of the tongue. This may have a survival value, because many bitter substances, including alkaloids produced by a variety of plants, are strongly poisonous. Many of the organic molecules with a bitter taste differ from those with a sweet taste by only minor chemical groups. A few substances, such as pepper, primarily stimulate pain rather than taste receptors when present in foods.

The distribution on the tongue of regions of strongest taste does not mean that the taste receptor cells in these areas are limited to detecting only sweet, salty, sour, or bitter substances; all regions of the tongue can detect molecules of each type to at least some extent.

Traditionally, the wide range of different flavors that humans can differentiate, which easily amounts to thousands, has been considered to be the result of subtle combinations of the four primary flavors: sweet, salty, sour, and bitter. There are indications, however, that the picture may be considerably more complex than this. Persons can be "taste-blind" for certain very specific, single molecules, such as the chemical phenylthiocarbamide (PTC). The ability to taste this substance, which has a bitter flavor, is hereditary; some persons can taste PTC, and some cannot. The pattern of inheritance suggests that a membrane protein able to combine with PTC is present in some persons and not in others. Persons taste-blind for PTC do not have the specific membrane protein and cannot respond to the presence of the chemical even though other bitter flavors can be detected. It is possible that there are a wide variety of specific membrane proteins like the one responsible for detecting PTC distributed in the surface membranes of the taste receptor cells of the tongue.

The chemoreceptors responsible for the other chemical sense, the sense of smell, are located within the head at the roof of the nasal cavity. The receptor cells detecting odors, called olfactory cells, are distributed among supportive cells in a double patch of tissue totaling about 5 square centimeters in area. Although limited to this area, the olfactory region contains between 10 and 100 million olfactory cells in the average person.

Each olfactory cell bears between ten and twenty fine, fibrous extensions that protrude into a layer of mucus that covers the olfactory area. The membranes of the extensions contain the protein molecules that recognize and combine with chemicals to trigger a nerve impulse by an olfactory cell. In order to reach the fibrous extensions, molecules detected as odors must dissolve in the mucous solution covering the olfactory region.

The opposite ends of the olfactory cells penetrate directly into the cranial cavity through microscopic channels in the shelf of bone separating the top of the nasal cavity from the base of the brain. On the brain side of the bony shelf, the extensions of the olfactory cells make connections with nerve cells of the brain. The region of the brain connecting with the olfactory cells consists of two narrow swellings, the olfactory bulbs, which extend along the lower surface of the brain. Olfactory cells are the only receptor cells known to make direct connections in this way with nerve cells of the brain. All other sensory receptors make indirect connections to the brain via sensory nerves and, in most cases, other nerve cells that make interconnections in the spinal cord. The extensions of olfactory cells making connections with the olfactory bulbs are known collectively as the olfactory or first cranial nerve.

Efforts to identify primary odors equivalent to the primary sweet, salty, sour, and bitter flavors have been largely unsuccessful. Humans can detect and identify thousands or even tens of thousands of different substances by smell, some in concentrations of only a few molecules per olfactory cell. There are thousands of different substances that individuals may be unable to recognize. These observations indicate that, as with the receptors for taste, many different kinds of specific receptor molecules in the olfactory cell membranes recognize and combine with molecules of odorous substances to trigger nerve impulses. There seems to be little rhyme or reason to the types and classes of molecules registering as different odors: Molecules of widely different sizes and structure may smell the same, and closely related molecules that differ only in minor chemical groups, or in the folding arrangement of the same chemical groups, may smell quite different.

Applications

The chemoreceptors responsible for the senses of taste and smell typically adapt rapidly to continued stimulation by the same molecules. In adaptation, a receptor cell generates nerve impulses most rapidly when first stimulated; with continued stimulation at the same intensity, the frequency of nerve impulses drops steadily until a baseline of a relatively few impulses per second is reached. Adaptation for the senses of taste and smell also involves complex interactions in the brain, because discernment of tastes and smells continues to diminish even after chemoreceptors reach their baselines.

For the sense of taste, adaptation is reflected in the fact that the first bite of food, for example, has the most intensely perceived taste. As stimulation by the same food continues, the intensity of the taste and a person's perception of the flavor steadily decrease. If a second food is tasted, the initial intensity of its taste is high, but again intensity drops off with continued stimulation. If the first food is retasted, however, its flavor will again seem stronger. This effect occurs because adaptation of the receptors detecting the initial taste lessens during the period during which the second food is tasted. If sufficient time passes before the first food is retasted, the flavor will appear to be almost as strong as its first taste. For this reason, one gains greater appreciation of a meal if foods are alternated rather than eaten and finished separately.

Taste receptor cells have a life expectancy of about ten days. As they degenerate, they are constantly replaced by new taste cells that continually differentiate from tissue at the sides of taste buds. As humans reach middle age, the rate of replacement drops off, so that the total number of taste receptor cells declines steadily after the age of about forty-five. This may account for the fact that, as people get older, nothing ever tastes as good as it did in childhood. Smoking also decreases the sensitivity of taste receptor cells, and thereby decreases a person's appreciation and appetite for foods.

Olfactory cells also adapt rapidly to the continued presence of the same molecules and slow or stop generating nerve impulses if the concentration of the odoriferous substances is maintained. This response is also reflected in common experience. When engaged in an odor-generating activity such as cooking or interior painting, a person is strongly aware of the odors generated by the activity only initially. After exposure for more than a few minutes, the person's perception of the odor lessens and eventually disappears almost completely. If the person leaves the odoriferous room for a few minutes, however, allowing the olfactory receptors and brain centers to lose their adaptation, the person is usually surprised at the strength of the odor if he or she returns to the room.

The region at the top of the nasal cavity containing the olfactory cells lies outside the main stream of air entering the lungs through the mouth and nose. As a result, the molecules dissolving in the mucous layer covering the olfactory cells are carried to this region only by side eddies of the airflow through the nose. Flow to the olfactory region is greatly improved by sniffing, a response used by all air-breathing vertebrates as a way to increase the turbulence in the nasal passages and thereby to intensify odors from the environment. Head colds interfere with people's sense of smell through congestion and blockage of the nasal cavity, which impedes airflow to the olfactory region.

Although humans are not nearly as sensitive to odors as are many other animals, their ability to detect some substances by smell is still remarkable, particularly in the case of smells generated by putrefaction. Some of the mercaptans, for example, which are generated in decaying flesh, can be detected in concentrations in air as small as 0.0000000002 milligram per milliliter. One of these substances, methyl mercaptan, is mixed in low concentration in natural gas. The presence of this mercaptan allows people to detect natural gas, which otherwise would be odorless, by smell.

Context

The idea that taste and smell receptors operate by recognizing specific molecular types is an old one, dating back to the first century B.C., when Titus Lucretius Carus proposed that the sense of smell depends on recognition of atomic shapes. Definitive experimental demonstration of this mechanism for the sense of smell, however, was not obtained until 1991, when Linda Buck and Richard Axel finally isolated members of a large family of membrane proteins that can actually do what Lucretius proposed: They recognize and bind specific molecular types and trigger responses by olfactory cells. Axel and Buck have obtained indications that there are hundreds of different proteins in the family responsible for molecular recognition in the sense of smell.

One of the many interesting features of the family is that, as with the sense of taste, many people inherit a deficiency in one or more of the membrane proteins so that they are congenitally unable to detect a particular odor. There are in fact many thousands of different odors to which persons may be insensitive, which directly supports the idea that the family of membrane proteins responsible for detecting individual molecular types is very large indeed. Another interesting feature of the mechanism is that there are many odors for which people must be "educated." People cannot recognize them on first encounter, but later learn to discern them. This indicates that membrane proteins recognizing previously unknown molecules may be induced; that is, they may be newly synthesized and placed in olfactory cell membranes in response to encountering a new chemical in the environment. People can also smell, and often taste, totally new artificial substances never before encountered by humans or indeed any other animal. Thus, the chemoreceptors have membrane proteins capable of recognizing molecules never encountered in animal evolution.

Both taste and smell receptors are linked through nerve connections to regions of the brain stem that control visceral responses, as well as to the areas of the cerebral cortex registering conscious sensations. As a result, different odors and tastes may give rise to a host of involuntary responses, such as salivation, appetite, thirst, pleasure, excitement, sexual arousal, nausea, or even vomiting, as well as to consciously perceived sensations. The odor of a once-enjoyed food may make someone ill in the future if the person became sick after eating the food; previously unobjectionable or even pleasant odors and tastes may become unpleasant and nauseating to women during pregnancy. The odor of other foods, such as some of the ranker cheeses, may be repulsive at first experience but later appetizing as a person learns to enjoy them. The degree to which many substances are perceived as pleasant or unpleasant is also related to their concentration. Many substances perceived as pleasantly sweet in low concentration, for example, taste bitter and unpleasant at higher concentrations.

A part of the perception of pleasantness or unpleasantness in taste or smell is related to the body's nutritional needs. Persons who are deficient in the insulin hormone, for example, so that their cells cannot metabolize glucose, develop a craving for sweets. Several studies have shown that children, if left to themselves, will select a combination of foods that generally satisfies their nutritional needs.

Bibliography

Akins, Kathleen, ed. *Perception*. New York: Oxford University Press, 1996.

Berne, Robert M., and Matthew Levy, eds. *Physiology*. 2d ed. St. Louis: C. V. Mosby, 1988. Chapter 12, "Chemical Senses," in this standard college physiology text outlines the anatomy and physiology of the systems integrated in the senses of taste and smell. Includes a discussion of the neural connections and regions of the brain involved in the perception of taste and smell. Intended for students at the college level, but clearly written; should be accessible to readers at the high school level.

Coren, Stanley, *Sensation and Perception*. New York: Academic Press, 1979. A simply written, easily understood discussion of the senses, sensory cells, and routes traveled by sensory information through the spinal cord to the brain. Provides a clear and interesting description of the basics of perception in the cerebral cortex.

Guyton, Arthur C. *Textbook of Medical Physiology*. 7th ed. Philadelphia: W. B. Saunders,

1986. Chapter 48, "Sensory Receptors and Their Basic Mechanisms of Action," in this readable and clearly written text outlines the fundamental activities of sensory receptors. Chapter 62, "The Chemical Senses—Taste and Smell," presents more detailed information on the chemoreceptors active in detection of taste and smell, and the connections between these receptors and the brain. Intended for college and medical students, but easily understood by readers at the high school level.

Milne, Lorus Johnson, and Margery Milne. *The Senses of Animals and Men*. New York: Atheneum, 1962. A simple and entertaining survey of the senses and their importance in humans and other animals, written for a popular audience. Provides interesting and thought-provoking comparisons between the sensory systems of humans and of other animals.

Schmidt-Nielsen, Knut. *Animal Physiology, Adaptation, and Environment*. 4th ed. New York: Cambridge University Press, 1990. A standard college text by one of the greatest animal physiologists. Provides a deeply perceptive comparison of sensory systems in humans and other animals. Chapter 8 describes the senses. The text is remarkable for its lucid and entertaining description of animal physiology.

Stephen L. Wolfe

See also:

The Auditory System, 82; Sensation and Perception, 535; Touch and Pressure, 627; Visual Development, 638; The Visual System, 643.

SOCIAL LEARNING
Albert Bandura

Type of psychology: Personality
Fields of study: Behavioral and cognitive models; cognitive learning

Albert Bandura's social learning theory, later called social cognitive theory, provides a theoretical framework for understanding and explaining human behavior; the theory embraces an interactional model of causation and accords central roles to cognitive, vicarious, and self-regulatory processes.

Principal terms

DETERMINISM: the doctrine that behavior is caused by events independent of one's will

MODEL: a person whose behavior is imitated by another person

MODELING: giving verbal or written instructions and/or demonstrating a behavior for teaching purposes

OBSERVATIONAL LEARNING: the acquisition of a behavior by imitating someone else's performance (also called vicarious learning)

OUTCOME EXPECTANCIES: the consequences expected to result from an action

RECIPROCAL DETERMINISM: an interactional model proposing that environment, personal factors, and behavior all operate as interacting determinants of one another

REINFORCEMENT: a contingency by which a response produces a desirable consequence, which increases the future probability of that response

SELF-EFFICACY: the perception or judgment of one's ability to perform a certain action successfully

Overview

Social learning theory, later amplified as social cognitive theory by its founder, social psychologist Albert Bandura, provides a unified theoretical framework for analyzing the psychological processes that govern human behavior. Its goal is to explain how behavior develops, how it is maintained, and through what processes it can be modified. It seeks to accomplish this task by identifying the determinants of human action and the mechanisms through which they operate.

Bandura lays out the conceptual framework of his approach in his book *Social Learning Theory* (1977). His theory is based on a model of reciprocal determinism. This means that Bandura rejects both the humanist/existentialist position viewing people as free agents and the behaviorist position viewing behavior as controlled by the environment. Rather, external determinants of behavior (such as rewards and punishments) and internal determinants (such as thoughts, expectations, and beliefs) are considered part of a system of interlocking determinants that influence not only behavior but also the various other parts of the system. In other words, each part of the system—behavior, cognition, and environmental influences—affects each of the other parts. People are neither free agents nor passive reactors to external pressures. Instead, through self-regulatory processes, they have the ability to exercise some measure of control over their own actions. They can affect their behavior by setting goals, arranging environmental inducements, generating cognitive strategies, evaluating goal attainment, and mediating consequences for their actions. Bandura accepts that these self-regulatory functions initially are learned as the result of external rewards and punishments. Their external origin, however, does not invalidate the fact that, once internalized, they in part determine behavior.

As self-regulation results from symbolic processing of information, Bandura in his theorizing has assigned an increasingly prominent role to cognition. This is reflected in his book *Social Foundations of Thought and Action: A Social Cognitive Theory* (1986), in which he no longer refers to his approach as social learning but as social cognitive theory. People, unlike lower animals, use verbal and nonverbal symbols (language and images) to process information and preserve experiences in the form of cognitive representations. This encoded information serves as a guide for future behavior. Without the ability to use symbols, people would have to solve problems by enacting various alternative solutions until, by trial and error, they learned which ones resulted in rewards or punishments. Through their cognitive abilities, however, people can think through different options, imagine possible outcomes, and guide their behavior by anticipated consequences. Symbolic capabilities provide people with a powerful tool to regulate their own behavior in the absence of external reinforcements and punishments.

According to Bandura, the most central of all mechanisms of self-regulation is self-efficacy, defined as the belief that one has the ability, with one's actions, to bring about a certain outcome. Self-efficacy beliefs function as determinants of behavior by influencing motivation, thought processes, and emotions in ways that may be self-aiding or self-hindering. Specifically, self-efficacy appraisals determine the goals people set for themselves, whether they anticipate and visualize scenarios of success or failure, whether they embark on a course of action, how much effort they expend, and how long they persist in the face of obstacles. Self-efficacy expectations are different from outcome expectations. While outcome expectancies are beliefs that a given behavior will result in a certain outcome, self-efficacy refers to the belief in one's ability to bring about this outcome. To put it simply, people may believe that something can happen, but whether they embark on a course of action depends on their perceived ability to make it happen.

Perhaps the most important contribution of social learning theory to the understanding of human behavior is the concept of vicarious, or observational, learning, also termed learning through modeling. Before the advent of social learning theory, many psychologists assigned a crucial role to the process of reinforcement in learning. They postulated that without performing responses that are followed by reinforcement or punishment, a person cannot learn. In contrast, Bandura asserted that much of social behavior is not learned from the consequences of trial and error but is acquired through symbolic modeling. People watch what other people do and what happens to them as a result of their actions. From such observations, they form ideas of how to perform new behaviors, and later this information guides their actions.

Symbolic modeling is of great significance for human learning because of its enormous efficiency in transmitting information. Whereas trial-and-error learning requires the gradual shaping of the behavior of individuals through repetition and reinforcement, in observational learning, a single model can teach complex behaviors simultaneously to any number of people. According to Bandura, some elaborate and specifically human behavior patterns, such as language, might even be impossible to learn if it were not for symbolic modeling. For example, it seems unlikely that children learn to talk as a result of their parents' reinforcing each correct utterance they emit. Rather, children probably hear and watch other members of their verbal community talk and then imitate their behavior. In a similar vein, complex behaviors such as driving a car or flying a plane are not acquired by trial and error. Instead, prospective drivers or pilots follow the verbal rules of an instructor until they master the task.

In summary, Bandura's social learning theory explains human action in terms of the interplay among behavior, cognition, and environmental influences. The theory places particular emphasis on cognitive mediating factors such as self-efficacy beliefs and outcome expectancies. Its greatest contribution to a general theory of human learning has been its emphasis on learning by observation or modeling. Observational learning has achieved the status of a third learning principle, next to classical and operant conditioning.

Applications

From its inception, social learning theory has served as a useful framework for the under-standing of both normal and abnormal human behavior. A major contribution that has important implications for the modification of human behavior is the theory's distinction between learning and performance. In a now-classic series of experiments, Bandura and his associates teased apart the roles of observation and reinforcement in learning and were able to demonstrate that people learn through mere observation.

In a study on aggression, an adult model hit and kicked a life-size inflated clown doll (a "Bobo" doll), with children watching the attack in person or on a television screen. Other children watched the model perform some innocuous behavior. Later, the children were allowed to play in the room with the Bobo doll. All children who had witnessed the aggression, either in person or on television, viciously attacked the doll, while those who had observed the model's innocuous behavior did not display aggression toward the doll. Moreover, it was clearly shown that the children modeled their aggressive behaviors after the adult. Those who had observed the adult sit on the doll and hit its face, or kick the doll, or use a hammer to pound it, imitated exactly these behaviors. Thus, the study accomplished its purpose by demonstrating that observational learning occurs in the absence of direct reinforcement.

In a related experiment, Bandura showed that expected consequences, while not relevant for learning, play a role in performance. A group of children watched a film of an adult model behaving aggressively toward a Bobo doll and being punished, while another group observed the same behavior with the person being rewarded. When the children sub-sequently were allowed to play with the Bobo doll, those who had watched the model being punished displayed fewer aggressive behaviors toward the doll than those who had seen the model being rewarded. When the experimenter then offered a reward to the children for imitating the model, however, all children, regardless of the consequences they had ob-served, attacked the Bobo doll. This showed that all children had learned the aggressive behavior from the model but that observing the model being punished served as an inhibiting factor, which was removed by the promise of a reward. Again, this study showed that children learn without reinforcement, simply by observing how others behave. Whether they then engage in the behavior, however, depends on the consequences they expect will result from their actions.

Models not only teach people novel ways of thinking and behaving but also can strengthen or weaken inhibitions. Seeing models punished may inhibit similar behavior in observers, while seeing models carry out feared or forbidden actions without negative consequences may reduce their inhibitions.

The most striking demonstrations of the disinhibitory effects of observational learning come from therapeutic interventions based on modeling principles. Baudura, in his book *Principles of Behavior Modification* (1969), shows how social learning theory can provide a conceptual framework for the modification of a wide range of maladaptive behaviors. For example, a large number of laboratory studies of subjects with a severe phobia of snakes showed that phobic individuals can overcome their fear of reptiles when fearless adult models demonstrate how to handle a snake and directly assist subjects in coping successfully with whatever they dread.

In later elaborations, the scope of social learning theory was amplified to include self-efficacy theory. Self-efficacy is now considered the principal mechanism of behavior change, in that all successful interventions are assumed to operate by strengthening a person's self-perceived efficacy to cope with difficulties.

How can self-efficacy be strengthened? Research indicates that it is influenced by four sources of information. The most important influence comes from performance attainments, with successes heightening and failures lowering perceived self-efficacy. Thus, having people enact and master a difficult task most powerfully increases their efficacy percepts. A second influence comes from vicarious experiences. Exposing people to models works because seeing people similar to oneself successfully perform a difficult task raises one's own efficacy expectations. Verbal persuasion is a third way of influencing self-efficacy. Convincing people that they have the ability to perform a task can encourage them to try harder, which indeed may lead to successful performance. Finally, teaching people coping strategies to lower emotional arousal can also increase self-efficacy. If subsequently they approach a task more calmly, the likelihood of succeeding at it may increase.

Bandura and his associates conducted a series of studies to test the idea that vastly different modes of influence all improve coping behavior by strengthening self-perceived efficacy. Severe snake phobics received interventions based on enactive, vicarious, cognitive, or emotive treatment modalities. The results confirmed that the degree to which people changed their behavior toward the reptiles was closely associated with increases in self-judged efficacy, regardless of the method of intervention. It is now widely accepted among social learning theorists that all effective therapies ultimately work by strengthening people's self-perceptions of efficacy.

Context

Social learning theory was born into a climate in which two competing and diametrically opposed schools of thought dominated psychology. On the one hand, psychologists who advocated psychodynamic theories postulated that human behavior is governed by motivational forces operating in the form of largely unconscious needs, drives, and impulses. These impulse theories tended to give circular explanations, attributing behavior to inner causes that were inferred from the very behavior they were supposed to cause. They also tended to

provide explanations after the fact, rather than predicting events, and had very limi _
empirical support.

On the other hand, there were various types of behavior theory that shifted the focus of
the causal analysis from hypothetical internal determinants of behavior to external, publicly
observable causes. Behaviorists were able to show that actions commonly attributed to inner
causes could be produced, eliminated, and reinstated by manipulating the antecedent
(stimulus) and consequent (reinforcing) conditions of the person's external environment.
This led to the proposition that people's behavior is caused by factors residing in the
environment.

Social learning theory presents a theory of human behavior that to some extent incorporates both viewpoints. According to Bandura, people are neither driven by inner forces nor
buffeted by environmental stimuli; instead, psychological functioning is best explained in
terms of a continuous reciprocal interaction of internal and external causes. This assumption, termed reciprocal determinism, became one of the dominant viewpoints in psychology.

An initial exposition of social learning theory was presented in Albert Bandura and
Richard H. Walters' text *Social Learning and Personality Development* (1963). This formulation drew heavily on the procedures and principles of operant and classical conditioning.
In his book *Principles of Behavior Modification,* Bandura placed much greater emphasis on
symbolic events and self-regulatory processes. He argued that complex human behavior
could not be satisfactorily explained by the narrow set of learning principles behaviorists
had drived from animal studies. He incorporated principles derived from developmental,
social, and cognitive psychology into social learning theory.

During the 1970's, psychology had grown increasingly cognitive. This development was
reflected in Bandura's 1977 book, *Social Learning Theory,* which presented self-efficacy
theory as the central mechanism through which people control their own behavior. Over the
following decade, the influence of cognitive psychology on Bandura's work grew stronger.
In his book *Social Foundations of Thought and Action: A Social Cognitive Theory,* he finally
disavowed his roots in learning theory and renamed his approach "social cognitive theory."
This theory accorded central roles to cognitive, vicarious, self-reflective, and self-regulatory
processes.

Social learning/social cognitive theory became the dominant conceptual approach within
the field of behavior therapy. It has provided the conceptual framework for numerous
interventions for a wide variety of psychological disorders and probably will remain popular
for a long time. Its founder, Albert Bandura, was honored with the Award for Distinguished
Scientific Contributions to Psychology from the American Psychological Foundation in
1980 in recognition of his work.

Bibliography

Bandura, Albert. *Principles of Behavior Modification.* New York: Holt, Rinehart and
    Winston, 1969. Presents an overview of basic psychological principles governing human
    behavior within the conceptual framework of social learning. Reviews theoretical and
    empirical advances in the field of social learning, placing special emphasis on self-
    regulation and on symbolic and vicarious processes. Applies these principles to the
    conceptualization and modification of a number of common behavior disorders such as
    alcoholism, phobias, and sexual deviancy.

_____. *Social Foundations of Thought and Action: A Social Cognitive Theory.* Englewood Cliffs, N.J.: Prentice-Hall, 1986. Presents a comprehensive coverage of the tenets of current social cognitive theory. Besides addressing general issues of human nature and causality, provides an impressive in-depth analysis of all important aspects of human functioning, including motivational, cognitive, and self-regulatory processes.

_____. *Social Learning Theory.* Englewood Cliffs, N.J.: Prentice-Hall, 1977. Lays out Bandura's theory and presents a concise overview of its theoretical and experimental contributions to the field of social learning. Redefines many of the traditional concepts of learning theory and emphasizes the importance of cognitive processes in human learning.

Evans, Richard I. *Albert Bandura, the Man and His Ideas: A Dialogue.* New York: Praeger, 1989. An edited version of an interview with Bandura. Easy to read, presenting Bandura's thoughts on the major aspects of his work in a very accessible form. The spontaneity of the discussion between Evans and Bandura gives a glimpse of Bandura as a person.

Grusec, Joan E. "Social Learning Theory and Developmental Psychology: The Legacies of Robert Sears and Albert Bandura." *Developmental Psychology* 28, no. 5 (September, 1992): 776-787.

Rotgers, Frederick. "Social-Learning Theory, Philosophy of Science, and the Identity of Behavior Therapy." In *Paradigms in Behavior Therapy: Present and Promise,* edited by Daniel B. Fishman, Frederick Rotgers, and Cyril M. Franks. New York: Springer-Verlag, 1988. Places Bandura's social learning theory in the context of contemporary behavior theory and examines its philosophical roots. Difficult because it requires some basic understanding of the philosophy of science, but provides an excellent analysis of the philosophical underpinnings of Bandura's theory.

Schultz, Duane. *Theories of Personality.* 4th ed. Pacific Grove, Calif: Brooks/Cole, 1990. Chapter 15 of this book contains an excellent summary of Bandura's work. Gives an easy-to-read overview of his philosophical position (reciprocal determinism), discusses his theory (including observational learning and self-regulatory processes), and presents a summary of relevant research conducted within the framework of social cognitive theory. An ideal starting point for anyone who would like to become familiar with Bandura's work.

Edelgard Wulfert

See also:

Aggression, 31; Behaviorism, 98; Cognitive Psychology, 146; Cognitive Therapy, 153; Learning, 364; Personality Theory: Major Issues, 453; Psychoanalytic Psychology, 471; Radical Behaviorism: B. F. Skinner, 501; Self: Definition and Assessment, 524; Social Psychological Models: Erich Fromm, 565; Social Psychological Models: Karen Horney, 571.

SOCIAL PSYCHOLOGICAL MODELS
Erich Fromm

Type of psychology: Personality
Fields of study: Humanistic-phenomenological models; psychodynamic and neoanalytic models

Erich Fromm studied the effects of political, economic, and religious institutions on human personality. Fromm's work provides powerful insights into the causes of human unhappiness and psychopathology as well as ideas about how individuals and social institutions could change to maximize mental health and happiness.

Principal terms

DYNAMIC ADAPTATION: changes in thoughts, feelings, and/or behaviors that have enduring consequences for an individual's personality

ESCAPE FROM FREEDOM: the unconscious adoption of personality traits that reduce anxiety at the expense of one's individuality

FREEDOM FROM: freedom from external constraints such as prison, hunger, and homelessness

FREEDOM TO: freedom to maximize individual potential through productive love and productive work

MENTAL HEALTH: to Fromm, this means maximizing individual potential

PERSONALITY: the manner in which individuals dynamically adapt to physical and social circumstances in order to survive and reduce anxiety

PRODUCTIVE LOVE: interpersonal relationships based on mutual trust, respect, and cooperation

PRODUCTIVE WORK: daily activities that allow creative expression and engender self-esteem

Overview

The approach of Erich Fromm (1900-1980) to the study of human personality starts from an evolutionary perspective. Specifically, Fromm maintained that humans, like all other living creatures, are motivated to survive and that survival requires adaptation to their physical surroundings. Humans are, however, unique in that they substantially alter their physical surroundings through the creation and maintenance of cultural institutions. Consequently, Fromm believed that human adaptation is primarily in response to the demands of political, economic, and religious institutions.

Fromm made a distinction between adaptations to physical and social surroundings that have no enduring impact on personality (static adaptation—for example, an American learning to drive on the left side of the road in England) and adaptation that does have an enduring impact on personality (dynamic adaptation—for example, a child who becomes humble and submissive in response to a brutally domineering, egomaniacal parent). Fromm consequently defines personality as the manner in which individuals dynamically adapt to their physical and social surroundings in order to survive and reduce anxiety.

Human adaptation includes the reduction of anxiety for two reasons. First, because humans are born in a profoundly immature and helplessly dependent state, they are especially prone to anxiety, which, although unpleasant, is useful to the extent that it results in signs of distress (such as crying) which alert others and elicit their assistance. Second, infants eventually mature into fully self-conscious human beings who, although no longer helpless and dependent, recognize their ultimate mortality and essential isolation from all other living creatures.

Fromm believed that humans have five basic inorganic needs (as opposed to organic needs associated with physical survival) resulting from the anxiety associated with human immaturity at birth and eventual self-consciousness. The need for relatedness refers to the innate desire to acquire and maintain social relationships. The need for transcendence suggests that human beings have an inherent drive to become creative individuals. The need for rootedness consists of a sense of belonging to a social group. The need for identity is the need to be a unique individual. The need for a frame of orientation refers to a stable and consistent way of perceiving the world.

Mental health for Fromm consists of realizing one's own unique individual potential, and it requires two kinds of freedom that are primarily dependent on the structure of a society's political, economic, and religious institutions. Freedom from external constraints refers to practical concerns such as freedom from imprisonment, hunger, and homelessness. This is how many people commonly conceive of the notion of freedom. For Fromm, freedom from external constraints is necessary, but not sufficient, for optimal mental health, which also requires the freedom to maximize one's individual potential.

Freedom to maximize individual potential entails productive love and productive work. Productive love consists of interpersonal relationships based on mutual trust, respect, and cooperation. Productive work refers to daily activities that allow for creative expression and provide self-esteem. Fromm hypothesized that people become anxious and insecure if their need for transcendence is thwarted by a lack of productive work and love. Many people, he believed, respond to anxiety and insecurity by an "escape from freedom": the unconscious adoption of personality traits that reduce anxiety and insecurity at the expense of individual identity.

Fromm described five personality types representing an escape from freedom. The authoritarian type reduces anxiety and insecurity by fusing himself or herself with another person or a religious, political, or economic institution. Fromm distinguished between sadistic and masochistic authoritarians: The sadistic type needs to dominate (and often hurt and humiliate) others, while the masochistic type needs to submit to the authority of others. The sadist and the masochist are similar in that they share a pathetic dependence on each other. Fromm used the people in Nazi Germany (masochists) under Adolf Hitler (a sadist) to illustrate the authoritarian personality type.

Destructive individuals reduce anxiety and insecurity by destroying other persons or things. Fromm suggested that ideally people derive satisfaction and security through constructive endeavors, but noted that some people lack the skill and motivation to create, and therefore engage in destructive behavior as an impoverished substitute for constructive activities.

Withdrawn individuals reduce anxiety and insecurity by willingly or unwillingly refusing to participate in a socially prescribed conception of reality; instead, they withdraw into their own idiosyncratic versions of reality. In one social conception, for example, many devout Christians believe that God created the Earth in six days, that Christ was born approximately two thousand years ago, and that He has not yet returned to Earth. The withdrawn individual might singularly believe that the earth was hatched from the egg of a giant bird a few years ago and that Christ had been seen eating a hamburger yesterday. Psychiatrists and clinicians today would generally characterize the withdrawn individual as psychotic or schizophrenic.

Self-inflated people reduce anxiety and insecurity by unconsciously adopting glorified images of themselves as superhuman individuals who are vastly superior to others. They are arrogant, strive to succeed at the expense of others, are unable to accept constructive criticism, and avoid experiences that might disconfirm their false conceptions of themselves.

Finally, Fromm characterized American society in the 1940's as peopled by automaton conformists, who reduce anxiety and insecurity by unconsciously adopting the thoughts and feelings demanded of them by their culture. They are then no longer anxious and insecure, because they are like everyone else around them. According to Fromm, automaton conformists are taught to distrust and repress their own thoughts and feelings during childhood through impoverished and demoralizing educational and socializing experiences. The result is the acquisition of pseudothoughts and pseudo-feelings, which people believe to be their own but which are actually socially infused. For example, Fromm contended that most Americans vote the same way that their parents do, although very few would claim that parental preference was the cause of their political preferences. Rather, most American voters would claim that their decisions are the result of a thorough and rational consideration of genuine issues (a pseudo-thought) instead of a mindless conformity to parental influence (a genuine thought—or, in this case, a nonthought).

Applications

In *Escape from Freedom* (1941), Fromm applied his theory of personality to a historical account of personality types by a consideration of how political, economic, and religious changes in Western Europe from the Middle Ages to the twentieth century affected "freedom from" and "freedom to." Fromm argued that the feudal political system of the Middle Ages engendered very little freedom from external constraints. Specifically, there was limited physical mobility; the average person died in the same place that he or she was born, and many people were indentured servants who could not leave their feudal lord even if they had somewhere to go. Additionally, there was no choice of occupation: One's job was generally inherited from one's father.

Despite the lack of freedom from external constraints, however, economic and religious institutions provided circumstances that fostered freedom to maximize individual potential through productive work and productive love. Economically, individual craftsmanship was the primary means by which goods were produced. Although this was time-consuming and inefficient by modern standards, craftsmen were responsible for the design and production of entire products. A shoemaker would choose the design and materials, make the shoes, and sell the shoes. A finished pair of shoes thus represented a tangible manifestation of the creative energies of the producer, thus providing productive work.

Additionally, the crafts were regulated by the guild system, which controlled access to apprenticeships and materials and set wages and prices in order to guarantee maximum employment and a fair profit to the craftsmen. The guilds encouraged relatively cooperative behavior between craftsmen and consequently engendered productive love. Productive love was also sustained by the moral precepts of the then-dominant Catholic church, which stressed the essential goodness of humankind, the idea that human beings had free will to choose their behavior on Earth and hence influence their ultimate fate after death, the need to be responsible for the welfare of others, and the sinfulness of extracting excessive profits from commerce and accumulating money beyond that which is necessary to exist comfortably.

The dissolution of the feudal system and the consequent transition to parliamentary democracy and capitalism provided the average individual with a historically unprecedented amount of freedom from external constraints. Physical mobility increased dramatically as the descendants of serfs were able to migrate freely to cities to seek employment of their choosing; however, according to Fromm, increased freedom from external constraints was acquired at the expense of the circumstances necessary for freedom to maximize individual potential through productive work and productive love.

Capitalism shifted the focus of commerce from small towns to large cities and stimulated the development of fast and efficient means of production, but assembly-line production methods divested the worker of opportunities for creative expression. The assembly-line worker has no control over the design of a product, does not engage in the entire production of the product, and has nothing to do with the sale and distribution of the product. Workers in a modern automobile factory might put on hub caps or install radios for eight hours each day as cars roll by on the assembly line. They have no control over the process of production and no opportunity for creative expression, given the monotonous and repetitive activities to which their job confines them.

In addition to the loss of opportunities to engage in productive work, the inherent competitiveness of capitalism undermined the relatively cooperative interpersonal relationships engendered by the guild system, transforming the stable small-town economic order into a frenzied free-for-all in which people compete with their neighbors for the resources necessary to survive, hence dramatically reducing opportunities for people to acquire and maintain productive love. Additionally, these economic changes were supported by the newly dominant Protestant churches (represented by the teachings of John Calvin and Martin Luther), which stressed the inherent evilness of humankind, the lack of free will, and the notion of predetermination—the idea that God had already decided prior to one's birth if one is to be consigned to heaven or hell after death. Despite the absence of free will and the idea that an individual's fate was predetermined, Protestant theologians claimed that people could get a sense of God's intentions by their material success on Earth, thus encouraging people to work very hard to accumulate as much as possible (the so-called Protestant work ethic) as an indication that God's countenance is shining upon them.

In summary, Fromm argued that the average person in Western industrial democracies has freedom from external constraints but lacks opportunities to maximize individual potential through productive love and productive work; the result is pervasive feelings of anxiety and insecurity. Most people respond to this anxiety and insecurity by unconsciously adopting personality traits that reduce anxiety and insecurity, but at the expense of their individuality, which Fromm referred to as an escape from freedom. For Fromm, psychopathology is the general result of the loss of individuality associated with an escape from freedom. The specific manifestation of psychopathology depends on the innate characteristics of the individual in conjunction with the demands of the person's social environment.

Fromm argued that while escaping from freedom is a typical response to anxiety and insecurity, it is not an inevitable one. Instead, he urged people to embrace positive freedom through the pursuit of productive love and work, which he claimed would require both individual and social change. Individually, Fromm advocated a life of spontaneous exuberance made possible by love and being loved. He described the play of children and the behavior of artists as illustrations of this kind of lifestyle. Socially, Fromm believed strongly that the fundamental tenets of democracy should be retained but that capitalism in its present form must be modified to ensure every person's right to live, to distribute resources more equitably, and to provide opportunities to engage in productive work.

Context

Fromm's ideas reflect the scientific traditions of his time as well as his extensive training in history and philosophy, in addition to his psychological background. Fromm is considered a neo-Freudian (along with Karen Horney, Harry Stack Sullivan, and others) because of his acceptance of some of Freud's basic ideas (specifically, the role of unconsciously motivated behaviors in human affairs and the notion that anxiety-producing inclinations are repressed or prevented from entering conscious awareness) while rejecting Freud's reliance on the role of biological instincts (sex and aggression) for understanding human behavior. Instead, the neo-Freudians were explicitly concerned with the influence of the social environment on personality development.

Additionally, Fromm was very much influenced by Charles Darwin's theory of evolution, by existential philosophy, and by the economic and social psychological ideas of Karl Marx. Fromm's use of adaptation in the service of survival to define personality is derived from basic evolutionary theory. His analysis of the sources of human anxiety, especially the awareness of death and perception of isolation and aloneness, is extracted from existential philosophy. The notion that human happiness requires productive love and work and that capitalism is antithetical to mental health was originally proposed by Marx. Fromm's work has never received the attention that it deserves in America because of his open affinity for some of Marx's ideas and his insistence that economic change is utterly necessary to ameliorate the unhappiness and mental illness that pervade American society. Nevertheless, his ideas are vitally important from both a theoretical and practical perspective.

Bibliography

Becker, Ernest. *The Birth and Death of Meaning.* 2d ed. New York: Free Press, 1971. Becker presents a general description of Fromm's ideas embedded in a broad interdisciplinary consideration of human social psychological behavior.

Cortina, Mauricio, and Michael Maccoby, eds. *A Prophetic Analyst: Erich Fromm's Contribution to Psychoanalysis.* Northvale, N.J.: Jason Aronson, 1996.

Fromm, Erich. *Anatomy of Human Destructiveness.* New York: Holt, Rinehart and Winston, 1973. An in-depth examination of the destructive personality type.

_____. *The Art of Loving.* New York: Harper, 1956. A detailed analysis of how to love and be loved. Distinguishes between genuine love and morbid dependency.

_____. *Escape from Freedom*. New York: Farrar & Rinehart, 1941. Fromm's early seminal work, in which his basic theory about the relationship between political, economic, and religious institutions and personality development was originally articulated. All of Fromm's later books are extensions of ideas expressed here.

_____. *Marx's Concept of Man*. New York: Frederick Ungar, 1961. An introduction to Marx's ideas, including a translation of Marx's economic and philosophical manuscripts of 1844.

_____. *The Revolution of Hope: Toward a Humanized Technology*. New York: Harper & Row, 1968. A detailed discussion of how capital-based economies can be transformed to provide opportunities for productive work without sacrificing productive efficiency, technological advances, or democratic political ideals.

Sheldon Solomon

See also:

Analytical Psychology: Carl G. Jung, 49; Dream Analysis, 206; Ego Psychology: Erik Erikson, 223; Individual Psychology: Alfred Adler, 296; Personality Theory: Major Issues, 453; Psychoanalytic Psychology, 471; Psychoanalytic Psychology and Personality: Sigmund Freud, 478; Radical Behaviorism: B. F. Skinner, 501; Social Learning: Albert Bandura, 559; Social Psychological Models: Karen Horney, 571.

SOCIAL PSYCHOLOGICAL MODELS
Karen Horney

Type of psychology: Personality

Fields of study: Personality theory; psychodynamic and neoanalytic models; psychodynamic therapies

Karen Horney's social psychoanalytic theory focuses on how human relationships and cultural conditions influence personality formation; the theory describes how basic anxiety, resulting from childhood experiences, contributes to the development of three neurotic, compulsive, rigid personality styles: moving toward others, moving away from others, and moving against others. Normal personality is characterized by flexibility and balance among interpersonal styles.

Principal terms

BASIC ANXIETY: a feeling of insignificance, helplessness, and being threatened in a world that is perceived as hostile because of one's childhood experiences

EXTERNALIZATION: experiencing unresolved, repressed inner turmoil as occurring outside oneself; holding external factors responsible for one's problems

IDEALIZED SELF: alienation from the real self that is characterized by grandiose, unrealistic conceptions of the self and unattainable standards

NEUROSIS: inflexible behaviors and reactions, or discrepancies between one's potential and one's achievements

NEUROTIC TRENDS: unconscious, compulsive patterns of neurotic behavior that are exhibited through the three patterns of moving toward, moving away from, and moving against people

SEARCH FOR GLORY: compulsive and insatiable efforts to fulfill the demands of the idealized self

SELF-REALIZATION: development of one's inherent capacities and real self

TYRANNY OF THE SHOULD: rigid or overly difficult inner dictates or commands that emerge out of the idealized image

Overview

Karen Horney (1885-1952) spent the major part of her career explaining how personality patterns, especially neurotic patterns, are formed, how they operate, and how they can be changed in order to increase individual potential. In contrast to Sigmund Freud's view that people are guided by instincts and the pleasure principle, Horney proposed that people act out desires to achieve safety and satisfaction in social relationships. She was optimistic about the possibility for human growth and believed that, under conditions of acceptance and care, people move toward self-realization, or the development of their full potential. She wrote almost exclusively, however, about personality problems and methods for solving them.

Horney believed that it is impossible to understand individuals or the mechanisms of neurosis apart from the cultural context in which they exist. Neurosis varies across cultures, as well as within the same culture, and it is influenced by socioeconomic class, gender, and historical period. For example, in *The Neurotic Personality of Our Time* (1937), Horney noted that a person who refuses to accept a salary increase in a Western culture might be seen as neurotic, whereas in a Pueblo Indian culture, this person might be seen as entirely normal.

The neurotic person experiences culturally determined problems in an exaggerated form. In Western culture, competitiveness shapes many neurotic problems because it decreases opportunities for cooperation, fosters a climate of mistrust and hostility, undermines self-esteem, increases isolation, and encourages people to be more concerned with how they appear to others than with fulfilling personal possibilities. It fosters the overvaluing of external success, encourages people to develop grandiose images of superiority, and leads to intensified needs for approval and affection as well as to the distortion of love. Moreover, the ideal of external success is contradicted by the ideal of humility, which leads to further internal conflict and, in many cases, neurosis.

Cultural patterns are replicated and transmitted primarily in family environments. Ideally, a family provides the warmth and nurturance that prepares children to face the world with confidence. When parents have struggled unsuccessfully with the culture, however, they create the conditions that lead to inadequate parenting. In its most extreme form, the competitiveness of the larger culture leads to child abuse, but it can also lead to parents' preoccupation with their own needs, an inability to love and nurture effectively, or a tendency to treat children as extensions of themselves. Rivalry, overprotectiveness, irritability, partiality, and erratic behavior are other manifestations of parental problems.

Within this negative environment, children experience fear and anger, but they also feel weak and helpless beside more powerful adults. They recognize that expressing hostility directly might be dangerous and result in parental reprisals or loss of love. As a result, children repress legitimate anger, banishing it to the unconscious. By using the defense mechanism of reaction formation, they develop emotions toward parents that are the opposite of anger, and they experience feared parents as objects of admiration. Children unconsciously turn their inner fears and anger against themselves and lose touch with their real selves. As a result, they develop basic anxiety, or the feeling of being alone and defenseless in a world that seems hostile.

In order to cope with basic anxiety, individuals use additional defensive strategies or neurotic trends to cope with the world. These involve three primary patterns of behavior: moving away from others, moving toward others, and moving against others. In addition, neurotic individuals develop an idealized self, an unrealistic, flattering distortion of the self-image that encourages people to set unattainable standards, shrink from reality, and compulsively search for glory rather than accept themselves as they are.

Applications

One of Karen Horney's most significant contributions revolved around her practical discussion of three frequently observed constricting behavior patterns that represent neurotic trends. She wrote about these in rich detail in *Our Inner Conflicts: A Constructive Theory of Neurosis* (1945), a highly readable book. The person who moves toward others believes:

"If I love you or give in, you will not hurt me." The person who moves against others believes: "If I have power, you will not hurt me." The person who moves away from others thinks: "If I am independent or withdraw from others, they will not hurt me."

The person who moves toward others has chosen a dependent or compliant pattern of coping. The person experiences strong needs for approval, belonging, and affection, and strives to live up to the expectations of others through behavior that is overconsiderate and submissive. This person sees love as the only worthwhile goal in life and represses all competitive, hostile, angry aspects of the self. The moving-against type, who has adopted an aggressive, tough, exploitive style, believes that others are hostile, that life is a struggle, and that the only way to survive is to win and to control others. This person sees herself or himself as strong and determined, and represses all feelings of affection for fear of losing power over others. Finally, the moving-away type, who has adopted a style of detachment and isolation, sees himself or herself as self-sufficient, private, and superior to others. This person represses all emotion and avoids any desire or activity that would result in dependency on others.

The interpersonal patterns that Horney discussed are no longer known as neurotic styles, but as personality disorders. Many of the behaviors that she described can be seen in descriptions of current diagnostic categories that appear in the American Psychiatric Association's *Diagnostic and Statistical Manual of Mental Disorders* (rev. 3d ed., 1987, DSM-III-R), such as dependent personality disorder, narcissistic personality disorder, and obsessive-compulsive personality disorder. Like Horney's original criteria, these categories describe inflexible and maladaptive patterns of behavior and thinking that are displayed in various environments and result in emotional distress and/or impaired functioning.

In her practice of psychoanalysis, Karen Horney used free association and dream analysis to bring unconscious material to light. In contrast to Freud's more passive involvement with patients, she believed that the psychoanalyst should play an active role not only in interpreting behavior but also in inquiring about current behaviors that maintain unproductive patterns, suggesting alternatives, and helping persons mobilize energy to change.

Horney also made psychoanalysis more accessible to the general population. She suggested that, by examining oneself according to the principles outlined in her book *Self-Analysis* (1942), one could increase self-understanding and gain freedom from internal issues that limit one's potential. Her suggestions indicate that a person should choose a problem that one could clearly identify, engage in informal free association about the issue, reflect upon and tentatively interpret the experience, and make specific, simple choices about altering problematic behavior patterns. Complex, longstanding issues, however, should be dealt with in formal psychoanalysis.

Context

Karen Horney was one of the first individuals to criticize Freud's psychology of women. In contrast to Freudian instinct theory, she proposed a version of psychoanalysis that emphasized the role that social relationships and culture play in human development. She questioned the usefulness of Freud's division of the personality into the regions of the id, ego, and superego, and viewed the ego as a more constructive, forward-moving force within the person.

Horney's work was enriched by her contact with psychoanalysts Harry Stack Sullivan,

Clara Thompson, and Erich Fromm, who also emphasized the role of interpersonal relationships and sociocultural factors and were members at Horney's American Institute of Psychoanalysis when it was first established. Horney's work also resembled Alfred Adler's personality theory. Her concepts of the search for glory and idealized self are similar to Adler's concepts of superiority striving and the superiority complex. Furthermore, Adler's ruling type resembles the moving-against personality, his getting type is similar to the moving-toward personality, and his avoiding type is closely related to the moving-away personality.

Horney anticipated many later developments within cognitive, humanistic, and feminist personality theory and psychotherapy. Abraham Maslow, who was inspired by Horney, built his concept of self-actualization on Horney's optimistic belief that individuals can move toward self-realization. Carl Rogers' assumptions that problems are based on distortions of real experience and discrepancies between the ideal and real selves are related to Horney's beliefs that unhealthy behavior results from denial of the real self as well as from conflict between the idealized and real selves. In the field of cognitive psychotherapy, Albert Ellis' descriptions of the mechanisms of neurosis resemble Horney's statements. He borrowed the phrase "tyranny of the should" from Horney and placed strong emphasis on how "shoulds" influence irrational, distorted thinking patterns. Finally, Horney's notion that problems are shaped by cultural patterns is echoed in the work of feminist psychotherapists, who believe that individual problems are often the consequence of external, social problems.

Bibliography

Horney, Karen. *Neurosis and Human Growth: The Struggle Toward Self-Realization*. New York: W. W. Norton, 1950. Presents Horney's theory in its final form. Describes the ways in which various neurotic processes operate, including the tyranny of the should, neurotic claims, self-alienation, and self-contempt. Discusses faulty, neurotic solutions that are developed as a way to relieve internal tensions through domination, dependency, resignation, or self-effacement.

_____. *The Neurotic Personality of Our Time*. New York: W. W. Norton, 1937. Outlines the manner in which culture influences personality difficulties and describes typical behavior problems that result from the exaggeration of cultural difficulties in one's life.

_____. *New Ways in Psychoanalysis*. New York: W. W. Norton, 1939. Describes major areas of agreement and disagreement with Freud, as well as important elements of her own theory; highly controversial when first published.

_____. *Our Inner Conflicts: A Constructive Theory of Neurosis*. New York: W. W. Norton, 1945. Identifies and describes, through rich detail and examples, the three neurotic trends of moving toward others, moving away from others, and moving against others; highly readable and a good introduction to Horney's main ideas.

_____. *Self-Analysis*. New York: W. W. Norton, 1942. Provides guidance for readers who may wish to engage in informal free association, self-discovery, and personal problem solving.

Paris, Bernard J. *Karen Horney: A Psychoanalyst's Search for Self-Understanding*. New Haven, Conn.: Yale University Press, 1994.

Quinn, Susan. *A Mind of Her Own: The Life of Karen Horney*. New York: Summit Books,

1987. Readable, honest, fascinating biography of Horney's life; provides insights into personal factors that influenced Horney's theoretical and clinical work.

Westkott, Marcia. *The Feminist Legacy of Karen Horney*. New Haven, Conn.: Yale University Press, 1986. This book integrates Karen Horney's earlier papers on the psychology of women with the more complete personality theory that emerged over time.

Carolyn Zerbe Enns

See also:

Analytical Psychology: Carl G. Jung, 49; Dream Analysis, 206; Ego Psychology: Erik Erikson, 223; Individual Psychology: Alfred Adler, 296; Personality Theory: Major Issues, 453; Psychoanalytic Psychology, 471; Psychoanalytic Psychology and Personality: Sigmund Freud, 478; Radical Behaviorism: B. F. Skinner, 501; Social Learning: Albert Bandura, 559; Social Psychological Models: Erich Fromm, 565.

SPEECH DISORDERS

Type of psychology: Language
Fields of study: Behavioral therapies; infancy and childhood; organic disorders

Speech disorders may have an organic or learned origin, and they often affect a person's ability to communicate efficiently. As a result of a speech disorder, a person may exhibit a number of behavioral effects, such as the avoidance of talking with others and low self-esteem.

Principal terms

COMMUNICATION: the exchange of information and ideas between participants, often in the form of speech
SELF-ESTEEM: the evaluative part of the self-concept; self-worth
SOCIAL INTERACTION: a communication act from one individual directed toward another
SPEECH: the process of producing sounds in the form of words
THERAPY: the systematic habilitation of a disorder
VOCAL FOLDS: folds of skin found in the larynx and attached to cartilage that vibrate to make speech; often called vocal cords

Overview

The ability to communicate is one of the most basic human characteristics. Communication is essential to learning, working, and, perhaps most important, social interaction. Normal communication involves hearing sounds, interpreting and organizing sounds, and making meaningful sounds. The ear first takes in sounds, changes them into electrical impulses, and relays these impulses to the brain. The brain interprets the impulses, assigns meaning, and prepares a response. This response is then coded into the precisely coordinated changes in muscles, breath, vocal folds, tongue, jaw, lips, and so on that produce understandable speech.

Between 5 and 10 percent of Americans experience speech and/or language difficulties, often referred to as speech disorders. For these individuals, a breakdown occurs in one of the processes of normal communication described above. People with speech disorders may exhibit one or more of the following problems: They may be difficult to understand, use and produce words incorrectly, consistently use incorrect grammar, be unable to hear appropriately or to understand others, consistently speak too loudly, demonstrate a hesitating speech pattern, or simply be unable to speak. Speech disorders can be categorized as one of three disorder types: disorders of articulation, of fluency, or of voice. Articulation disorders are difficulties in the formation and stringing together of sounds to produce words. Fluency disorders, commonly referred to as stuttering, are interruptions in the flow or rhythm of speech. Finally, voice disorders are characterized by deviations in a person's voice quality, pitch, or loudness.

Articulation disorders are the most common types of speech errors in children. Articulation errors may take the form of substitutions, omissions, or distortions of sounds. An example of a substitution would be if the *w* sound were substituted for the *r* sound, as in "wabbit" for "rabbit." Substitutions are the most common form of articulation errors. An example of an omission would be if the *d* sound was left out of the word "bed," as in "be___." Finally, sounds can also be distorted, as in "shleep" for "sleep."

Stuttering is defined as an interruption in the flow or rhythm of speech. Stuttering can be characterized by hesitations, interjections, repetitions, or prolongations of a sound, syllable, word, or phrase. "I wa-wa-want that" is an example of a part-word repetition, while "I, I, I want that" is an example of a whole-word repetition. When a word or group of words such as "uh," "you know," "well," or "oh" is inserted into an utterance, it is termed an interjection. "I want uh, uh, you know, uh, that" is an example of a sentence containing interjections. There may also be secondary behaviors associated with stuttering. In order for an individual to extricate himself or herself from a stuttering incident, secondary behaviors may be used. A stutterer may blink the eyes, turn the head, tap his or her leg, look away, or perform some other interruptive behavior to stop the stuttering. In therapy, secondary behaviors are very difficult to extinguish.

While articulation disorders and stuttering are often seen in children, voice disorders are common among adults. Voice disorders are categorized into disorders of pitch, intensity, nasality, and quality. A person with a voice disorder of pitch may have a vocal pitch which is too high. A person may speak too softly and thus exhibit a voice disorder of intensity. Still others may sound as though they talk through their nose (hypernasality) or always have a cold (hyponasality). The most common voice disorder is a disorder of quality. Examples of disorders of vocal quality include a voice that sounds hoarse, breathy, harsh, or rough. This type of voice disorder may be caused by vocal abuse, or an overusage of the voice, and might be found among singers, actors, or other individuals who abuse or overuse their voices. If the vocal abuse continues, vocal nodules (like calluses) may appear on the vocal folds. Vocal nodules may be surgically removed, and a person may be put on an extended period of vocal rest.

Speech disorders may be caused by a variety of factors. They may result from physical problems, health problems, or other problems. Physical problems such as cleft lip and palate, misaligned teeth, difficulty in controlling movements of the tongue, injury to the head, neck, or spinal cord, poor hearing, mental retardation, and cerebral palsy can contribute to poor articulation. The exact causes of stuttering are not known; however, a variety of factors are thought to be involved, including learning problems, emotional difficulties, biological defects, and neurological problems. Problems with voice quality can be caused by too much strain on the vocal folds (for example, yelling too much or clearing the throat too often), hearing loss, inflammation or growths on the vocal folds (vocal nodules), or emotional problems.

Applications

Speaking, hearing, and understanding are essential to human communication. A disorder in one or more of these abilities can interfere with a person's capacity to communicate. Impaired communication can influence all aspects of a person's life, creating many problems for an individual. Behavioral effects resulting from the speech disorder can be found in both children and adults. Children with speech disorders can experience difficulties in learning and find it hard to establish relationships with others. Speech disorders in adults can adversely affect social interactions and often create emotional problems, which may interfere with a person's ability to earn a living. Disorders such as those described above can interfere with a person's relationships, independence, well-being, and ability to learn. People who have trouble communicating thoughts and ideas may have trouble relating to others, possibly resulting in depression and isolation. Furthermore, job opportunities are often limited for people who cannot communicate effectively. Thus, they may have trouble leading independent, satisfying lives. Emotional problems may develop in people who exhibit speech disorders as a result of embarrassment, rejection, or poor self-image. Finally, learning is difficult and frustrating for people with speech disorders. As a consequence, their performance and progress at school and on the job can suffer.

When trying to communicate with others, individuals with speech disorders may experience other negative behavioral effects as a result of the disorder. These effects include frustration, anxiety, guilt, and hostility. The emotional experience of speech-disordered persons is often a result of their experiences in trying to communicate with others. Both the listener and the speech-disordered person react to the disordered person's attempts to communicate. In addition, the listener's reactions may influence the disordered individual. These reactions may include embarrassment, guilt, frustration, and anger and may cause the disordered individual to experience a sense of helplessness that can subsequently lower the person's sense of self-worth. Many speech-disordered people respond to their problem by being overly aggressive, by denying its existence, by projecting reactions in listeners, and/or by feeling anxious or timid.

Treatment of speech disorders attempts to eliminate or minimize the disorder and related problems. Many professionals may be involved in providing therapy, special equipment, or surgery. In therapy, specialists teach clients more effective ways of communicating. They may also help families learn to communicate with the disordered individual. Therapy may also include dealing with the negative behavioral effects of having a speech disorder, such as frustration, anxiety, and a feeling of low self-worth. In some cases, surgery can correct structural problems that may be causing speech disorders, such as cleft palate or misaligned teeth. For children with articulation disorders, therapy begins with awareness training of the misarticulations and the correct sound productions. After awareness is established, the new sound's productions are taught. For individuals who exhibit voice disorders, therapy is designed to find the cause of the disorder, eliminate or correct the cause, and retrain the individuals to use their voices correctly. Therapy for stutterers, however, is an entirely different matter. There are many methods for treating stuttering. Some are self-proclaimed "cures," while others help individuals live with their stuttering. Still other types of stuttering therapy help the stutterer overcome his or her fear of communicating, or help him or her develop a more normal breathing pattern.

Though there are many ways to treat speech disorders, disorder prevention is even more important. Certain things can be done to help prevent many speech disorders. All the methods focus on preventing speech disorders in childhood. Children should be encouraged to talk, but they should not be pushed into speaking. Pushing a child may cause that child to associate anxiety or frustration with communicating. Infants do not simply start talking; they need to experiment with their voice, lips, and tongue. This experimentation is often called babbling, and it should not be discouraged. Later on, one can slowly introduce words and help with correct pronunciation. When talking with young children, one should talk slowly and naturally, avoiding "baby talk" and gibberish. Children will have difficulty distinguishing between the baby-talk word (for example, "baba") and the real word ("bottle"). Having children point to and name things in picture books and in real-world surroundings allows the child to put labels (words) on the objects in his or her environment. Increases in the number of labels the child has learned can subsequently increase the number of topics about which the child can communicate. It is most important to listen to what the child is trying to say rather than to how the child is saying it. Such prevention strategies will encourage positive behavioral effects regarding the act of communicating. These positive effects include feelings of self-efficiency, independence, and a positive self-image.

Context
Early identification of a speech disorder improves the chances for successful treatment, and early treatment can help prevent a speech disorder from developing into a lifelong handicap. Professionals who identify, evaluate, and treat communication disorders in individuals have preparations in the field of speech-language pathology. A speech-language pathologist is a professional who has been educated in the study of human communication, its development, and its disorders. By evaluating the speech and language skills of children and adults, the speech-language pathologist determines if communication problems exist and decides on the most appropriate way of treating these problems.

Speech-language pathology services are provided in many public and private schools, community clinics, hospitals, rehabilitation centers, private practices, health departments, colleges and universities, and state and federal governmental agencies. There are more than fourteen hundred clinical facilities and hundreds of full-time private practitioners providing speech services to people throughout the United States. Service facilities exist in many cities in every state. A speech-language pathologist will have a master's or doctoral degree and should hold a Certificate of Clinical Competence (CCC) from the American Speech-Language-Hearing Association and/or a license from his or her state.

Responsibilities of a speech-language pathologist include evaluation and diagnosis, therapy, and referral to other specialists involved with speech disorders. By gathering background information and by direct observation and testing, the speech-language patholo-gist can determine the extent of the disorder as well as a probable cause. The speech-language pathologist chooses an appropriate treatment to correct or lessen the communica-tion problem and attempts to help the patient and family understand the problem. When other treatment is needed to correct the problem, the patient is referred to another specialist. Audiologists, special educators, psychologists, social workers, neurologists, pediatricians, otolaryngologists (also known as ear, nose, and throat specialists), and other medical and dental specialists may be involved in the diagnosis and treatment of a speech disorder. For example, psychologists may be best suited to treat the emotional or behavioral aspects of having a speech disorder (that is, anxiety, frustration, anger, denial, and so on). Otolaryn-gologists are often involved in the diagnosis of voice disorders. Audiologists determine whether an individual's hearing is affecting or causing a speech disorder.

Speech disorders can affect anyone at any time. The chances are good that everyone at one time has either had, or known someone with, a speech disorder. Since communication is so overwhelmingly a part of life, disordered speech is not something to take lightly. With good prevention, early identification, and early treatment, lifelong difficulties with commu-nication can be prevented.

Bibliography

Curlee, Richard F. "Counseling in Speech, Language, and Hearing." *Seminars in Speech and Language* 9, no. 3 (1988). In his introductory article to this issue, Curlee presents a clear and interesting overview of counseling strategies for the speech-language pathologist. Counseling of parents and spouses of persons with speech disorders is detailed.

Duffy, Joseph R. *Motor Speech Disorders: Substrates, Differential Diagnosis, and Management.* St. Louis, Mo.: Mosby, 1995.

Kirshner, Howard S., ed. *Handbook of Neurological Speech and Language Disorders.* New York: Marcel Dekker, 1995.

Riekehof, Lottie L. *The Joy of Signing.* Springfield, Mo.: Gospel Publishing House, 1987. A comprehensive book of sign language. Includes origins of the signs, usage of the signs, and sign variations.

Shames, George H., and Elizabeth H. Wiig, eds. *Human Communication Disorders.* Columbus, Ohio: Charles E. Merrill, 1986. This general text covers a wide range of communication disorders. Includes a section on speech-language pathology as a profession. Also includes sections on cleft palate, aphasia, and cerebral palsy.

The Speech Foundation of America. *Counseling Stutterers.* Memphis, Tenn.: Author, 1989. The Speech Foundation of America is a nonprofit, charitable organization dedicated to the prevention and treatment of stuttering. It provides a variety of low-cost publications about stuttering and stuttering therapy. This publication is written to give clinicians a better understanding of the counseling aspect of therapy and to suggest ways in which it can be used most effectively.

_____. *Therapy for Stutterers.* Memphis, Tenn.: Author, 1989. A general guide to help those who work or plan to work in therapy with adult and older-adolescent stutterers.

Jennifer A. Sanders Wann
Daniel L. Wann

See also:

Language: The Developmental Sequence, 346; Language Acquisition Theories, 352; Motor Development, 410.

THE CONCEPT OF STRESS

Type of psychology: Stress
Fields of study: Coping; critical issues in stress; stress and illness

The stress response consists of physiological arousal, subjective feelings of discomfort, and the behavioral changes people experience when they confront situations that they appraise as dangerous or threatening. Because exposure to extreme situational or chronic stress causes emotional distress and may impair physical functioning, it is important to learn effective stress coping strategies.

Principal terms

COGNITIVE APPRAISAL: an assessment of the meaningfulness of an event to an individual; events that are appraised as harmful or potentially harmful elicit stress

EMOTION-FOCUSED COPING: minimizing negative emotions elicited by a stressor by using techniques such as relaxation and denial and paying little attention to the stressor itself

LEARNED HELPLESSNESS: motivational, cognitive, and emotional deficits resulting from exposure to a stressor that is perceived to be uncontrollable

PROBLEM-FOCUSED COPING: minimizing negative emotions elicited by a stressor by changing or avoiding the stressor

STRESSOR: an event that is appraised as dangerous or threatening and that elicits a stress response

Overview

In the past, the term "stress" designated both a stimulus (a force or pressure) and a response (adversity, affliction). More recently, it has usually been used to denote a set of changes that people undergo in situations that they appraise as threatening to their well-being. These changes involve physiological arousal, subjective feelings of discomfort, and overt behaviors. The terms "anxiety" and "fear" are also used to indicate what people experience when they appraise circumstances as straining their ability to cope with them.

The external circumstances that induce stress responses are called stressors. Stressors have a number of important temporal components. Exposure to them may be relatively brief with a clear starting and stopping point (acute stressors) or may persist for extended periods without clear demarcation (chronic stressors). Stressors impinge on people at different points in their life cycles, sometimes occurring "off time" (at times that are incompatible with personal and societal expectations of their occurrence) or at a "bad time" (along with other stressors). Finally, stress may be induced by the anticipation of harmful circumstances that one thinks one is likely to confront, by an ongoing stressor, or by the harmful effects of stressors already encountered. All these factors affect people's interpretations of stressful events, how they deal with them, and how effective they are at coping with them.

Although there are some situations to which almost everyone responds with high levels of stress, there are individual differences in how people respond to situations. Thus, though most people cringe at the thought of having to parachute from an airplane, a substantial minority find this an exciting, challenging adventure. Most people avoid contact with snakes, yet others keep them as pets. For most people, automobiles, birds, and people with deep voices are largely neutral objects, yet for others they provoke a stress reaction that may verge on panic.

The key concept is cognitive appraisal. Situations become stressors for an individual only if they are construed as threatening or dangerous by that individual. As demonstrated in a study of parachuters, by psychologists Walter D. Fenz and Seymour Epstein, stress appraisals can change markedly over the course of exposure to a stressor, and patterns of stress arousal differ as a function of experience with the stressor. Fenz and Epstein found that fear levels of veteran jumpers (as evaluated by a self-report measure) were highest the morning before the jump, declined continuously up to the moment of the jump, and then increased slightly until after landing. Fear levels for novice jumpers, in contrast, increased up to a point shortly before the jump and then decreased continuously. For both groups, the peak of stress occurred during the anticipatory period rather than at the point of the greatest objective danger (the act of jumping).

Stress reactions are measured in three broad ways: by means of self-report, through behavioral observations, and on the basis of physiological arousal. The self-report technique is the technique most commonly used by behavioral scientists to evaluate subjective stress levels. The State Anxiety Scale of the State-Trait Anxiety Inventory, developed by psychologist Charles Spielberger, is one of the most widely used self-report measures of stress. Examples of items on this scale are "I am tense," "I am worried," and "I feel pleasant." Subjects are instructed to respond to the items in terms of how they currently feel.

Self-report state anxiety scales may be administered and scored easily and quickly. Further, they may be administered repeatedly and still provide valid measures of momentary changes in stress levels. They have been criticized by some, however, because they are face valid (that is, their intent is clear); therefore, people who are motivated to disguise their stress levels can readily do so.

Overt behavioral measures of stress include direct and indirect observational measures. Direct measures focus on behaviors associated with stress-related physiological arousal such as heavy breathing, tremors, and perspiration; self-manipulations such as nail biting, eyeblinks, and postural orientation; and body movement such as pacing.

Speech disturbances, both verbal (for example, repetitions, omissions, incomplete sentences, and slips of the tongue) and nonverbal (for example, pauses and hand movements), have been analyzed intensively, but no single measure or pattern has emerged as a reliable indicant of stress. Another way in which people commonly express fear reactions is by means of facial expressions. This area has been studied by psychologists Paul Ekman and Wallace V. Friesen, who concluded that the facial features that take on the most distinctive appearance during fear are the eyebrows (raised and drawn together), the eyes (open, lower lid tensed), and the lips (stretched back).

Indirect observational measures involve evaluating the degree to which people avoid feared objects. For example, in one test used by clinical psychologists to assess fear level, an individual is instructed to approach a feared stimulus (such as a snake) and engage in increasingly intimate interactions with it (for example, looking at a caged snake from a distance, approaching it, touching it, holding it). The rationale is that the higher the level of fear elicited, the earlier in the sequence the person will try to avoid the feared stimulus. Other examples include asking claustrophobics (people who are fearful of being closed in) to remain in a closed chamber as long as they can and asking acrophobics (people who fear heights) to climb a ladder and assessing their progress.

Physiological arousal is an integral component of the stress response. The most frequently monitored response systems are cardiovascular responses, electrodermal responses, and muscular tension. These measures are important in their own right as independent indicants of stress level, and in particular as possible indices of stress-related diseases.

Applications

The concept of stress has been used to help explain the etiology of certain diseases. Diseases that are thought to be caused in part by exposure to stress or poor ability to cope with stress are called psychophysiological or psychosomatic disorders. Among the diseases that seem to have strong psychological components are ulcers and coronary heart disease. The role of stress in ulcers was highlighted in a study by Joseph V. Brady known as the "executive monkey" study. In this study, pairs of monkeys were yoked together in a restraining apparatus. The monkeys received identical treatment except that one member of each pair could anticipate whether both of them would be shocked (he was given a warning signal) and could control whether the shock was actually administered (if he pressed a lever, the shock was avoided). Thus, one monkey in each pair (the "executive monkey") had to make decisions constantly and was responsible for the welfare of both himself and his partner. Twelve pairs of monkeys were tested, and in every case the executive monkey died of peptic ulcers within weeks, while the passive member of each pair remained healthy. This experiment was criticized because of flaws in its experimental design, but it nevertheless brought much attention to the important role that chronic stress can play in the activation of physiological processes (in this case, the secretion of hydrochloric acid in the stomach in the absence of food) that can be damaging or even life threatening.

Although being in the position of a business executive who has to make decisions constantly can be very stressful, research indicates that it may be even more damaging to be exposed to stress over long periods and not have the opportunity to change or control the source of stress. People and animals who are in aversive situations over which they have little or no control for prolonged periods are said to experience "learned helplessness." This concept was introduced by psychologist Martin E. P. Seligman and his colleagues. In controlled research with rats and dogs, he and his colleagues demonstrated that exposure to prolonged stress that cannot be controlled produces emotional, motivational, and cognitive deficits. The animals show signs of depression and withdrawal, they show little ability or desire to master their environment, and their problem-solving ability suffers.

Learned helplessness has also been observed in humans. Seligman refers to Bruno Bettelheim's descriptions of some of the inmates of the Nazi concentration camps during World War II, who, when faced with the incredible brutality and hopelessness of their situation, gave up and died without any apparent physical cause. Many institutionalized patients (for example, nursing home residents and the chronically ill) also live in environments that are stressful because they have little control over them. Seligman suggests that the stress levels of such patients can be lowered and their health improved if they are given maximum control over their everyday activities (such as choosing what they want for breakfast, the color of their curtains, and whether to sleep late or wake up early).

Research findings have supported Seligman's suggestions. For example, psychologists

Ellen Langer and Judith Rodin told a group of elderly nursing home residents that they could decide what they wanted their rooms to look like, when they wanted to go see motion pictures, and with whom they wanted to interact. A second comparable group of elderly residents, who were randomly assigned to live on another floor, were told that the staff would care for them and try to keep them happy. It was found that the residents in the first group became more active and reported feeling happier than those in the second group. They also became more alert and involved in different kinds of activities, such as attending movies and socializing. Further, during the eighteen-month period following the intervention, 15 percent of the subjects in the first group died, whereas 30 percent of the subjects in the second group died.

Altering people's perception of control and predictability can also help them adjust to transitory stressful situations. Studies by psychologists Stephen Auerbach, Suzanne Miller, and others have shown that for people who prefer to deal with stress in active ways (rather than by avoiding the source of stress), adjustment to stressful surgical procedures and diagnostic examinations can be improved if they are provided with detailed information about the impending procedure. It is likely that the information enhances their sense of predictability and control in an otherwise minimally controllable situation. Others, who prefer to control their stress by "blunting" the stressor, show better adjustment when they are not given detailed information.

Context

Physiologist Walter B. Cannon was among the first scientists to describe how people respond to stressful circumstances. When faced with a threat, one's body mobilizes for "fight or flight." One's heart rate increases, one begins to perspire, one's muscles tense, and one undergoes other physiological changes to prepare for action—either to confront the stressor or to flee the situation.

Physician Hans Selye examined the fight-or-flight response in more detail by studying physiological changes in rats exposed to stress. He identified three stages of reaction to stress, which he collectively termed the general adaptation syndrome (GAS). This includes an initial alarm reaction, followed by a stage of resistance, and finally by a stage of exhaustion, which results from long-term unabated exposure to stress and produces irreversible physiological damage. Selye also brought attention to the idea that not only clearly aversive events (for example, the death of a spouse or a jail sentence) but also events that appear positive (for example, a promotion at work or meeting new friends) may be stressful because they involve changes to which people must adapt. Thus, these ostensibly positive events (which he called eustress) will produce the nonspecific physiological stress response just as obviously negative events (which he called distress) will.

How an individual cognitively appraises an event is the most important determinant of whether that event will be perceived as stressful by that person. Psychologist Richard S. Lazarus has delineated three important cognitive mechanisms (primary appraisals, secondary appraisals, and coping strategies) that determine perceptions of stressfulness and how people alter appraisals. Primary appraisal refers to an assessment of whether a situation is neutral, challenging, or potentially harmful. When a situation is judged to be harmful or threatening, a secondary appraisal is made of the coping options or maneuvers that the individual has at his or her disposal. Actual coping strategies that may be used are problem focused (those that involve altering the circumstances that are eliciting the stress response) or emotion focused (those that involve directly lowering physiological arousal or the cognitive determinants of the stress response). Psychologists have used concepts such as these to develop stress management procedures that help people control stress in their everyday lives.

Bibliography

Brady, Joseph Vincent. "Ulcers in Executive Monkeys." *Scientific American* 199 (October, 1958): 95-98. This article describes a classic series of studies in which monkeys subjected to psychological stress in a laboratory apparatus developed gastrointestinal lesions.

Kaplan, Howard B., ed. *Psychosocial Stress: Perspectives on Structure, Theory, Life-Course, and Methods.* New York: Academic Press, 1996.

Lazarus, Richard S., and Susan Folkman. *Stress, Appraisal, and Coping.* New York: Springer, 1984. Lazarus and Folkman review the history and development of the concepts of stress and coping. The book, which is organized around their cognitive appraisal theory of emotion, includes sections on coping and health and adaptation, and on approaches to stress management.

Rodin, Judith. "Managing the Stress of Aging." In *Coping and Health,* edited by Seymour Levine and Holger Ursin. New York: Plenum Press, 1980. In this chapter, Rodin emphasizes that stress produced by the perception of loss of personal control is particularly prevalent among the elderly. She describes interventions and coping-skills training techniques that have been useful in enhancing the sense of control and reducing the stress levels of institutionalized older people.

Seligman, Martin E. P. *Helplessness: On Depression, Development, and Death.* San Francisco: W. H. Freeman, 1975. Seligman describes how being placed in a situation in which one is powerless to influence important outcomes produces "learned helplessness" and associated stress and depression. Many examples from studies with animals and humans are given. Ways of combating learned helplessness by giving people progressively greater control are also described.

Toates, Fredrick, and Milton Keynes. *Stress: Conceptual and Biological Aspects.* New York: John Wiley & Sons, 1996.

Stephen M. Auerbach

See also:

Stress: Behavioral and Psychological Responses, 586; Stress: Physiological Responses, 592; Stress-Related Diseases, 598.

STRESS
Behavioral and Psychological Responses

Type of psychology: Stress
Fields of study: Coping; critical issues in stress; stress and illness

Stress is an adaptive reaction to circumstances that are perceived as threatening. It motivates people and can enhance performance. Learning to cope with adversity is an important aspect of normal psychological development, but exposure to chronic stress can have severe negative consequences if effective coping mechanisms are not learned.

Principal terms

COPING STRATEGIES: techniques used to lower one's stress level

DAILY HASSLES: seemingly minor everyday events that are a constant source of stress

PHOBIAS: stresses induced by unrealistic fear of specific situations

STATE ANXIETY: often used interchangeably with *fear* and *stress;* denotes a momentary, transitory reaction to a situation that is perceived as threatening or dangerous

TRAIT ANXIETY: relatively stable individual differences in proneness to experience state anxiety; people high in trait anxiety are especially threatened by situations involving fear of failure or social/interpersonal threats

Overview

The term "stress" is used to designate how human beings respond when they confront circumstances that they appraise as dangerous or threatening and that tax their coping capability. Stressful events (stressors) elicit a wide range of responses in humans. They not only bring about immediate physiological changes but also affect one's emotional state, the use of one's intellectual abilities and one's efficiency at solving problems, and one's social behavior. When experiencing stress, people take steps to do something about the stressors eliciting the stress and to manage the emotional upset they are producing. These maneuvers are called coping responses. Coping is a key concept in the study of the stress process. Stress-management intervention techniques are designed to teach people the appropriate ways to cope with the stressors that they encounter in their everyday lives.

The emotional state most directly affected by stress is anxiety. In fact, the term "state anxiety" is often used interchangeably with the terms "fear" and "stress" to denote a transitory emotional reaction to a dangerous situation. Stress, fear, and state anxiety are distinguished from trait anxiety, which is conceptualized as a relatively stable personality disposition or trait. According to psychologist Charles Spielberger, people high in trait or "chronic" anxiety interpret more situations as dangerous or threatening than do people who are low in trait anxiety, and they respond to them with more intense stress (state anxiety) reactions. Instruments that measure trait anxiety ask people to characterize how they usually feel, and thus they measure how people characteristically respond to situations. Measures of trait anxiety (such as the trait anxiety scale of the State-Trait Anxiety Inventory) are especially useful in predicting whether people will experience high levels of stress in situations involving threats to self-esteem or threat of failure at evaluative tasks.

Common phobias or fears of specific situations, however, especially when the perceived threat has a strong physical component, are not related to individual differences in general trait anxiety level. Measures of general trait anxiety are therefore not good predictors of people's stress levels when they are confronted by snakes, an impending surgical operation, or the threat of electric shock. Such fears can be reliably predicted only by scales designed to evaluate proneness to experience fear in these particular situations.

Seemingly minor events that are a constant source of irritation can be very stressful, as can more focalized events that require major and sometimes sudden readjustments. Psychologists Richard Lazarus and Susan Folkman have dubbed these minor events "daily hassles." The media focus attention on disasters such as plane crashes, earthquakes, and epidemics that suddenly disrupt the lives of many people, or on particularly gruesome crimes or other occurrences that are likely to attract attention. For most people, however, much of the stress of daily life results from having to deal with ongoing problems pertaining to jobs, personal relationships, and everyday living circumstances. According to Lazarus and Folkman, exposure to such daily hassles is actually more predictive of negative health outcomes than is frequency of exposure to major life events.

People often have no actual experience of harm or unpleasantness regarding things that they come to fear. For example, most people are at least somewhat uneasy about flying on airplanes or about the prospect of having a nuclear power plant located near them, though few people have personally experienced harm caused by these things. Although people tend to pride themselves on how logical they are, they are often not very rational in appraising how dangerous or risky different events actually are. For example, there is great public concern about the safety of nuclear reactors, though they in fact have caused very few deaths. The same general public that smokes billions of cigarettes (a proved carcinogen) per year also supported banning an artificial sweetener because of a minuscule chance that it might cause cancer.

People tend to think of stress as being uniformly negative—something to be avoided or at least minimized as much as possible. Psychologists Carolyn Aldwin and Daniel Stokols point out, however, that studies using both animals and humans have indicated that exposure to stress also has beneficial effects. Rats handled as infants are less fearful, are more exploratory, are faster learners, and have more robust immune systems later in life. In humans, physical stature as adults is greater in cultures that expose children to stress (for example, circumcision, scarification, sleeping apart from parents) than in those that are careful to prevent stress exposure—even when nutrition, climate, and other relevant variables are taken into account. Although failure experiences in dealing with stressful circumstances can inhibit future ability to function under stress, success experiences enable learning of important coping and problem-solving skills that are then used to deal effectively with future stressful encounters. Such success experiences also promote a positive self-concept and induce a generalized sense of self-efficacy that in turn enhances persistence in coping with future stressors.

Psychologists Stephen Auerbach and Sandra Gramling note that stress is a normal, adaptive reaction to threat. It signals danger and prepares people to take defensive action.

Over time, individuals learn which coping strategies are successful for them in particular situations. This is part of the normal process of personal growth and maturation. Stress can, however, cause psychological problems if the demands posed by stressors overwhelm a person's coping capabilities. If a sense of being overwhelmed and unable to control events persists over a period of time, one's stress signaling system ceases to work in an adaptive way. One misreads and overinterprets the actual degree of threat posed by situations, makes poor decisions as to what coping strategies to use, and realizes that one is coping ineffi-ciently; a cycle of increasing distress and ineffective coping may result. Some people who have experienced high-level stress for extended periods or who are attempting to deal with the aftereffects of traumatic stressors may become extremely socially withdrawn and show other signs of severe emotional dysfunction.

Applications

The fact that stress has both positive and negative effects can be exemplified in many ways. Interpersonally, stress brings out the worst and the best in people. A greater incidence of negative social behaviors, including less altruism and cooperation and more aggression, has generally been observed in stressful circumstances. Psychologist Kent Bailey points out that, in addition to any learning influences, this may result from the fact that stress signals real or imagined threats to survival and is therefore a potent elicitor of regressive, self-serving survival behaviors. The highly publicized murder of Kitty Genovese in Queens, New York, a number of years ago, which was witnessed by thirty-eight people (from the safety of their apartments) who ignored her pleas for help, exemplifies this tendency, as does the behavior during World War II of many Europeans who either did not stand up for the Jews and other minorities who were oppressed by the Nazis or conveniently turned their heads. Everyone has heard, however, of selfless acts of individual heroism being performed by seemingly ordinary people who in emergency situations rose to the occasion and risked their own lives to save others. Even in a Europe dominated by Adolf Hitler, there were people who risked great harm to themselves and their families to save others. In addition, in stressful circumstances in which cooperation and altruism have survival value for all concerned, as in the wake of a natural disaster, helping-oriented activities and resource sharing are among the most common short-term reactions.

Stress may enhance as well as hinder performance. For example, the classic view of the relationship between stress and performance is represented in the Yerkes-Dodson inverted-U model, which posits that both low and high levels of arousal decrease performance, whereas intermediate levels enhance performance. Although this model has not been unequivocally validated, it seems to be at least partially correct, and its correctness may depend upon the circumstances. On the one hand, psychologists Gary Evans and Sheldon Cohen concluded that, in learning and performance tasks, high levels of stress result in reduced levels of working-memory capacity and clearly interfere with performance of tasks that require rapid detection, sustained attention, or attention to multiple sources of input. On the other hand, psychologist Charles Spielberger found that in less complex tasks, as learning progresses, high stress levels may facilitate performance.

Psychologist Irving Janis examined the relationship between preoperative stress in surgical patients and how well they coped with the rigors of the postoperative convalescent period. He found that patients with moderate preoperative fear levels adjusted better after surgery than those with low or high preoperative fear. He reasoned that patients with moderate fear levels realistically appraised the situation, determined how they would deal with the stressful aspects of the recovery period, and thus were better able to tolerate those stressors. Patients low in preoperative fear engaged in unrealistic denial and thus were unprepared for the demands of the postoperative period, whereas those high in preoperative fear became overanxious and carried their inappropriately high stress levels over into the recovery period, in which that stress continued to inhibit them from realistically dealing with the demands of the situation. The negative effect of unrealistically low fear levels is also exemplified in the description by psychologists Walter Fenz and Seymour Epstein of two first-time sky divers who surprised everyone with their apparent total lack of concern during training and on the morning of their first jump. Their reactions changed dramatically, however, once they entered the aircraft. "One began vomiting, and the other developed a coarse tremor. Both pleaded for the aircraft to be turned back. Upon leaving, they stated that they were giving up jumping."

Janis' investigation was particularly influential because it drew attention to the question of how psychologists can work with people to help them cope with impending stressful events, especially those (such as surgery) that they are committed to confronting and over which they have little control. Findings by psychologists Thomas Strentz and Stephen Auerbach indicate that in such situations it may be more useful to teach people emotion-focused coping strategies (those designed to minimize stress and physiological arousal directly) than problem-focused strategies (those designed to change the stressful situation itself). In a study with volunteers who were abducted and held hostage for four days in a stressful simulation, they found that hostages who were taught to use emotionfocused coping techniques (such as deep breathing, muscular relaxation, and directed fantasy) adjusted better and experienced lower stress levels than those who were taught problem-focused techniques (such as nonverbal communication, how to interact with captors, and how to gather intelligence).

Context

Stress has many important adaptive functions. The experience of stress and learning how to cope with adversity is an essential aspect of normal growth and development. Coping strategies learned in particular situations must be generalized appropriately to new situations. Exposure to chronic stress that cannot be coped with effectively can have severe negative consequences. Work by pioneering stress researchers such as Hans Selye brought attention to the physiological changes produced by exposure to chronic stress, which contribute to diseases such as peptic ulcers, high blood pressure, and cardiovascular disorders. Subsequent research by psychiatrists Thomas Holmes and Richard Rahe and their colleagues indicated that exposure to a relatively large number of stressful life events is associated with the onset of other diseases such as cancer and psychiatric disorders, which are less directly a function of arousal in specific physiological systems.

Studies by these researchers have led psychologists to try to understand how best to teach people to manage and cope with stress. Learning to cope with stress is a complex matter because, as Richard Lazarus has emphasized, the stressfulness of given events is determined by how they are cognitively appraised, and this can vary considerably among individuals. Further, the source of stress may be in the past, the present, or the future. The prospect of an impending threatening encounter (such as a school exam) may evoke high-level stress, but people also experience stress when reflecting on past unpleasant or humiliating experiences or when dealing with an immediate, ongoing danger. Sometimes, people deal with past, present, and future stressors simultaneously.

It is important to distinguish among present, past, and future stressors, because psychological and behavioral responses to them differ, and different kinds of coping strategies are effective in dealing with them. For example, for stressors that may never occur but are so aversive that people want to avoid them if at all possible (for example, cancer or injury in an automobile accident), people engage in preventive coping behavior (they stop smoking, or they wear seat belts) even though they are not currently experiencing a high level of anxiety. In this kind of situation, an individual's anxiety level sometimes needs to be heightened in order to motivate coping behavior.

When known stressors are about to affect one (for example, a surgical operation the next morning), it is important for one to moderate one's anxiety level so that one can function effectively when actually confronting the stressor. The situation is much different when one is trying to deal with a significant stressor (such as sexual assault, death of a loved one, or a war experience) that has already occurred but continues to cause emotional distress. Some persons who cannot adjust adequately are diagnosed as having "post-traumatic stress disorder." Important aspects of coping with such stressors include conceptualizing one's response to the situation as normal and rational rather than "crazy" or inadequate, and reinstatement of the belief that one is in control of one's life and environment rather than subject to the whims of circumstance.

Bibliography

Auerbach, Stephen M. "Assumptions of Crisis Theory and Temporal Model of Crisis Intervention." In *Crisis Intervention with Children and Families,* edited by Stephen M. Auerbach and Arnold L. Stolberg. Washington, D.C.: Hemisphere, 1986. This chapter examines some basic issues pertaining to psychological responses to extremely stressful events, including the role of the passage of time, individual differences, and previous success in dealing with stressful events. Crisis intervention and other stress-management programs are also reviewed.

_____. "Temporal Factors in Stress and Coping: Intervention Implications." In *Personal Coping: Theory, Research, and Application,* edited by B. N. Carpenter. Westport, Conn.: Praeger, 1991. Focuses on how behavioral and psychological stress responses differ depending on whether the stressor is anticipated, currently ongoing, or has already occurred. The types of coping strategies that are likely to be most effective for each kind of stressor are described, and many examples are given.

Briere, John. *Psychological Assessment of Adult Posttraumatic States.* Washington, D.C.: American Psychological Association, 1997.

Driskell, James E., and Eduardo Salas, eds. *Stress and Human Performance.* Hillsdale, N.J.: Lawrence Erlbaum, 1996.

Greenberg, Jerrold S. *Comprehensive Stress Management.* Dubuque, Iowa: Wm. C. Brown, 1990. An easy-to-read text giving an overview of psychological and physiological stress responses and stress-management techniques. Separate sections on applications to occupational stress, the college student, the family, and the elderly.

Janis, Irving Lester. *Psychological Stress.* New York: John Wiley & Sons, 1958. Describes some of Janis' early investigations evaluating relationships between stress and behavior. The focus is on his pioneering study evaluating the relationship between preoperative stress levels in surgical patients and their ability to adapt to the rigors of the postoperative convalescent period.

Monat, Alan, and Richard S. Lazarus, eds. *Stress and Coping.* 2d ed. New York: Columbia University Press, 1985. This anthology consists of twenty-six brief readings under the headings of effects of stress, stress and the environment, coping with the stresses of living, coping with death and dying, and stress management. The selections are readable as well as informative, and the editors give a useful overview prior to each section in which they summarize the relevance and importance of each reading.

Silver, R. L., and C. Wortman. "Coping with Undesirable Life Events." In *Human Helplessness,* edited by Judy Garber and Martin E. P. Seligman. New York: Academic Press, 1980. Silver and Wortman examine the behavioral consequences of encountering and adjusting to cataclysmic stressful events such as a disabling accident, a serious illness, or the death of a loved one. They review different theoretical formulations of reactions to stressful events and examine whether people's actual emotional and behavioral reactions are consistent with theories. They emphasize social support, the ability to find meaning in the outcome of the event, and experience with other stressors as important factors that determine how well people adjust.

Stephen M. Auerbach

See also:

The Concept of Stress, 581; Phobias, 459; Stress: Physiological Responses, 592; Stress-Related Diseases, 598.

STRESS
Physiological Responses

Type of psychology: Stress
Fields of study: Biology of stress; critical issues in stress; stress and illness

The human body contains a number of regulatory mechanisms that allow it to adapt to changing conditions. Stressful events produce characteristic physiological changes that are meant to enhance the likelihood of survival. Because these changes sometimes present a threat to health rather than serving a protective function, researchers seek to determine relations between stressors, their physiological effects, and subsequent health.

Principal terms

FIGHT-OR-FLIGHT RESPONSE: a sequence of physiological changes, described by Walter B. Cannon, that occur in response to threat and prepare the organism to flee from or fight the threat

GENERAL ADAPTATION SYNDROME: a physiological process by which the organism responds to stressors and attempts to reestablish homeostasis; consists of three stages: alarm, resistance, and exhaustion

HOMEOSTASIS: the tendency of the human body to strive toward an optimal or balanced level of physiological functioning

PARASYMPATHETIC NERVOUS SYSTEM: a branch of the nervous system responsible for maintaining or reestablishing homeostasis

STRESS RESPONSE: the physiological, emotional, cognitive, and/or behavioral changes that result from a stressful event, including increased heart rate, anxiety, confused thinking, and/or avoidance behaviors

STRESSOR: any psychological or physical event that produces the physiological, emotional, cognitive, and/or behavioral changes characteristic of a stress response

SYMPATHETIC NERVOUS SYSTEM: a branch of the nervous system that is responsible for activating the fight-or-flight response

Overview

Although the term "stress" is commonly used (if not overused) by the general population to refer to various responses to events that individuals find taxing, the concept involves much more. For centuries, scientific thinkers and philosophers have been interested in learning more about the interactions between the environment (stressful events), emotions, and the body. Much is now known about this interaction, although there is still much left to discover. In the late twentieth century, particularly, much has been learned about how stressful events affect the activity of the body (or physiology); for example, it has been established that these physiological responses to stressors sometimes increase the risk of development or exacerbate a number of diseases. In order best to understand the body's response to stressful events (or stressors), the general sequence of events and the specific responses of various organ systems must be considered.

Almost all bodily responses are mediated at least partially by the central nervous system: the brain and spinal cord. The brain takes in and analyzes information from the external environment as well as from the internal environment (the rest of the body), and it acts to regulate the activities of the body to optimize adaptation or survival. When the brain detects a threat, a sequence of events occurs to prepare the body to fight or to flee the threat. Walter B. Cannon, in the early twentieth century, was the first to describe this "fight-or-flight" response of the body. It is characterized by generalized physiological activation. Heart rate, blood pressure, and respiration increase to enhance the amount of oxygen available to the tissues. The distribution of blood flow changes to optimize efficiency of the tissues most needed to fight or flee: Blood flow to the muscles, brain, and skin increases, while it decreases in the stomach and other organs less important for immediate survival. Increased sweating and muscle tension help regulate the body's temperature and enhance movement if action is needed. Levels of blood glucose and insulin also increase to provide added energy sources, and immune function is depressed. Brain activity increases, resulting in enhanced sensitivity to incoming information and faster reactions to this information.

Taken together, these physiological changes serve to protect the organism and to prepare it to take action to survive threat. They occur quite rapidly and are controlled by the brain through a series of neurological and hormonal events. When the brain detects a threat (or stressor), it sends its activating message to the rest of the body through two primary channels, the sympathetic nervous system (SNS) and the pituitary-adrenal axis. The SNS is a branch of the nervous system that has multiple, diffuse, neural connections to the rest of the body. It relays activating messages to the heart, liver, muscles, and other organs that produce the physiological changes already described. The sympathetic nervous system also stimulates the adrenal gland to secrete two hormones, epinephrine and norepinephrine (formerly called adrenaline and noradrenaline), into the bloodstream. Epinephrine and norepinephrine further activate the heart, blood vessels, lungs, sweat glands, and other tissues.

Also, the brain sends an activating message through its hypothalamus to the pituitary gland, at the base of the brain. This message causes the pituitary to release hormones into the bloodstream that circulate to the peripheral tissues and activate them. The primary "stress" hormone released by the pituitary gland is adrenocorticotropic hormone (ACTH), which in turn acts upon the adrenal gland to cause the release of the hormone cortisol. The actions of cortisol on other organs cause increases in blood glucose and insulin, among many other reactions.

In addition to isolating these primary stress mechanisms, research has demonstrated that the body secretes naturally occurring opiates—endorphins and enkephalins—in response to stress. Receptors for these opiates are found throughout the body and brain. Although their function is not entirely clear, some research suggests that they serve to buffer the effects of stressful events by counteracting the effects of the SNS and stress hormones.

One can see that the human body contains a very sophisticated series of mechanisms that have evolved to enhance survival. When stressors and the subsequent physiological changes that are adaptive in the short run are chronic, however, they may produce long-term health risks. This idea was first discussed in detail in the mid-twentieth century by physiologist Hans Selye, who coined the term "general adaptation syndrome" to describe the body's physiological responses to stressors and the mechanisms by which these responses might result in disease. Selye's general adaptation syndrome involves three stages of physiological response: alarm, resistance, and exhaustion. During the alarm stage, the organism detects a stressor and responds with SNS and hormonal activation. The second stage, resistance, is characterized by the body's efforts to neutralize the effects of the stressor. Such attempts are meant to return the body to a state of homeostasis, or balance. (The concept of homeostasis, or the tendency of the body to seek to achieve an optimal, adaptive level of activity, was developed earlier by Walter Cannon.) Finally, if the resistance stage is prolonged, exhaustion occurs, which can result in illness. Selye referred to such illnesses as diseases of adaptation. In this category of diseases, he included hypertension, cardiovascular disease, kidney disease, peptic ulcer, hyperthyroidism, and asthma.

Selye's general adaptation syndrome has received considerable attention as a useful framework within which to study the effects of stressors on health, but there are several problems with his theory. First, it assumes that all stressors produce characteristic, widespread physiological changes that differ only in intensity and duration. There is compelling evidence, however, that different types of stressors can produce very different patterns of neural and hormonal responses. For example, some stressors produce increases in heart rate, while others can actually cause heart rate deceleration. Thus, Selye's assumption of a nonspecific stress response must be questioned. Also, Selye's theory does not take into account individual differences in the pattern of response to threat. Research during the later twentieth century has demonstrated that there is considerable variability across individuals in their physiological responses to identical stressors. Such differences may result from genetic or environmental influences. For example, some studies have demonstrated that normotensive offspring of hypertensive parents are more cardiovascularly responsive to brief stressors than individuals with normotensive parents. Although one might conclude that the genes responsible for hypertension have been passed on from the hypertensive parents, these children might also have different socialization or learning histories that contribute to their exaggerated cardiovascular reactivity to stressors. Whatever the mechanism, this research highlights the point that individuals vary in the degree to which they respond to stress and in the degree to which any one organ system responds.

Applications

Coinciding with the scientific community's growing acknowledgment that stressful events have direct physiological effects, much interest has developed in understanding the relations between these events and the development and/or maintenance of specific diseases. Probably the greatest amount of research has focused on the link between stress and heart disease, the primary cause of death in the United States. Much empirical work also has focused on gastrointestinal disorders, diabetes, and pain (for example, headache and arthritis). Researchers are beginning to develop an understanding of the links between stress and immune function. Such work has implications for the study of infectious disease (such as flu and mononucleosis), cancer, and acquired immune deficiency syndrome (AIDS).

A number of types of research paradigms have been employed to study the effects of stressors on health and illness. Longitudinal studies have identified a number of environmental stressors that contribute to the development or exacerbation of disease. For example, one study of more than four thousand residents of Alameda County, California, spanning two decades, showed that a number of environmental stressors such as social isolation were significant predictors of mortality from all causes. Other longitudinal investigations have linked stressful contexts such as loud noise, crowding, and low socioeconomic status with the onset or exacerbation of disease.

A major drawback of such longitudinal research is that no clear conclusions can be made about the exact mechanism or mechanisms by which the stressor had its impact on health. Although it is possible, in the Alameda County study, that the relationship between social isolation and disease was mediated by the SNS/hormonal mechanisms already discussed, individuals who are isolated also may be less likely to engage in health care behaviors such as eating healthy diets, exercising, and maintaining preventive health care. Thus, other research paradigms have been used to try to clarify the causal mechanisms by which stressors may influence particular diseases. For example, laboratory stress procedures are used by many scientists to investigate the influence of brief, standardized stressors on physiology. This type of research has the advantage of being more easily controlled. That is, the researcher can manipulate one or a small number of variables (for example, noise) in the laboratory and measure the physiological effects. These effects are then thought to mimic the physiological effects of such a variable in the natural environment.

This research primarily is conducted to ask basic questions about the relations between stressors, physiology, and subsequent health. The findings also have implications, however, for prevention and intervention. If a particular stressor is identified that increases risk of a particular disease, prevention efforts could be developed to target the populations exposed to this stressor. Prevention strategies might involve either modifying the stressor, teaching people ways to manage more effectively their responses to it, or both.

During the last two or three decades, applied researchers have attempted to develop intervention strategies aimed at controlling the body's physiological responses to stress. This work has suggested that a number of stress management strategies can actually attenuate physiological responsivity. Most strategies teach the individual some form of relaxation (such as deep muscle relaxation, biofeedback, hypnosis, or meditation), and most of this work has focused on populations already diagnosed with a stress-related disease, such as hypertension, diabetes, or ulcer. The techniques are thought to produce their effects by two possible mechanisms: lowering basal physiological activation (or changing the level at which homeostasis is achieved) and/or providing a strategy for more effectively responding to acute stressors to attenuate their physiological effects. Research has not proceeded far enough to make any statements about the relative importance of these mechanisms. Indeed, it is not clear whether either mechanism is active in many of the successful intervention studies. While research does indicate that relaxation strategies often improve symptoms of stress-related illnesses, the causal mechanisms of such techniques remain to be clarified.

Context

The notion that the mind and body are connected has been considered since the writings of ancient Greece. Hippocrates described four bodily humors (fluids) that he associated with differing behavioral and psychological characteristics. Thus, the road was paved for scientific thinkers to consider the interrelations between environment, psychological state, and physiological state (that is, health and illness). Such considerations developed most rapidly in the twentieth century, when advancements in scientific methodology permitted a more rigorous examination of the relationships among these variables.

In the early twentieth century, as noted already, Walter B. Cannon was the first to document and discuss the "fight or flight response" to threatening events. He also reasoned that the response was adaptive, unless prolonged or repeated. In the 1940's, two physicians published observations consistent with Cannon's of an ulcer patient who had a gastric fistula, enabling the doctors to observe directly the contents of the stomach. They reported that stomach acids and bleeding increased when the patient was anxious or angry, thus documenting the relations between stress, emotion, and physiology. Shortly after this work was published, Selye began reporting his experiments on the effects of cold and fatigue on the physiology of rats. These physical stressors produced enlarged adrenal glands, small thymus and lymph glands (involved in immune system functioning), and increased ulcer formation.

Psychiatrists took this information, along with the writings of Sigmund Freud, to mean that certain disease states might be associated with particular personality types. Efforts to demonstrate the relationship between specific personality types and physical disease endpoints culminated in the development of a field known as psychosomatic medicine. Research, however, does not support the basic tenet of this field, that a given disease is linked with specific personality traits; thus, psychosomatic medicine has not received much support from the scientific community. The work of clinicians and researchers in psychosomatic medicine paved the way for late twentieth century conceptualizations of the relations between stress and physiology. Most important, biopsychosocial models that view the individual's health status in the context of the interaction between his or her biological vulnerability, psychological characteristics, and socio-occupational environment have been developed for a number of physical diseases.

Future research into individual differences in stress responses will further clarify the mechanisms by which stress exerts its effects on physiology. Once these mechanisms are identified, intervention strategies for use with patients or for prevention programs for at-risk individuals can be identified and implemented. Clarification of the role of the endogenous opiates in the stress response, for example, represents an important dimension in developing new strategies to enhance individual coping with stressors. Further investigation of the influence of stressors on immune function should open new doors for prevention and intervention, as well.

Much remains to be learned about why individuals differ in their responses to stress. Research in this area will seek to determine the influence of genes, environment, and behavior on the individual, elucidating the important differences between stress-tolerant and stress-intolerant individuals. Such work will provide a better understanding of the basic mechanisms by which stressors have their effects, and should lead to exciting new prevention and intervention strategies that will enhance health and improve the quality of life.

Bibliography

Briere, John. *Psychological Assessment of Adult Posttraumatic States.* Washington, D.C.: American Psychological Association, 1997.

Craig, Kenneth D., and Stephen M. Weiss, eds. *Health Enhancement, Disease Prevention, and Early Intervention: Biobehavioral Perspectives.* New York: Springer, 1990. Includes, among other chapters of interest, an excellent chapter by Neal Miller (the "father of biofeedback") on how the brain affects the health of the body.

Feist, Jess, and Linda Brannon. *Health Psychology: An Introduction to Behavior and Health.* Belmont, Calif.: Wadsworth, 1988. Written for undergraduate students. A very readable overview of the field of health psychology. Provides the reader with chapters on stress and health, and various stress-related diseases.

Fuller, M. G., and V. L. Goetsch. "Stress and Stress Management." In *Behavior and Medicine,* edited by Danny Wedding. New York: Mosby-Year Book, 1990. Provides an overview of the field, focusing particularly on the physiological response to stress.

Jacobson, Edmund. *You Must Relax.* New York: McGraw-Hill, 1934. A rare classic which may be available in the special collections section of the library. Jacobson is considered the father of modern relaxation training. This book is worth seeking for the pictures of Jacobson's patients after undergoing his relaxation procedure as well as for Jacobson's thoughtful insights.

Ornstein, Robert, and D. S. Sobel. "The Brain as a Health Maintenance Organization." In *The Healing Brain: A Scientific Reader,* edited by Robert Ornstein and Charles Swencionis. New York: Guilford Press, 1990. Discusses the body's responses to stressors from an evolutionary perspective.

Selye, Hans. *The Stress of Life.* New York: McGraw-Hill, 1956. A thoroughly readable account of Selye's work and thinking about stress and health. Available at most bookstores, a must for those interested in learning more about stress.

Toates, Fredrick, and Milton Keynes. *Stress: Conceptual and Biological Aspects.* New York: John Wiley & Sons, 1996.

Virginia L. Goetsch
Kevin T. Larkin

See also:

The Concept of Stress, 581; The Endocrine System, 248; Stress: Behavioral and Psychological Responses, 586; Stress-Related Diseases, 598.

STRESS-RELATED DISEASES

Type of psychology: Stress
Field of study: Stress and illness

As a person experiences stress, physical responses occur that have been associated with a host of physical diseases. Understanding the stress-disease relationship, including how to control and lower stress levels, is important in maintaining a healthful life.

Principal terms

BIOFEEDBACK: a procedure in which one's biological functions are monitored and immediately fed back to the person so that control over these functions can be learned

GENERAL ADAPTATION SYNDROME: a general pattern of biological reactions to stressors consisting of three stages—the alarm stage, the resistance stage, and the exhaustion stage

LOCUS OF CONTROL: beliefs concerning the sources of power over one's life; persons who believe they can generally control the direction of their lives have an internal locus of control, and those who believe that their lives are influenced more by fate have an external locus of control

STRESSOR: the agent, circumstance, or demand that causes stress TYPE A PERSONALITY: a set of personality characteristics that includes impatience, competitiveness, hostility, cynicism, and a sense of constant pressure

TYPE B PERSONALITY: a set of personality characteristics that includes low levels of impatience, competitiveness, hostility, and cynicism, and a more relaxed, easygoing attitude toward life

Overview

The term "stress," as it is used in the field of psychology, may be defined as the physical or psychological disturbance an individual experiences as a result of what that individual perceives to be an adverse or challenging circumstance. Four observations concerning this definition of stress should be made. First, stress is what the individual experiences, not the circumstance causing the stress (the stressor). Second, individuals differ in what they perceive to be stressful. What may be very stressful for one individual may not be at all stressful for another. Hans Selye, the researcher who did more than anyone else to make the medical community and the general population aware of the concept and consequences of stress, once noted that, for him, spending the day on the beach doing nothing would be extremely stressful. This difference in people's perceptions is behind the familiar concept that events do not cause stress. Instead, stress comes from one's perception or interpretation of events.

Third, stress occurs in response to circumstances that are seen as negative, but stress may also arise from challenging circumstances, even positive ones. The well-known Social Readjustment Rating Scale developed by Thomas Holmes and Richard Rahe includes both positive and negative life events. A negative event, such as the death of a spouse, is clearly stressful; however, marriage, generally viewed as a positive life event, can also be stressful. Fourth, stressors can lead to stress-related disturbances that are psychological, physiological, or both. The psychological response is rather unpredictable. A given stressor may result in one individual responding with anger, another with depression, and another with a new determination to succeed.

The physiological response is more predictable. Beginning in the 1930's, Selye began studying the human response to stressors. Eventually he identified what he termed the general adaptation syndrome (GAS) to describe the typical pattern of physical responses. Selye divided the GAS into three stages: alarm, resistance, and exhaustion.

The first stage begins when an individual becomes frightened, anxious, or even merely concerned. The body immediately undergoes numerous physical changes to cope with the stressor. Metabolism speeds up. Heart and respiration rates increase. The hormones epinephrine, norepinephrine, and cortisol are secreted. Sugar is released from the liver. The muscles tense. Blood shifts from the internal organs to the skeletal musculature. These and a host of other changes are aimed at helping the body cope, but the price paid for this heightened state of arousal typically includes symptoms such as headache, upset stomach, sleeplessness, fatigue, diarrhea, and loss of appetite. The body's increase in alertness and energy is accompanied by a lowered state of resistance to illness.

Obviously, people cannot remain in the alarm stage for long. If the stressor is not removed, the body enters the resistance stage—a stage which may last from minutes to days or longer. During this stage, the body seeks to adapt to the stressor. The physical changes that occurred during the alarm stage subside. Resistance to illness is actually increased to above-normal levels. Because the body is still experiencing stress, however, remaining in this stage for a long period will eventually lead to physical and psychological exhaustion—the exhaustion stage.

Selye has noted that over the course of life, most people go through the first two stages many, many times. Such is necessary to adapt to the demands and challenges of life. The real danger is found in not eliminating the stressor. During the exhaustion stage, the body is very vulnerable to disease and in extreme cases may suffer collapse and death. Although newer research has found subtle differences in the stress response, depending on the stressor involved, the basic findings of Selye have continued to be supported. Moreover, specific illnesses are caused or promoted by stress.

For many years Americans have been aware of the relationship between stress and heart disease. The biochemical changes associated with stress lead to higher blood pressure, an increased heart rate, and a release of fat into the bloodstream. If the fat is completely consumed by the muscles through physical activity (for example, defending oneself from an attacker), no serious health consequences follow. If, however, a person experiences stress without engaging in physical activity (a more common scenario in Western culture), the fat is simply deposited on the walls of the blood vessels. As these fatty deposits accumulate, life is threatened.

The work of two cardiologists, Meyer Friedman and Ray Rosenman, is of particular importance to a discussion of heart disease and stress. Friedman and Rosenman demonstrated, based originally on personal observation and subsequently on clinical research, that there is a personality type that is particularly prone to heart disease. The personality type that is at the greatest risk was found to be one which is highly stressed—impatient, hostile, hard-driving, and competitive. They termed this a Type A personality. The low-risk person, the Type B personality, is more patient, easygoing, and relaxed.

Numerous studies have examined health based on the Type A-Type B concept. Virtually all have supported Friedman and Rosenman's conclusions. One major report, however, did not; subsequent analysis of that report and other research generally has indicated that the aspects of the Type A personality which are threatening to one's health are primarily the hostility, cynicism, and impatience, not the desire to achieve.

Stomach ulcers are another health problem long known to be caused or aggravated by stress. Stress leads to an increase in the production of digestive acids and pepsinogen. When pepsinogen levels are abnormally high, the lining of the stomach is destroyed. Research with laboratory rats has demonstrated that even rats, when placed under high levels of stress, produce additional pepsinogen and develop stomach ulcers. Thus, the adage sometimes spoken by gastroenterologists, "It's not what you eat, it's what eats you," has merit.

A newer area of research that is even more fundamental to understanding how stress is related to disease involves the immune system. As the physiological changes associated with stress occur, the immune system is suppressed. The immune system has two primary functions: to identify and destroy hazardous foreign materials called antigens (these include bacteria, viruses, parasites, and fungi) and to identify and destroy the body's own cells that have undergone changes associated with malignancy. Thus, if the immune system is suppressed, the body is less able to detect and defend against a host of diseases. An example of this effect again involves research with laboratory rats. One such investigation involved placing tumor cells in the bodies of rats. Some of the rats were then exposed to an abundance of stress. Those that were given this treatment were less resistant to the cancer. Their tumors were larger, and they developed sooner than those found in the "low-stress" rats.

As research continues, the number of specific diseases that can be linked to stress grows. A partial alphabetical listing of stress-related diseases and disorders for which recent research is available would include acne, asthma, cancers (many types), coronary thrombosis, diabetes mellitus, gastric ulcers, herpes simplex (types 1 and 2), human immunodeficiency virus (HIV) infection, infertility, migraine headache, mononucleosis syndrome, rheumatoid arthritis, streptococcal infection, stroke, systemic lupus erythematosus, and tuberculosis.

It should be emphasized that few, if any, of these physical problems are caused solely by stress. Many other factors influence risk, including genetic composition, gender, race, environmental conditions, nutritional state, and so forth. Nevertheless, stress is frequently an important factor in determining initial resistance as well as the subsequent course of a given disease.

Applications

Why is it that some individuals who appear to live with many stressors generally avoid physical and psychological illness? Understanding the answer to that question is important, because it can provide insight as to what the average person can and should do to lower stress levels. Dispositional factors (optimistic versus pessimistic, easygoing versus hard-driving, friendly versus hostile) are probably most important in determining one's stress level. The Type A-Type B research noted above is an example of research demonstrating the influence of dispositional factors.

Research with twins has found that temperament is largely inborn; however, any individual can choose to be more optimistic, generous, and patient. Norman Cousins is often cited as an example of a person who decided to change his outlook and mental state in order to preserve his life. He had read Selye's *The Stress of Life* (1956), which describes how negative emotions can cause physical stress and subsequent disease. Cousins, who had a rare and painful illness from which he was told he would likely never recover, decided that if negative emotions could harm one's health, then positive emotions could possibly return one's health.

As Cousins describes his experience in *Anatomy of an Illness as Perceived by the Patient* (1979), he left his hospital room for a more pleasant environment, began trading massive doses of drugs for television comedies and laughter, and decided to stop worrying. To the surprise of his medical team, his recovery began at once. Though this now-classic example is only anecdotal, the research on disposition and stress would support the assumption that Cousins' decision to change his mental state and stop worrying—not his avoidance of traditional medical care—was the truly important influence.

A related area of research has investigated how psychological hardiness helps people resist stress. Studies by Suzanne Kobasa and her colleagues examined business executives who all had an obvious abundance of stressors in their lives. In comparing those hardy individuals who handled the stressors well with the nonhardy individuals, the researchers found that the two groups differed in three important but basic ways.

The first was commitment. Stress-resistant executives typically possessed a clear sense of values. They had clear goals and a commitment to those goals. Less hardy executives were more likely to feel alienation. The second was challenge. The hardy executives welcomed challenges and viewed change rather than stability as the norm in life. Their less healthy counterparts viewed change with alarm. The third factor was control. The hardy executives felt more in control of their lives. This aspect of Kobasa's research overlaps with research conducted since the 1960's involving a concept known as the "locus of control." People with an internal locus of control are those individuals who believe they are influential rather than powerless in controlling the direction of their lives. This area of research has also found that such a belief lowers stress.

Many years ago it was estimated that more than a thousand studies had been completed that examined the relationship between physical fitness and mental health. What has emerged from this heavily researched area is a clear conclusion: Exercise can lower stress levels. Though regular, sustained aerobic exercise is generally advocated, research has found that even something as simple as a daily ten-minute walk can have measurable beneficial effects. Why does exercise lower stress levels? There are several possible explanations—the increased production of neurotransmitters (such as the endorphins that influence mood), the emotional benefit of feeling more physically fit, and the benefit of distracting one's mind from immediate problems are commonly suggested; however, the research as to why exercise is beneficial is still inconclusive.

Another approach to reducing stress involves learning to evoke a physical "relaxation response," a term coined by Harvard Medical School cardiologist Herbert Benson. Benson became intrigued by the ability of some people who practice meditation to lower their blood pressure, heart rate, and oxygen consumption voluntarily. He discovered that the process is not at all mystical and can be easily taught. The process involves getting comfortable, closing the eyes, breathing deeply, relaxing muscles, and relaxing one's mind by focusing on a simple word or phrase.

Others are helped by using an electronic device which closely monitors subtle physiological changes. By observing these changes (typically on a monitor), a person can, for example, learn to slow down a heart rate. This is known as biofeedback training. Many other techniques and suggestions arising from research as well as common sense can lower stress. A strong social support system has been found to be very important; disciplining oneself not to violate one's own value system is essential. Even having a pet that needs love and attention has been found to lower stress.

Context

A general recognition that a relationship exists between mind and body is at least as old as the biblical Old Testament writings. In the book of Proverbs, for example, one reads, "A cheerful heart is good medicine,/ but a crushed spirit dries up the bones" (Proverbs 17:22). Hippocrates (460-377 B.C.), generally considered the "father of medicine," sought to understand how the body could heal itself and what factors could slow or prevent this process. He clearly perceived a relationship between physical health and what we now term "stress," though his understanding was shallow.

Several physiologists of the nineteenth century made contributions; however, it was not until the twentieth century that the classic studies of American physiologist Walter B. Cannon proved the link scientifically. Cannon and his student Phillip Bard began their analysis of stress and physiological arousal to disprove the idea espoused by others, that emotion follows physiological arousal.

Cannon found a variety of stressors that led to the release of the hormones adrenaline and noradrenaline (or, properly now, epinephrine and norepinephrine). Heat, cold, oxygen deprivation, and fright all led to hormonal changes as well as a number of additional physiological adaptations. Cannon was excited about this discovery and impressed with the body's remarkable ability to react to stressors. All these changes were aimed at preparing the body for what Cannon termed the "fight-or-flight" response. It was Selye's task to build on Cannon's work. His description of the reaction subsequently termed the general adaptation syndrome first appeared in a scientific journal in 1936. As knowledge of the stress concept began to spread, interest by the public as well as the research community increased.

Literally tens of thousands of stress research studies conducted throughout the world have been completed during the last half of the twentieth century. Of particular importance was the discovery by three American scientists that the brain produces morphinelike antistress substances. The discovery of these substances, named endorphins, won the 1977 Nobel Prize for the scientists involved and opened a whole new area of research.

The hope remains that someday an endorphin-type drug could be used to counter some of the unhealthy effects of stress, ensuring better health and longer lives. Better health and longer lives are available even today, however, for all people who are willing to make lifestyle changes based on current knowledge.

Bibliography

Brown, Barbara B. *Between Health and Illness*. Boston: Houghton Mifflin, 1984. One of many books available for the nonprofessional who simply wants an overview of stress and its consequences. This easy-to-read book is full of accurate information and practical suggestions.

Cooper, Cary L., ed. *Handbook of Stress, Medicine, and Health*. Boca Raton, Fla.: CRC Press, 1995.

Friedman, Meyer, and Diane Ulmer. *Treating Type A Behavior—and Your Heart*. New York: Knopf, 1984. This is an easily read book on preventing heart disease by changing one's lifestyle. Presents the results of a large research project and relates relevant research. The first author, Meyer Friedman, along with fellow cardiologist Ray Rosenman, also authored the classic *Type A Behavior and Your Heart* (New York: Alfred A. Knopf, 1974).

Lovallo, William R. *Stress and Health: Biological and Psychological Interactions*. Thousand Oaks, Calif.: Sage Publications, 1997.

Managing Stress: From Morning to Evening. Alexandria, Va.: Time-Life Books, 1987. A very good introduction to understanding and managing stress. Written in clear, simple language and widely available, it provides an overview of the sources of stress, the physiological changes associated with stress, the effects of stress on the immune system, the way to assess one's own stress level, and suggestions for numerous approaches to managing stress. Full of illustrations and photographs. A weakness is that the book fails to address adequately the importance of dispositional factors, focusing too heavily on some stress-reduction techniques that few are likely to use.

Pelletier, Kenneth R. *Mind as Healer, Mind as Slayer*. New York: Dell Books, 1977. This well-known work examines how stress contributes to heart disease, cancer, arthritis, migraine, and respiratory disease. Sources of stress, evaluation of personal stress levels, profiles of unhealthy personality traits, and means of preventing stress-related diseases are addressed.

Selye, Hans. *The Stress of Life*. Rev. ed. New York: McGraw-Hill, 1976. Originally published in 1956, this is the most influential book ever written about stress. It focuses on the relationship between a stressful life and subsequent illness, but it is very technical. Those wanting a less difficult introduction to Selye's writings and work should read his *Stress Without Distress*.

_____. *Stress Without Distress*. New York: New American Library, 1975. Written by the pioneering researcher who discovered and named what is known as the general adaptation syndrome. Describes that syndrome and discusses how to handle stress so as not to suffer the physical declines that so often arise from excessive stress.

Timothy S. Rampey

See also:

The Concept of Stress, 581; The Endocrine System, 248; Stress: Behavioral and Psychological Responses, 586; Stress: Physiological Responses, 592.

SUBSTANCE ABUSE

Type of psychology: Psychopathology
Fields of study: Biological treatments; nervous system; substance abuse

Substance abuse is the use of any substance in amounts or frequencies that violate social, personal, or medical norms for physical or behavioral health; these substances are often addictive.

Principal terms

DEPENDENCE: the presence of withdrawal signs when use of a substance is discontinued

HALLUCINOGENS: drugs that can alter perception, including LSD, PCP, peyote, psilocybin, and possibly marijuana

INHALANTS: volatile drugs, including glue, gasoline, propellants, and some anesthetics

OPIATES: substances derived from the opium poppy, including morphine, heroin, codeine, and Demerol

SEDATIVES/HYPNOTICS: nonopiate substances that cause a slowing of behavioral arousal, including alcohol, tranquilizers, and barbiturates

SELF-MEDICATION: a theory that substance abuse is a form of self-treatment in order to alleviate measured or perceived pain/dysphoria

STIMULANTS: drugs that cause behavioral and/or physiological stimulation, including amphetamine, cocaine, and their respective derivatives; caffeine; nicotine; and some antidepressants

TOLERANCE: the need for greater amounts of a substance over time in order to achieve a previous effect

Overview

Substance abuse is studied in psychology from personality, social, and biological perspectives. Social and personality studies of the substance abuser have produced theories with four principal themes: The abuser displays inability to tolerate stress, immaturity in the form of inability to delay gratification, poor socialization, and/or environmental problems. Biological theories of substance abuse maintain that at least two major factors can result in abusive disorders: the need to relieve some form of pain and the seeking of pleasure or euphoria. Pain is broadly defined as any feeling of dysphoria. Because both pain and euphoria can be produced by psychosomatic or somatopsychic events, these two biological categories can subsume most of the stated nonbiological correlates of substance abuse.

There are several forms of substance abuse, including chronic abuse, intermittent abuse (sprees), active abuse that involves drug seeking, and passive abuse that involves unintentional repeated exposure to drugs. In each case, abuse is determined by a physical or psychological reaction or status that violates accepted professional or personal health norms.

Substance abuse may or may not involve the development of tolerance or physical dependence and may or may not result in easily detectable symptomatology. Tolerance, the need for greater amounts or more frequent administration of a substance, can develop over time or can be acute. In addition, the amount of a substance needed to produce tolerance varies widely among drugs and among individuals. Similarly, the withdrawal signs that indicate dependence need not be the same among individuals and are not always obvious, even to the abuser. Thus, an individual can be an "invisible" abuser.

There are several types of abused substances, and some of these are not typically viewed as problematic. Major categories include sedatives/hypnotics, such as alcohol; opiates, such as heroin; stimulants, including cocaine and caffeine; inhalants, such as nitrous oxide ("laughing gas"); and hallucinogens, including phencyclidine (PCP or "angel dust"). Food is an example of a substance not usually considered a substance of abuse, but it has definite abuse potential.

The experience of pain or the seeking of euphoria as causes of substance abuse can be measured physically or can be perceived by the individual without obvious physical indicators. The relative importance of pain and euphoria in determining the development and maintenance of substance abuse requires consideration of the contributions of at least five potential sources of behavioral and physical status: genetic predisposition, dysregulation during development, dysregulation from trauma at any time during the life span, the environment, and learning. Any of these can result in or interact to produce the pain or feelings of euphoria that can lead to substance abuse.

The key commonality in pain-induced substance abuse is that the organism experiences pain that it does not tolerate. Genetic predisposers of pain include inherited diseases and conditions that interfere with normal pain tolerance. Developmental dysregulations include physical and behavioral arrests and related differences from developmental norms. Trauma from physical injury or from environmental conditions can also result in the experience of pain, as can the learning of a pain-producing response.

Several theories of pain-induced substance abuse can be summarized as self-medication theories. In essence, these state that individuals abuse substances in order to correct an underlying disorder that presumably produces some form of dysphoria. Self-medication theories are useful because they take into account the homeostatic (tendency toward balance) nature of the organism and because they include the potential for significant individual differences in problems with pain.

Relief from pain by itself does not account entirely for drug use that goes beyond improvement in health or reachievement of normal status and certainly cannot account entirely for drug use that becomes physically self-destructive (an exception occurs when pain becomes more motivating than the need to preserve life). Thus, the desire for euphoria is also studied. This type of substance abuse can be distinguished from the possible pleasure produced by pain relief because it does not stop when such relief is achieved.

Euphoria-induced substance use, or pleasure seeking, is characteristic of virtually all species tested. The transition from pleasurable use to actual abuse is also widespread, but often limited in other species when life-threatening conditions are produced. Some theorists have proposed that pleasure seeking is an innate drive not easily kept in check even by socially acceptable substitutes. Thus, euphoria-induced substance abuse is conceived of as pleasure seeking gone awry. Other theorists believe that euphoria-induced substance abuse is related to biological causes such as evolutionary pressure. For example, some drug-abuse researchers believe that organisms that could eat rotten, fermented fruit (partly alcohol) may have survived to reproduce when others did not.

Applications

Laboratory studies of the biological bases of substance abuse involve clinical (human) and preclinical (animal) approaches. Such research has demonstrated that there are areas of the brain that can provide powerful feelings of euphoria when stimulated, indicating that the brain is primed for the experience of pleasure. Direct electrical stimulation of some areas of the brain, including an area first referred to as the medial forebrain bundle, produced such strong addictive behaviors in animals that they ignored many basic drives including those for food, water, mating, and care of offspring.

Later research showed that the brain also contains highly addictive analgesic and euphoriant chemicals that exist as a normal part of the neural milieu. Thus, the brain is also predisposed to aid in providing relief from pain and has coupled such relief in some cases with feelings of euphoria. It is not surprising, therefore, that substance abuse and addictive behaviors can develop so readily in so many organisms.

The effects of typical representatives of the major categories of abused substances can be predicted. Alcohol, a sedative/hypnotic, can disrupt several behavioral functions. It can slow reaction time, movement, and thought processes and can interfere with needed rapid eye movement (REM) sleep. It can also produce unpredictable emotionality, including violence. Abusers of alcohol develop tolerance and dependence, and withdrawal can be life-threatening. Heroin, an opiate, has analgesic (pain-killing) and euphoriant effects. It is also highly addictive, but withdrawal seldom results in death. Marijuana, sometimes classified as a sedative, sometimes as a hallucinogen, has many of the same behavioral effects as alcohol. Stimulants vary widely in their behavioral effects. Common to all is some form of physiological and behavioral stimulation. Some, such as cocaine and the amphetamines (including crystal methamphetamine, or "ice"), are extremely addictive and seriously life-threatening and can produce violence. Others, such as caffeine, are relatively mild in their euphoriant effects. Withdrawal from stimulants, especially the powerful forms, can result in profound depression. Hallucinogens are also a diverse group of substances that can produce visual, auditory, tactile, olfactory, or gustatory hallucinations, but most do so in only a small percentage of the population. Some, such as PCP, can produce violent behavior, while others, such as lysergic acid diethylamide (LSD), are not known for producing negative emotional outbursts. Inhalants usually produce feelings of euphoria, but they are seldom used by individuals beyond the adolescent years.

It is noteworthy that some of the pharmacological effects of very different drugs are quite similar. Marijuana and alcohol affect at least three of the same brain biochemical systems. Alcohol can become a form of opiate in the brain following some specific chemical transformations. These similarities raise an old question in substance abuse: Is there a fundamental addictive mechanism common to everyone that differs only in the level and nature of expression? Older theories of drug-abuse behavior approached this question by postulating the "addictive personality," a type of person who would become indiscriminately addicted as a result of his or her personal and social history. With advances in neuroscience have come theories concerning the possibility of an "addictive brain," which refers to a neurological status that requires continued adjustment provided by drugs. This is a modification of self-medication theories.

An example of the workings of the addictive brain might be a low-opiate brain that does not produce normal levels of analgesia or normal levels of organismic and behavioral euphoria (joy). The chemical adjustment sought by the brain might be satisfied by use or abuse of any drug that results in stimulation of the opiate function of the brain. As discussed above, several seemingly unrelated drugs can produce a similar chemical effect. Thus, the choice of a particular substance might depend both on brain status and on personal or social experience with the effects and availability of the drug used.

The example of the opiate-seeking brain raises at least two possibilities for prevention and treatment, both of which have been discussed in substance-abuse literature: regulation of the brain and substitution. So far, socially acceptable substitutes or substitute addictions offer some promise, but reregulation of the dysregulated brain is still primarily a hope of the future. An example of a socially acceptable substitute might be opiate production by excessive running, an activity that can produce some increase in opiate function. The success of such a substitution procedure, however, depends upon many variables that may be quite difficult to predict or control. The substitution might not produce the required amount of reregulation, the adjustment might not be permanent, and tolerance to the adjustment might develop. There are a host of other possible problems.

Context

Use and probable abuse of psychoactive substances date from the earliest recorded history and likely predate it. Historical records indicate that many substances with the potential for abuse were used in medicinal and ceremonial or religious contexts, as tokens in barter, for their euphoriant properties during recreation, as indicators of guilt or innocence, as penalties, and in other practices.

Substance abuse is widespread in virtually all countries and cultures, and it can be extremely costly, both personally and socially. There is no doubt that most societies would like to eliminate substance abuse, but current practices have been relatively unsuccessful in doing so. It is obvious that economic as well as social factors contribute both to abusive disorders and to the laws regulating substance use, and possibly create some roadblocks in eliminating abuse.

In psychology, the systematic and popular study of substance abuse became most extensive during the period when such abuse was most popular, the 1960's and 1970's. Research into psychological, social, environmental, therapeutic, and some biological aspects of abuse proliferated during these years, and the reasons proposed to explain abuse disorders were almost as numerous as the authors proposing them. During the early 1980's, drug-abuse research experienced a somewhat fallow period, but with discoveries of the brain mechanisms involved in many disorders, a resurgence has occurred. Many disorders previously thought to be the result of nonbiological factors are now known to have strong neural determinants. Both psychosomatic and somatopsychic events affect the nervous system, and the resurgence of brain-oriented research reflects this understanding.

Future research on substance abuse is likely to focus on more of the biological determinants and constraints on the organism and to try to place substance-abuse disorders more in the contexts of biological self-medication and biological euphoria. Many people erroneously consider biological explanations of problematic behaviors to be an excuse for such behaviors, not an explanation. In fact, discoveries regarding the neural contributions to such behaviors are the basis on which rational therapies for such behaviors can be developed. Recognizing that a disorder has a basis in the brain can enable therapists to address the disorder with a better armamentarium of useful therapeutic tools. In this way, simple management of such disorders can be replaced by real solutions to the problems created by substance abuse.

Bibliography

Bukstein, Oscar Gary. *Adolescent Substance Abuse: Assessment, Prevention, and Treatment.* New York: John Wiley & Sons, 1995.

Gomberg, Edith S. Lisanky, and Ted D. Nirenberg, eds. *Women and Substance Abuse.* Norwood, N.J.: Ablex, 1993.

Jaffe, Jerome H. "Drug Addiction and Drug Abuse." In *Goodman and Gilman's the Pharmacological Basis of Therapeutics,* edited by Alfred Goodman Gilman, Louis S. Goodman, et al. 7th ed. New York: Macmillan, 1985. A standard reference for students interested in an overview of the pharmacological aspects of selected addictive drugs. Of greater interest to those interested in pursuing the study of substance abuse from a neurological and physiological perspective.

Julien, Robert M. *A Primer of Drug Action.* 5th ed. New York: W. H. Freeman, 1988. An introductory treatment of types and actions of many abused and therapeutic substances. A useful, quick reference guide for psychoactive effects of drugs used in traditional pharmacological therapy for disorders and of abused substances. Contains good reference lists and appendices that explain some of the anatomy and chemistry required to understand biological mechanisms of substance abuse.

Leavitt, Fred. *Drugs and Behavior.* 2d ed. New York: John Wiley & Sons, 1982. Inclusive coverage from a psychological perspective of the effects of drugs on many types of behaviors. Includes sections on licit and illicit drugs, theories of drug use and abuse, prevention and treatment, and development of drugs. Important because it considers the effects of drug use on a large range of behaviors and physical states and because it presents a relatively integrated view of biopsychological information on drugs.

Ray, Oakley Stern, and Charles Ksir. *Drugs, Society, and Human Behavior.* 4th ed. St. Louis: Times Mirror/Mosby, 1987. A good text for the newer student of substance abuse who not only wishes to understand the substances and their biological significance but also is interested in current methods of prevention and treatment. Of special interest are the interspersed history and comments regarding the social aspects of abused substances.

United States Department of Health and Human Services. *Drug Abuse and Drug Abuse Research: The First in a Series of Triennial Reports to Congress.* Rockville, Md.: National Institute on Drug Abuse, 1984. An excellent summary of research on selected substances of abuse. The rest of the series should also be of great interest to the reader interested in substance-abuse research. The strength of this series is the understandable language and style used to convey recent research. Treatment, prevention, and specific drug research are summarized, and a well-selected reference list is provided for each chapter.

United States Department of Health and Human Services. *Theories on Drug Abuse: Selected Contemporary Perspectives.* Edited by Dan J. Lettieri, Mollie Sayers, and Helen Wallenstein Pearson. Rockville, Md.: National Institute on Drug Abuse, 1980. An older but good compendium of theoretical positions related to the question of substance abuse. Theories covered include the gamut of empirical and nonempirical thought concerning the predisposition to, development of, maintenance of, and possible termination of abuse disorders. Perspectives are biological, personal, and social. Of interest are a quick guide to theory components and an extensive list of references.

Rebecca M. Chesire

See also:
Abnormality, 1; Anxiety Disorders, 65; Depression, Clinical, 194; Suicide, 610.

Suicide

Type of psychology: Psychopathology
Field of study: Depression

Suicide is the intentional taking of one's own life; roughly twelve per 100,000 Americans commit suicide annually. Suicide rates are higher for males than females and increase with age; risk for suicide also increases with clinical depression, so suicide may be considered the most severe consequence of any psychological disorder.

Principal terms

ALTRUISTIC SUICIDE: a suicide that occurs in response to societal demands; introduced by Émile Durkheim as one of the three basic types of suicide

ANOMIE: the experience of alienation or disorientation following a major change in one's social relationships

EGOISTIC SUICIDE: a suicide that occurs because of insufficient ties between the individual and society

EPIDEMIOLOGICAL RESEARCH: the study of the frequency of a condition in a population and its relationship to characteristics of the population

PSYCHOLOGICAL AUTOPSY: an attempt to determine the reasons for suicide, through interviewing the victim's friends and family members and examining personal records

SUICIDAL GESTURE: an apparent attempted suicide, the primary purpose of which is to call attention to oneself in order to gain sympathy or assistance

Overview

Suicide is the intentional taking of one's own life. Psychologists have devoted much effort to its study, attempting to identify those at greatest risk for suicide and to intervene effectively to prevent suicide.

Sociologist Émile Durkheim introduced what has become a well-known classification of suicide types. Altruistic suicides, according to Durkheim, are those that occur in response to societal demands (for example, the soldier who sacrifices himself to save his comrades). Egoistic suicides occur when the individual is isolated from society and so does not experience sufficient societal demands to live. The third type is the anomic suicide. Anomie is a sense of disorientation or alienation which occurs following a major change in one's societal relationships (such as the loss of a job or the death of a close friend); the anomic suicide occurs following such sudden and dramatic changes.

Research supports Durkheim's ideas that suicide is associated with social isolation and recent loss. Many other variables, both demographic and psychological, have also been found to be related to suicide. Numerous studies have shown that the following demographic variables are related to suicide: sex, age, marital status, employment status, urban/rural dwelling, and race. Paradoxically, more females than males attempt suicide, but more males than females commit suicide. The ratio in both cases is about three to one. The difference between the sex ratios for attempted and completed suicide is generally explained by the fact that males tend to employ more lethal and less reversible methods than do females (firearms and hanging, for example, are more lethal and less reversible than ingestion of drugs).

Age is also related to suicide. In general, risk for suicide increases with increasing age; however, even though suicide risk is higher in older people, much attention has been devoted to suicide among children and adolescents. This attention is attributable to two factors. First, since 1960, there has been an increase in the suicide rate among people under twenty-five years of age. Second, suicide has become one of the leading causes of death among people under twenty-one, whereas suicide is surpassed by many illnesses as a cause of death among older adults. Other demographic variables are related to suicide. Suicide risk is higher for divorced than married people. The unemployed have a higher suicide rate than those who are employed. Urban dwellers have a higher suicide rate than rural dwellers. Caucasians have a higher suicide rate than African Americans.

In addition to these demographic variables, several psychological or behavioral variables are related to suicide. Perhaps the single best predictor of suicide is threatening to commit suicide. Most suicide victims have made some type of suicide threat (although, in some cases, the threat may be veiled or indirect, such as putting one's affairs in order or giving away one's belongings). For this reason, psychologists consider seriously any threat of suicide. A related index of suicide risk is the detailedness or clarity of the threat. Individuals who describe a suicide method in detail are at greater risk than those who express an intent to die but who describe the act only vaguely. Similarly, the lethality and availability of the proposed method provide additional measures of risk. Suicide risk is higher if the individual proposes using a more lethal method and if the individual has access to the proposed method.

Another useful indicator of suicide risk is previous suicide attempts. People who have made prior attempts are at higher risk for suicide than people who have not. The lethality of the method used in the prior attempt is a related indicator. An individual who survives a more lethal method (a gunshot to the head) is considered at higher risk than one who survives a less lethal attempt (swallowing a bottle of aspirin).

Suicide risk is associated with particular behavioral or psychological variables: depression, isolation, stress, pain or illness, recent loss, and drug or alcohol use. These factors may help explain why certain of the demographic variables are related to suicide. For example, people who are unemployed may experience higher levels of stress, depression, and isolation than people who are employed. Similarly, divorced people may experience more stress and isolation than married people. The elderly may experience more isolation, depression, and pain or illness than younger people.

Although the demographic and psychological variables summarized above have been found to be related to suicide, the prediction of suicide remains extremely difficult. Suicide is a statistically rare event; according to basic laws of probability, it is very difficult to predict such rare occurrences. What happens in actual attempts to predict suicide is that, in order to identify the "true positives" (individuals who actually attempt suicide), one must accept a very large number of "false positives" (individuals who are labeled suicidal but who in fact will not attempt suicide).

Applications

Several methods have been used to study the psychology of suicide. Epidemiological research determines the distribution of demographic characteristics among suicide victims.

Another method is to study survivors of suicide attempts. This enables psychologists to examine intensively their psychological characteristics. A third method is to analyze suicide notes, which may explain the individual's reasons for suicide. A final method is the psychological autopsy. This involves interviewing the victim's friends and family members and examining the victim's personal materials (such as diaries and letters) in an attempt to identify the psychological cause of the suicide.

Although all these approaches have been widely used, each has its limitations. The epidemiological method focuses on demographic characteristics and so may overlook psychological influences. Studying survivors of suicide attempts has limitations because survivors and victims of suicide attempts may differ significantly. For example, some suicide attempts are regarded as suicidal gestures, or "cries for help," the intent of which is not to die but rather to call attention to oneself to gain sympathy or assistance. Thus, what is learned from survivors may not generalize to suicide victims. The study of suicide notes is limited by the fact that, contrary to popular belief, most suicide victims do not leave notes. For example, in a study of all suicides in Los Angeles County in a single year, psychologists Edwin Shneidman and Norman Farberow found that only 35 percent of the males and 39 percent of the females left notes. Finally, the psychological autopsy is limited in that the victim's records and acquaintances may not shed light on the victim's thought processes.

In 1988, Harry Hoberman and Barry Garfinkel conducted an epidemiological study to identify variables related to suicide in children and adolescents. They examined death records in two counties in Minnesota over an eleven-year period for individuals who died at age nineteen or younger. Hoberman and Garfinkel examined in detail the death records of 225 suicide victims. They noted that 15 percent of their sample had not been identified as suicides by the medical examiner, but had instead been listed as accident victims or as having died of undetermined causes. This finding suggests that official estimates of suicide deaths in the United States are actually low.

Consistent with other studies, Hoberman and Garfinkel found that suicide was related to both age and sex. Males accounted for 80 percent of the suicides, females for only 20 percent. Adolescents aged fifteen to nineteen years composed 91 percent of the sample, with children aged fourteen and under only 9 percent. In addition, Hoberman and Garfinkel found that a full 50 percent of the sample showed evidence of one or more psychiatric disorders. Most common were depression and alcohol and drug abuse. Finally, Hoberman and Garfinkel found that a substantial number of the suicide victims had been described as "loners," "lonely," or "withdrawn." Thus, several of the indicators of suicide in adults also are related to suicide in children and adolescents.

Psychiatrist Aaron Beck and his colleagues developed the Hopelessness Scale in 1974 to assess an individual's negative thoughts of self and future. In many theories of suicide, an individual's sense of hopelessness is related to risk for suicide. Beck and others have demonstrated that hopelessness in depressed patients is a useful indicator of suicide risk. For example, in 1985, Beck and his colleagues reported a study of 207 patients who were hospitalized because of suicidal thinking. Over the next five to ten years, fourteen patients committed suicide. Only one demographic variable, race, differed between the suicide and nonsuicide groups: Caucasian patients had a higher rate of suicide (10.1 percent) than African-American patients (1.3 percent). Of the psychological variables assessed, only the Hopelessness Scale and a measure of pessimism differed between suicide victims and other patients. Patients who committed suicide were higher in both hopelessness and pessimism than other patients. Beck and his colleagues determined the Hopelessness Scale score which best discriminated suicides from nonsuicides. Other mental health professionals can now use this criterion to identify those clinically depressed patients who are at greatest risk for suicide.

Several approaches have been developed in efforts to prevent suicide. Shneidman and Farberow developed what may be the most well-known suicide-prevention program, the Los Angeles Suicide Prevention Center. This program, begun in 1958, helped popularize telephone suicide hotlines. Staff members are trained to interact with individuals who are experiencing extreme distress. When an individual calls the center, staff members immediately begin to assess the caller's risk for suicide, considering the caller's demographics, stress, lifestyle, and suicidal intent. Staff members attempt to calm the caller, so as to prevent an immediate suicide, and to put the person into contact with local mental health agencies so that the individual can receive more extensive follow-up care.

Psychologists William Fremouw, Maria de Perczel, and Thomas Ellis published a useful guide for those who work with suicidal clients. Among their suggestions are to talk openly and matter-of-factly about suicide, to avoid dismissing the client's feelings or motives in a judgmental or pejorative way, and to adopt a problem-solving approach to dealing with the client's situation.

Suicide-prevention programs are difficult to evaluate. Callers may not identify themselves, so it is difficult to determine whether they later commit suicide. Still, such programs are generally thought to be useful, and suicide-prevention programs similar to that of Shneidman and Farberow have been developed in many communities.

Context

Suicide is one of the most extreme and drastic behaviors faced by psychologists. Because of its severity, psychologists have devoted considerable effort to identifying individuals at risk for suicide and to developing programs that are effective in preventing suicide.

Psychological studies of suicide have shown that many popular beliefs about suicide are incorrect. For example, many people erroneously believe that people who threaten suicide never attempt suicide; that all suicide victims truly wish to die; that only the mentally ill commit suicide; that suicide runs in families; and that there are no treatments that can help someone who is suicidal. Because of these and other popular myths about suicide, it is especially important that psychological studies of suicide continue and that the results of this study be disseminated to the public.

Suicide risk increases in clinically depressed individuals. In depressed patients, suicide risk has been found to be associated with hopelessness: As one's sense of hopelessness increases, one's risk for suicide increases. Since the 1970's, Beck's Hopelessness Scale has been used in efforts to predict risk for suicide among depressed patients. Although the suicide rate has been relatively stable in the United States throughout the 1900's, the suicide rate of young people has increased since the 1960's. For this reason, depression and suicide among children and adolescents have become major concerns of psychologists. Whereas childhood depression received relatively little attention from psychologists before the 1970's, psychologists have devoted considerable attention to this condition since then. Much of this attention has concerned whether biological, cognitive, and behavioral theories of the causes of depression and approaches to the treatment of depression, which were originally developed and applied to depressed adults, may generalize to children.

In the 1980's, psychologists developed several innovative programs that attempt to identify youths who are depressed and experiencing hopelessness, and so may be at risk for suicide; evaluations and refinements of these programs will continue.

Bibliography

Durkheim, Émile. *Suicide*. Reprint. Glencoe, Ill.: Free Press, 1951. In this work, originally published in 1897, Durkheim introduced his classification system of suicide types— altruistic, egoistic, and anomic suicides—and examined the relationship of suicide to isolation and recent loss.

Fairbairn, Gavin J. *Contemplating Suicide: The Language and Ethics of Self-Harm*. New York: Routledge, 1995.

Fremouw, William J., Maria de Perczel, and Thomas E. Ellis. *Suicide Risk: Assessment and Response Guidelines*. New York: Pergamon Press, 1990. This book presents useful guidelines, based on both research and clinical practice, for working with suicidal individuals.

Hawton, Keith. *Suicide and Attempted Suicide Among Children and Adolescents*. Beverly Hills, Calif.: Sage Publications, 1986. This work overviews research results concerning the causes of youth suicide and treatment programs for suicidal youngsters.

Hendin, Herbert. *Suicide in America*. Rev. ed. New York: W. W. Norton, 1995.

Holinger, Paul C., and J. Sandlow. "Suicide." In *Violent Deaths in the United States,* edited by Paul C. Holinger. New York: Guilford Press, 1987. This chapter presents epidemiological information on suicide in the United States, from 1900 to 1980. It also addresses demographic variables and their relationship to suicide.

Lann, Irma S., Eve K. Moscicki, and Ronald Maris, eds. *Strategies for Studying Suicide and Suicidal Behavior*. New York: Guilford Press, 1989. This book examines the various research methods used to study suicide. Considers the relative strengths and weaknesses and offers examples of each method.

Lester, David, ed. *Current Concepts of Suicide*. Philadelphia: Charles Press, 1990. A useful overview of research results on the possible causes of suicide and on programs designed both to prevent suicide and to treat suicidal patients.

Peck, Michael L., Norman L. Farberow, and Robert E. Litman, eds. *Youth Suicide*. New York: Springer, 1985. A useful overview of the psychological influences on youth suicide and on the treatment and prevention programs that have been used with suicidal youths.

Shneidman, Edwin S., Norman L. Farberow, and Robert E. Litman. *The Psychology of Suicide*. New York: Science House, 1970. This is a collection of articles, some of which are now regarded as classics in the study of suicide.

Stengel, Erwin. *Suicide and Attempted Suicide*. Rev. ed. Harmondsworth, England: Penguin Books, 1973. This classic work summarizes the demographic and psychological variables that were known at the time to be associated with suicide.

Michael Wierzbicki

See also:

SURVEY RESEARCH
Questionnaires and Interviews

Type of psychology: Psychological methodologies
Fields of study: Descriptive methodologies; experimental methodologies; methodological issues

Psychologists use survey research techniques including questionnaires and interviews to evaluate specific attitudes about social or personal issues, and to find out about people's behaviors directly from those people. Questionnaires are self-administered and in written form; interviews consist of the psychologist asking questions of the respondent. There are strengths along with limitations for both of these data collection methods.

Principal terms

ATTITUDES: a person's thoughts and beliefs about something in the world or about him- or herself

DEMOGRAPHICS: statistical features of populations, such as age, income, race, and marital status

INTERVIEW: a data collection technique involving one-to-one verbal communication, either face-to-face or by means of a telephone, between the interviewer and respondent

POPULATION: all people in a definable group

QUESTIONNAIRE: a data collection technique in which the questions are in written format and the respondents write down their answers

RESPONDENT: a person (subject) who provides answers to a questionnaire or in an interview

SAMPLE: the number of people who participate in a study and are part of a population

SURVEY RESEARCH: the collection of data from people by means of questionnaires or interviews

Overview

Survey research is common in both science and daily life. Most everyone in today's society has been exposed to survey research in one form or another. Researchers ask questions about the political candidate one favors, the television programs one watches, the soft drink one prefers, whether there should be a waiting period prior to purchasing a handgun, and so on.

There are many ways to obtain data about the social world; among them are observation, field studies, and experimentation. Two key methods for obtaining data—questionnaires and interviews—are survey research methods. Most of the social research conducted or published involves these two data collection devices.

In general, when using survey methods, the researcher gets information directly from each person (or respondent) by using self-report measurement techniques to ask people about their current attitudes, behaviors, and demographics, in addition to past experiences and future goals. In questionnaires, the questions are in written format and the subjects write down their answers. In interviews, there is one-to-one verbal communication, either face-to-face or by means of a telephone, between the interviewer and respondent. Both techniques are flexible and adaptable to the group of people being studied and the particular situation. Both can range from being highly structured to highly unstructured.

Questionnaires can be completed in groups or self-administered on an individual basis. They can also be mailed to people. They are generally less expensive than conducting interviews. Questionnaires also allow greater anonymity of the respondents. One drawback is that a questionnaire requires that the subjects understand exactly what the questions are asking. Also, there may be a problem of motivation with the filling out of questionnaires, because people may get bored or find it tedious to fill out the forms on their own. The survey researcher must therefore make sure that the questionnaire is not excessively long.

In contrast, with an interview there is a chance that the interviewer and subject will have good communication and that all questions will be understood. Telephone interviews are less expensive than face-to-face interviews; still, questionnaires tend to be less costly. In an interview, the respondent is presented with questions orally, whereas in the questionnaire, regardless of type or form, the respondent is presented with a written question. Each data collection device has pros and cons. The decision to use questionnaires versus interviews would basically depend on the purpose of the study, the type of information needed, the size of the sample, the resources for conducting the study, and the variable(s) to be measured. Overall, the interview is probably the more flexible device of the two.

When creating a questionnaire, the researcher must give special thought to writing the specific questions. Researchers must avoid questions that would lead people to answer in a biased way, or ones that might be easily misinterpreted. For example, the questions "Do you favor eliminating the wasteful excesses in the federal budget?" and "Do you favor reducing the federal budget?" might well result in different answers.

Questions are either closed- or open-ended, depending on the researcher's choice. In a closed-ended question, a limited number of fixed response choices are provided to subjects. With open-ended questions, subjects are able to respond in any way they like. Thus, a researcher could ask a person "Where would you like a swimming pool to be built in this town?" versus "Which of the following locations is your top choice for a swimming pool to be built in this town?" The first question allows the person to provide any answer; the second provides a fixed number of alternative answers from which the person must choose. Use of closed-ended questions is a more structured approach, allowing greater ease of analysis because the response alternatives are the same for everyone. Open-ended questions require more time to analyze and are therefore more costly. Open-ended questions, however, can provide valuable insights into what the subjects are actually thinking.

A specialized type of interview is the clinical, or therapeutic, interview. The specific goal of a particular clinical interview depends on the needs and the condition of the particular individual being interviewed. There is a distinction between a therapeutic interview, which attempts both to obtain information and to remedy the client's problem, and a research interview, which attempts solely to obtain information about people at large. Because the clinical interview is a fairly unstructured search for relevant information, it is important to be aware of the factors that might affect its accuracy and comprehensiveness. Research on hypothesis confirmation bias suggests that it is difficult to search for unbiased and comprehensive information in an unstructured setting such as the clinical interview. In the context of the clinical interview, clinicians are likely to conduct unintentionally biased searches for information that confirms their early impressions of each client. Research on self-fulfilling prophecies suggests a second factor that may limit the applicability of interviews in general. This research suggests that the interviewer's expectations affect the behavior of the person being interviewed, and that respondents may change their behavior to match the interviewer's expectations.

Applications

Knowing what to believe about research is often related to understanding the scientific method. The two basic approaches to using the scientific method, the descriptive and the experimental research approaches, differ because they seek to attain different types of knowledge. Descriptive research tries to describe particular situations; experimental research tries to determine cause-and-effect relationships. Independent variables are not manipulated in descriptive research. For that reason, it is not possible to decide if one thing causes another. Instead, survey research uses correlational techniques, which allow the determination of whether behaviors or attitudes are related to one another and whether they predict one another. For example, how liberal a person's political views are might be related to that person's attitudes about sexuality. Such a relationship could be determined using descriptive research.

Survey research, as a widely used descriptive technique, is defined as a method of collecting standardized information by interviewing a representative sample of some population. All research involves sampling of subjects. That is, subjects must be found to participate in the research whether that research is a survey or an experiment. Sampling is particularly important when conducting survey research, because the goal is to describe what a whole population is like based on the data from a relatively small sample of that population.

One famous survey study conducted in the mid-1930's was the interviewing done by Alfred Kinsey and his colleagues. Kinsey studied sexual behavior. Until that time, most of what was known about sexual behavior was based on what biologists knew about animal sex, what anthropologists knew about sex among natives in non-Western, nonindustrialized societies, or what Freud learned about sexuality from his emotionally disturbed patients. Kinsey and his colleagues were the first psychological researchers to interview volunteers about their sexual behaviors. The research was hindered by political investigations and threats of legal action against them. In spite of the harassment encountered by the scientists on the project, the Kinsey group published *Sexual Behavior in the Human Male* in 1948 and *Sexual Behavior in the Human Female* in 1953. The findings of the Kinsey group have benefited the public immensely. As a result, it is now known that the majority of people (both males and females) interviewed by the Kinsey group masturbated at various times, but that more males than females said they masturbated. Data collected by the Kinsey group on oral-genital sexual practices have allowed researchers to discover that, since the 1930's, attitudes toward oral-genital sex have become more positive. Their research also shocked the nation with the discovery that the majority of brides at that time were not virgins.

When scientific sampling techniques are used, the survey results can be interpreted as an accurate representation of the entire population. Although Kinsey and his associates helped to pave the way for future researchers to be able to investigate sexual behaviors and attitudes, there were some problems with the research because of its lack of generalizability. The Kinsey group research is still the largest study of sexual behavior ever completed. They interviewed more than ten thousand people; however, they did not attempt to select a random or representative sample of the population of the United States, which meant that the responses of middle-class, well-educated Caucasians were overrepresented. There is also a problem with the accuracy of the respondents' information, because of memory errors, exaggerations, or embarrassment about wanting to tell an interviewer personal, sensitive information. Despite these limitations, the interviewing conducted by Kinsey and associates made great strides for the study of sexuality and great strides for psychology in general.

When research is intended to reveal very precisely what a population is like, careful sampling procedures must be used. This requires defining the population and sampling people from the population in a random fashion so that no biases will be introduced into the sample. In order to learn what elderly people think about the medical services available to them, for example, a careful sample of the elderly population is needed. Obtaining the sample only from retirement communities in Arizona would bias the results, because these individuals are not representative of all elderly people in the population.

Thus, when evaluating survey data, a researcher must examine how the responses were obtained and what population was investigated. Major polling organizations such as the Gallup organization typically are careful to obtain representative samples of people in the United States. Gallup polls are frequently conducted to survey the voting public's opinions about the popularity of a presidential candidate or a given policy. Many other surveys, however, such as surveys that are published in popular magazines, have limited generalizability because the results are based on people who read the particular magazine and are sufficiently motivated to complete and mail in the questionnaire. When *Redbook*, for example, asks readers to write in to say whether they have ever had an affair, the results may be interesting but would not give a very accurate estimate of the true extent of extramarital sexual activity in the United States. An example of an inaccurate sampling technique was a survey by *Literary Digest* (a now defunct magazine) sampling almost ten million people. The results showed that Alfred Landon would beat Franklin D. Roosevelt by a landslide in the 1936 presidential election. Although it was large, the sample was completely inaccurate.

Context

One of the earliest ways of obtaining psychological information using descriptive techniques was through clinical interviewing. The early interviews conducted by Sigmund Freud in the late 1800's were based on question-and-answer medical formats, which is not surprising, considering that Freud was originally a physician. Later, Freud relied on the less structured free-association technique. In 1902, Adolf Meyer developed a technique to assess a client's mental functioning, memory, attention, speech, and judgment. Independent of the style used, all the early clinical interviews sought to get a psychological portrait of the person, determine the source of the problem, make a diagnosis, and formulate a treatment. More detailed studies of interviews were conducted in the 1940's and 1950's to compare and contrast interviewing styles and determine how much structure was necessary. During the 1960's, much research came about as a result of ideas held by Carl Rogers, who emphasized the interpersonal elements he thought were necessary for the ideal therapeutic relationship; among them are warmth, positive regard, and genuineness on the part of the interviewer.

In the 1800's and early 1900's, interviews were used mainly by psychologists who were therapists helping people with problems such as fear, depression, and hysteria. During that same period, experimental psychologists had not yet begun to use survey research methods. Instead, they used introspection to investigate their own thought processes. For example, experimental psychologist Hermann Ebbinghaus gave himself lists of pronounceable nonsense syllables to remember; he then tested his own memory and attempted to improve it methodically. Many experimental psychologists during this period relied upon the use of animals such as dogs and laboratory rats to conduct behavioral research.

As mentioned above, one of the first attempts by experimental psychologists to study attitudes and behaviors by means of the interview was that of the Kinsey group in the 1930's. At about that same time, Louis Thurstone, an experimental social psychologist, formalized and popularized the first questionnaire methodology for attitude measurement. Thurstone devised a set of questionnaires, or scales, that have been widely used for decades. He is considered by many to be the "father" of attitude scaling. Soon thereafter, Rensis Likert made breakthroughs in questionnaire usage with the development of what are known as Likert scales. A Likert scale provides a series of statements to which subjects can indicate degrees of agreement or disagreement. Using the Likert technique, the respondent answers by selecting from predetermined categories ranging from "strongly agree" to "strongly disagree." It is fairly standard to use five categories (strongly agree, agree, uncertain, disagree, strongly disagree), but more categories can be used if necessary. An example of a question using this technique might be, "Intelligence test scores of marijuana users are higher on the average than scores of nonusers." The respondent then picks one of the five categories mentioned above in response. Likert scales have been widely used and have resulted in a vast amount of information about human attitudes and behaviors.

Bibliography

Alreck, Pamela L., and Robert Settle. *The Survey Research Handbook: Guidelines and Strategies for Conducting a Survey.* 2d ed. Chicago: Irwin Professional Publishing, 1995.

Berdie, Douglas R., and John F. Anderson. *Questionnaires: Design and Use.* Metuchen, N.J.: Scarecrow Press, 1974. Provides extensive, detailed information that guides the reader through the process of questionnaire creation. Also helps the novice learn how to administer a questionnaire correctly.

Bordens, Kenneth S., and Bruce B. Abbott. *Research Design and Methods: A Process Approach.* Mountain View, Calif.: Mayfield, 1988. Places the techniques of surveys, interviews, and questionnaires for collecting data in the context of conducting research as a process from start to finish. A well-received textbook in psychology.

Converse, Jean M., and Stanley Presser. *Survey Questions: Handcrafting the Standardized Questionnaire.* Beverly Hills, Calif.: Sage, 1986. Provides explicit, practical details which would be of use to a person who needs to put together a questionnaire for any of a variety of reasons. Stresses the art of questionnaire creation.

Cozby, Paul C. *Methods in Behavioral Research.* 4th ed. Mountain View, Calif.: Mayfield, 1989. Examines the importance of survey research in the context of conducting experiments and doing research in psychology in general. Allows the reader to understand the research process from a broader perspective.

Kidder, Louise H., and Charles M. Judd. *Research Methods in Social Relations.* 5th ed. New

York: Holt, Rinehart and Winston, 1986. A popular book whose writing style is exceptionally clear. Offers thorough information that introduces the reader to the process of doing research in psychology, including how to get an idea for a research topic, how to collect the information, how to be ethical with subjects, and how to report the results. Detailed information is provided on questionnaires and interviews.

Schweigert, Wendy A. *Research Methods and Statistics for Psychology*. Pacific Grove, Calif.: Brooks/Cole, 1994.

Stewart, Charles J., and William B. Cash, Jr. *Interviewing Principles and Practices*. 3d ed. Dubuque, Iowa: Wm. C. Brown, 1982. A "hands-on" introduction to interviewing which provides practical suggestions and tips along with background information.

Weisberg, Herbert F., Jon A. Krosnick, and Bruce D. Bowen. *An Introduction to Survey Research, Polling, and Data Analysis*. Thousand Oaks, Calif.: Sage Publications, 1996.

Deborah R. McDonald

See also:

Case-Study Methodologies, 110; Psychological Experimentation, 484.

THOUGHT
Study and Measurement

Type of psychology: Cognition
Fields of study: Cognitive processes; thought

The study of thought is probably as old as thought itself. Although the measurement of thought did not originate in psychology, cognitive psychology is primarily dedicated to the study and measurement of thought processes.

Principal terms

COGNITIVE PSYCHOLOGY: an area of study that investigates mental processes; areas within cognitive psychology include attention, perception, language, learning, memory, problem solving, and logic

EBBINGHAUS FORGETTING CURVE: an empirical demonstration that suggests that as time passes, memory performance decreases

HIGHER MENTAL FUNCTIONS: a phrase used to describe advanced thinking processes believed to be mostly limited to humans, such as reasoning, logic, decision making, problem solving, and language use

INFORMATION PROCESSING MODEL: a method of characterizing the processing of the human mind that finds the mind's approach similar to the basic processing of a computer

PARALLEL PROCESSING: a theory concerning how people scan information in memory that suggests the ability to comprehend simultaneously all the components in immediate memory

PERCENT SAVINGS: a formula developed by Hermann Ebbinghaus for the precise measure of memory and forgetting; the higher the percent savings, the less time Ebbinghaus had to spend rememorizing nonsense syllables he had forgotten

PERSONAL EQUATION: an equation developed by astronomers in the 1800's that allowed them to account and compensate for individual differences in tracking the movement of stars across the sky

SERIAL PROCESSING: a theory concerning how people scan information in memory that suggests that as the number of items in memory increases, so does the amount of time taken to determine whether an item is present in memory.

SUBTRACTION TECHNIQUE: a method developed by the Dutch physiologist Frans C. Donders to measure the various components of a complex cognitive task

Overview

Cognitive psychologists study many processes basic to human nature and everyday life. Mental processes are central to who people are, what they do, and how they survive. In cognitive psychology, the study of thought necessitates its measurement. For example, much effort has been put forth in cognitive psychology to study how people understand and process information in their environment. One popular approach is to use the idea of a human information-processing system, analogous to a computer. Computers are information-processing devices that use very specific instructions to achieve tasks. A computer receives input, performs certain internal operations on the data (including memory operations), and outputs certain results. Cognitive psychologists often use the information-processing metaphor in describing human operations. People must "input" information from the environment; this process includes sensory and perceptual systems, the recognition of certain common patterns of information, and attention processes.

Once this information has entered the "system," a vast number of operations can be performed. Much of the work by cognitive psychologists has centered on the storage of information during this process—that is, on memory. While memory processes have been of interest since ancient times, it was not until the 1880's that scientists, notably Hermann Ebbinghaus, first systematically and scientifically studied memory. Scientists studying memory today talk about concepts such as short-term and long-term memory as well as about the distinction between episodic and semantic memory systems. The function of memory is essential to human thought and ultimately to the measurement of thought.

In terms of measuring what happens to incoming information, more than memory storage occurs; people manipulate these data. They make decisions based on the information available, and they have capabilities (often referred to as higher mental processes) that in many ways differentiate humans from other animals. Some of the functions commonly studied and measured include reasoning, problem solving, logic, decision making, and language development and use. The information-processing analogy is completed with the "output" of information. When a person is asked a question, the response is the output; it is based on the information stored in memory, whether those items be personal experiences, knowledge gained from books, or awareness of social customs. People do these things so effortlessly, day in and day out, that it is difficult to stop, appreciate, and comprehend how thoughts work. Psychologists have pondered these questions for many years and are only beginning to discover the answers.

Applications

Some of the earliest systematic studies of thought and the accompanying desire to measure it came from astronomy, not psychology or philosophy. From this beginning, Dutch physiologist Frans C. Donders set out specifically to measure a sequence of mental process—thought—in the middle of the nineteenth century. His technique was simple yet elegant in its ability to measure how much time mental processes consume; the procedure developed by Donders is typically referred to as the subtraction technique.

The subtraction technique begins with the timing and measurement of a very basic task. For example, a person might be asked to press a button after hearing a tone. Donders realized that it was fairly easy to time accurately how long subjects took to perform this task. He believed that two cognitive (thought) processes would be operating: perception of the tone and the motor response of pressing the button. Once the time of this simple task was known, Donders would make the task more difficult. If a discrimination task were added, he believed, the time taken to complete the task would increase compared to the basic perception-motor response sequence. In this discrimination task, for example, Donders might tell a person to press the button only after hearing a high-pitched sound. That person is now faced with an added demand—to make a decision about pitch. Donders believed that with this discrimination stage, the processing of the information would require more mental effort and more time; he was right. More important, Donders could now measure the amount of extra thought required for the decision by subtracting the simple-task time from the discrimination-task time. In a general sense, Donders had a method for measuring thought.

Donders also had the ability to measure and manipulate specific components of the thought process. He even added another component to the sequence of tasks, what he called choice time. For example, the task could be changed so that for a high tone the subject should press the right button, and for a low tone, press the left button. By subtracting the discrimination time from this new choice time, he could estimate how long the added choice contributed to the overall thought process. Through these ingenious methods, Donders inspired generations of cognitive psychologists to study thought in terms of the time it takes to think.

The first recognized work done in psychology on the measurement of thought processes was Hermann Ebbinghaus' work on memory capacity and forgetting. Working independently in the 1880's in Germany, Ebbinghaus set out to study memory processes, particularly the nature of forgetting. Being the first psychologist to study the issue, he had no precedent as to how to proceed, so Ebbinghaus invented his own procedures for measuring memory. To his credit, those procedures were so good that they are still commonly used. Before describing his measurement of memory, Ebbinghaus made two important decisions about methods for studying memory. First, he studied only one person's memory—his own. He believed he would have better control over situational and contextual variables that way.

Second, Ebbinghaus decided that he could not use everyday words in his memory studies, because they might have associations that would make them easier to study. For example, if one were memorizing a poem, the story and the writing style might help memory, and Ebbinghaus was interested in a pure measure of memory and forgetting. To achieve this, Ebbinghaus pioneered the use of nonsense syllables. He used three-letter combinations of consonant-vowel-consonant so that the items were pronounceable but meaningless. Nonsense syllables such as "geb," "fak," "jit," "zab," and "buh" were used.

Ebbinghaus used a vigorous schedule of testing and presented himself with many lists of nonsense syllables to be remembered at a later time. In fact, he spent five years memorizing various lists until he published his seminal work on the topic, *Über das Gedächtnis* (1885; *Memory: A Contribution to Experimental Psychology,* 1913). He systematically measured memory by memorizing a list, letting some time pass, and testing himself on the list. He devised a numerical measurement for memory called percent savings. Percent savings was a measure of the degree of forgetting that occurred over time. For example, it might take him ten minutes to memorize a list perfectly. He would let forty-eight hours pass, then tell himself to recall the list. Forgetting occurs during that time, and only some items would be remembered. Ebbinghaus would then look at the original list and rememorize it until he knew it perfectly; this might take seven minutes or so. He always spent less time rememorizing the list. Said another way, there was some savings from the earlier experience fortyeight hours before. This percent savings was his measure of memory. The higher the percentage of savings, the more items remembered (or the less forgotten), and Ebbinghaus could remember the list in less time.

Ebbinghaus then varied the time between original list learning and later list recall. He found that percent savings drops over time; that is, the longer one waits to remember something, the less one saves from the prior experience, so the more time he had to spend rememorizing the list. Ebbinghaus found fairly good percent savings two or nine hours later, but percent savings dropped dramatically after two or three days. Plotted on a graph, this relationship looks like a downward sloping curve, and it is called the Ebbinghaus forgetting curve. Simply stated, it means that as time passes, memories become poorer. Although this effect is not surprising today, Ebbinghaus was the first (in 1885) to demonstrate this phenomenon empirically.

Another example of the work in the area of cognitive psychology comes from the studies of Saul Sternberg in the 1960's at Bell Laboratories. Sternberg examined how additional information in memory influences the speed of mental operations in retrieving information stored in memory. Sternberg's task was fairly simple. He presented people with a list of numbers; the list might range from one to six numbers. After the people saw this initial list, a single number (called a probe) was presented. People were asked to identify whether the probe number was on the initial list of numbers. The list might be "2935," for example, and the probe might be "3."

Sternberg's primary interest was in studying how the length of the initial list affected the time it took to make the required yes-or-no decision. Two possibilities typically emerge when people consider this problem. The concept called serial processing holds that the comparison of the probe to each number in the initial list takes up a little bit of time, so that the more items in the initial list, the longer the memory search takes. An alternative idea, parallel processing, suggests that people instantaneously scan all the items in the memory set, and the number of items in the initial list does not make a difference. Another way of saying this is that all the items are scanned at once, in parallel fashion. Sternberg found that people search their memories using the technique of serial processing. In fact, he was able to calculate precisely the amount of additional search time needed for each added item in the memory set—38 milliseconds (a millisecond is a thousandth of a second). Although the search may seem fast, even instantaneous, the more there is to think about, the more time it takes to think.

Context

The study of thought, and particularly its measurement, is a relatively recent development. For centuries, the thinking processes of humans were believed to be somewhat mystical, and certainly not available for scientific inquiry. Most philosophers were concerned more with the mind and its relationship to the body or the world than with how people think. The study of thought, although it was generally considered by the ancient Greek philosophers, did not merit serious attention until the emergence of the "personal equation" by astronomers and the realization that thought processes are indeed measurable and can be measured accurately and precisely.

The story of the first recorded measurements of thought begins with the royal astronomer to England, Nevil Maskelyne, and his assistant, David Kinnebrook, in 1794. Astronomers of the day were mostly concerned with stellar transits (measuring the movement of stars across the sky). Using telescopes and specialized techniques, the goal of the astronomer was to measure the time taken for a particular star to move across a portion of the telescopic field. Using a complicated procedure that involved listening to a beating clock and viewing the sky, astronomers could measure the transit time of a star fairly accurately, to within one-tenth or two-tenths of a second. These measurements were particularly important because the clocks of that period were based on stellar transits.

Maskelyne and Kinnebrook often worked together in recording the movement of the stars. While Kinnebrook had no problems during 1794, in 1795 Maskelyne began to notice that Kinnebrook's times varied from his own by as much as one-half of a second—considered a large and important difference. By early 1796, the difference between the astronomers' times had grown to eight-tenths of a second. This was an intolerable amount of error to Maskelyne, and he fired his assistant Kinnebrook.

About twenty years later, a German astronomer named Friedrich Bessel came across the records of these incidents and began to study the "error" in the differing astronomers' measurements. He believed that the different measurements were attributable in part to differences between people and that this difference was not necessarily an error. He found that even the most famous and reliable astronomers of the day differed from one another by more than two-tenths of a second.

This incident between Maskelyne and Kinnebrook, and its later study by Bessel, led to some important conclusions. First, measurements in astronomy would have to consider the specific person making the measurement. Astronomers even went to the lengths of developing what became known as the personal equation. The personal equation is a verified, quantified account of how each astronomer's thought processes worked when measuring stellar transits. In essence, the personal equation was a measurement of the thought process involved and a recognition of differences between people. Second, if astronomers differed in their particular thought processes, then many people differ in other types of thinking processes as well. Finally, and perhaps most important in the long run, this incident laid the groundwork for the idea that thought could be measured accurately and the information could be put to good use. No longer was thinking a mystical or magical process that was unacceptable for study by scientists.

It is from this historical context that the field of cognitive psychology has emerged. Cognitive psychology is chiefly concerned with the thought processes and, indeed, all the general mental processing of organisms (most often humans). The interests of a cognitive psychologist can be quite varied: learning, memory, problem solving, reasoning, logic, decision making, linquistics, cognitive development in children, and other topics. Each area of specialization continues to measure and examine how people think, using tasks and procedures as ingenious as those of Donders, Ebbinghaus, and Sternberg. The study and measurement of thought (or, more generally, the field of cognitive psychology) will continue to play an important and vital role. Not many questions are more basic to the study of human behavior than how people think, what processes are involved, and how researchers can scientifically study and measure these processes.

Bibliography

Anderson, John R. *Cognitive Psychology and Its Implications*. 3d ed. New York: W. H. Freeman, 1990. This text is a long-standing leader in the field of cognitive psychology. Provides a wonderful overview of the fundamental issues of cognitive psychology, including attention and perception, basic principles of human memory, problem solving, the development of expertise, reasoning, intelligence, and language structure and use.

Ashcraft, Mark H. *Human Memory and Cognition*. Glenview, Ill.: Scott, Foresman, 1989.

A cognitive psychology textbook that heavily emphasizes the human information-processing metaphor. Arranged differently from Anderson's text, it too provides good coverage of all the basic areas of cognitive psychology.

Boring, Edwin G. *A History of Experimental Psychology.* 2d ed. Englewood Cliffs, N.J.: Prentice-Hall, 1950. This text is the foremost authority on the development and history of psychology up until 1950. Contains detailed accounts of the work of early philosophers and astronomers who contributed to the study of thought, and even contains an entire chapter devoted to the personal equation. This can be a difficult text to read, but it is the authoritative overview of the early history of psychology.

Calvin, William H. *The Cerebral Code: Thinking a Thought in the Mosaics of the Mind.* Cambridge, Mass.: MIT Press, 1996.

Garnham, Alan, and Jane Oakhill. *Thinking and Reasoning.* Cambridge, Mass.: Blackwell, 1994.

Lachman, Roy, Janet L. Lachman, and Earl C. Butterfield. *Cognitive Psychology and Information Processing: An Introduction.* Hillsdale, N.J.: Lawrence Erlbaum, 1979. One of the earliest texts that adequately captures the coming importance and influence of cognitive psychology. There are outstanding chapters that trace the influences of other disciplines and traditions on what is now known as cognitive psychology. Topic areas within the field are discussed as well.

Laszlo, Ervin, et al. *Changing Visions: Human Cognitive Maps: Past, Present, and Future.* Westport, Conn.: Praeger, 1996.

Mayer, Richard E. *Thinking, Problem Solving, and Cognition.* 2d ed. New York: W. H. Freeman, 1992. A book primarily dedicated to the topic of problem solving, which is unusual. The format is interesting and creative, covering the historical perspective of problem solving, basic thinking tasks, information-processing analysis, and implications and applications. The focus on thought and its measurement is seen throughout, especially in sections discussing mental chronometry.

Schultz, Duane P., and Sydney Ellen Schultz. *A History of Modern Psychology.* 4th ed. San Diego: Harcourt Brace Jovanovich, 1987. A readable and understandable treatment of the history of psychology. Touches on the importance of the contributions of the astronomers as well as Donders in the study and measurement of thought.

R. Eric Landrum

See also:

The Cerebral Cortex, 121; Cognitive Psychology, 146; Logic and Reasoning, 376; Memory, Theories of, 383; Neural Anatomy and Cognition, 415; Neuropsychology, 422.

TOUCH AND PRESSURE

Type of psychology: Sensation and perception
Field of study: Auditory, chemical, cutaneous, and body senses

Receptors of touch and pressure are mechanoreceptors that convert mechanical energy into the electrical energy of nerve impulses. Touch receptors detect objects coming into light contact with the body surface and allow a person to reconstruct the size, shape, and texture of objects even if they are unseen; pressure receptors detect heavier contacts, weights, or forces and provide a sense of the position of body parts.

Principal terms

ADAPTATION: a reduction over time of the nerve impulses sent by a sensory receptor under a constant stimulus

EXPANDED-TIP TACTILE RECEPTOR: a touch receptor located in both hairy and nonhairy regions of the skin

FREE NERVE ENDING: a mechanoreceptor located primarily in the skin and acting as a touch receptor

HAIR END ORGAN: a touch receptor formed by sensory nerve branches surrounding a hair root in the skin; detects displacement of the hair shaft

MECHANORECEPTOR: a sensory receptor that detects mechanical energy and converts it into the electrical energy of nerve impulses

MEISSNER'S CORPUSCLE: a highly sensitive touch receptor located in nonhairy regions of the skin

PACINIAN CORPUSCLE: a pressure receptor located just under the skin and in deeper body regions

PROPRIORECEPTION: the sense of the position of the body parts

RUFFINI'S END ORGAN: a pressure receptor located in deeper body regions and in the connective tissue capsules surrounding the joints

SOMATIC SENSORY CORTEX: the region of the cerebrum receiving and integrating signals from sensory receptors

Overview

The human body is supplied with an abundance of sensory receptors that detect touch and pressure. These receptors are members of a larger group of what are called mechanoreceptors; they are able to detect energy in mechanical form and convert it to the energy of nerve impulses. Mechanoreceptors occur both on body surfaces and in the interior, and they detect mechanical stimuli throughout the body. Touch receptors are located over the entire body surface; pressure receptors are located only under the skin and in the body interior. The two sensations are closely related. A very light pressure on the body surface is sensed by receptors in the skin and is felt as touch. As the pressure increases, mechanoreceptors in and immediately below the skin and at deeper levels are stimulated, and the sensation is felt as pressure.

Several different types of mechanoreceptors are located in the skin and primarily detect touch. One type, known as free nerve endings, consists simply of branched nerve endings without associated structures. Although located primarily in the skin, some mechanoreceptors of this type are also found to a limited extent in deeper tissues, where they detect pressure. A second mechanoreceptor type, termed Meissner's corpuscles, consists of a ball of nerve endings enclosed within a capsulelike layer of cells. These mechanoreceptors, which are exquisitely sensitive to the lightest pressure, occur in nonhairy regions of the skin, such as the lips and fingertips. A third mechanoreceptor type, the expanded-tip tactile receptor, occurs in the same nonhairy regions as Meissner's corpuscles and, in smaller numbers, in parts of the skin that are covered with hair. These mechanoreceptors often occur in clusters that are served by branches of the same sensory nerve cell. Meissner's corpuscles and the expanded-tip tactile receptors, working together in regions such as the fingertips, are primarily responsible for a person's ability to determine the size, surface texture, and other tactile features of objects touched. A fourth type of mechanoreceptor consists of a network of nerve endings surrounding the root of a hair. The combined nerve-hair root structure, called a hair end organ, is stimulated when body hairs are displaced. These mechanoreceptors, because hairs extend from the body surface, give an early warning that the skin of a haired region of the body is about to make contact with an object.

The remaining mechanoreceptors of this group are located in deeper regions of the body; because of their location, they detect pressure rather than touch. Pacinian corpuscles, which occur just under the skin and in deeper regions of the body, consist of a single sensory nerve ending buried inside a fluid-filled capsule. The capsule is formed by many layers of connective tissue cells, which surround the nerve ending in concentric layers, much like the successive layers of an onion. Pressure displaces the capsule and deforms its shape; the deforming pressure is transmitted through the capsule fluid to the surface of the sensory nerve ending. In response, the sensory nerve generates nerve impulses. The remaining type of pressure receptor, Ruffini's end organ, consists of a highly branched group of nerve endings enclosed in a capsule. These mechanoreceptors occur below the skin, in deeper tissues, and in the connective tissue capsules surrounding the joints. They detect heavy pressures on the body that are transmitted to deeper layers, and, through their locations in the joints, contribute to proprioception—the sense of the position of the body's limbs.

The various types of mechanoreceptors are believed to convert mechanical energy into the electrical energy of nerve impulses by essentially the same mechanism. In some manner, as yet incompletely understood, the mechanical forces deforming the cell membranes of sensory nerve endings open channels in the membranes to the flow of ions. The ions, which are electrically charged particles, produce the electrical effects responsible for generating nerve impulses.

The different mechanoreceptor types exhibit the phenomenon of adaptation to varying degrees. In adaptation, the number of nerve impulses generated by a sensory receptor drops off with time if the stimulus remains constant. In the pacinian corpuscle, for example, which is highly adaptive, adaptation results from flow of the capsule fluid. If pressure against the corpuscle is held at steady levels, deforming the capsule in one direction, the fluids inside the capsule flow in response to relieve the pressure. The new fluid distribution compensates for the applied pressure, and the nerve impulses generated by the pacinian corpuscle drop in frequency. Any change in the pressure, however, is transmitted through the fluid to the sensory nerve ending before the fluid has a chance to shift in response. As a result, a new volley of nerve impulses is fired by the sensory neuron on a change of pressure until the fluid in the corpuscle shifts again to compensate for the new pressure. In pacinian corpuscles, compensating movements of the fluid take place within hundredths or even thousandths of a second. Meissner's corpuscles and the hair end organs also adapt quickly.

The expanded-tip tactile receptors and Ruffini's end organs adapt significantly more slowly than the other mechanoreceptors. Expanded-tip tactile receptors adapt initially to a steady touch or pressure, but reach a base level at which they continue to generate nerve impulses under steady pressure. The Ruffini's end organs adapt only to a limited extent. The continuing nerve impulses arriving from these mechanoreceptors provide continuous monitoring of a constant stimulus. Thus, some of the mechanoreceptors are specialized to detect changes in touch or pressure and some to keep track of constant stimuli.

Applications

The combined effects of touch and pressure receptors, along with the varying degrees of adaptation of different receptor types, allow the detection of a range of stimuli, varying from the lightest, most delicate, glancing touch, through moderate pressures, to heavy pressures that stimulate both the body surfaces and interior. People can explore the surface, texture, and shape of objects and can interpret the various levels of touch and pressure so well that they can reconstruct a mental image of objects touched by the fingers with their eyes closed.

Much of this mechanosensory ability depends on the degree to which the different receptor types adapt. The rapid adaptation of Meissner's corpuscles and the hair end organs explains why, if a steady, light to moderate pressure (not heavy enough to cause pain) is maintained on the body surface, the sensation of pressure quickly diminishes. If the pressure is heavy enough to cause pain, a person continues to be aware of the painful sensation, because pain receptors are very slow to adapt. If the degree or location of the pressure is altered, a person again becomes acutely aware of the pressure.

Awareness of continued touch depends primarily on the expanded-tip tactile receptors, which initially adapt but then continue to send nerve impulses when a light surface pressure is held constant. This allows a person to continue to be aware, for example, that some part of the body surface is touching an object. The limited adaptation of Ruffini's corpuscles keeps a person aware of stronger pressures that are felt deeply in the body. Through their locations in joints, these slow-adapting mechanoreceptors also help keep a person continually aware of the positions of the limbs.

The sensory effects of the fast-and slow-adapting mechanoreceptors can be demonstrated by a simple exercise such as pinching the skin on the back of the hand with a steady pressure only strong enough to cause slight pain. The feeling of pressure dissipates rapidly; however, one remains aware of the touch and pain. The rapid dissipation of the sensation of pressure is caused by the fast adaptation of Meissner's corpuscles and any pacinian corpuscles that may have been stimulated. Some degree of touch sensation is maintained, however, by residual levels of nerve impulses sent by the expanded-tip tactile receptors. The sensation of pain continues at almost steady levels because, in contrast to most of the mechanoreceptors, pain receptors adapt very little. If the pressure is released, the pain stops, and another intense sensation of pressure is felt as all the receptor types fire off a burst of nerve impulses in response to the change.

Mechanoreceptors located at deeper levels keep a person constantly aware of the positions of body parts and the degree of extension of the limbs with respect to the trunk. Ruffini's and pacinian corpuscles located within the connective tissue layers covering the bones, and within the capsules surrounding the joints, keep track of the angles made by the bones as they are pulled to different positions by the muscles. Ruffini's and pacinian corpuscles are among the most important mechanoreceptors keeping track of these movements.

Context

Touch and pressure receptors represent only a part of the body's array of mechanoreceptors. Other mechanoreceptors located more deeply in the body help monitor the position of body parts and detect the degree of stretch of body cavities.

In addition to the Ruffini's and pacinian corpuscles detecting the positions of the bones and joints, two further types of mechanoreceptors constantly track the tension developed by the muscles moving the limbs. One is buried within the muscle itself, and one is in the tendons connecting the muscles to the bones. The mechanoreceptors buried within muscles, called muscle spindles, consist of a specialized bundle of five to twelve small muscle cells enclosed within a capsule of connective tissue. Sensory nerve endings surround the muscle cells in a spiral at the midpoint of the capsule and also form branched endings among the muscle cells of the capsule. Because of their position within the muscle spindle, the nerve endings are stretched, and generate nerve impulses, when the surrounding muscle tissue contracts.

The mechanoreceptors of tendons, called Golgi tendon organs, are formed by nerve endings that branch within the fibrous connective tissue cells forming a tendon. The nerve endings of Golgi tendon organs detect both stretch and compression of the tendon as the muscles connected to them move and place tension on the limbs. The combined activities of the deeply located mechanoreceptors keep a person aware of posture, stance, and positions of the limbs. They also allow a person to perform feats such as bringing the thumbs or fingers together behind the back, or touching the tip of the nose with the forefinger with the eyes closed.

Mechanoreceptors are one of five different types of sensory receptors that also include thermoreceptors, which detect changes in the flow of heat to or from the body; nocioreceptors, which detect tissue damage and whose nerve impulses are integrated and perceived in the brain as pain; chemoreceptors, which detect chemicals in locations such as the tongue, where they are responsible for the sense of taste, and in the nasal cavity, where they contribute to the sense of smell; and photoreceptors, which detect light. The mechanoreceptors, thermoreceptors, and nocioreceptors together form what are known as the somatic or body senses.

Sensory nerve tracts originating from mechanoreceptors, particularly those arising from the body surfaces, and their connecting neurons within the spinal cord and the brain are held in highly organized register with one another. Sensory fibers and their connecting nerves originating from the hand, for example, are located in a position near those originating from the wrist. In the cerebral cortex, the organization is retained, so that there is a projection of the body parts over a part of the cerebrum called the somatic sensory cortex. In this region, which occupies a band running from the top to the lower sides of the brain along anterior segments of the parietal lobes, segments corresponding to major body parts trace out a distorted image of the body from the top of the brain to the sides, with the genitalia, feet, and legs at the top, the arms and hands at the middle region, and the head, lips, tongue, and teeth at the bottom. Sensory information from the right side of the body is received and integrated in the somatic sensory cortex on the left side of the brain, and information from the left side of the body is received and integrated on the right side of the brain. The area of the somatic sensory cortex integrating signals from various body regions depends on the numbers of touch and other sensory receptors in the body regions. The lips and fingers, for example, which are generously supplied with sensory receptors, are represented by much larger areas in the somatic sensory cortex than the arms and legs. Reception and integration of signals in the somatic sensory cortex is partly under conscious control; a person can direct attention to one body part or another and concentrate on the signals arriving from the selected region. The activities of touch, pressure, and other sensory receptors, integrated and interpreted in the somatic sensory cortex, supply people's link to the world around them and supply the information people require to survive and interact with the environment.

Bibliography

Berne, Robert M., and Matthew N. Levy, eds. *Physiology*. 2d ed. St. Louis: C. V. Mosby, 1988. Chapter 9 in this standard college physiology text, "The Somatosensory System," outlines the anatomy and physiology of the systems integrated in the detection of touch and pressure, with emphasis on the somatic sensory cortex of the brain and the nerve tracts of the spinal cord connecting sensory receptors with the brain. Intended for students at the college level, but clearly enough written to be accessible to readers at the high school level.

Coren, Stanley. *Sensation and Perception*. New York: Academic Press, 1979. A simply written text providing an easily understood discussion of the senses, sensory cells, and routes traveled by sensory information through the spinal cord to the brain. Includes a clear and interesting description of the basics of perception in the cerebral cortex.

Guyton, Arthur C. *Textbook of Medical Physiology*. 7th ed. Philadelphia: W. B. Saunders, 1986. Chapter 48 in this readable and clearly written text, "Somatic Sensory Receptors and Their Basic Mechanisms of Action," outlines the fundamental activities of sensory receptors. Chapter 49, "Somatic Sensations: I. The Mechanoreceptive Sensations," presents more detailed information on the types of touch and pressure receptors and the nerve tracts connecting them to the somatic sensory cortex of the brain. Intended for college and medical students, but comprehensible to readers at the high school level.

Kruger, Lawrence, ed. *Pain and Touch*. San Diego, Calif.: Academic Press, 1996.

Milne, Lorus Johnson, and Margery Milne. *The Senses of Animals and Men*. New York: Atheneum, 1962. A simple and entertaining survey of the senses and their importance in humans and other animals. Provides interesting and thought-provoking comparisons between the sensory systems of humans and other animals. Written for a popular audience.

Schmidt-Nielsen, Knut. *Animal Physiology, Adaptation, and Environment*. 4th ed. New York: Cambridge University Press, 1990. This standard college text, by one of the greatest animal physiologists, provides a deeply perceptive comparison of sensory systems in humans and other animals. Chapter 8 describes information and the senses. The text is remarkable for its lucid and entertaining description of animal physiology.

Streri, Arlette. *Seeing, Reading, Touching: The Relations Between Vision and Touch in Infancy.* Translated by Tim Pownall and Susan Kingerlee. Cambridge, Mass.: MIT Press, 1993.

Stephen L. Wolfe

See also:

The Auditory System, 82; The Central and Peripheral Nervous Systems, 115; The Cerebral Cortex, 121; Sensation and Perception, 535; Smell and Taste, 553; Visual Development, 638; The Visual System, 643.

Trust, Autonomy, Initiative, and Industry

Type of psychology: Developmental psychology
Field of study: Infancy and childhood

Children's self-perception, according to Erik Erikson, is formulated at a very early age. Should the early developmental needs of a child be denied, there is a likelihood that later psychological and behavioral problems will occur.

Principal terms

AUTONOMY: a child's self-assertion toward a parent without in any way harming the parent-child relationship

EGO: a unifying principle which makes sense of the many diverse experiences facing the growing child

IDENTITY: a reciprocal acceptance on the part of children to act and think like those on whom they depend

INDUSTRY: the recognition that building, creating, or making is a satisfactory and self-imaging activity

INITIATIVE: a child's instigation of a new game or decision on the next activity

PSYCHE: the soul or essential being of humankind

SELF-IMAGE: an accepted view of how one appears to the world

TRUST: the first stage of Erikson's model, in which the helpless infant knows that all basic needs will be met

Overview

Psychoanalyst Erik Erikson was one of the first to undertake intensive study of human development as it occurs over the course of the entire lifetime. He divided human development into eight "psychosocial" stages. The first four of these stages occur between birth and puberty, and they involve trust (versus mistrust), autonomy (versus shame and doubt), initiative (versus guilt), and industry (versus inferiority).

From the day they are born, infants will show whether they are contented or discontented—whether they sense that their needs are being fully met by a parent or other caregiver. A sense that their most basic needs are not being met will be reflected in unsettled sleep or continual crying. Continual reinforcement by the mother demonstrating that the infant's needs will be met provides the infant with a rudimentary sense of personal identity. Erikson postulates that infants look for and require a certain degree of uniformity in their handling and that this consistency on the part of the handler, in most cases the mother, creates and reinforces a sense of trust. Trust would seem a natural occurrence from a caring and nurturing mother, yet within this mother-child paradigm the possibility of mistrust exists.

The trust versus mistrust stage deals with the oral-sensory experiences of the small child. Eating and sleeping are the only major concerns. During this stage, the basis of trust or mistrust will develop. While feeding and caring for the infant are important, what seems more important during this period is the quality of the mother's attentiveness to the child. From the basic premise and understanding of trust, the growing infant will necessarily move into the next stage, which Erikson describes as the muscular-anal stage, during which the child begins to experience autonomy—a greater awareness of being an individual. This is not the first stage of being an individual, in the true sense, but is the early prototype model of how children will later perceive themselves. This is a point at which young infants realize that they can be autonomous from their principal provider yet feel relatively safe in what is still perceived as a hostile environment.

Erikson defines a sharp and concise relationship between the growth of the child and the ability to perform more advanced physical functions. During the period that is characterized by basic trust, bodily functions are enacted satisfactorily but without control. The child is not hindered by this lack of physical control, because the mothering figure takes care of all basic needs. Along with muscular development, mobility increases, and the growing child discovers more ways of becoming physically independent, although in a limited way. A definite sense of autonomy is experienced by the child between the ages of one and three. Assuming that the child has received nurturing, this newfound physical freedom will set up a dynamic within the child's psychic awareness that will most likely contradict those earlier childhood experiences. Wanting to be more autonomous is natural, but the fear of shame and doubt follow quickly behind this yearning to experience a more independent role in life.

At this stage, the infant must not feel compromised as more interesting experiences are presented to him or her. Since all the child's basic needs have been met, the appearance of wanting to be independent will not cause a loss of caregiving. The underpinning of trust must still be present and reinforced so that the exploring infant can take a more active and independent role in the world. Transition from the oral to the muscular stage need not be traumatic, as long as the caregiver is supportive and continues to reinforce the already present acceptance of trust. The consequence of moving into the muscular-anal stage is that the child gains more autonomy and thus a greater sense of identity, which will eventually lead to an understanding of himself or herself as a fully realized individual.

Shame and doubt develop in a child who feels unable to venture beyond the confines of the caregiver. Able to experiment with the social modalities of holding on and letting go, children learn how to regulate their infantile impulses. Allowing the child to experience and experiment in a caring environment will allow autonomous living to begin. Conversely, if the child continues to be forced into feeling a sense of shame during this period, the child's understanding of being a separate person will be severely restricted.

The third stage, that of initiative versus guilt, is reached in the growth and development of the child around the time of entering kindergarten (sometimes earlier), and it continues to about the child's seventh birthday. New ideas are presented that allow the possibility of further exploration of both the social and the phenomenal world. A major characteristic of this stage is the willingness on the part of the child to forget failure quickly and move on to the next endeavor. There is probably no other period in a young child's life that is more important than this stage, which is characterized by a yearning to learn and become a more integrated member of the child's immediate family and circle of friends. There is a strong sense that the child wants to share new ideas and become a part of the larger world, especially in terms of emulating the ideas of the schoolteacher.

Between the ages of six or seven and eleven years, the child enters an intense period of industry and activity; this is the fourth stage. What has been learned from earlier childhood experiences, both in the home and at school, will form the base for further exploration. Whereas play was an activity in and of itself, now the child wishes to produce and create something tangible from what was originally a play situation. At this stage, the child begins using prototypal tools, implements, and utensils, which may in some way reflect the type of work the child will experience in adulthood.

Applications

The first four stages of Erikson's eight-stage model of development deal with the child from birth to about eleven years of age. The other four stages deal with identity during the adolescent years, intimacy as a young adult, growth as an adult, and ego integrity as an older adult. For a child to develop a healthy and well-adjusted view of life, Erikson believes, the growing child must pass through each of these early stages. Each stage builds on the one immediately before.

When the basic tenets of trust, autonomy, initiative, and industry are fully integrated into the life of the child, there is unlikely to be a serious problem in later life. When one or all of these particular aspects of a child's growth meets its counterpart or negative side of these tenets (basic mistrust, shame and doubt, guilt, and inferiority), however, certain psychological imbalances become apparent in adulthood.

Studies of infantile schizophrenia probably best illustrate the denial of trust in the first two years of the infant's life. Should there be a lifelong denial of trust, the person will exhibit a definite schizoid or schizotypal personality disorder. Often this personality disorder will be accompanied by various states of depression. Depression can, in severe cases, lead to suicide or repeated suicide attempts. Such is the need and effect of trust on young children that their whole identities, in some psychic way, are tied up with the personal love and care given to them by their mother during this time. Basic mistrust and a later sense of insecurity will characterize the child who has not fully experienced basic trust in his or her parents.

In stage 2, shame and doubt act as the shadow side to autonomy and the ability to act in an individual, responsible way in society. Erikson maintains that the child who does not experience a well-regulated sense of autonomy will soon develop manipulative characteristics. At a time when the child should be exploring the environment and discovering new facets of that environment, there is a tendency to overmanipulate. The object or plaything no longer is interesting in terms of any intrinsic value but becomes something over which the child can project some authority and power. This is the basis for later neurotic disorders such as certain compulsive behavior patterns.

A child who is not given the room within a normal caring and monitored environment to express feelings of frustration and anger will tend to stifle these natural responses. Later in life, when similar stressful situations occur, the person may not have the coping skills to be able to deal properly with these same feelings. These inhibitors to normal expression and natural well-being are formulated when the child is growing up. Parents who cannot tolerate any form of aggressive behavior will create a problem for their child. When the child becomes an adult, he or she will need to be assertive in given situations; there is a high likelihood that this will not happen, because of the childhood inhibitions about confronting stressful situations. Instead, in order to inhibit the natural adaptive response to outside aggression, the person will appear overly agreeable and accommodating.

Again, the suppression of those earlier fears is evident. The normal coping skills are nonfunctional because their natural expression was inhibited during the early formative years. A person who adopts a neurotic style will rarely be able to conceal the underlying stress. Doubt and shame take on a broader and more potent meaning in adulthood. When initiative is called upon, the inhibitory devices first learned as a child become dominant. Instead of taking responsibility and acting in an independent manner, the individual will exhibit a childlike incompetence. An adult may even be unable and unsuited to take up a worthwhile position in society; industry, rather than being a part of the life experience, becomes something to be shunned. What develops is a feeling of inferiority and an inability to enter into the workplace fully as a productive and useful individual.

Context

Erik Erikson's *Childhood and Society* (1963) quickly became the seminal study on child growth and development. Erikson studied and practiced psychoanalysis; he was himself psychoanalyzed by Anna Freud while at the Vienna Psychoanalytic Institute. Erikson's work is comparable in significance to that undertaken by Jean Piaget, a Swiss psychologist who postulated that children learn through a series of cognitive stages. While Piaget was almost entirely concerned with how a child perceives the world in a cognitive sense, Erikson viewed the growth of the child in terms of an emotional and sensory perception of the world.

What Erikson's pioneering models and theories attempted to do was to lessen the many disparities between the accepted understanding of psychoanalysis, which mostly concentrated on the disturbed psyche of a person, and the broader influences of society. In an attempt to synthesize the two, Erikson added to the understanding of personality theories, which continue to be refined.

Erikson's works receive perhaps their broadest acknowledgment within the field of educational psychology; he is certainly one of the most widely read of American psychiatrists. Educators find Erikson's work relevant to the training of teachers, and it is very often coupled with the work of Piaget. Unfortunately, the two schools of thought tend to become intermingled, with the boundaries between Piaget's cognitive theories and Erikson's behavioral models becoming less than distinct. Erikson did not confine his work or his theories to the early years. Another important area of inquiry for Erikson was the issues and concerns facing the adolescent, especially as they relate to peer groups and school influences.

Overall, Erikson's views on childhood and his theory of identity crisis affected the main schools of psychotherapy only peripherally. While the behaviorist will acknowledge that a suppressed childhood can and often does lead to a maladjusted life in adulthood, Erikson is not considered any kind of final authority on the matter. What did become important in the study of the personality was Erikson's view of the ego and ego identity. Erikson was the first to see the inherent dangers of child psychoanalysis. A merely clinical approach to children's problems did not go far enough, in Erikson's view, and thus he became an early advocate of psychohistroy. In his reaction to Freudian analysis, Erikson created a more humane approach to psychoanalysis. The eight stages of psychosocial development devised by Erikson continue to receive wide acknowledgment within the field of educational psychology and will continue to be used by educators and counseling psychologists alike.

Bibliography

Coles, Robert. *Erik H. Erikson: The Growth of His Work*. Boston: Little, Brown, 1970. This complete and scholarly work attempts to unify and examine the writings and teachings of Erikson. While the style is somewhat polemic at times, the book is quite valuable as a biography and source.

Erikson, Erik H. *Childhood and Society*. New York: W. W. Norton, 1963. In this classic study, Erikson presents his views and theories on identity and identity crisis—a phrase which he coined—as well as the psychosexual development of the child. The main view is that children grow through a series of progressive crises which should establish a sense of trust, autonomy, initiative, and competence.

_____. *Identity: Youth and Crisis*. New York: W. W. Norton, 1968. Using his own theory of identity crises developed in *Childhood and Society,* Erikson applies his understanding to those who are experiencing the uncertainty and confusion of adolescence. This work concentrates on such issues as peer culture, the school environment, and the inner feelings of adolescents.

_____. *Insight and Responsibility*. New York: W. W. Norton, 1964. This work acts in many ways as a source for Erikson's ideas. It consists of lectures that were given before 1964 and contains his essential ideas concerning psychotherapy, identity crises, the ego, and the beginnings of what later came to be known as psychohistory. Allows the reader a concise yet detailed introduction to Eriksonian therapy.

Evans, Richard I. *Dialogue with Erik Erikson*. Reprint. Northvale, N.J.: Jason Aronson, 1995.

Psychoanalysis and Contemporary Thought 19, no. 2 (1996). A special issue entitled "Ideas and Identities: The Life and Work of Erik Erikson," edited by Robert S. Wallerstein. A variety of insightful perspectives on Erikson; includes a selection of photographs.

Roazen, Paul. *Erik H. Erikson: The Power and Limits of a Vision*. New York: Free Press, 1976. While Erikson tried to distance himself from the psychoanalytic approaches of Freud, Roazen shows that Erikson's views still have a basis in that movement. Contains further discussion on the life cycle, normality, and identity.

Tribe, Carol. *Profile of Three Theories: Erikson, Maslow, Piaget*. Dubuque, Iowa: Kendall Hunt Publishing, 1995.

Richard G. Cormack

See also:

Adolescence: Cognitive Skills, 13; Adolescence: Sexuality, 19; Aging: Cognitive Changes, 37; Cognitive Development Theory: Jean Piaget, 135; Ego Psychology: Erik Erikson, 223; Gender-Identity Formation, 254; Generativity in Adulthood, 260; Identity Crises, 284; Integrity, 315; Intimacy in Adulthood, 340; Moral Development, 399; Psychoanalytic Psychology, 471.

VISUAL DEVELOPMENT

Type of psychology: Sensation and perception
Field of study: Vision

Visual development involves the changes in the functioning of the human visual system that occur with age. Research has shown that even newborns can see well enough to start to learn about the world; by eight months of age, infants' visual functioning is comparable to that of adults.

Principal terms

ACUITY: the ability to detect very small details in a pattern

DEPTH CUE: a source of information in the two-dimensional retinal image that makes depth perception possible by specifying the three-dimensional characteristics of the scene being viewed

DEPTH PERCEPTION: the ability to see three-dimensional features, such as the distance of an object from oneself and the shape of an object

DETECTION: the ability to see that a surface is patterned

DISCRIMINATION: the ability to see that two patterns differ in some way

PATTERN: any two-dimensional picture consisting of an arrangement of black-and-white lines

RECOGNITION: the ability to know that a pattern being viewed has been seen before

Overview

Researchers studying visual development pursue two major goals. First, they try to describe the visual capacities of humans at different ages, beginning with the newborn infant. Second, they attempt to explain what causes the changes in visual functioning that occur with age. For centuries, young infants' inability to describe verbally how they see the world made it impossible to pursue these goals through direct scientific study. Philosophers and early psychologists based their assertions about visual development on logical arguments and indirect evidence from experiments with adults.

In the 1960's, Robert Fantz made it possible for scientists to investigate these claims directly by developing procedures that measure three basic visual capacities in infants: the "detection," "discrimination," and "recognition" of two-dimensional patterns. Detection refers to the ability to see that a surface is patterned rather than uniform. Discrimination refers to the somewhat more complex ability of distinguishing between two (or more) patterns. Finally, recognition refers to the still more complex ability to determine whether a pattern has been seen previously.

Infants' detection of visual patterns has been tested by measuring their visual acuity. Visual acuity refers to the ability to see very small objects such as closely spaced, thin black stripes on a white background. An infant's acuity can be determined by using the "preferential-looking procedure" developed by Fantz. This procedure is based on the observation that infants consistently prefer to look at black stripes rather than a plain gray field. An infant is shown a striped pattern next to a plain gray field. If the infant consistently prefers to look at the striped side, then he or she must detect the stripes; otherwise, the striped pattern would look the same to him or her as the gray field, and the infant would not show a preference for it.

Visual acuity is influenced by two factors: spatial frequency and contrast. Spatial frequency refers roughly to the fineness or coarseness of a pattern. For the striped patterns described above, the smaller the space between stripes, the higher the spatial frequency of the pattern. Contrast refers to the difference between the brightest part of the white space in a pattern and the darkest part of the black space.

There is a dramatic improvement in acuity between birth and eight months of age. In addition, there are age-related changes in the spatial frequencies that are most easily detected. Newborns are best at detecting very low spatial frequencies. This means that, at birth, infants can most easily see coarse outlines such as a person's hairline. With age, visual acuity becomes best at progressively higher spatial frequencies. As a result, older infants and adults can detect details such as the eyes, nose, and mouth of a person's face. By eight months of age, an infant's visual acuity is about as good as an adult who could see better if he or she wore glasses but does not usually bother to do so.

Infants' discrimination of visual patterns has also been assessed by using the preferential-looking procedure. An infant is shown two patterns that differ in some way. If the infant consistently looks more at one pattern than the other, he or she must be able to discriminate between them on the basis of this difference. Many studies have documented that infants can discriminate patterns from birth onward. Before three months of age, an infant will look more at the pattern that appears to have the greater total amount of contrast. After three months, infants' preferences are more often based on the complexity and familiarity of the patterns. Among the preferred stimuli at this age are human faces, especially one's own mother.

Infants' recognition of visual patterns has been assessed by using the "habituation procedure," which was also developed by Fantz. This method involves two phases: a familiarization phase and a test phase. In the familiarization phase, infants are shown a pattern repeatedly. When infants become so bored that they no longer look at this pattern much, the test phase occurs. In this phase, infants are shown both the old pattern and a new one. Infants who are only a few days old will often remain bored with the old pattern but exhibit interest in the new pattern. This indicates that they must be able to discriminate between the old pattern and the new pattern. They also must be able to recognize the old pattern; otherwise, they would never be bored with it.

No one knows whether infants' recognition of a repeatedly shown picture is conscious. It is, however, surprisingly robust. Even two weeks after they are repeatedly shown a particular pattern, two-month-olds continue to prefer a different pattern.

Applications

The development of methods to test infants' ability to detect, discriminate, and recognize patterns led investigators to apply these same methods in other ways. Researchers have investigated infants' ability to see features of the world other than patterns. The same methods have also proved useful for diagnosing infants suspected of having abnormal vision.

For example, researchers have discovered that "saccadic" and "smooth pursuit" eye movements develop very early. When one's eyes are stationary, the picture one sees, called the visual field, has very sharp detail only in its center. Saccadic eye movements quickly shift the eyes from one position to another in order to move an object of interest to the center of the visual field where it can be seen most clearly. If the object then moves, smooth-pursuit eye movements keep it in the center of the visual field by steadily following it.

Even newborns perform saccadic eye movements. With age, infants become able to move their eyes to objects increasingly far from the center of the visual field. Infants are also capable of smooth-pursuit eye movements by two months of age. Before that time, they look at the location where an object has been for a second or two after it moves away. Then they quickly shift their eyes forward to a position roughly in line with the object's new location.

Mark Bornstein used the habituation procedure to show that infants' color vision is similar to that of adults. Adults see particular ranges of wavelengths of light as a single unique category of color; for example, they see wavelengths of 450 to 480 nanometers as blue. During the familiarization phase, Bornstein repeatedly presented four-month-olds with a particular wavelength of light until they lost interest. Infants then viewed two new wavelengths in the test phase. These were equally far from the original in terms of their wavelengths. To adults, however, one of the new wavelengths looked like a different color from the original wavelength, whereas the other was the same color. Infants looked more at the wavelength that adults saw as the different color than at the one that adults saw as the same color. This indicates that infants could see the color of the original wavelength and saw that one of the new wavelengths was the same color. Like adults, infants saw the other new wavelength as a new color. As a result, it was more interesting to them and they looked longer at it.

Finally, researchers have found that depth perception, the ability to see the distance and three-dimensional shape of objects, develops early in infancy. When one looks at an object, light enters the eye and is displayed on the retina, a light-sensitive structure at the back of the eye. The display of light on the retina is two-dimensional, however, somewhat like a picture. In order to see in three dimensions, the adult visual system uses three types of information contained in the flat retinal image: kinetic, binocular, and pictorial depth cues. The ability to use these three types of depth cues appears to develop in the same sequence for all individuals: Kinetic cues are used soon after birth, binocular cues start to be used at four months of age, and pictorial cues start to be used at around seven months.

Kinetic cues are based on how the retinal image moves over time. For example, as an object approaches, it fills an increasing portion of the visual field. Infants can use this expansion of the retinal image to see the approach of an object in the first month of life. Binocular cues are based on the fact that, because eyes in humans are several centimeters apart, the display of light on the two retinas almost always differs. By four months of age, infants can use the difference in the two retinal images of an object being observed to form an impression of how far away the object is. Pictorial cues were originally described by Leonardo da Vinci as ways of conveying distance in paintings. By seven months of age, infants are able to use pictorial cues such as perspective and shading to see the distance and shape of objects.

The methods of visual-development research have also been used successfully to diagnose infants with suspected visual abnormalities. For example, the absence of saccadic or smooth-pursuit eye movements may signal a visual deficit. In addition, the preferential-looking procedure for testing visual acuity has been used to determine whether an infant's vision is sufficiently impaired to require corrective surgery. This procedure has been standardized and used to diagnose children with problems such as cataracts, muscular weakness in the eyelids, and crossed eyes.

In some cases, infants who are suspected of being blind are found to have vision within normal limits. This saves the children's parents months of unnecessary worrying and prevents these infants from being treated as blind. In other cases, testing confirms that a child has a visual impairment. This often allows surgery to be performed early enough to be maximally effective.

Context

Philosophers concerned with questions about human nature and the origins of knowledge speculated for centuries about the visual capacities of infants. A central problem for many was the "nature versus nurture" issue. This refers to the question of whether visual abilities are inborn as part of the human biological heritage (the nature account) or learned through experience (the nurture account).

In the eighteenth and nineteenth centuries, empiricist philosophers such as John Locke, David Hume, Bishop Berkeley, and John Stuart Mill suggested that mature vision was primarily a learned skill. They maintained that infants at first see the world as a flat mosaic of lines and color. Gradually, by reaching for and manipulating objects and by moving around in the world, infants learn which parts of this mosaic constitute objects and surfaces. Eventually, they learn to infer other properties of these objects, such as how far away they are. This concept of impoverished initial endowment led the great early psychologist William James to write in 1890 that infants experience the world as "one great blooming, buzzing, confusion."

Research on visual development has had a dramatic impact on the age-old nature/nurture debate. It has shown that, like adults, even young infants are able to extract important information about the world. Because this competence is present before infants actively reach for objects, the traditional empiricist account is no longer tenable.

The research is more consistent with the view of the nature side of the nature/nurture debate, sometimes referred to as the "nativist theory." This view holds that people are biologically prepared to see the world. Many important visual abilities are present at birth, and others emerge in the first several months of infancy. For example, J. J. Gibson and Eleanor Gibson note that humans, like all animals, evolved in a world of objects and events. To survive, younger as well as older animals need to see the world in terms of these basic units and not as a meaningless mosaic of lines and colors. The Gibsons believe that, because they are essential to survival, many visual abilities are "built into" the infant.

Visual-development researchers now recognize two important qualifications to the nativist theory. First, it is unlikely that experience cannot have an effect on visual development. For example, animals raised in extremely abnormal conditions, such as complete darkness, fail to develop many visual abilities. Second, while many basic capacities seem to be inborn, there are certainly measurable changes in visual abilities in the first year. Some of these are probably caused by changes in the parts of the brain that are concerned with vision. Others, such as early improvements in visual acuity, are caused by changes in the optics and anatomy of the eye.

Bibliography

Bornstein, M. H. "Chromatic Vision in Infancy." In *Advances in Child Development and Behavior,* edited by H. W. Reese and L. P. Lipsitt. New York: Academic Press, 1978. Bornstein argues against the view that the division of wavelengths into colors is determined by the culture in which one lives. Instead, he reviews research with infants indicating that biological makeup plays a critical role in the way people perceive colors.

Daw, Nigel W. *Visual Development*. New York: Plenum Publishing, 1995.

Granrud, C. E., ed. *Visual Perception and Cognition in Infancy*. Hillsdale, N.J.: Lawrence Erlbaum, 1991. A collection of chapters by leading researchers in the field, this book covers a wide range of topics in visual development. The authors review their own research findings and consider the theoretical implications of their work. The writing is mostly nontechnical but challenging.

Haith, Marshall M. *Rules That Babies Look By*. Hillsdale, N.J.: Lawrence Erlbaum, 1980. This book presents an entertaining description of how infants choose where to look and how their eye movements change with age. Easily the most readable summary of eye-movement research.

Maurer, Daphne, and Charles Maurer. *The World of the Newborn*. New York: Basic Books, 1988. This book won the American Psychological Association book award for 1988. The award was well deserved, because the book is both readable and informative in describing how newborns see as well as hear, feel, and think.

Mehler, Jacques, and Robin Fox, eds. *Neonate Cognition: Beyond the Blooming, Buzzing, Confusion*. Hillsdale, N.J.: Lawrence Erlbaum, 1985. This collection of chapters by leading researchers in the field is the predecessor of the more recent volume edited by Granrud, listed above. Presents many intriguing examples of the capabilities possessed by infants in the first eight months after birth.

Wandell, Brian A. *Foundations of Vision*. Sunderland, Mass.: Sinauer Associates, 1995.

Yonas, A., and C. E. Granrud. "The Development of Sensitivity to Kinetic, Binocular, and Pictorial Depth Information in Human Infants." In *Brain Mechanisms and Spatial Vision,* edited by David J. Ingle, David N. Lee, and Marc Jeannerod. Boston: Nijhoff, 1985. Describes a program of research that shows that infants begin to use the three types of depth cues at different ages. Summarizes many experiments and includes useful illustrations that make it easy to understand how infants' depth perception is studied.

Lincoln G. Craton

See also:

The Auditory System, 82; Sensation and Perception, 535; Smell and Taste, 553; Touch and Pressure, 627; The Visual System, 643.

THE VISUAL SYSTEM

Type of psychology: Sensation and perception
Field of study: Vision

The anatomy of the visual system uniquely enables humans to perceive an astounding array of complex information over varying distances in a brief moment of time. An understanding of this system provides insights into visual impairments and how to overcome them, as well as the development of artificial vision in humans and machines.

Principal terms

ACCESSORY EYE STRUCTURES: those parts of the eye that contribute to focusing light onto the retina; principal ones are the cornea, iris, pupil, and lens

ACCOMMODATION: the ability of the lens to focus light on the retina by changing its shape

FOVEA: the central part of the retina that is densest in cone cells and is therefore the area of sharpest visual acuity

PHOTORECEPTOR: a specialized nerve cell that can transform light into a neural message; rods are specialized for black-and-white vision, cones for color vision

RETINA: the thin membrane on the back of the eye that contains photoreceptors

TRANSDUCTION: the process of changing physical energy, such as light, into neural messages

VISUAL CORTEX: the top six cell layers in the back of the brain that are specialized for organizing and interpreting visual information

Overview

Humans have three senses capable of detecting information at a distance: audition, smell, and vision. While smell depends on simple stimuli (odors), and hearing depends on time (sounds must change over time for meaningful audition to occur), the visual system is capable of analyzing complex stimuli, such as three dimensions, and may capture a multitude of diverse information in a brief moment of time (one picture may indeed be worth more than a thousand words). It is little wonder that most people consider vision their most prized sense. Indeed, the importance of the eye to the body is demonstrated by how well it is protected: It is encased in a bony socket, able to be covered reflexively or voluntarily by eyelids, and bordered by eyebrows and eyelashes to keep foreign matter from entering the open eye. What the visual system does that is so important is to transform a form of energy known as electromagnetic radiation (light) into a neurological experience that people call sight. How light becomes sight can be broken down into three phases: focusing, transduction, and neurological processing.

Focusing light is the primary responsibility of the accessory structures of the eye, depicted in section A of the figure on the next page. Light first enters the eye through a thin, transparent membrane called the cornea, which bends light waves to a narrower focus on the retina. The remainder of the eye is covered by the sclera, a protective tough white membrane. Light next passes through a chamber containing the aqueous humor, a transparent watery fluid that nourishes the cornea and the front of the eye.

Light then enters a second, larger chamber through a small opening called the pupil. The size of the pupil is controlled by two pigmented muscles called the iris. These muscles, which provide one's eye color, regulate the amount of light entering the second chamber. When illumination is low, the iris dilates (widens) the pupil to allow more light in, and it constricts (narrows) the pupil as light brightens. Once light passes through the pupil, it enters a flexible structure called the lens, the shape of which can be changed by ciliary muscles. The lens flattens in order to focus light from distant objects on the retina and becomes rounder in order to focus closer objects on the retina. The focusing process resulting from the ability of the lens to change its shape is called accommodation.

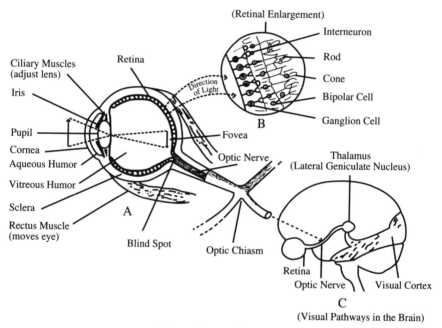

VISUAL SYSTEM ANATOMY

After light rays are refracted (bent) by the lens, they are projected onto the retina, a thin membrane on the back of the eye that contains cells that record the light images. The light rays must pass through another nourishing fluid, the vitreous humor, that keeps the main chamber from collapsing. In the center of the retina is an area called the fovea, which contains the greatest number of light-sensitive cells. Vision is usually best when light falls directly on the fovea; consequently, people are constantly moving their eyes with rectus muscles to ensure that the image from what they are viewing falls directly on the retina.

Transforming electromagnetic radiation into neural activity is accomplished in the retina by photoreceptor cells (section B of the figure). Light passes through several cell layers in the retina until it strikes the two main types of photoreceptors: the approximately 6 million cones, which are specialized for day and color vision and are primarily located in the fovea, and the approximately 125 million rods, which are specialized for black-and-white and night vision and increase in number farther away from the fovea. When a photon (light particle) strikes a photoreceptor, it causes a chemical contained in the rod or cone to split in two, creating a neural impulse (message). Photoreceptors connect with bipolar cells, which in turn connect with ganglion cells, whose axons (output "wires") form the optic nerve sending retinal information to the brain. Interneurons form interconnections among these three types of retinal cells and sharpen the image. There are no photoreceptors where the optic nerve leaves the eye, resulting in a small blind spot in the retina.

After exiting the retina, half the optic nerve fibers, from the inside half (nearest the nose) of each eye's visual field, cross to the opposite hemisphere of the brain at the optic chiasm (section C of the figure). The fibers from the outer half of each eye's visual field do not cross over. Thus, if one looks straight ahead with one's right eye and puts a finger in front of that eye, dividing the visual field in half, information from the left half of the field would go to the left hemisphere; that from the right half would go to the right hemisphere. From the optic chiasm, nerve messages go to the lateral geniculate nucleus of the thalamus, which combines and analyzes such information as form, color, depth, and movement from both eyes before sending information to the visual cortex. In the visual cortex (the occipital lobe), many cells (called feature detectors) appear to respond only to specific visual stimuli, such as dots, lines, or movement. This "feature-detection" model assumes that the brain "sees" by putting together the simple features of light. An alternative, the "spatial frequency-filter" model, suggests that thousands of brain cells are simultaneously engaged in analyzing broad patterns of light and dark rather than synthesizing simple stimuli. However the brain deals with retinal information, one thing is certain: People interpret what their eyes detect in their brains.

Applications

Given the complex anatomical route that transpires before light becomes sight, it is remarkable that humans see as well as they do. Malfunctions anywhere in the visual system can cause distortions in visual perception. Retracing the pathway of the visual system, one can identify some common visual problems associated with anatomical defects and the corrective steps that can alleviate some of these problems.

Light first enters the cornea, which must remain transparent for visual clarity. If the aqueous humor chemical balance is upset, it can result in the cornea becoming cloudy. This can be corrected by a number of procedures, the most severe of which is a corneal transplant. The aqueous humor must recycle approximately every four hours to remain clear. If too much aqueous humor is produced or it is blocked from exiting, pressure builds up inside the eye, resulting in glaucoma. This disease can lead to blindness if not treated early.

The pupil allows light passing through the aqueous humor to enter the lens. As people age, it is common that the pupil does not open as wide, letting less light in, thus causing "night blindness," or difficulty in seeing under low illumination, a major problem. Another consequence of aging is the hardening of the lens, making it more difficult to accommodate to close objects. This is the reason why many adults, usually beginning in their forties, need reading glasses. Two other widespread problems associated with the lens are astigmatism, caused by surface and shape defects of the lens, and cataracts, a clouding of the lens that is present at birth in some but is most common in the elderly, affecting in varying degrees 75 percent of people over sixty-five years of age. Astigmatism can be corrected by lenses;

cataracts by surgery.

The eye's shape is also important to proper vision. The vitreous humor, in conjunction with the sclera, helps to maintain the round shape of the eye. Sometimes impurities circulating through this fluid result in seeing spots before one's eyes. If the eyeball elongates between the lens and retina, nearsightedness (difficulty with distance vision) results; if the eyeball narrows between the lens and retina, farsightedness (difficulty with close vision) results. These two common problems are usually corrected with glasses or contact lenses. Continued eyestrain, such as from long periods of reading without resting one's eyes, may result in an elongation of the eyeball, leading to or worsening nearsightedness.

Retinal factors account for differences between day and night vision and problems with color vision. People see better at night by looking slightly to the side of an object, directing light slightly away from the fovea, thus using more rods than cones (which do not work well under dim illumination). Rods are connected to many ganglion cells; a small amount of light striking many rods can therefore effectively stimulate the ganglion cell which is connected to those rods. During daylight illumination, one sees best by looking straight at something, focusing light on the fovea. Acuity (visual sharpness) is best at the fovea, because cones are more densely packed there. Furthermore, because most cones are connected to only one ganglion cell, this ensures great acuity, since little information about which cone is being stimulated is lost. Cones are also responsible for color vision; animals such as dogs, which do not have cones, do not perceive color. In humans, many of the different defects in color vision are caused by having the wrong photopigments or by an absence of photopigments in the cones.

Defects in the optic nerve that prevent messages from the retina from reaching the visual cortex result in blindness. Researchers have wondered whether vision could be restored if a way could be found to bypass the damaged area and stimulate the visual cortex. William Dobelle and his associates reported in a 1977 study that such a possibility is more than science fiction. They found that if many electrodes (terminals that conduct electrical current into an area) were implanted in the visual cortices of blind volunteers' brains, stimulation of these electrodes would result in the volunteers reporting glowing patterns of light "before" their eyes. Advances in artificial vision techniques of this nature could have obvious benefits for the blind.

Research in the early 1960's by David Hubel and Torsten Wiesel demonstrated that cell development in the visual cortex is greatly affected by early experience. Studies with kittens and monkeys demonstrated that deprivation of early visual experience led to incomplete cell development in the visual cortex, thus leading to deficits in visual perception. If visual defects such as astigmatism or being cross-eyed in young children are not corrected early in life, the usual result is some type of permanent visual deficiency.

Context

It is interesting that those scientists who spent long nights observing light in the heavens, astronomers, produced the first valid insights into the function of the human eye. Johannes Kepler (1571-1630) is credited with being the first to suggest that the photoreceptive tissue of the eye is located in the retina. Christoph Scheiner, in 1625, demonstrated that the lens is the primary focusing device of the eye.

Scientific knowledge about the functioning of retinal cells began in 1876, when Franz

Boll discovered in his research with fish eyes that the retina was a different color where light had shined on it. This discovery implicated a photochemical process as being crucial for visual transduction. Selig Hecht, in 1929, was among the first to describe how this process worked. In the meantime, Johannes von Kries had presented his duplicity theory of photoreceptors. Von Kries's theory, in 1895, distinguished between the functions of rods and cones. Haldan Keffer Hartline discovered the important function of the retinal interneurons in 1932; Hartline demonstrated how inhibitory messages coming from these cells help to sharpen visual perception.

While it had been known for many years that retinal cells send their messages to the visual areas of the brain's cortex, little was known about the organization and functioning of these cells until the work of David Hubel and Torsten Wiesel was first published in the early 1960's. Hubel and Wiesel, who won a Nobel Prize for their work, found that different areas in the visual field have corresponding receptive areas in the visual cortex. In other words, a kind of map of what one sees in one's field of vision is represented in the visual cortex. They also found that different layers of cortical cells are responsible for different types of visual stimulation.

As knowledge of the anatomy of the visual system increases, there are important benefits to humans and machines. The more they know about how the eye works, the more researchers and physicians can help the visually impaired. For example, advancements based on Dobelle's work with artificial vision may enable the totally blind to have increasingly more sophisticated visual experiences. Similarly, gains in knowledge about the visual system enable people to build machines that can respond more "intelligently" to their visual environments. Such developments are particularly useful in the field of robotics. Whether it exists in humans or machines, the vision of the future is one of fascinating possibilities.

Bibliography

Cohen, David. *The Secret Language of the Mind: A Visual Inquiry into the Mysteries of Consciousness*. San Francisco: Chronicle Books, 1996.

Goldstein, E. Bruce. *Sensation and Perception*. 3d ed. Belmont, Calif.: Wadsworth, 1989. Goldstein's book is an advanced introduction to the field of sensation and perception, with more than half the chapters concerned with vision. An interesting chapter entitled "What Can Go Wrong with Your Eyes" contains information not commonly found in sensation and perception books. May be somewhat difficult reading for the layperson or high school student.

Gregory, Richard Langton. *Eye and Brain*. 4th ed. Princeton, N.J.: Princeton University Press, 1990. This inexpensive paperback is considered a classic in the field of visual perception. The book is written in a style that is easily accessible. Gregory's book contains many excellent illustrations. If one were to read one book on vision, this would be the book.

Keller, Helen. *The Story of My Life*. New York: Airmont, 1965. For anyone who has wondered what life would be like without a functioning visual system, this is a fascinating book to read. Presents the intriguing and courageous story of Keller's own triumph over adversity. The psychological consequences of visual disability are particularly notable.

MacKay, Donald MacCrimmon. *Behind the Eye*. Cambridge, Mass.: Basil Blackwell, 1991.

Based on the Gifford lectures, given at the University of Glasgow by an expert in the field of visual processing in the brain. MacKay's book uniquely combines an understanding of neurophysiology and philosophy to approach not only the question of how the mind perceives but also the more fundamental question of what the mind is. Suitable for advanced undergraduates, but also accessible to the nonspecialist.

Matlin, Margaret W. *Perception*. 2d ed. Boston: Allyn & Bacon, 1988. Like Goldstein's book, this presents a general introduction to the field of perception. The chapters concerning vision are written in a scholarly style, but with more wit and style than most texts in the field. Matlin's book is probably easier fare for the layperson or high school student than Goldstein's.

Tovee, Martin J. *An Introduction to the Visual System*. New York: Cambridge University Press, 1996.

Wolfe, Jeremy M., ed. *The Mind's Eye: Readings from Scientific American*. New York: W. H. Freeman, 1986. Twelve articles from *Scientific American* concerned with vision are featured in this book. The articles are divided into three sections: "Eyes," "Pathways to the Mind's Eye," and "In the Mind's Eye." The original writings of researchers in the field may sometimes be challenging reading for the nonspecialist, but the book is a valuable resource.

Paul J. Chara, Jr.

See also:

The Auditory System, 82; The Cerebral Cortex, 121; Sensation and Perception, 535; Smell and Taste, 553; Touch and Pressure, 627; Visual Development, 638.

GLOSSARY

Absolute threshold: The smallest amount of stimulus that elicits a sensation 50 percent of the time.

Accommodation: In Piaget's theory of development, adjusting the interpretation (schema) of an object or event to include a new instance; in vision, the ability of the lens to focus light on the retina by changing its shape.

Acetylcholine (ACh): A cholinergic neurotransmitter important in producing muscular contraction and in some autonomic nerve transmissions.

Achievement motivation: The tendency for people to strive for moderately difficult goals because of the relative attractiveness of success and repulsiveness of failure.

Acquisition: In learning, the process by which an association is formed in classical or operant conditioning; in memory, the stage at which information is stored in memory.

Action potential: A rapid change in electrical charges across a neuron's cell membrane, with depolarization followed by repolarization, leading to a nerve impulse moving down an axon; associated with nerve and muscle activity.

Actor-observer bias: The tendency to infer that other people's behavior is caused by dispositional factors but that one's own behavior is the product of situational causes.

Actualizing tendency: The force toward maintaining and enhancing the organism, achieving congruence between experience and awareness, and realizing potentials.

Adaptation: Any heritable characteristic that presumably has developed as a result of natural selection and thus increases an animal's ability to survive and reproduce.

Addiction: Physical dependence on a substance; components include tolerance, psychological dependence, and physical withdrawal symptoms.

Adolescence: The period extending from the onset of puberty to early adulthood.

Adrenal glands: The suprarenal glands, small, caplike structures sitting each on top of one kidney; in general, they function in response to stress, but they are also important in regulating metabolic and sexual functions.

Affect: A class name given to feelings, emotions, or dispositions as a mode of mental functioning.

Affective disorders: Functional mental disorders associated with emotions or feelings (also called mood disorders); examples include depression and bipolar disorders.

Afferent: A sensory neuron or a dendrite carrying information toward a structure; for example, carrying sensory stimuli coming into the reticular formation.

Affiliation motive: The motive to seek the company of others and to be with one's own kind, based on such things as cooperation, similarity, friendship, sex, and protection.

Aggression: Behavior intended to harm or injure another person or thing.

Agoraphobia: An intense fear of being in places or situations in which help may not be available or escape could be difficult.

Allele: One of the many forms of a gene; it may be dominant (needing only one copy for the trait to appear) or recessive (needing two copies).

Altruism: A phenomenon in human and animal behaviors in which individuals unselfishly sacrifice their own genetic fitness in order to help other individuals in a group.

Alzheimer's disease: A form of presenile dementia, characterized by disorientation, loss of memory, speech disturbances, and personality disorders.

Amplitude: The peak deviation from the rest state of the movement of a vibrating object, or the ambient state of the medium through which vibration is conducted.

Anal stage: According to Freud, the second psychosexual stage of personality development, approximately from ages two to four; sexual energy is focused on the anus and on pleasures and conflicts associated with retaining and eliminating feces.

Analgesia: The reduction or elimination of pain.

Analytic psychology: A school of psychology founded by Carl Jung that views the human mind as the result of prior experiences and the preparation of future goals; it deemphasizes the role of sexuality in psychological disorders.

Androgens: Male sex hormones secreted by the testes; testosterone, the primary mammalian male androgen, is responsible for the development and maturation of male sexual structures and sexual behaviors.

Androgyny: The expression of both traditionally feminine and traditionally masculine attributes.

Anorexia nervosa: An eating disorder characterized by an obsessive-compulsive concern for thinness achieved by dieting; often combined with extreme exercising and sometimes part of a binge-purge cycle.

Anterograde amnesia: An inability to form new memories after the onset of amnesia.

Antidepressants: Drugs that are used in the treatment of depression, many of which affect or mimic neurotransmitters; classes of antidepressants include the tricyclics and MAO inhibitors.

Antisocial personality disorder: A personality disorder characterized by a history of impulsive, risk-taking, and perhaps chronic criminal behavior, and by opportunistic interpersonal relations.

Anxiety: A chronic fearlike state that is accompanied by feelings of impending doom and that cannot be explained by an actual threatening object or event.

Aphasia: Partial or total loss of the use of language as a result of brain damage, characterized by an inability to use and/or comprehend language.

Applied research: Research intended to solve existing problems, as opposed to "basic research," which seeks knowledge for its own sake.

Aptitude: The potential to develop an ability with training and/or experience.

Archetypes: In Jung's theory, universal, inherited themes—such as the motifs of the self, hero, and shadow—that exercise an influence on virtually all human beings.

Archival data: Information collected at an earlier time by someone other than the present researcher, often for purposes very different from those of the present research.

Artificial intelligence: The use of computers to simulate aspects of human thinking and, in some cases, behavior.

Assimilation: The interpretation of a new instance of an object or event in terms of one's preexisting schema or understanding; the fit, never perfect, is close enough.

Attachment: An emotional bond between infant and caregiver based on reciprocal interaction patterns.

Attention: The ability to focus mentally.

Attitude: A relatively stable evaluation of a person or thing; it can be either positive or negative, can vary in level of intensity, and has an affective, cognitive, and behavioral component.

Attribution: The process by which one gathers information about the self and others and interprets it to determine the cause of an event or behavior.

Attributional biases: Typical motivational and cognitive errors in the attribution process; tendencies that are shared among people in using information in illogical or unwarranted ways.

Autonomic nervous system: The division of the peripheral nervous system that regulates basic, automatically controlled life processes such as cardiovascular function, digestive function, and genital function.

Availability heuristic: A decision-making heuristic whereby a person estimates the probability of some occurrence or event depending on how easily examples of that event can be remembered.

Aversion therapy: A therapy that involves pairing something negative (such as electric shock) with an undesired behavior (such as drinking alcohol or smoking cigarettes).

Axon: The single fiberlike extension of a neuron that carries information away from the cell body toward the next cell in a pathway.

Beck Depression Inventory (BDI): A brief questionnaire used to measure the severity of depression; developed by Aaron Beck.

Behavior therapy: A branch of psychotherapy narrowly conceived as the application of classical and operant conditioning to the alteration of clinical problems, but more broadly conceived as applied experimental psychology in a clinical context.

Behaviorism: A theoretical approach which states that the environment is the primary cause of behavior and that only external, observable stimuli and responses are available to objective study.

Between-subject designs: Experimental plans in which different participants receive each level of the independent variable.

Bilingual: A person who has enough control of two languages to function well with both languages in a number of different contexts.

Binocular cues: Visual cues that require the use of both eyes working together.

Biofeedback: A psychophysiological technique in which an individual monitors a specific, supposedly involuntary, bodily function such as blood pressure or heart rate and consciously attempts to control this function through the use of learning principles.

Bipolar disorder: A disorder characterized by the occurrence of one or more manic episodes, usually interspersed with one or more major depressive episodes.

Bottom-up processing: Information processing guided by simple stimulus features of units rather than by a person's general knowledge, beliefs, or expectations.

Brain stem: The lower part of the brain, between the brain and spinal cord, which activates the cortex and makes perception and consciousness possible; it includes the midbrain, pons, medulla, and cerebellum.

Bystander effect: The tendency for an individual to be less likely to help as the number of other people present increases.

Cardinal trait: According to Allport's theory of personality, a single outstanding characteristic that dominates a person's life; few individuals are characterized by a cardinal disposition.

Case study: An in-depth method of data collection in which all available background data on an individual or group are reviewed; typically used in psychotherapy.

Catecholamines: A neurotransmitter group derived from the amino acid tyrosine that includes dopamine, epinephrine, and norepinephrine; they are activated in stressful situations.

Catharsis: A reduction of psychological tension and/or physiological arousal by expressing (either directly or vicariously) repressed aggressive or sexual anxieties.

Cell body: The principal portion of a cell such as a neuron, which contains genetic material and most of the cell cytoplasm.

Central nervous system: The nerve cells, fibers, and other tissues associated with the brain and spinal cord.

Central traits: According to Allport's theory, the relatively few (five to ten) distinctive and descriptive characteristics that provide direction and focus to a person's life.

Cephalocaudal development: A pattern of early physical growth consisting of motor development that proceeds from head to foot.

Cerebellum: The portion of the brain that controls voluntary muscle activity, including posture and body movement; located behind the brain stem.

Cerebral commissures: Fiber tracts, such as the corpus callosum and anterior commissure, that connect and allow neural communication between the cerebral hemispheres.

Cerebral cortex: The outer layer of the cerebrum; controls higher-level brain functions such as thinking, reasoning, motor coordination, memory, and language.

Cerebral hemispheres: Two anatomically similar hemispheres that make up the outer surface of the brain (the cerebral cortex); separated by the cerebral longitudinal fissure.

Cerebrospinal fluid: A fluid, derived from blood, that circulates in and around the ventricles of the brain and the spinal cord.

Cerebrum: The largest and uppermost portion of the brain; the cerebrum performs sensory and motor functions and affects memory, speech, and emotional functions.

Chaining: The process by which several neutral stimuli are presented in a series; they eventually assume reinforcing qualities by being ultimately paired with an innate reinforcer.

Children's Depression Inventory (CDI): A modified version of the Beck Depression Inventory (BDI) that was developed to measure the severity of depression in children; developed by Maria Kovacs.

Chromosomes: Microscopic threadlike bodies in the nuclei of cells; they carry the genes, which convey hereditary characteristics.

Circadian rhythm: A cyclical variation in a biological process or behavior that has a duration of about a day; in humans under constant environmental conditions, the rhythm usually reveals its true length as being slightly more than twenty-four hours.

Classical conditioning: A form of associative learning in which a neutral stimulus, called the conditioned stimulus (CS), is repeatedly paired with a biologically significant unconditioned stimulus (UCS) so that the CS acquires the same power to elicit response as the UCS; also called Pavlovian conditioning.

Clinical psychologist: A person with a Ph.D. in psychology, specially trained to assess and treat mental disorders and behavior problems.

Cochlea: The snail-shell-shaped portion of the inner ear, which contains the nerve connections to the auditory nerve.

Code-switching: A speech style used by many bilinguals that is characterized by rapid shifts back and forth between two languages within a single conversation or sentence.

Cognition: Mental processes involved in the acquisition and use of knowledge, such as attention, thinking, problem solving, and perception; cognitive learning emphasizes these processes in the acquisition of new behaviors.

Cognitive appraisal: An assessment of the meaningfulness of an event to an individual; events that are appraised as harmful or potentially harmful elicit stress.

Cognitive behavior therapy: Therapy that integrates principles of learning theory with cognitive strategies to treat disorders such as depression, anxiety, and other behavioral problems (such as smoking or obesity).

Cognitive dissonance theory: Leon Festinger's theory that inconsistencies among one's cognitions cause tension and that individuals are motivated to reduce this tension by changing discrepant attitudes.

Cognitive map: A mental representation of an external area that is used to guide one's behavior.

Cognitive processes: The processes of thought, which include attending to an event, storing information in memory, recalling information, and making sense of information; they enable people to perceive events.

Cognitive psychology: An area of study that investigates mental processes; areas within cognitive psychology include attention, perception, language, learning, memory, problem solving, and logic.

Cognitive science: A multidisciplinary approach to the study of cognition from the perspectives of psychology, computer science, neuroscience, philosophy, and linguistics.

Cohort: An identifiable group of people; in developmental research, group members are commonly associated by their birth dates and shared historical experiences.

Collective unconscious: In Jung's theory, memory traces of repeated experiences that have been passed down to all humankind as a function of evolutionary development; includes inherited tendencies to behave in certain ways and contains the archetypes.

Color: The brain's interpretation of electromagnetic radiation of different wavelengths within the range of visible light.

Color blindness: An inability to perceive certain colors; the most common type is green-minus color blindness, involving a defect in the eyes' green cones.

Compensation: In Adler's theory, a defense mechanism for overcoming feelings of inferiority by trying harder to excel; in Freud's theory, the process of learning alternative ways to accomplish a task while making up for an inferiority—a process that could involve dreams that adjust psychologically for waking imbalances.

Complementary color: Light that complements another light in that their addition produces white light and their juxtaposition produces high contrast.

Compulsions: Ritualistic patterns of behavior that commonly follow obsessive thinking and that reduce the intensity of the anxiety-evoking thoughts.

Concrete operations stage: The third stage of Piaget's theory, during which children acquire basic logical rules and concrete concepts; occurs between the ages of seven and eleven.

Conditioned response (CR): In Pavlovian conditioning, the behavior and emotional quality that occurs when a conditioned stimulus is presented; related to but not the same as the unconditioned response.

Conditioned stimulus (CS): A previously neutral stimulus (a sight, sound, touch, or smell) that, after Pavlovian conditioning, will elicit the conditioned response (CR).

Conditioned taste aversion: An avoidance of a food or drink that has been followed by illness when consumed in the past.

Conditioning: A type of learning in which an animal learns a concept by associating it with some object or by the administration of rewards and/or punishments.

Conditions of worth: In Rogers' theory, externally based conditions for love and praise; the expectation that the child must behave in accordance with parental standards in order to receive love.

Cone: One type of visual receptor found in the retina of the eye; primarily for color vision and acute daytime vision.

Confounding of variables: The variation of other variables along with the independent variable of interest, as a result of which any effects cannot be attributed with certainty to the independent variable.

Consciousness: A level of awareness that includes those things of which an individual is aware at any given moment, such as current ideas, thoughts, accessed memories, and feelings.

Consensual validation: The verification of subjective beliefs by obtaining a consensus among other people.

Consensus information: Information concerning other people's responses to an object; in attribution theory, high consensus generally leads people to attribute situational rather than personal causes to a behavior.

Conservation: In Piaget's theory, understanding that the physical properties (number, length, mass, volume) remain constant even though appearances may change; a concrete-operational skill.

Consistency information: Information concerning a person's response to an object over time. In attribution theory, high consistency implies that behavior is dispositional or typical of a person.

Consolidation: A neural process by which short-term memories become stored in long-term memory.

Construct: A formal concept representing the relationships between variables or processes such as motivation and behavior; may be empirical (observable) or hypothetical (inferred).

Construct validity: A type of validity that assesses the extent to which a test score (variable) correlates with other tests (variables) already established as valid measures of the item.

Consumer psychology: The subfield of psychology that studies selling, advertising, and buying; the goal of its practitioners is generally to communicate clearly and to persuade consumers to buy products.

Context dependence: The phenomenon in which memory functions more effectively when material is recalled in the same environment in which it was originally learned, compared with recall in a different environment.

Contingency: A relationship between a response and its consequence or between two stimuli; sometimes considered a dependency.

Contingency management: A method of behavior modification that involves providing or removing positive rewards in accordance with whether the individual being treated engages in the expected behavior.

Continuous reinforcement: A schedule in which each response is followed by a reinforcer.

Control group: A group of subjects that are like the experimental groups in all ways except that they do not experience the independent variable; used as a comparison measure.

Control variable: An extraneous factor that might influence the dependent variable, making it difficult to evaluate the effect of the independent variable; in an experiment, attempts are made to isolate or control such effects systematically.

Convergence: In perception, the turning of the eyes inward from parallel lines of sight to look at a nearby object; a depth cue.

Convergent thinking: Creative thinking in which possible solutions to a problem are systematically eliminated in search for the best solution; the type of ordinary thinking in which most people generally engage.

Conversion disorder: A psychological disorder in which a person experiences physical symptoms, such as the loss or impairment of some motor or sensory function (paralysis or blindness, for example), in the absence of an organic cause.

Coping: Responses directed at dealing with demands (in particular, threatening or stressful ones) upon an organism; these responses may either improve or reduce long-term functioning.

Correlation: The degree of relatedness or correspondence between two variables, expressed by a coefficient that can range from +1.00 to -1.00; 0.00 signifies no correspondence.

Cortex: The surface (or outer layer) of the brain, which receives sensory input, interprets it, and relates behavior to external stimuli; responsible for perception and conscious thought.

Cortical brain centers: The portions of the brain making up the cerebral cortex and controlling voluntary behavior, higher reasoning, and language skills; they develop rapidly during the first two years of life.

Countertransference: The phenomenon in which an analyst either shifts feelings from his or her past onto a patient or is affected by the client's emotional problems; caused by a patient's perceived similarity to individuals or experiences in the analyst's life.

Creativity: Cognitive abilities in areas such as fluency, flexibility, originality, elaboration, visualization, metaphorical thinking, and problem definition; the ability to originate something that is both new and appropriate.

Criterion group: A group used to validate a measurement instrument; in the case of interest inventories, it refers to persons in a particular occupational group.

Critical period: A time during which the developing organism is particularly sensitive to the influence of certain inputs or experiences necessary to foster normal development; in nonhuman animals, a specific time period during which a certain type of learning such as imprinting must occur.

Cross-sectional design: A design in which subgroups of a population are randomly sampled; the members of the sample are then tested or observed.

Cue-producing response: A response that serves as a cue for other responses; words (speech) can cue behaviors, and thoughts can cue other thoughts.

Cutaneous sense: Relating to the skin sense, as in responses to touch or temperature.

Cyclothymia: A milder version of a cyclical mood disorder in which mood swings can occur but are not as intense as in bipolar disorder.

Daily hassles: Seemingly minor everyday events that are a constant source of stress.

Dark adaptation: An increase in the sensitivity of rods and cones to light through an increase in the concentration of light-absorbing pigments.

Data: A collection of observations from an experiment or survey.

Death instinct: The unconscious desire for death and destruction in order to escape the tensions of living.

Debriefing: Discussing an experiment and its purpose with subjects after its completion; required if the experiment involved deception.

Decay: The disappearance of a memory trace.

Deduction: A type of logic by which one draws a specific conclusion from one or more known truths or premises; often formed as an "if/then" statement.

Defense mechanism: According to Freud, a psychological strategy by which an unacceptable sexual or aggressive impulse may be kept from conscious thought or expressed in a disguised fashion.

Deindividuation: The loss of self-awareness and evaluation apprehension that accompanies situations that foster personal and physical anonymity.

Delusion: A symptom of psychosis that consists of a strong irrational belief held despite considerable evidence against it; types include delusions of grandeur, reference, and persecution.

Dementia: Globally impaired intellectual functioning (memory reasoning) in adults as a function of brain impairment; it does not mean "craziness," but a loss or impairment of mental power.

Dendrite: A branching extension of a neuron through which information enters the cell; there may be one or many dendrites on a neuron.

Dependent variable: The outcome measure in a study; the effect of the independent variable is measured by changes in the dependent variable.

Depolarization: A shift in ions and electrical charges across a cell membrane, causing loss of resting membrane potential and bringing the cell closer to the action potential.

Depression: A psychological disorder characterized by extreme feelings of sadness, hopelessness, or personal unworthiness, as well as loss of energy, withdrawal, and either lack of sleep or excessive sleep.

Depth perception: The ability to see three-dimensional features, such as the distance of an object from oneself and the shape of an object.

Descriptive statistics: Procedures that summarize and organize data sets; they include mean, median, range, correlation, and variability.

Desensitization: A behavioral technique of gradually removing anxiety associated with certain situations by associating a relaxed state with these situations.

Determinism: The theory or doctrine that acts of the will, occurrences in nature, or social or psychological phenomena are causally determined by preceding events or natural laws.

Development: The continuous and cumulative process of age-related changes in physical growth, thought, perception, and behavior of people and animals; a result of both biological and environmental influences.

Developmental psychology: The subfield of psychology that studies biological, social, and intellectual changes as they occur throughout the human life cycle.

Deviancy: The quality of having a condition or engaging in behavior that is atypical in a social group and is considered undesirable.

Diagnosis: The classification or labeling of a patient's problem within one of a set of recognized categories of abnormal behavior, determined with the aid of interviews and psychological tests.

Diagnostic and Statistical Manual of Mental Disorders (DSM-III-R): A system created by the American Psychiatric Association for diagnosing and classifying mental disorders; used by mental health professionals and insurance companies.

Dichotic listening: A technique in which two different messages are simultaneously played through earphones, with a different message to each ear.

Diffusion of responsibility: The reduction of personal responsibility that is commonly experienced in group situations; diffusion of responsibility increases as the size of the crowd increases.

Discounting: Reducing the role of a particular cause in producing a behavior because of the presence of other plausible causes.

Discrimination: In perception, the ability to see that two patterns differ in some way; in intergroup relations, behavior (usually unfavorable) toward persons that is based on their group membership rather than on their individual personalities.

Discriminative stimulus: A stimulus that signals the availability of a consequence, given that a response occurs.

Dispersion: A statistical measure of variability; a measure (range, semi-interquartile range, standard deviation, or variance) that provides information about the difference among the scores.

Displacement: According to Freud, a defense mechanism by which a person redirects his or her aggressive impulse onto a target that may substitute for the target that originally aroused the person's aggression.

Display: A visual dance or series of movements or gestures by an individual or animal to communicate such things as dominance, aggression, and courtship to other individuals.

Display rules: Culturally determined rules regarding the appropriate expression of emotions.

Dispositional: Relating to disposition or personality rather than to situation.

Dissociative disorder: A disorder that occurs when some psychological function, such as memory, is split off from the rest of the conscious mind; not caused by brain dysfunction.

Dissonance: An unpleasant psychological and physiological state caused by an inconsistency between cognitions.

Distal stimulus: An object or other sensory element in the environment.

Distinctiveness information: Information concerning a person's response to an object under given conditions; in attribution theory, high distinctiveness suggests that individuals are behaving uniquely toward a given target/object.

Diurnal enuresis: The presence of enuretic episodes when the individual is awake.

Divergent thinking: Thinking that results in new and different responses that most people cannot, or do not, offer; the type of thinking most clearly involved in creativity.

Domestic violence: Physical, emotional, psychological, or sexual abuse perpetrated by a family member toward another family member; typically the abuse follows a repetitive, predictable pattern.

Dominance hierarchy: An ordered arrangement of dominant to subordinate individuals in an animal population that serves numerous social functions, including protection; a pecking order.

Dopamine: One type of neurotransmitter, a chemical that is released from one nerve cell and stimulates receptors on another, thus transferring a message between them; associated with movement and with treatment of depression.

Double bind: A form of communication that often occurs when a family member sends two messages, requests, or commands that are logically inconsistent, contradictory, or impossible, resulting in a "damned if one does, damned if one doesn't" situation; a hypothesis about the development of schizophrenia.

Double-blind method: A procedure in which neither the experimenter nor the subjects know who is receiving treatment and who is not; this controls for subject and experimenter biases and expectations.

Down syndrome: A chromosomal abnormality that causes mental retardation as well as certain physical defects, such as extra eyelid folds and a thick tongue; caused by an extra (third) chromosome on chromosome pair 21.

Drive: The tendency of a person or animal to engage in behaviors brought about by some change or condition inside that organism; often generated by deprivation (hunger or thirst) or exposure to painful or other noxious stimuli.

Drive-reduction hypothesis: The idea that a physiological need state triggers a series of behaviors aimed at reducing the unpleasant state; drive reduction is reinforcing.

Dysfunctional family: A family grouping that is characterized by the presence of disturbed interactions and communications; particularly an abusive, incestuous, or alcoholic family.

Dyslexia: A type of reading disability in which one is unable to process written symbols effectively

Dysphoria: A symptom of clinical depression; extreme sadness.

Dysthymic disorder: A form of depression in which mild to moderate levels of depressive symptoms persist chronically.

Early recollections: A projective technique in which the patient attempts to remember things that happened in the distant past; these provide clues to the patient's current use of private logic.

Eating disorders: Afflictions resulting from dysfunctional relationships to hunger, food, and eating.

Echoic memory: Sensory memory for sound.

Echolalia: An involuntary and parrotlike repetition of words or phrases spoken by others.

Eclectic therapy: Therapy in which a combination of models and techniques is employed, rather than a single approach.

Educational psychology: The subfield of psychology that studies the effectiveness of education, usually formal education; educational psychologists seek to develop new educational techniques and to improve the learning process.

Efferent nerve: A motor neuron or an axon carrying information away from a structure; for example, in the transmission of stimuli from the reticular formation to the cerebral cortex.

Ego: In psychoanalytic theory, the part of the personality responsible for perceiving reality and thinking; mediates between the demands of the pleasure-seeking id, the superego, and reality.

Egocentric thought: A cognitive tendency in childhood in which the child assumes that everyone shares his or her own perspective; the cognitive inability to understand the different perspective of another.

Elaborative rehearsal: Giving meaning to information to enable encoding it in memory.

Electroconvulsive therapy (ECT): A treatment for severe depression in which an electric current is passed through the brain of the patient.

Electroencephalogram (EEG): The graphic recording of the electrical activity of the brain (brain waves).

Electroencephalography: Measurement of the electrical output of the brain, which may then sometimes be brought under voluntary control by biofeedback and relaxation.

Embryonic phase: The period of rapid prenatal change that follows the zygote period; extends from the second to the eighth week after conception.

Emotion: A psychological response that includes a set of physiological changes, expressive behaviors, and a subjective experience.

Empathy: In therapy, the therapist's ability to focus attention on the needs and experience of the client; also refers to the therapist's ability to communicate an understanding of the client's emotional state.

Empirical evidence: Data or information derived objectively from the physical senses, without reliance on personal faith, intuition, or introspection.

Empiricism: A philosophy holding that knowledge is learned through experience and that infants begin life like blank slates, learning about their environment through experience.

Encoding: The transformation of incoming sensory information into a form of code that the memory system can accept and use.

Endocrine gland: A gland that produces one or more hormones and secretes them into the blood so that they can serve as intercellular messengers.

Endocrine system: A system of ductless glands in the bodies of vertebrate animals that secretes hormones which travel through the bloodstream to target tissues, whose functioning is altered by the hormones.

Endogenous behavior: An innate, or inborn, behavior that is established by the animal's inherited genetic code (DNA) and that is not influenced by the animal's experiences or environment.

Endorphins: A group of endogenous, opiatelike neuropeptides of the central nervous system that simulate analgesia and interfere with transmission of pain impulses; the brain's own morphine.

Enkephalins: Peptides containing five amino acids, within the endorphin group, that may act as neurotransmitters; the first of the endorphins to be discovered.

Enmeshment: An excessively close relationship between parent and child in which adult concerns and needs are communicated and in which overdependence on the child is apparent.

Entitlement: The expectation of special or unusually favorable treatment by others; commonly seen among narcissistic personalities.

Entropy: In Jung's analytic theory, a concept maintaining that aspects of a person's psychic energy which are not in balance will tend to seek a state of equilibrium.

Enuresis: The inability to control the discharging of urine; nocturnal enuresis is also called bed-wetting.

Environmental psychology: The subfield of psychology that studies the relationship between the environment and behavior, particularly the effects of the physical and social environments (such as noise or crowding) on behavior.

Environmental stressor: A condition in the environment, such as crowding, noise, toxic chemicals, or extreme temperatures, that produces stress (bodily or mental tension).

Epilepsy: A disorder of the nervous system in which the cortex produces electrical firing that causes convulsions and other forms of seizures; thought by some to be linked to the reticular formation.

Epinephrine: The neurotransmitter released from the adrenal gland as a result of innervation of the autonomic nervous system; formerly called adrenaline.

Episodic memory: A form of long-term memory involving temporal and spatial information, including personal experiences.

Equipotentiality: In Pavlovian conditioning, the idea that any stimulus paired with an effective unconditioned stimulus will come to elicit a conditioned response with equal facility.

Equity theory: A theory in attraction and work motivation that contends that individuals are motivated to remain in relationships they perceive to be fair, just, and equitable—that is, where one's outcomes are proportional to one's inputs, particularly when contrasted with others in the relationship.

Equivalence: A principle stating that an increase in energy or value in one aspect of the psyche is accompanied by a decrease in another area.

Estradiol: The primary sex hormone of mammalian females, which is responsible for the menstrual cycle and for development of secondary sex characteristics; a primary estrogen, secreted by the corpus luteum.

Ethnocentrism: An attitude of uncritically assuming the superiority of the in-group culture.

Ethology: A branch of zoology that studies animals in their natural environments; often concerned with investigating the adaptive significance and innate basis of behaviors.

Etiology: The factors that are thought to cause or contribute to the development of a particular disorder.

Eustress: Positive arousal or stress, appraised as a challenge rather than as a threat.

Evoked potential: A brain response triggered by electroencephalography using discrete sensory stimuli.

Excitation transfer: The theory that arousal from one source can intensify an emotional reaction to a different source (for example, that sexual arousal can increase the response to an aggressive cue).

Existentialism: A philosophical viewpoint emphasizing human existence and the human situation in the world that gives meaning to life through the free choice of mature values and commitment to responsible goals; the critical goal involves finding one's true self and living according to this potential.

Exogenous substances: Substances not normally occurring in the body, present only when administered; exogenous substances include substances such as drugs or synthetic test compounds mimicking endogenous substances.

Expectancy confirmation bias: Interpreting ambiguous information as being supportive of expectations; mistakenly "seeing" what is expected.

Expectancy theory: A cognitive motivation model which proposes that people choose to perform behaviors they believe to be the most likely to lead to positive outcomes; in work theory, workers are more motivated when they perceive congruence between their efforts, products, and rewards.

Experiment: One of several data collection methods; requires systematically manipulating the levels of an independent variable under controlled conditions in order to measure its impact on a dependent variable.

Experimenter bias: Biases introduced into a research study as a result of the expectations of the experimenter.

Expressive aphasia: Difficulties in expressing language, usually after damage to Broca's area in the left frontal lobe of the cerebral cortex.

External validity: The extent to which the results of a research study can be generalized to different populations, settings, or conditions.

Externalization: A defense mechanism in which one experiences unresolved, repressed inner turmoil as occurring outside oneself; holding external factors responsible for one's problems.

Extinction: A process by which the probability of a response is decreased; in classical or Pavlovian conditioning, a process in which the temporal contiguity of the conditioned stimulus and the unconditioned stimulus is disrupted and the learned association is lost; in operant or instrumental conditioning, a process in which undesirable behavior is not followed by reinforcement.

Extraneous variable: A variable that has a detrimental affect on a research study, making it difficult to determine if the result is attributable to the variable under study or to some unknown variable not controlled for; for example, in jury decision making, the effect of defendant attractiveness.

Extrinsic motivation: Motivation to perform an activity only because the activity leads to a valued outcome external to the activity itself.

Extrinsic religion: An immature religious orientation that uses religion for self-serving purposes such as security or a sense of social or economic well-being.

Factor analysis: A statistical technique wherein a set of correlated variables can be re-grouped in terms of the degree of commonality they share.

Family therapy: A type of psychotherapy that focuses on correcting the faulty interactions among family members that maintain children's psychological problems.

Farsightedness: An inability to focus clearly on nearby objects that is caused by the point of focus of the lens falling behind the retina.

Feminist analysis: The examination of the ways in which inequality, injustice, or oppression devalues women and/or limits their potential, both individually and collectively.

Fetal phase: The third period of prenatal development, extending from the ninth week of pregnancy until birth.

Fetishism: A sexual behavior in which a person becomes aroused by focusing on an inanimate object or a part of the human body.

Field research: An approach in which evidence is gathered in a "natural" setting, such as the workplace; by contrast, laboratory research involves an artificial, contrived setting.

Fight-or-flight syndrome: A sequence of physiological changes, described by Walter B. Cannon, that occurs in response to threat and prepares the organism to flee from or fight the threat; includes increases in heart rate, blood pressure, and respiration.

Fixation: In psychoanalytic theory, an inability to progress to the next level of psychosexual development because of overgratification or undergratification of desires at a particular stage.

Flashback: A type of traumatic reexperiencing in which a person becomes detached from reality and thinks, feels, and acts as if a previous traumatic experience were happening again.

Flocking: A defensive maneuver in many mammalian and bird species in which a scattered group of individuals implodes into a compact cluster at the approach of a predator.

Flooding: A type of therapy in which a phobic person imagines his or her most-feared situation until fear decreases.

Fluid intelligence: The form of intelligence that reflects speed of information processing, reasoning, and memory capacity rather than factual knowledge (crystallized intelligence); associated with Raymond Cattell.

Forebrain: A developmentally defined division of the brain that contains structures such as the cerebral hemispheres, the thalamus, and the hypothalamus.

Forensic psychology: The application of psychological skills in the legal profession—for example, in jury selection, sanity determination, and assessing competency to stand trial.

Forgetting: The loss of information from memory.

Formal operations: According to Piaget, the fourth stage of cognitive development, reached at adolescence; characterized by the ability to engage in abstract thinking, hypothetical constructs, and unobserved logical possibilities.

Fovea: The central part of the retina, which is densest in cone cells and is therefore the area of sharpest visual acuity.

Free association: The psychoanalytic method in which a patient talks spontaneously without restriction; thought to reveal repressed conflicts of the unconscious.

Frequency: The number of complete back-and-forth movements or pressure changes (cycles) from the rest or ambient state that occur each second; measured in units called hertz.

Frequency distribution: The pairing of a measurement or score with the number of people or subjects obtaining that measurement.

Frontal lobe: The anterior portion of each cerebral hemisphere, containing control of motor areas and most of the higher intellectual functions of the brain, including speech.

Frustration: A psychological state of arousal that results when a person is prevented from attaining a goal.

Frustration-aggression hypothesis: A concept pioneered by John Dollard stating that aggressive behavior is born of frustration in attempting to reach a goal.

Fugue state: A flight from reality in which the individual develops amnesia, leaves his or her present situation, travels to a new location, and establishes a new identity.

Function word: A word that has little meaning in itself yet signals grammatical relationships between other words in a sentence, such as an article ("the" or "a") or a preposition (for example, "in," "on," "of").

Functional autonomy: A concept, pioneered by Gordon W. Allport, that many adult motives are independent in purpose from their childhood origins.

Functional disorders: Signs and symptoms for which no organic or physiological basis can be found.

Functional fixedness: An inability to think of novel uses for objects because of a fixation on their usual functions.

Functionalism: An early school of American psychology that argued for the study of the human mind from the standpoint of understanding consciousness in terms of its purpose rather than its elements.

Fundamental attribution error: Underestimating the influence of situations and overestimating the influence of personality traits in causing behavior.

Fundamental frequency: The lowest frequency in a harmonic series of complex overtones; the overtones are integer multiples of the fundamental.

Gamete: A reproductive sex cell; the female cell is known as the ovum, and the male cell is known as the sperm.

Gamma-Aminobutyric acid (GABA): The most common neurotransmitter in the brain, derived from the amino acid glutamic acid; an inhibitor that seems to affect mood and emotion.

Gender: Social maleness or femaleness, reflected in the behaviors and characteristics that society expects from people of one biological sex.

Gender identity: A child's accurate labeling of himself or herself by gender; also, a person's inner sense of femaleness or maleness.

Gender schema: A general knowledge framework that organizes information and guides perceptions related to males and females.

Gene: The basic unit of heredity; a segment of a DNA molecule that contains hereditary instructions for an individual's physical traits and abilities and for the cell's production of proteins.

General adaptation syndrome: The three-stage physiological response pattern of the body to stress that was proposed by Hans Selye; the three stages are the alarm reaction, resistance stage, and exhaustion stage.

Generalization: The process by which behavior learned in one situation transfers to new situations.

Generativity: In Erikson's theory of personality, the seventh stage, associated with the desire to leave a legacy; the need to take care of future generations through the experiences of caring, nurturing, and educating.

Genetics: The biochemical basis of inherited characteristics.

Genital stage: In Freud's theory, the fifth psychosexual stage, beginning at adolescence and extending throughout adulthood; the individual learns to experience sexual gratification with a partner.

Genotype: The genetic makeup of an individual.

Gestalt: A German word, for which there is no precise translation, that is generally used to refer to a form, a whole, or a configuration.

Gestalt school of psychology: A school of psychology which maintains that the overall configuration of a stimulus array, rather than its individual elements, forms the basis of perception.

Gestalt therapy: A form of psychotherapy, initiated by Fritz Perls, that emphasizes awareness of the present and employs an active therapist-client relationship.

Giftedness: A marked ability to learn more rapidly, perform more intricate problems, and solve problems more rapidly than is normally expected for a given age; operationally defined as an IQ score above 130 on an individually administered test.

Goal setting: A motivational technique used to increase productivity in which employees are given specific performance objectives and time deadlines.

Gray matter: Unmyelinated neurons that make up the cerebral cortex, so called because they lack the fatty covering (myelin) found on neurons of the white matter.

Group dynamics: The study of how groups influence individual functioning.

Gustation: The sense of taste.

Gyrus: A convolution on the surface of the brain that results from the infolding of the cortex (surface).

Habit: An association or connection between a cue and a response, such as stopping (the response) at a red light (the cue).

Habituation: A decrease in response to repeated presentations of a stimulus that is not simply caused by fatigued sensory receptors.

Hallucinogen: A drug that can alter perception (vision and audition, in particular); examples include LSD, PCP, peyote, psilocybin, and possibly marijuana.

Hardiness: A constellation of behaviors and perceptions, characterized by perceptions of control, commitment, and challenge, that are thought to buffer the effects of stress; introduced by Suzanne Kobasa.

Hawthorne effect: A phenomenon that occurs when a subject's behavior changes after the subject discovers that he or she is being studied.

Hedonic: Associated with the seeking of pleasure and the avoidance of pain.

Helplessness: The belief that one has little or no control over the events in one's life; viewed by Martin Seligman as an important cause of depression.

Heredity: The transmission of characteristics from parent to offspring through genes in the chromosomes.

Heuristic: A shortcut or rule of thumb used for decision making or problem solving that often leads to, but does not guarantee, a correct response.

Higher-order conditioning: The linking of successive conditioned stimuli, the last of which elicits the conditioned response; higher-order associations are easily broken.

Hindbrain: A developmentally defined division of the brain that contains the pons, medulla, and cerebellum.

Hippocampus: A structure located in the temporal lobe (lateral cortical area) of the brain that has important memory functions.

Homeostasis: A term referring to the idea that the body tries to maintain steady states—that is, to maintain physiological characteristics within relatively narrow and optimum levels.

Homophobia: A fear, prejudice, or hatred toward homosexuals, usually based upon irrational stereotyping.

Hormone: A chemical "messenger," usually composed of protein or steroids, that is produced and secreted by an endocrine gland and released into the bloodstream; it targets specific genes in certain body tissue cells.

Hostile aggression: Aggressive behavior that is associated with anger and is intended to harm another.

Hue: The chromatic or color sensation produced by a certain wavelength of light.

Humanistic psychology: A branch of psychology that emphasizes the human tendencies toward growth and fulfillment, autonomy, choice, responsibility, and ultimate values such as truth, love, and justice; exemplified by the theories of Carl Rogers and Abraham Maslow.

Hypermetropia: Hereditary farsightedness caused by the length of the eyeball in the anterior-posterior direction being too short.

Hypnagogic hallucination: A vivid auditory or visual hallucination that occurs at the transition from wakefulness to sleep or from sleep to wakefulness; associated with narcolepsy.

Hypnosis: An altered state of consciousness brought on by special induction techniques (usually progressive relaxation instructions) and characterized by varying degrees of responsiveness to suggestions.

Hypnotic susceptibility: A subject's measured level of responsiveness to hypnotic suggestions on standardized scales.

Hypochondriasis: A psychological disorder in which the person is unrealistically preoccupied with the fear of disease and worries excessively about his or her health.

Hypothalamus: A small region near the base of the brain that controls the pituitary gland, autonomic nervous system, and behaviors important for survival, including eating, drinking, and temperature regulation.

Hypothesis: An educated guess about the relationship between two or more variables, derived from inductive reasoning; often tested by an experiment.

Iconic memory: Brief sensory memory for vision.

Id: The part of the psyche that contains the instincts and is directed solely by pleasure seeking; it is the most primitive part of the psyche and was thought by Freud to fuel the ego and superego.

Idealized self: Alienation from the real self that is characterized by grandiose, unrealistic conceptions of the self and unattainable standards; part of Karen Horney's psychology.

Identification: The internalization of parental or societal values, behaviors, and attitudes; in Freudian theory, a defense and resolution of incestuous feelings toward the opposite-sex parent that is important in the development of the superego.

Identity: A personal configuration of occupational, sexual, and ideological commitments; according to Erikson, the positive pole of the fifth stage of psychosocial development.

Identity crisis: According to Erikson, the central developmental issue in adolescence; encompasses a struggle between an integrated core identity and role confusion.

Idiographic study: The study of the unique patterns of the individual through methods such as case studies, autobiographies, and tests that examine patterns of behavior within a single person.

Illusions: Beliefs that are unsupported by evidence or that require facts to be perceived in a particular manner.

Imagery: The use of visualization to imagine the physical movements involved in executing a skill.

Imitation: The performance of behaviors that were learned by observing the actions of others.

Immune response: The body's response to invasion by disease-producing organisms; proteins (antibodies) are produced that mark the unwanted cells for destruction.

Immutable characteristics: Physical attributes (such as gender) that are present at birth and that other people assume gives them information as to the kind of person they are seeing.

Implosion therapy: A therapy in which the patient imagines his or her feared situation, plus elements from psychodynamic theory that the therapist thinks are related to the fear until fear decreases.

Impression management: The attempt to control the impressions of oneself that others form; synonymous with "self-presentation."

Imprinting: The innate behavioral attachment that a young animal forms with another individual (for example, its mother), with food, or with an object during a brief critical period shortly after birth; especially seen in ducks and chicks.

In-group: A social group to which a person belongs or with which a person is identified, thereby forming part of the self-concept.

In-group bias: The tendency to discriminate in favor of one's own group.

Incentive: A motivating force or system of rewards that is presented to an individual if he or she behaves or successfully performs specified tasks according to the norms of society; a goal object.

Incompetency: The legally established lack of sufficient knowledge and judgment to maintain a given right or responsibility.

Incongruence: In Rogers' theory, inconsistency or distortion between one's real and ideal self; a lack of genuineness.

Independent variable: The factor that is manipulated by the experimenter in order to assess its causal impact on the dependent variable.

Individual psychology: Alfred Adler's school of personality theory and therapy; stresses the unity of the individual and his or her striving for superiority to compensate for feelings of inferiority.

Induction: A type of logic by which one arrives at a general premise or conclusion based on generalization from a large number of known specific cases.

Industrial and organizational (I/O) psychology: The subfield of psychology that studies behavior in business and industry; practitioners analyze placement, training, and supervision of personnel, study organizational and communication structures, and explore ways to maximize efficiency.

Inflection: An addition to the stem of a word which indicates subtle modulations in meaning, such as plurality (more than one) or tense (present time or past time); in English, inflections are all suffixes.

Information processing model: The approach of most modern cognitive psychologists; it interprets cognition as the flow of information through interrelated stages (input, processing, storage, and retrieval) in much the same way that information is processed by a computer.

Innate: A term describing any inborn characteristic or behavior that is determined and controlled largely by the genes.

Insanity: A legal term for having a mental disease or defect so great that criminal intent or responsibility and punishability are not possible; it renders one incompetent.

Insight: A sudden mental inspiration or comprehension of a problem that was previously unsolved.

Insomnia: Difficulty in falling asleep or in remaining asleep for sufficient periods.

Instinct: An innate or inherited tendency that motivates a person or animal to act in often complex sequences without reasoning, instruction, or experience; in Freudian theory, a biological source of excitation that directs the development of personality into adulthood, such as the life instinct (Eros) and death instinct (Thanatos).

Institutional racism: The behavior patterns followed in organizations and in society at large that produce discrimination against members of racial minorities regardless of the prejudice or lack thereof of individuals.

Instrumental aggression: Aggressive behavior that is a by-product of another activity; instrumental aggression occurs only incidentally, as a means to another end.

Instrumental conditioning: The learning of the relationship between a voluntary action and the reinforcements or punishments that follow that action; also known as operant conditioning.

Integration: The function of most of the neurons of the cerebral cortex; summarizing incoming sensory information and producing a consensus as to what the nervous system will do next.

Intelligence: The ability to perform various mental tasks, including reasoning, knowledge, comprehension, memory, applying concepts, and manipulating figures; thought to reflect one's learning potential.

Intelligence quotient (IQ): A measure of a person's mental ability (as reflected by intelligence test scores) in comparison with the rest of the population at a comparable age.

Intensity: A measure of a physical aspect of a stimulus, such as the frequency of a sound or the brightness of a color.

Interest inventory: A type of test designed to determine areas of interest and enjoyment, often for the purpose of matching a person with a career.

Interference: The loss or displacement of a memory trace because of competing information that is presented.

Intermittent reinforcement: Any reinforcement schedule in which some but not all responses are rewarded; particularly difficult to extinguish.

Internal validity: The extent to which the dependent variable is caused by the independent variable; if relevant plausible rival alternative hypotheses can be ruled out, the study has strong internal validity.

Interneuron: A neuron that receives information from a sensory neuron and transmits a message to a motor neuron; very common in the brain and important in integration.

Interrater reliability: The obtained level of agreement between two observers when scoring the same observations with the same behavioral taxonomy.

Interval schedule: A schedule in which reinforcer delivery is contingent upon performance of a response after a specified amount of time has elapsed.

Intrinsic motivation: Motivation based on the desire to achieve or perform a task for its own sake, because it produces satisfaction or enjoyment, rather than for external rewards.

Introspection: The self-report of one's own sensations, perceptions, experiences, and thoughts; analyses of and reports on the content of one's own conscious experiences.

Irradiation: Nervous excitement generated in a specific brain center by an unconditioned stimulus that spreads to surrounding areas of the cerebral cortex.

Kinesthetic: Related to the sensation of body position, presence, or movement, resulting mostly from the stimulation of sensory nerves in muscles, tendons, and joints.

Korsakoff syndrome: Alcohol-induced brain damage that causes disorientation, impaired long-term memory, and production of false memories to fill memory gaps.

Latency: In Freud's theory, the period between approximately age six and adolescence, when sexual instincts are not strongly manifested; strictly speaking, not a psychosexual stage.

Latent content: According to psychoanalytic theory, the hidden content of a dream, camouflaged by the manifest content.

Lateral geniculate nucleus: A subdivision of the thalamus in the brain, which receives the nerve impulse from the retina; it assembles visual information.

Laterality: Specialization by sides of almost symmetrical structures; speech is lateralized in human brains, because it is mainly controlled by the left hemispheres of almost all right-handed people.

Law of effect: Thorndike's basic law of instrumental conditioning, which holds that responses followed by certain events will be either more or less likely to recur.

Leakage: Nonverbal behavior that reveals information that a person wishes to conceal; especially useful in deception detection.

Learned helplessness: The hypothesized result of experiences in which behavior performed seems to bear no relationship to the appearance or control of a stressor.

Learning: A modification in behavior as the result of experience that involves changes in the nervous system which are not caused by fatigue, maturation, or injury.

Lesion: Damage or injury to brain tissue that is caused by disease or trauma or produced experimentally using mechanical, electrical, or chemical methods.

Levels-of-processing model: The perspective that holds that how well something is remembered is based on how elaborately incoming information is mentally processed.

Libido: The energy used to direct behavior that is pleasurable either for the self or others; directed toward the self, it results in self-gratification, follows the pleasure principle, and is immature.

Limbic system: An integrated set of cerebral structures (including the amygdala, hypothalamus, hippocampus, and septal area) that play a vital role in the regulation of emotion and motivation.

Linguistic relativity hypothesis: The idea that the structure of particular languages that people speak affects the way they perceive the world.

Linguistics: A field of inquiry that focuses on the underlying structure of language; linguists study phonology (the sound system), syntax (sentence structure), and semantics (meaning), among other topics.

Lipids: Fats and oils.

Lithium carbonate: An alkaline compound that modulates the intensity of mood swings and is particularly effective in the dampening of symptoms of manic excitability.

Loci method: A serial-recall mnemonic consisting of visualizing items to be remembered along a known path of distinct locations.

Locus of control: Beliefs concerning the sources of power over one's life; persons who believe they can generally control the direction of their lives have an internal locus of control, whereas those who believe that their lives are influenced more by fate have an external locus of control.

Long-term memory: A memory system of unlimited capacity that consists of more or less permanent knowledge.

Longitudinal study: A research methodology that requires the testing of the same subjects repeatedly over a specified period of time.

Loudness: The strength of sound as heard; related to sound pressure level but also affected by frequency.

Magnitude estimation: A technique for measuring perceptual experience by having persons assign numbers to indicate the "magnitude" of an experience.

Main effect: A statistically significant difference in behavior related to different levels of a variable and not affected by any other variable.

Major depressive episode: A disorder of mood and functioning, meeting clearly specified criteria and present for at least two weeks, which is characterized by dysphoric mood or apathy.

Mania: A phase of bipolar disorder in which the mood is one of elation, euphoria, or irritability; a disorder in which manic symptoms occur, including hyperactivity, agitation, restlessness, and grandiosity, and then are followed by a return to a normal mood state.

Manifest content: In Freudian theory, the content of a dream just as it is experienced or recalled; masks the dream's latent content.

Masculine protest: The denying of inferiority feelings through rebelliousness, violence, or maintaining a tough exterior.

Maturation: Development attributable to one's genetic timetable rather than to experience.

Mean: The arithmetic average of all the data measuring one characteristic; it can be used as a descriptive or inferential statistic.

Mechanoreceptor: A sensory receptor that is sensitive to mechanical stimulation, such as touch, movement of a joint, or stretching of a muscle.

Medical model: A view in which abnormality consists of a number of diseases that originate in bodily functions, especially in the brain, and have defined symptoms, treatments, and outcomes.

Medulla oblongata: The bulbous portion of the brain stem that directly connects with the spinal cord; controls cardiac and respiratory activity.

Melatonin: A hormone produced by the pineal gland within the forebrain that is usually released into the blood during the night phase of the light-dark cycle.

Memory: The mental processes that are involved in storing and recalling previously experienced images, information, and events.

Mere exposure: A psychological phenomenon in which liking tends to increase as a person sees more of something or someone.

Meta-analysis: A set of quantitative (statistical) procedures used to evaluate a body of empirical literature.

Metastasis: The transfer of disease from one part of the body to an unrelated part, often through the bloodstream or lymphatic system.

Midbrain: The section of the brain just above the hindbrain; influences auditory and visual processes and arousal.

Middle temporal gyrus (MT): The region of the occipital lobe in which motion perception is integrated.

Midlife crisis: A sense of reevaluation, and sometimes panic, that strikes some individuals during middle age; impulsive behavior, reassessment of goals, and career changes can result.

Mind-body problem: A psychological question originating from philosophy and religion that concerns how to understand the relationship between a physical body or brain and a nonphysical mind or subjective experience.

Mineralocorticoids: The proinflammatory hormones aldosterone and desoxycorticosterone, secreted by the adrenal cortex and having a role in salt metabolism.

Misattribution: Attributing an event to any factor other than the true cause.

Mnemonics: Strategies for improving memory through placing information in an organized context.

Monoamine oxidase (MAO) inhibitors: A class of antidepressant drugs.

Monoamines: A group of neurotransmitters derived from a single amino acid; they include serotonin and the catecholamines.

Monocular cue: A visual cue available to each eye separately; often used by artists to portray depth.

Monosynaptic reflex: A reflex system that consists of only one synapse, the synapse between the sensory input and motor output.

Monotic: Referring to the stimulation of only one ear.

Morpheme: The smallest part of a word that has a discernible meaning.

Morphology: The rules in a given language that govern how morphemes can be combined to form words.

Motivation: A hypothetical construct used to explain behavior and its direction, intensity, and persistence.

Motor neurons: The cells of the central nervous system responsible for causing muscular activity.

Multiple personality disorder: A rare mental disorder characterized by the development and existence of two or more relatively unique and independent personalities in the same individual.

Myopia: Hereditary nearsightedness caused by the length of the eyeball in the anteriorposterior direction being too long.

Nanometer: A billionth of a meter.

Narcolepsy: A condition in which an individual is prone to fall suddenly into a deep sleep.

Nativism: A philosophy which holds that knowledge is innate and that the neonate enters the world prepared for certain kinds of environmental inputs.

Natural selection: The process by which those characteristics of a species that help it to survive or adapt to its environment tend to be passed along by members that live long enough to have offspring.

Need: A state of an organism attributable to deprivation of a biological or psychological requirement; it is related to a disturbance in the homeostatic state.

Negative reinforcement: The procedure whereby the probability of a response is increased by the contingent removal of an aversive stimulus.

Neo-Freudian: A term for psychoanalysts who place more emphasis on security and interpersonal relations as determining human behavior than on the exclusively biological theories of Freud; Neo-Freudians include Adler, Jung, Horney, Sullivan, and Erikson.

Nerve impulse: Electrical activity transmitted through a nerve fiber.

Nervous system: An array of billions of neurons (conducting nerve cells) that transmits electrical information throughout the body and thereby controls practically all bodily processes.

Neurologist: A physician who specializes in the diagnosis and treatment of disorders of the nervous system.

Neuron: An individual nerve cell, the basic unit of the nervous system; receives and transmits electrical information and consists of a cell body, dendrites, and an axon.

Neuropsychology: The study of brain-behavior relationships, usually by using behavioral tests and correlating results with brain areas.

Neuropsychopharmacology: The field of study of the relationship among behavior, neuronal functioning, and drugs.

Neurosis: Any functional disorder of the mind or the emotions, occurring without obvious brain damage and involving anxiety, phobic responses, or other abnormal behavior symptoms.

Neurotransmitter: A chemical substance released from one nerve cell that communicates activity by binding to and changing the activity of another nerve cell, muscle, or gland; some stimulate, others inhibit.

Nomothetic study: A research approach that compares groups of people in order to identify general principles; the dominant method of personality research.

Nonparticipant observation: A field technique in which the researcher passively observes the behavior of the subjects, trying not to get involved in the setting.

Nonverbal communication: Communication through any means other than words; includes facial expression, tone of voice, and posture.

Normal distribution: A bell-shaped curve that often provides an accurate description of the distribution of scores obtained in research; it forms the basis of many statistical tests.

Observational learning: Learning that results from observing other people's behavior and its consequences.

Observational study: A research technique in which a scientist systematically watches for and records occurrences of the phenomena under study without actively influencing them.

Obsessions: Intrusive, recurrent, anxiety-provoking thoughts, ideas, images, or impulses that interfere with an individual's daily functioning.

Obsessive-compulsive disorder: A chronic, debilitating anxiety disorder characterized by continuous obsessive thinking and frequent compulsive behaviors.

Occipital lobe: The posterior portion of each cerebral hemisphere, where visual stimuli are received and integrated.

Oedipal complex: In Freudian theory, sexual attraction to the parent of the opposite sex, and jealousy of and fear of retribution from the parent of the same sex; first manifested in the phallic stage (in girls, sometimes called the "Electra complex").

Olfaction: The sense of smell.

Operant: The basic response unit in instrumental conditioning; a response which, when emitted, operates upon its environment and is instrumental in providing some consequences.

Operant conditioning: Learning in which a behavior increases or decreases depending on whether the behavior is followed by reward or punishment; also known as instrumental conditioning.

Operational definition: A description of a measurement or manipulation in terms that are unambiguous, observable, and easily identified.

Opiates: A class of drugs that relieve pain; opiates include morphine, heroin, and several naturally occurring peptides.

Oral stage: In Freudian theory, the first stage of psychosexual development, from birth to approximately age two; sexual energy focuses on the mouth, and conflicts may arise over nursing, biting, or chewing.

Organic disorder: A symptomatology with a known physiological or neurological basis.

Organizational effects: The early and permanent effects of a hormone; for example, the sex hormones, which produce differentiation in the developing embryo of primordial gonads, internal reproductive structures, and external genitalia.

Ossicle: Any of the three bones of the middle ear (the hammer, anvil, and stirrup) that are involved in conduction of sound into the inner ear.

Out-group: Any social group to which an individual does not belong and which, as a consequence, may be viewed in a negative way.

Overextension: The application of a word to more objects than ordinary adult usage allows; for example, when children refer to all small four-legged animals as "dog."

Overjustification effect: The tendency of external factors that are perceived to be controlling an individual's behavior to undermine the individual's intrinsic motivation to engage in that behavior.

Overtone: One of several sine waves simultaneously generated by most sound sources; these pure tones are all integer multiples of the fundamental.

Papilla: A small bundle of taste receptor cells surrounded by supportive cells and communicating with the exterior through a small pore.

Paradoxical intervention: A therapeutic technique in which a therapist gives a patient or family a task that appears to contradict the goals of treatment.

Parallel distributed processing (PDP): A neurally inspired model in which information is processed in a massively parallel and interactive network; the course of processing is determined by the connection strengths between units of the network.

Paranoia: A psychosis characterized by delusions, particularly delusions of persecution, and pervasive suspiciousness; paranoia rarely involves hallucinations.

Parasympathetic nervous system: A branch of the autonomic nervous system; responsible for maintaining or reestablishing homeostasis.

Parietal lobe: The side and upper-middle part of each cerebral hemisphere and the site of sensory reception from the skin, muscles, and other areas; also contains part of the general interpretive area.

Pavlovian conditioning: Learning in which two stimuli are presented one after the other, and the response to the first changes because of the response automatically elicited by the second; also called classical conditioning.

Penis envy: In Freudian theory, the strong envy that females develop of the male organ because they subconsciously believe they have been castrated; Freud proposed that penis envy dominates the female personality.

Perception: The psychological process by which information that comes in through the sense organs is meaningfully interpreted by the brain.

Perceptual constancy: The tendency to perceive figures as constant and stable in terms of shape, color, size, or brightness.

Peripheral nervous system: All the nerves located outside the bones of the skull and spinal cord.

Persona: A major Jungian archetype representing one's public personality; the mask that one wears in order to be acceptable to society at large.

Personality: An individual's unique collection of behavioral responses (physical, emotional, and intellectual) that are consistent across time and situations.

Personality disorder: A disorder involving deep-rooted behavior patterns that are inflexible and maladaptive and that cause distress in an individual's relationships with others.

Personality trait: A stable disposition to behave in a given way over time and across situations.

Phallic stage: In Freudian theory, the third stage of psychosexual development, from approximately age four to age six; sexual energy focuses on the genitals.

Phenomenology: An approach that stresses openness to direct experience in introspective or unsophisticated ways, without using analysis, theory, expectations, or interpretation.

Pheromone: A hormone or other chemical that is produced and released from the tissues of one individual and targets tissues in another individual, usually with a consciously or unconsciously detectable scent.

Phobia: An anxiety disorder involving an intense irrational fear of a particular thing (such as horses) or situation (such as heights).

Phoneme: A minimal unit of sound that can signal a difference in meaning.

Phonology: The specification for a given language of which speech sounds may occur and how they may be combined, as well as the pitch and stress patterns that accompany words and sentences.

Photoreceptor: A specialized nerve cell that can transform light into a neural message; rods are specialized for black-and-white vision, cones for color vision.

Pineal gland: A light-sensitive endocrine gland that is located toward the back of the brain and that controls reproductive cycles in many mammalian species.

Pitch: The highness or lowness of a sound as heard; related to frequency but also affected by loudness.

Pituitary: An endocrine gland located in the brain that controls several other endocrine glands and that cooperates with the hypothalamus of the nervous system in controlling physiology.

Placebo: A substance or treatment (such as a pill or an injection) that has no intrinsic effect but is presented as having some effect.

Placebo effect: The relief of pain or the causing of a desired behavioral effect as a result of a patient's belief that a substance or treatment which has no known psychological or biological effect will in fact be effective; for example, a sugar pill may relieve a backache if given by a trusted doctor.

Plasticity: The ability of neurons and neural networks to grow into specific patterns based partially upon the organism's genetics and partially upon the organism's learned experience; in the brain, neurons can modify the structural organization in order to compensate for neural damage.

Play therapy: A system of individual psychotherapy in which children's play is utilized to explain and reduce symptoms of their psychological disorders.

Pons: A part of the brain stem that serves as the nerve connection between the cerebellum and the brain stem.

Population: All members of a specified group that a researcher is interested in studying.

Positive reinforcement: A procedure used to increase the frequency of a response by presenting a favorable consequence following the response.

Positron emission tomography (PET) scanning: A brain-imaging technique that allows blood flow, energy metabolism, and chemical activity to be visualized in the living human brain.

Post-traumatic stress disorder (PTSD): A pathological condition caused by severe stress such as an earthquake or a divorce; it has an acute stage and a chronic stage, and symptoms involve reexperiencing the traumatic event.

Postsynaptic potential: A chemical stimulus produced in a postsynaptic cell; may excite the cell to come nearer to electrical firing, or may inhibit firing.

Power law: A statement of the lawful relationship between two variables that expresses one of them as the other raised to some exponent.

Pragmatism: A philosophical position that provided the framework of functionalism by proposing that the value of something lies in its usefulness.

Prejudice: Liking or disliking of persons based on their category or group membership rather than on their individual personalities; predominantly refers to unfavorable reactions.

Preoperational stage: In Piaget's theory, a transitional stage of the preschool child (ages two to seven, approximately), after mental representations (symbols) are acquired but before they can be logically manipulated.

Preparedness: The idea that, through evolution, animals have been genetically prepared to learn certain things important to their survival.

Presbyopia: Farsightedness resulting from decreased flexibility of the lens of the eye and other age-related factors.

Primacy effect: The tendency for things that are seen or received first to be better recalled and more influential than things that come later.

Primary motive: A motive that arises from innate, biological needs and that must be met for survival.

Primary reinforcer: A stimulus that acts as a natural, unlearned reinforcer.

Primary sex characteristics: The physiological features of the sex organs.

Priming: An increase in the availability of certain types of information in memory in response to a stimulus.

Prisoner's dilemma: A laboratory game used by psychologists to study the comparative strategies of cooperation and competition.

Probability: The proportion of times a particular event will occur; also, the study of uncertainty that is the foundation of inferential statistics.

Progesterone: A female sex hormone secreted by the corpus luteum of the ovary; maintains the lining of the uterus during pregnancy and the second half of the menstrual cycle.

Programmed instruction: A self-paced training program characterized by many small, increasingly difficult lessons separated by frequent tests.

Progressive muscle relaxation: A relaxation technique that systematically works through all the major muscle groups of the body by first tensing, then relaxing each group and paying attention to the changes.

Projective task: Any task that provides an open-ended response that may reveal aspects of one's personality; tasks or tests commonly include standard stimuli that are ambiguous in nature.

Proposition: A mental representation based on the underlying structure of language; a proposition is the smallest unit of knowledge that can be stated.

Prosocial behavior: Behavior intended to benefit another; can be motivated by either egoistic or altruistic concern.

Prototype: A "best example" of a concept—one that contains the most typical features of that concept.

Proxemics: The use of space as a special elaboration of culture; it is usually divided into the subfields of territory and personal space.

Proximo-distal development: Motor development that proceeds from the center of the body to its periphery.

Psychoactive drugs: Chemical substances that act on the brain to create psychological effects; usually classified as depressants, stimulants, narcotics (opiates), hallucinogens, or antipsychotics.

Psychoanalytic theory: A set of theories conceived by Sigmund Freud that see the roots of human behavior and mental disorders in unconscious motivation and early adulthood conflict.

Psychobiology: The study of the interactions between biological and psychological processes.

Psychogenic disorder: An illness that is attributable primarily to a psychological conflict or to emotional stress.

Psychometrics: The theory or technique of psychological measurement; the measurement of psychological differences among people and the statistical analysis of those differences.

Psychophysics: The study of the relationship between physical units of a stimulus, such as amplitude, and its sensory, experienced qualities, such as loudness.

Psychophysiology: The study of the interaction between the psyche (mind and emotions) and the physiology (physical processes such as blood pressure and heart rate) of the organism.

Psychosis: A general term referring to a severe mental disorder, with or without organic damage, characterized by deterioration of normal intellectual and social function and by partial or complete withdrawal from reality; includes schizophrenia and mood disorders such as bipolar disorder.

Psychosocial crisis: In Erikson's theory, a turning point in the process of development precipitated by the individual having to face a new set of social demands and new social relationships.

Psychosomatic disorder: A physical disorder that results from, or is worsened by, psychological factors; synonymous with psychophysiological disorder and includes stress-related disorders.

Psychosurgery: Brain surgery conducted to alter an inappropriate or maladaptive behavior.

Psychotherapy: A general category of treatment techniques for mental disorders; most psychotherapy uses talking as a tool and centers on the client-psychotherapist relationship to develop awareness and provide support.

Punishment: The procedure of decreasing the probability of a behavior by the response-contingent delivery of an aversive stimulus.

Pure tone: A sound produced by a vibration of a single frequency, the amplitude of which changes over time as a sinusoidal function; a sine wave.

Quasi-experiment: An experiment that does not allow subjects to be assigned randomly to treatment conditions.

Random assignment: The most common technique for establishing equivalent groups by balancing subject characteristics through the assigning of subjects to groups through some random process.

Rapid eye movement (REM) sleep: A special stage of sleep that involves desynchronized electrical brain activity, muscle paralysis, rapid eye movements, and narrative dream recall.

Ratio schedule: A reinforcement schedule in which reinforcer delivery is contingent upon the performance of a specified number of responses.

Rational-emotive therapy: A cognitive-based psychotherapy, pioneered by Albert Ellis, that attempts to replace or modify a client's irrational, inappropriate, or problematic thought processes, outlooks, and self-concept.

Realistic conflict theory: A theory from social psychology that suggests that direct competition for scarce or valued resources can lead to prejudice.

Receptive aphasia: Difficulties in comprehending spoken and written material, usually after damage to Wernicke's area in the left temporal lobe of the cerebral cortex.

Receptive field: The region and pattern in space to which a single neuron responds.

Receptor: A specific protein structure on a target cell to which a neurotransmitter binds, producing a stimulatory or inhibitory response.

Recessive gene: A gene whose corresponding trait will not be expressed unless the gene is paired with another recessive gene for that trait.

Reciprocal determinism: An interactional model proposing that environment, personal factors, and behavior all operate as interacting determinants of one another.

Reductionism: An aspect of the scientific method which seeks to understand complex and often interactive processes by reducing them to more basic components and principles.

Reflex: An unlearned and automatic biologically programmed response to a particular stimulus.

Reflex arc: The simplest behavioral response, in which an impulse is carried by a sensory neuron to the spinal cord, crosses a synapse to a motor neuron, and stimulates a response.

Regression: An ego defense mechanism that a person uses to return to an earlier stage of development when experiencing stress or conflict.

Regulators: Facial gestures and expressions by listeners that are informative for speakers; they convey comprehension or acceptance, or indicate when the other person may speak.

Reinforcement: An operation or process that increases the probability that a learned behavior will be repeated.

Reinforcer: A stimulus or event that, when delivered contingently upon a response, will increase the probability of the recurrence of that response.

Relative deprivation: The proposition that people's attitudes, aspirations, and grievances largely depend on the frame of reference within which they are conceived.

Reliability: The consistency of a psychological measure, which can be assessed by means of stability over repeated administrations or agreement among different observers.

Representativeness: A heuristic in which an estimate of the probability of an event or sample is determined by the degree to which it resembles the originating process or population.

Repression: In psychoanalytic theory, a defense mechanism that keeps unacceptable thoughts and impulses from becoming conscious.

Response cost: Negative consequences that follow the commission of an undesired behavior, decreasing the rate at which the misbehavior will recur.

Response hierarchy: An arrangement of alternative responses to a cue, in a hierarchy from that most likely to occur to that least likely to occur.

Resting membrane potential: The maintenance of difference in electrical charges between the inside and outside of a neuron's cell membrane, keeping it polarized with closed ion channels.

Retardation: A condition wherein a person has mental abilities that are far below average; other skills and abilities, such as adaptive behavior, may also be marginal; measured by an IQ score of less than 70.

Reticular formation: A core of neurons extending through the medulla, pons, and midbrain that controls arousal and sleeping/waking, as well as motor functions such as muscle tone and posture.

Retina: The light-sensitive area at the back of the eye, containing the photoreceptors (rods and cones) that detect light.

Retrieval: The process of locating information stored in memory and bringing it into awareness.

Retrograde amnesia: The type of amnesia that involves an inability to remember things that occurred before the onset of the amnesia.

Rhodopsin: The visual pigment in the cells of the rods that responds to light.

Rod: A photoreceptor of the retina specialized for the detection of light without discrimination of color.

Role: A social position that is associated with a set of behavioral expectations.

Role Construct Repertory Test: George A. Kelly's test for determining the nature of a person's system of constructs and psychological problems, which are related to significant others in the life of the person.

Rule-governed behavior: Behavior that is under the discriminative control of formalized contingencies.

Sample: A subset of a population; a group of elements selected from a larger, well-defined pool of elements.

Sampling error: The extent to which population parameters deviate from a sample statistic.

Satiety: A feeling of fullness and satisfaction.

Schema: An active organization of prior knowledge, beliefs, and experience which is used in perceiving the environment, retrieving information from memory, and directing behavior (plural, schemata).

Schizophrenia: Any of a group of psychotic reactions characterized by withdrawal from reality with accompanying affective, behavioral, and intellectual disturbances, including illusions and hallucinations.

Schwann cell: A type of insulating nerve cell that wraps around neurons located peripherally throughout the organism.

Script: An event schema in which a customary sequence of actions, actors, and props is specified; for example, behavior at a restaurant.

Seasonal affective disorder (SAD): Bipolar disorder that undergoes a seasonal fluctuation resulting from various factors, including seasonal changes in the intensity and duration of sunlight.

Secondary reinforcement: A learned reinforcer that has acquired reinforcing qualities by being paired with other reinforcers.

Secondary sex characteristics: Physical features other than genitals that differentiate women and men; for example, facial hair.

Self: The unified and integrated center of one's experience and awareness, which one experiences both subjectively, as an actor, and objectively, as a recipient of actions.

Self-actualization: A biologically and culturally determined process involving a tendency toward growth and full realization of one's potential, characterized by acceptance, autonomy, accuracy, creativity, and community; pioneered by Abraham Maslow.

Self-concept: The sum total of the attributes, abilities, attitudes, and values that an individual believes defines who he or she is.

Self-efficacy: The perception or judgment of one's ability to perform a certain action successfully or to control one's circumstances.

Self-esteem: The evaluative part of the self-concept; one's feeling of self-worth.

Self-image: The self as the individual pictures or imagines it.

Self-perception: A psychological process whereby individuals infer the nature of their attitudes and beliefs by observing their own behavior.

Semantic memory: The long-term representation of a person's factual knowledge of the world.

Semicircular canals: The three structures in the inner ear that together signal acceleration of the head in any direction.

Sensation: The process by which the nervous system and sensory receptors receive and represent stimuli received from the environment.

Sensorimotor stage: The first of Piaget's developmental stages, lasting from birth to about two years of age, during which objects become familiar and are interpreted by appropriate habitual, motor, and sensory processes.

Sensory memory: The persistence of a sensory impression for less than a second; it allows the information to be processed further.

Serial processing: A theory concerning how people scan information in memory that suggests that as the number of items in memory increases, so does the amount of time taken to determine whether an item is present in memory.

Set point: An organism's personal homeostatic level for a particular body weight, which results from factors such as early feeding experiences and heredity.

Sex: Biological maleness or femaleness, determined by genetic endowment and hormones.

Sex typing: The process of acquiring traits, attitudes, and behaviors seen culturally as appropriate for members of one's gender; gender-role acquisition.

Sexual instinct: In Freud's theory, the innate tendency toward pleasure seeking, particularly through achieving sexual aims and objects.

Shaping: The acquiring of instrumental behavior in small steps or increments through the reinforcement of successively closer approximations to the desired final behavior.

Short-term memory: A memory system of limited capacity that uses rehearsal processes either to retain current memories or to pass them on to long-term memory.

Significance level: The degree of likelihood that research results are attributable to chance.

Skinner box: The most commonly used apparatus for studying instrumental conditioning; manipulation of a lever (for rats, monkeys, or humans) or an illuminated disk (for pigeons) produces consequences.

Social categorization: The classification of people and groups according to attributes that are personally meaningful.

Social cognition: The area of social psychology concerned with how people make sense of social events, including the actions of others.

Social comparison: Comparing attitudes, skills, and feelings with those of similar people in order to determine relative standing in a group or the acceptability of one's own positions.

Social facilitation: The enhancement of a person's most dominant response as a result of the presence of others; for some tasks, such as simple ones, performance is enhanced, while for others, such as novel tasks, performance is impaired.

Social identity theory: A theory maintaining that people are motivated to create and maintain a positive identity in terms of personal qualities and, especially, group memberships.

Social learning theory: The approach to personality that emphasizes the learning of behavior via observations and direct reward; exemplified by the theories of Albert Bandura, Walter Mischel, and Julian Rotter.

Social loafing: The tendency to expend less effort while in the presence of others; most likely to occur on additive tasks in which one's individual effort is obscured as a result of the collective efforts of the group.

Social phobia: A condition characterized by fear of the possible scrutiny or criticism of others.

Social psychology: A subfield of psychology that studies how individuals are affected by environmental factors and particularly by other people.

Social support: The relationships with other people that provide emotional, informational, or tangible resources that affect one's health and psychological comfort.

Socialization: The process of learning and internalizing social rules and standards.

Sociobiology: The application of the principles of evolutionary biology to the understanding of social behavior.

Somatization disorder: A mental syndrome in which a person chronically has a number of vague but dramatic medical complaints that apparently have no physical cause.

Somatoform disorders: A group of mental disorders in which a person has physical complaints or symptoms that appear to be caused by psychological rather than physical factors; for example, hypochondriasis.

Somnambulism: The scientific term for sleepwalking; formerly a term for hypnosis.

Spectrum analysis: The ability of a system, such as hearing, to decompose a complex wave into its sine-wave components and their respective amplitudes.

Spinal cord: The part of the central nervous system that is enclosed within the backbone; conducts nerve impulses to and from the brain.

Spontaneous recovery: The recovery of extinguished behaviors over time in the absence of any specific treatment or training.

Sports psychology: The subfield of psychology that applies psychological principles to physical activities such as competitive sports; frequently concerned with maximizing athletic performance.

Sprouting: A process that occurs when remaining nerve fibers branch and form new connections to replace those that have been lost.

Stage theory of development: The belief that development moves through a set sequence of stages; the quality of behavior at each stage is unique but is dependent upon movement through earlier stages.

Standard deviation: A measure of how variable or spread out a group of scores is from the mean.

Standardization: The administration, scoring, and interpretation of a test in a prescribed manner so that differences in test results can be attributed to the testee.

Statistical significance: Differences in behavior large enough that they are probably related to the subject variables or manipulated variables—differences too large to be caused by chance alone.

Stereogram: A two-dimensional image that appears three-dimensional when viewed binocularly, typically consisting of two images of the same scene as viewed from slightly disparate viewpoints; when special glasses are worn, the images are fused into one image with the full three-dimensional effect.

Stereotype: A set of beliefs, often rigidly held, about the characteristics of an entire group.

Stimulants: Drugs that cause behavioral and/or physiological stimulation, including amphetamines, cocaine, and their respective derivatives; caffeine; nicotine; and some antidepressants.

Stimulus: An environmental circumstance to which an organism may respond; it may be as specific as a physical event or as global as a social situation.

Stimulus generalization: The ability of stimuli that are similar to other stimuli to elicit a response that was previously elicited only by the first stimuli.

Storage: The stage of memory between encoding and retrieval; the period for which memories are held.

Strange situation: A particular experimental technique designed to measure the quality of the mother-infant attachment relationship.

Stress: The judgment that a problem exceeds one's available resources, resulting from a primary appraisal of the problem and a secondary appraisal of the coping resources.

Stressor: Anything that produces a demand on an organism.

Striate cortex: The region of the occipital lobe that reconstitutes visual images for recognition.

Stroke: A vascular accident resulting from either the rupture of a vessel or the blocking of blood flow in an artery.

Structuralism: An early school of psychology that sought to define the basic elements of mind and the laws governing their combination.

Sublimation: According to Freud, a defense mechanism by which a person may redirect aggressive impulses by engaging in a socially sanctioned activity.

Suffix: A morpheme that attaches to the end of a word.

Superego: In Freudian theory, the part of the psyche that contains parental and societal standards of morality and that acts to prohibit expression of instinctual drives; includes the conscience and the ego-ideal.

Syllogism: A logical argument constructed of a major premise, a minor premise, and a conclusion, the validity of which is determined by rules of inference.

Symbiotic relationship: An overprotective, often enmeshed relationship between a parent and child.

Sympathetic nervous system: A division of the autonomic nervous system that prepares the organism for energy expenditure.

Synapse: The junction between two neurons over which a nerve impulse is chemically transduced.

Synchronized electroencephalogram: A regular, repetitive brain-wave pattern that is caused by multitudes of neurons firing at the same time and the same rate in a given brain region.

Systematic desensitization: An exposure therapy in which the phobic person is gradually presented with a feared object or situation.

Systems theory: A concept in which the family grouping is viewed as a biosocial subsystem existing within the larger system of society; intrafamilial communications are the mechanisms of subsystem interchange.

Tachistoscope: An experimental apparatus for presenting visual information very briefly to the right or left visual field; sometimes called a T-scope.

Tardive dyskinesia: Slow, involuntary motor movements, especially of the mouth and tongue, which can become permanent and untreatable; can result from psychoactive drug treatment.

Temporal lobe: The lower portion on the side of each cerebral hemisphere, containing the sites of sensory interpretation, memory of visual and auditory patterns, and part of the general interpretive area.

Test-retest reliability: A common way of determining consistency, by administering the same test twice to the same persons.

Testosterone: The principal male sex hormone produced by the testes.

Thalamus: A portion of the diencephalon, located at the base of the forebrain, which receives sensory information from the body and relays these signals to the appropriate regions of the cerebrum.

Thematic Apperception Test (TAT): A personality test in which individuals demonstrate their needs by describing what is happening in a series of ambiguous pictures.

Theory: A model explaining the relationship between several phenomena; derived from several related hypotheses which have survived many tests.

Therapy: The systematic habilitation of a disorder.

Thermoreceptor: A sensory receptor specialized for the detection of changes in the flow of heat.

Threshold: The minimum stimulus intensity necessary for an individual to detect a stimulus; usually defined as that intensity detected 50 percent of the time it is presented.

Thyroxine: The major hormone produced and secreted by the thyroid gland; stimulates protein synthesis and the basal metabolic rate.

Timbre: The sound quality produced by the respective amplitude and frequency of the overtones, or underlying sine waves that make up a complex wave.

Top-down processing: A situation in which a person's perception of a stimulus is influenced by nonstimulus factors such as the person's general knowledge, beliefs, or expectations.

Trait theory: A way of conceptualizing personality in terms of relatively persistent and consistent behavior patterns that are manifested in a wide range of circumstances.

Transduction: The process of changing physical energy, such as light, into neural messages.

Transference: The phenomenon in which a person in psychoanalysis shifts thoughts or emotions concerning people in his or her past (most often parents) onto the analyst.

Transvestite: A person who, for fun or sexual arousal, often dresses and acts like a member of the opposite sex (going "in drag"); most are heterosexual males.

Tricyclics: A class of antidepressant drugs.

Turner's syndrome: A condition in which there is only one X sex chromosome, with no second female X or male Y; causes the development of female structures.

Two-factor theory: A behavioral theory of anxiety stating that fear is caused by Pavlovian conditioning and that avoidance of the feared object is maintained by operant conditioning.

Type A personality: A behavior pattern that describes individuals who are driven, competitive, high-strung, impatient, time-urgent, intense, and easily angered; some researchers have associated this pattern with increased risk of heart disease.

Unconditional positive regard: The attempt by a therapist to convey to a client that he or she genuinely cares for the client.

Unconditioned response (UR): An innate or unlearned behavior that occurs automatically following some stimulus; a reflex.

Unconditioned stimulus (US): A stimulus that elicits an unconditioned response; the relation between unconditioned stimuli and unconditioned responses is unlearned.

Unconscious: The deep-rooted aspects of the mind; Freud claimed that it includes negative instincts and urges that are too disturbing for people to be aware of consciously.

Unipolar depression: A disorder characterized by the occurrence of one or more major depressive episodes but no manic episodes.

Validity: A statistical value that tells the degree to which a test measures what it is intended to measure; the test is usually compared to external criteria.

Vicarious learning: Learning (for example, learning to fear something) without direct experience, either by observing or by receiving verbal information.

Visual cortex: The top six cell layers in the back of the brain, which are specialized for organizing and interpreting visual information.

Visual dyslexia: The lack of ability to translate observed written or printed language into meaningful terms.

Voyeurism: The derivation of sexual pleasure from looking at the naked bodies or sexual activities of others without their consent.

Wavelength: The distance traveled by a wave front in the time given by one cycle (the period of the wave); has an inverse relation to frequency.

White matter: The tissue within the central nervous system, consisting primarily of nerve fibers.

Within-subject design: An experimental plan in which each subject receives each level of the independent variable.

Working through: A psychoanalytical term that describes the process by which clients develop more adaptive behavior once they have gained insight into the causes of their psychological disorders.

Yerkes-Dodson law: The principle that moderate levels of arousal tend to yield optimal performance.

Zeitgeber: A German word meaning "time giver"; a factor that serves as a synchronizer or entraining agent, such as sunlight in the morning.

Psychology
Basics

LIST OF TITLES BY CATEGORY

INDEX

A